The Essential Guide to Doing Your Research Project

COMPANION WEBSITE

Visit the companion website at www.uk.sagepub.com/oleary to find a range of teaching and learning material for lecturers and students.

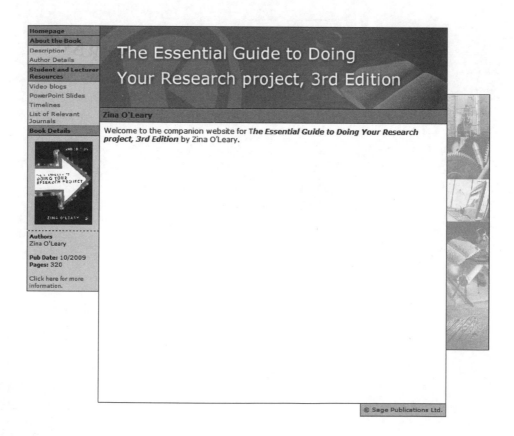

The Essential Guide to Doing Your Research Project

Zina O'Leary

Los Angeles | London | New Delhi
Singapore | Washington DC

First published in 2004 as *The Essential Guide to Doing Research*
Reprinted 2009, 2010

SAGE Publications Ltd
1 Oliver's Yard
55 City Road
London EC1Y 1SP

SAGE Publications Inc.
2455 Teller Road
Thousand Oaks, California 91320

SAGE Publications India Pvt Ltd
B 1/I 1 Mohan Cooperative Industrial Area
Mathura Road
New Delhi 110 044

SAGE Publications Asia-Pacific Pte Ltd
33 Pekin Street #02-01
Far East Square
Singapore 048763

Library of Congress Control Number: 2009923886

British Library Cataloguing in Publication data

A catalogue record for this book is available from
the British Library

ISBN 978-1-84860-010-2
ISBN 978-1-84860-011-9 (pbk)

Typeset by C&M Digitals Pvt Ltd, Chennai, India
Printed and bound in Great Britain by the MPG Books Group
Printed on paper from sustainable resources

Mixed Sources
Product group from well-managed
forests and other controlled sources
www.fsc.org Cert no. SGS-COC-2482
© 1996 Forest Stewardship Council
FSC

CONTENTS

Acknowledgements   xi

1   **Taking the Leap into the Research World**   **1**
    The challenge of tackling a research project   1
    So what is this thing called research and why do it?   2
        The need for research knowledge   2
        The potential of research knowledge   3
    Delving into the 'construct' of research   4
        Ontology and epistemology   4
        Competing positions   5
        The position of the reflexive researcher   7
    Getting help along the way   8
        The structure of the book   8
        How to get the most out of the book   10
    Further reading   10
    Chapter summary   12

2   **Getting Started**   **14**
    On your mark, get set, go!   14
    Navigating the process   15
        Understanding your programme   16
        Getting set up   18
        Getting the right advice   18
        Managing the workload   20
    Staying on course   22
        Finding a balance   22
        Dealing with 'crisis'   23
    Further reading   25
    Chapter summary   25

3   **Striving for Integrity in the Research Process**   **27**
    Power, politics, ethics, and research integrity   27
        Understanding the power game   28

Credibility: integrity in the production of knowledge 29
    Working with appropriate indicators 29
    Managing subjectivities 30
    Capturing 'truth' 34
    Approaching methods with consistency 37
    Making relevant and appropriate arguments 37
    Providing accurate and verifiable research accounts 39
Ethics: integrity and the 'researched' 40
    Legal obligations 40
    Moral obligations 40
    Ethical obligations 41
    Ethics approval processes 42
Integrity indicators and checklist 43
Further reading 44
Chapter summary 44

4   Developing Your Research Question   46
The importance of good questions 46
Defining your topic 48
    Curiosity and creativity 48
    Looking for inspiration 48
    Practicalities 50
From interesting topics to researchable questions 51
    Narrowing in 51
    The need to redefine 53
The hypothesis dilemma 55
    Hypothesis defined 55
    Appropriateness 56
Characteristics of good questions 56
Further reading 60
Chapter summary 60

5   Crafting a Research Proposal   61
The role of the proposal 61
    Demonstrating merits of the research question 62
    Demonstrating merits of the proposed methods 63
    Demonstrating merits of the researcher 63
Elements of the proposal 64
Writing a winning proposal 66
    Following guidelines 66
    Writing purposively 67
    Drafting and redrafting 67
Obstacles and challenges 68
    When your design does not fit proposal requirements 68
    When your design is emergent 68
    When want to or need to change direction/method 69

Further reading   70
Chapter summary   70

6   Working with Literature   **71**
The importance of literature   71
The role of literature   72
Sourcing relevant literature   75
    Types of literature   75
    Calling on 'experts'   76
    Honing your search skills   76
Managing the literature   77
    Assessing relevance   78
    Being systematic   78
    Annotating references   79
Writing the formal 'literature review'   81
    Purpose   81
    Coverage   82
    The writing process   83
Further reading   86
Chapter summary   86

7   Designing a Research Plan   **88**
Methodology, methods, and tools   88
    The relationship between methodology and methods   89
Moving from questions to answers   89
    Finding a path   90
    Hitting the target   91
Getting down to the nitty-gritty   98
    Fundamental questions   98
    Emergent methodological design   101
Further reading   102
Chapter summary   102

**8   Understanding Methodologies: Quantitative, Qualitative,
and 'Mixed' Approaches**   **104**
Understanding the quantitative/qualitative divide   104
The quantitative tradition   106
    Scientific/hypothetico–deductive methods   106
    Experimental design   107
    Exploring a population   110
The qualitative tradition   113
    Credibility in qualitative studies   114
    Ethnography   115
    Phenomenology   119
    Ethnomethodology   123
    Understanding feminist approaches   126

Mixed methodology   127
    Arguments for mixed methodology   127
    Perspectives and strategies   128
    Challenges and obstacles   130
Further reading   131
Chapter summary   133

**9   Understanding Methodologies: Evaluative, Action-Oriented,
      and Emancipatory Strategies   136**
Research that attempts to drive change   136
Evaluation research   137
    Summative/outcome evaluation   138
    Formative/process evaluation   140
    The politics of evaluative research   141
    Negotiating real-world challenges of evaluative research   142
Action research   145
    The scope of action research   147
    Key elements of action research   148
    Challenges associated with action research   151
Emancipatory research   152
    Participatory action research   154
    Critical ethnography   155
    Issues in emancipatory research   156
Further reading   156
Chapter summary   158

10   Seeking 'Respondents'   160
Who holds the answer?   160
Samples: selecting elements of a population   161
    Opportunities in working with a 'sample'   162
    Sample selection   162
    Random samples   166
    Non-random samples   168
Key informants: Working with experts and insiders   169
    Opportunities in working with key informants   171
    Informant selection   172
Cases: delving into detail   173
    Opportunities in working with cases   174
    Case selection   175
Further reading   177
Chapter summary   178

11   Direct Data Collection: Surveys and Interviews   180
The challenge of getting data directly from the source   180
Surveying   180
    Options and possibilities   181

Issues and complexities   182
The survey process   183
The survey instrument   186
Interviewing   194
Options and possibilities   194
Issues and complexities   196
The interview process   199
Conducting your interview   202
Further reading   205
Chapter summary   206

12   **Indirect Data Collection: Working with Observations**
     and Existing Text   **208**
The challenge of gathering indirect data   208
Observation   209
Options and possibilities   209
Issues and complexities   211
The observation process   213
Receiving, reflecting, recording, authenticating   215
Working with existing 'texts'   217
Options and possibilities   218
Issues and complexities   218
The process of textual analysis   221
Delving into documents, history, artefacts, and secondary data   223
Further reading   227
Chapter summary   228

13   **Analysing Quantitative Data**   **230**
Moving from raw data to significant findings   230
Keeping a sense of the overall project   230
Doing statistical analysis   232
Managing data and defining variables   233
Data management   233
Understanding variables – cause and effect   236
Understanding variables – measurement scales   236
Descriptive statistics   237
Measuring central tendency   237
Measuring dispersion   238
Measuring the shape of the data   239
Inferential statistics   240
Questions suitable to inferential statistics   241
Statistical significance   242
Understanding and selecting the right statistical test   243
Presenting quantitative data   244
Further reading   253
Chapter summary   254

14	**Analysing Qualitative Data**	**256**
	The promise of qualitative analysis	256
	Keeping the bigger picture in focus	257
	From raw data to significant findings	258
	QDA software	259
	The logic of QDA	260
	Balancing creativity and focus	260
	Moving between inductive and deductive reasoning	261
	The methods of QDA	262
	Identifying biases/noting impressions	263
	Reducing and coding into themes	264
	Looking for patterns and interconnections	265
	Mapping and building themes	265
	Developing theory	267
	Drawing conclusions	267
	Specific QDA strategies	269
	Presenting qualitative data	269
	Further reading	274
	Chapter summary	277
15	**The Challenge of Writing Up**	**278**
	The writing challenge	278
	Research as communication	279
	Knowing and engaging your audience	279
	Finding an appropriate structure and style	280
	The writing process	282
	Writing as analysis	283
	Constructing your 'story'	283
	Developing each section/chapter	285
	From first to final draft	288
	The need for exposure	292
	Attending conferences	293
	Giving presentations	293
	Writing and submitting articles	294
	The final word	294
	Further reading	294
	Chapter summary	295
	Bibliography	297
	Index	305

ACKNOWLEDGEMENTS

The first note of thanks needs to go to all the project students, both undergraduate and postgraduate, I've worked with at the University of Western Sydney, Sydney University, The University of New South Wales, The Australia and New Zealand School of Governance, The International Medical University of Malaysia, and The Polytechnic University of Hong Kong. I hope I've taught you as much as you've taught me. I'd also like to thank the research partners I've collaborated with in China, Fiji, Palau, Malaysia, and Vietnam over the past 10 or so years. You broaden my perspective and help me bring currency and innovation to my teaching. A special note of thanks must also go to Brent Powis who has been unwavering in his support of all my academic endeavours. The team at Sage Publications, particularly Patrick Brindle, Rachel Burrows and Anna Coatman, also need to be acknowledged. Their acute insights and their support make this a better work. Finally, I'd like to thank my children Scout and Dakota (as well as Sam, Loc and Kate) just for being themselves and making my world a better place.

1
TAKING THE LEAP INTO THE RESEARCH WORLD

CHAPTER PREVIEW

- The challenge of tackling a research project
- So what is this thing called research and why do it?
- Delving into the 'construct' of research
- Getting help along the way

THE CHALLENGE OF TACKLING A RESEARCH PROJECT

> **❝If we knew what it was we were doing, it would not be called research, would it?❞**
> *Albert Einstein*

Daunting isn't it? Tackling your own research project. You're no expert on research and suddenly you are confronted with a need to do the whole thing: pick a topic, develop a researchable question, navigate your way through ethics, work with literature, develop a methodological approach, design methods, construct a coherent proposal, find respondents, collect data, analyse that data, *and* write it up – all within a completely unrealistic timeframe! How in the world are you going to manage that?

Well, believe it or not, the answer is pretty straightforward. Whether you are tackling a one-semester project at the end of your undergraduate degree or undertaking a PhD, the answer is the same. You do it one step at a time. There is a logic and rhythm to doing research, a logic and rhythm that you need not only to become familiar with, but to be able to apply with some level of confidence and competence.

But it can be intimidating. Even if you do not consciously recognize it, 'doing' research represents a huge shift in your learning journey. Up until this point you have probably been limited to being a knowledge consumer. The information is already out there – you just need to find it, memorize it, engage it, synthesize it, and, as your skills build, form opinions about it and maybe even critique it. But undertaking research is a whole new world. You move from being a knowledge consumer to a knowledge producer, someone who is charged with capturing and reporting on 'truth'. And this means taking on a whole new realm of responsibility and gaining competence with a host of new skills. This is the challenge of 'doing', and not just knowing about, research.

SO WHAT IS THIS THING CALLED RESEARCH AND WHY DO IT?

It is easy to think you've got a broad grasp on this concept we call 'research'. After all, it's something you probably do in your daily life on a regular basis. You do 'research' when you are deciding what car to buy. You do 'research' to help you determine what university you should attend. And, of course, you do 'research' when you have to find things out for an assignment.

But there is a distinct difference between this kind of everyday research and the construct of research that you're about to tackle. The author Zora Neale Hurston once said, 'Research is formalized curiosity. It is poking and prying with a purpose' (1942). And this is certainly one part of it. Scientific research demands formalization, systemization, and rigorous processes. But it also requires that 'formalized curiosity' be done in order to make a *new* contribution to knowledge. As the *Oxford English Dictionary* (2007) puts it, research is 'the systematic study of materials and sources in order to establish facts and reach new conclusions'. So more than engaging in what might be haphazard processes to find out something *you* did not know, 'scientific research' is about systematically finding out something not known in the wider world. It is your opportunity to contribute to a body of knowledge.

If you think about it, that's actually quite exciting. Through research, you have the capability to uncover or discover new knowledge, new knowledge that just might impact on real change. After all, knowledge for knowledge's sake is a luxury many argue we cannot afford. Rarely is research undertaken simply to satisfy curiosity. Much more often we are after knowledge that can help us tackle pressing problems and issues – and unfortunately in our world, this is not something we are not short of.

The need for research knowledge

I know that for some of you, the main driver for undertaking a research project is simply the requirement that exists within your degree. But beyond requirements, the potential to have your research make a contribution to the betterment of some situation should be a real motivator. As the physicist Richard Feynman once said, '[w]e are at the very beginning of time for the human race. It is not unreasonable that we grapple with problems … Our responsibility is to do what we can, learn what we can, improve the solutions, and pass them on.' (Feynman, 1997)

Research can help us improve our world, a world where problems abound. Governments, for example, are riddled with problems – in fact, governments themselves can be a problem. The environment is under stress. Our planet is turning into a giant greenhouse, there is salinity in the soil, and we do not have enough clean/safe drinking water to go around. In fact, we can't find a way to distribute money, food, or medicine so that everyone with a need gets a share. Health care and education are far from adequate and/or equitable, and from the global arena to the local playground we cannot seem to overcome racism, sexism, prejudice, or discrimination. Domestic violence and child abuse occur daily in every corner of the world, and child pornography is a multi-billion-dollar industry.

We also have to deal with the threat of terrorism as well as our fear of that threat. We poison ourselves daily with toxic chemicals – from alcohol, cigarettes, factories, and automobiles. Children are starving – some due to war and political upheaval – some from mass-media-induced anorexia. Meanwhile, schools struggle with violence, drugs, sexual and racial tension.

And then there is the workplace where more than 6,000 people die every day due to work-related accidents and disease (International Labour Organization 2005). Meanwhile, 'survivors' deal with significant stress from the boss, massive bureaucratic inefficiencies, gross inequities, and the need to balance work with a thousand other responsibilities.

The potential of research knowledge

So what is the role of research in solving such problems? Well, research is the process of gathering data in order to answer a particular question(s); and these questions generally relate to a need for knowledge that can facilitate problem solving.

Does this then make research the answer to our problems? Well, unfortunately no – but research can be an instrumental part of problem resolution. Research can be a key tool in informed decision making. It can be central to determining what we should do, what we can do, how we will do it, and how well we have done it. Research may not be the answer to our problems, but it can supply some of the data necessary for us to begin to tackle the problems that challenge us all. Research can help us:

- *understand more about particular issues and problems* – including all the complexities, intricacies and implications thereof
- *find workable solutions* – vision futures, explore possibilities
- *work towards that solution* – implement real change
- *evaluate success* – find out if problem-solving/change strategies have been successful.

If you think about it, from local to global levels, all of these activities can be, and should be, informed by research. Research can be the key to finding out more: that is, uncovering and understanding the complexity of the issues that surround us. It can also help us in our quest for solutions. It can be key to assessing needs, visioning futures, and finding and assessing potential answers. It can also allow us to enact and learn from change through the use of 'action research' strategies. And finally, evaluative research can be central to monitoring and refining our attempts at problem solving. In short, research may not be the answer – but it is certainly a tool that can help us move forward.

Now as someone about to tackle a research project, it is important for you to keep in mind that while you might like to save the world's children from hunger, do away with the evils of terrorism, or put a stop to religious persecution, not many of you will be in a position to fully address these types of problems through your research processes. Generally speaking, conducting a research project will often see you engaged in issues, or aspects of issues, that, while still important and significant, are local, grounded, and practical. Even more so than projects that are overly grandiose and theoretical, there can be real value in projects that respond to real and tangible needs. Your goal should be doing what you can to add to a body of knowledge.

DELVING INTO THE 'CONSTRUCT' OF RESEARCH

Now that you have some sense of what research is and why you might be motivated to take it on, it is time to delve a bit deeper into the philosophical underpinning of the research game. You know, you're not alone if you are someone who questions whether or not this is really necessary. For many, the words 'philosophical underpinning' conjure up a place you simply do not want to go. But necessary it is – research is a fluid construct that potential researchers need to grapple with.

Only a few decades ago, the construct of research was without too much contention. Research was a technical enterprise that followed the rules of scientific method. The object of scientific enquiry might differ, i.e. chemistry, biology, physics, the social, etc., but research was united by common objectives, logic, presuppositions, and general methodological approaches. Social science fell under the scientific paradigm of the day (positivism) and worked within its assumptions.

Enter the later half of the twentieth century, however, and many of the assumptions related to the production of knowledge, and therefore research, began to be questioned, critiqued, and even denigrated. The implication has been a shift from sole reliance on approaches that follow 'positivist' rules of scientific method reliant on hypothesis testing to more 'post-positivist' approaches that can be participative, collaborative, inductive, idiographic, and exploratory.

Ontology and epistemology

Much of this shift can be understood through the exploration of two more words plenty of students would like to avoid. But here they are anyway. It is important to become familiar with these terms since they help us understand debates and diversity related to the production of knowledge, and consequently, the research processes you are about to engage in.

> **ONTOLOGY**
> The study of what exists, and how things that exist are understood and categorized.
>
> **EPISTEMOLOGY**
> How we come to have legitimate knowledge of the world; rules for knowing.

All right, so let's break this down. The main question addressed by ontology is 'what types of things actually exist?', while the main question addressed by epistemology is 'what are the rules for discovering what exists?' Now these two questions actually work in concert and have a tendency to lead to great debate. Because there are different rules for knowing (epistemologies), there can be quite varied conceptions of what exists or what is 'real' (ontology).

Consider the following. 'Empiricists' believe that all knowledge is limited to what can be observed by the senses (their epistemology). They therefore have a difficult time acknowledging anything that cannot be measured (their ontology). But there are other ways of knowing (competing epistemologies) which lead to differing conceptions of 'real' (alternate ontology). For example, those with religious epistemologies based on faith (rather than measurement) would say God is real even if you cannot physically touch him or her. Similarly, those with indigenous ways of knowing would accept myths and legends as truth. Postmodernists, however, may question whether there is any way we can find 'truth', and might suggest that 'truth' is a slippery concept that is always political.

In the world of social science research, the tension and debate between competing epistemologies and ontologies requires researchers to consider their own orientation to knowledge and truth. Even new researchers need to consider their positioning. For example, do you have an, 'empirical' epistemology, which leads you to believe that the only things we can know are external and physically observable, i.e. the truth is out there? And as a researcher, what limits will this put on your research? Or maybe you have a more 'postmodern' epistemology in which you believe that people play a large part in the 'construction' of knowledge, and truth is actually ambiguous, fluid, and relative. Certainly, holding that belief system will impact on how you go about 'fact finding'.

Within social science research the debate that rages between such differing ways of knowing is enormous, leading to an overly defensive, emotive, and often unproductive divide between empiricists and more postmodern researchers. Each believes they hold the key to legitimate knowing, which unfortunately lessens the potential for them to work together down a path of holistic knowing.

Competing positions

Let's pause here and have a quick look at some of the ways in which we can come to have an understanding of our world, and how a particular way of knowing might influence research processes. Now it would be nice if these terms were mutually exclusive – but given their varied disciplinary roots, many overlap, which, I know, can be confusing. I will give a brief overview here, but if you really want to get into the nitty-gritty of each of these 'isms', I would have a look at the readings recommended at the end of this chapter.

REALISM
The view that the external world exists independently of perception. In other words, the truth is out there whether we can see and understand it or not.

EMPIRICISM
The view that all knowledge is limited to what can be observed through the senses. The cornerstone of scientific method.

POSITIVISM
The view that all true knowledge is scientific, and is best pursued by scientific method.

These three terms present relatively straightforward approaches to knowing in which the world has single truth. In the conduct of research, they suggest that what we can know comes from sensory experience best served through scientific method. These three terms arguably represent the unquestioned landscape of research since the Enlightenment.

In recent decades, however, this black and white way of seeing has been called into question. Physicists now recognize the role of chaos and complexity in a universe that we may never 'capture'. And what about the nature of truth in the social world? Whose truth is it anyway? There are many 'post-positivist' philosophers and researchers alike who are questioning the assumptions of these ways of knowing and openly critique, oppose, and/or reject positivism's central tenets.

This has led to acceptance of alternate epistemologies that can be broadly classed under the umbrella of a 'postmodern' or 'post-positivist' worldview. For these ways of knowing, the certainty implied above is replaced by an acceptance of chaos, complexity, the unknown, incompleteness, diversity, plurality, fragmentation, and multiple realities. Ways of knowing that fall under this umbrella include:

RELATIVISM
The view that there are no universals, and that things like truth, morals, and culture can only be understood in relation to their own socio-historic context.

SOCIAL CONSTRUCTIONISM
Theories of knowledge that emphasize that the world is constructed by human beings as they interact and engage in interpretation.

SUBJECTIVISM
Emphasizes the subjective elements in experience and accepts that personal experiences are the foundation for factual knowledge.

The position of the reflexive researcher

Undeniably, there is a divide in the research world between those who accept chaos, complexity, the unknown, and multiple realities, and those who do not. But I would argue that this divide can and should be traversed. While many researchers feel a need to identify themselves with a particular way of knowing and only engage in methodological approaches that sit under their own epistemology, it's worth considering whether divergent, disparate, and distinct ways of knowing can each offer credible knowledge production.

In fact, I would argue that good research should be seen as a thinking person's game. It is a creative and strategic process that involves constantly assessing, reassessing, and making decisions about the best possible means for obtaining trustworthy information, carrying out appropriate analysis, and drawing credible conclusions.

Now there are many researchers who rely on, and even come to 'believe' in, particular methodological approaches. Janesick actually coined the term 'methodolatry' – a combination of method and idolatry that she defines as a 'preoccupation with selecting and defending methods to the exclusion of the actual substance of the story being told'; she describes methodolatry as a 'slavish attachment and devotion to methods' (2007: 48).

As a budding researcher, it is important to remember that there is no 'best type' of research. Particular research strategies are good or bad to the exact degree that they fit with the questions at hand. Good questions need to be matched with appropriate procedures of enquiry, and this is always driven by the researcher, not the methodology. The perspectives you will adopt and the methods you will use need to be as fluid, flexible, and eclectic as is necessary to answer the questions posed.

Box 1.1 highlights the advantages to not being pigeonholed. Each research situation and research question is unique, and assumptions can be as varied as the situations. The trick is to understand what assumptions you are working under and how they might affect your study.

BOX 1.1   BANANA CONSUMPTION ASSUMPTIONS!

I once had a student who wanted to explore whether recycled 'grey' water could be used to irrigate bananas. She did this in two phases. The first phase involved the formulation of a hypothesis that stated there would be no bio-physical differences between bananas irrigated with town water and those irrigated with recycled grey water. For this phase of the study she (quite appropriately) accepted the positivist assumptions, and conducted her research according to the 'rules' of scientific method – she was the consummate lab-based objective scientist.

(Continued)

(Continued)

Her second phase explored whether consumers would buy bananas irrigated with recycled water regardless of 'no difference' in quality. For this phase of the study, the student thoughtfully explored her assumptions and realized that in relation to this particular question, she found herself moving into 'post-positivist' territory. She struggled with her own subjectivity and realized that 'truth' and 'reality' can be two different things (many consumers who believed findings of 'no difference' claimed they still would not purchase the bananas irrigated with recycled water). There was no defined set of rules to best answer this question, but her willingness to 'think' her way through the process and be flexible in her approach allowed her to draw conclusions that were seen as both credible and valuable.

GETTING HELP ALONG THE WAY

By now you are probably getting some sense of why research is often referred to as a journey. You haven't even finished the first chapter of this book, and already there is a whole lot you have been asked to consider. And that's before you even start thinking about your own research project. But don't worry, you are not alone. The goal of this book is to be your guide. It is designed to accompany you on your journey; to lay out the processes and procedures you will need to engage with; to help you through the logic of research; to offer guidance on all the decisions that are part and parcel of conducting a research project; and to send you down the right road when you need to delve deeper into relevant methodologies and methods.

At the same time, it is important to know that this is not a 'recipe book'. It does not lay out sets of 'steps' that you blindly follow. Yes, it will logically work you through the processes and procedures, but this is a book that recognizes that good research is always reliant on reflexive researchers, researchers who must weigh up all decisions in light of a quest for credible data and findings, limited by unavoidable practicalities.

So whether you are about to tackle a small-scale project, or undertake a major thesis, this book is intended to accompany you on what is bound to be a journey of rich discovery, a journey that will have you unearth not only 'findings' related to your research question, but also the process of research, as well as the thorny challenges associated with project management.

The structure of the book

The Essential Guide to Doing Your Research Project consists of 15 chapters that will logically take you through all aspects of conducting a research project from conception to dissemination. In other words, the chapters mirror the processes necessary for the conduct of most research projects.

The first three chapters address the preliminaries. As well as introducing the book's objectives and offering guidelines for how to get the most out of the work, **Chapter 1** introduces you to some of the more fundamental and theoretical aspects of research including an understanding of how knowledge is understood and produced. This level of understanding can go a long way in helping to ground your own research approach. **Chapter 2** is about practicalities. This chapter acknowledges that undertaking research can be a difficult and alienating activity, and attempts to offer strategies for staying on top of the process. It covers: what you need to know to start your research journey; how to best navigate the research process; and how to stay on track. **Chapter 3** covers the concept of integrity. The chapter starts with an exploration of power and politics in research processes before moving on to traditional indicators of credibility as well as alternatives more appropriate to 'qualitative' data. The chapter then discusses ethical responsibilities and ethics approval processes.

The next three chapters are all about effective planning. **Chapter 4** takes you through the art and science of knowing what you want to know. It guides you through the process of defining a feasible, clearly articulated research question that acts to direct 'methods'. It is amazing how much simpler it is to adopt, adapt, or create appropriate methodological approaches when you are absolutely clear about what it is you want to know. **Chapter 5** covers research proposals and the opportunity they present to clarify thinking, bed down ideas, articulate thoughts in a way that provides a blueprint for future action, and, most importantly, 'sell your project'. **Chapter 6** explores the varied ways in which literature informs research. I often tell students that before 'doing' research, they need to convince me of three things: (1) that the questions they wish to answer are worthy of research; (2) that they are the right person to add to a body of knowledge (they know their stuff); and (3) their methodological approach is the best 'doable' way of getting the answers to their question. And to do this, they need to read. This chapter covers issues related to sourcing, managing, and utilizing the literature to its full potential.

The design of social science studies has become incredibly diverse over the past 30 or so years, and can be a daunting realm of exploration for those new to research. **Chapter 7** looks at designing your data study such that it grows from questions rather than falls from paradigms, and offers a framework for delving into the basic questions that drive method. Chapters 8 and 9 delve more specifically into methodologies with **Chapter 8** taking you through what are often described as qualitative, quantitative, and mixed methodologies, while **Chapter 9** explores more purposive approaches such as evaluative, action-oriented, and emancipatory strategies.

Data collection is the focus of the next three chapters. **Chapter 10** looks at 'respondents', and covers the logistics, challenges, and methods of defining and selecting samples, key informants, and cases. **Chapter 11** concentrates on the opportunities and challenges associated with direct data collection via surveys and interviews, while **Chapter 12** takes you through options for collecting and working with existing data sources.

Next comes making sense of, and presenting, your data. **Chapter 13** takes you through the basics of quantitative data management and analysis and covers variable types, measurement scales, descriptive and inferential statistics, the selection of statistical tests, and data presentation. **Chapter 14** focuses on qualitative data and takes you through the logic and methods of general qualitative analysis, as well as specific branches of analysis such as content, discourse, conversation, and narrative analysis; semiotics; and hermeneutics. The chapter concludes with examples of how to present qualitative data.

That leaves **Chapter 15**. This final chapter covers the ever-intimidating writing process and stresses the importance of seeing the write-up as a 'conversation' that needs to be mindful of its audience, have a logical structure, and communicate a clear storyline. Its goal is to offer you a host of practical strategies for getting through your write-up in ways that not only improve the overall quality of the project itself, but make the task much less daunting.

How to get the most out of the book ·

There are actually a few ways you can use this book and you may find yourself dipping in and out of these three strategies:

1   Read it through in order to become familiar with the process and procedures associated with research. I, for one, happen to think it is a pretty good knowledge book.
2   Use it as a reference. As you progress though your research project you will inevitably need to look things up. You are likely to find the answers within this book's 15 chapters. And if you can't, the recommended readings should give you some good leads.
3   Use this book as a companion to your research processes. This is where the book really comes into its own. While each chapter will introduce you to a new area of content, the main goal is to take you through the development processes you need to undertake when doing your own project. The emphasis is to arm you with the knowledge and skills you will need to get you from 'clueless' to 'completed'. When using the book in this way, a good approach is to read as you go. I would recommend starting here and working your way through to the last page of Chapter 15, when you will be ready to submit your work.

FURTHER READING

There are some heavy theoretical concepts in this chapter that you may want to explore in a bit more depth. Here are some accessible leads.

Empiricism

BonJour, L. (2005) *The Structure of Empirical Knowledge*. Cambridge, MA: Harvard University Press.
Carey, S. S. (2003) *A Beginner's Guide to Scientific Method*. Belmont, CA: Wadsworth.
Robinson, D. (2004) *Introducing Empiricism*. New York: Totem Books.

Epistemology

Steup, M. and Sosa, E. (eds) (2005) *Contemporary Debates In Epistemology.* Oxford: Blackwell.

Williams, M. (2001) *Problems of Knowledge: A Critical Introduction to Epistemology.* Oxford: Oxford University Press.

Ontology

Conee, E. and Sider, T. (2005) *Riddles of Existence: A Guided Tour of Metaphysics.* Oxford: Oxford University Press.

Jacquotte, D. (2002) *Ontology.* Montreal: McGill–Queen's University Press.

Paradigm

Guba, E. (ed.) (1990) *The Paradigm Dialog.* London: Sage.

Wallerstein, I. (2001) *Unthinking Social Science: The Limits of Nineteenth-Century Paradigms.* Philadelphia: Temple University Press.

Positivism

Schick, T. (ed.) (1999) *Readings in the Philosophy of Science: From Positivism to Postmodern.* Columbus, OH: McGraw-Hill.

Steinmetz, G. (ed.) (2005) *The Politics of Method in the Human Sciences: Positivism and Its Epistemological Others.* Durham, NC: Duke University Press.

Realism

Psillos, S. (1999) *Scientific Realism: How Science Tracks Truth.* London: Routledge.

Rescher, N. (2005) *Reason and Reality: Realism and Idealism in Pragmatic Perspective.* Lanham, MD: Rowman & Littlefield.

Relativism

Boghossian, P. A. (2006) *Fear of Knowledge: Against Relativism and Constructivism.* Oxford: Oxford University Press.

Hazelrigg, L. E. (1989) *Social Science and the Challenge of Relativism: A Wilderness of Mirrors: On Practices of Theory in a Gray Age.* Gainesville, FL: University Press of Florida.

(Continued)

(Continued)

Social constructionism

Berger, P. L. and Luckman, T. (1967) *The Social Construction of Reality: A Treatise in the Sociology of Knowledge.* New York: Anchor.
Burr, V. (2003) *Social Constructionism.* New York: Psychology Press.

Subjectivism

Brown, J. R. (1996) *The I in Science: Training to Utilize Subjectivity in Research.* Oslo: Scandinavian University Press.
Zahavi, D. (2007) *Subjectivity and Selfhood: Investigating the First-Person Perspective.* Cambridge MA: The MIT Press.

CHAPTER SUMMARY

- Research is the process of developing new knowledge by gathering data that answers a particular question. It is your opportunity to contribute to a body of knowledge and perhaps even influence change.
- Research can be a key tool in informed decision making. It can be central to determining what we should do, what we can do, how we will do it, and how well we have done it.
- Scientific research was born of 'positivism' and adopted the assumptions of that paradigm. These assumptions include: a knowable and predictable world; empirical and reductionist research; objective and expert researchers; hypothesis-driven methods; and statistically significant, quantitative findings.
- Over the past decades, the assumptions of positivism have been brought into question. Post-positivist researchers acknowledge: a world that is ambiguous and variable; research that can be intuitive and holistic; researchers who can be subjective and collaborative; methods that can be inductive and exploratory; and findings that can be idiographic and qualitative.
- Two theoretical questions even new researchers should consider are 'what types of things actually exist?' (ontology) and 'what are the rules for discovering what exists?' (epistemology).
- The traditional research landscape can be represented by concepts such as *realism* – that the external world exists independently of perception; *positivism* – that all true knowledge is scientific; and *empiricism* – that all knowledge is limited to what can be observed through the senses.
- An alternative 'postmodern' worldview accepts chaos, complexity, the unknown, incompleteness, diversity, plurality, fragmentation, and multiple realities. This can be represented by concepts such as *relativism* – that

things like truth, morals, and culture can only be understood in relation to their own socio-historic context; *social constructionism* – that the world is constructed by human beings as they interact and engage in interpretation; *subjectivism* – that personal experiences are the foundation for factual knowledge.

- Rather than positioning the researcher according to paradigmatic assumptions, the reflexive researcher can consider whether it is possible to explore the assumptions of various paradigms as they relate to particular research questions.
- While undertaking a research project can be somewhat intimidating, using this book as a guide to your journey will help you best navigate all the ins and outs of the research process.

2

GETTING STARTED

CHAPTER PREVIEW

- On your mark, get set, go!
- Navigating the process
- Staying on course

ON YOUR MARK, GET SET, GO!

> ❝ The secret of getting ahead is getting started. ❞
> *Mark Twain*

You know what would make Mark Twain's advice even more valuable? If we knew the best way to make a start. Most students getting ready to tackle a research project have little idea of how to make a start or what they need to get them on their way.

Well one thing is for sure, research does not just happen. Researching is a process that demands planning, forethought, commitment, and persistence. In fact, research is more of a journey than a task; and, like any journey, it needs to be managed, navigated, and negotiated from early conception to final destination. Now it is not unusual for students to question their ability to successfully navigate this journey. After all, researching is a skill that is only just beginning to develop, so the thought of embarking can be quite daunting. Some jump in without a strategic plan, while others wallow too long in the planning stages. Some will make a good start, but get lost or lose motivation along the way. As you begin to contemplate the task ahead, it's worth keeping in mind that completing a research project in good time is much more than a test of your intellectual ability; it is also a test of your persistence and tenacity.

As you travel on your journey, you are likely to find that your quest to produce new knowledge will be learning experience far richer than you might have ever expected. Conducting a research project allows you to:

- *Engage in 'problem-based learning'* – the thinking behind problem-based learning is that the best starting point for learning is working through a problem that needs to be solved in a hands-on fashion. The learning here is 'double loop'. Not only do you learn about a problem you are exploring, but you also learn how to tackle that problem, hopefully in a manner that will allow you to transfer problem-solving skills to a variety of new challenges. The nature of conducting research (and stumbling a bit along the way) embeds problem-based learning into the research process.

- *Engage in 'action learning'* – Kolb (1984) stressed the importance of the creation of knowledge through 'transformation of experience'. He suggested that experiential or action learning is dependent on cycles that include: (1) engagement in real experiences (concrete experimentation) that need to be followed by (2) thoughtful review and consideration (reflexive observation); as well as (3) broader theorizing (abstract conceptualization); and (4) attempts to improve action (active experimentation). Such processes are embedded in various aspects of conducting research. To 'do' research is to engage in cycles of action learning.

- *Enhance communication skills* – Gathering credible data is not a task for the shy or faint-hearted. It is a process that is highly dependent on your ability to communicate with others. Whether it is the challenge of gaining access, conducting interviews, or engaging in participant observation – boosting your communication skills is often a side benefit of doing research.

- *Develop research skills* – I know I write research methods texts, but I'll still tell you there is only so much you can learn from 'reading' about the conduct of research – the real learning comes from the 'doing'. Without a doubt, it is reflectively conducting research that will teach you how to do it.

- *Produce new knowledge* – You will find out something. You will hopefully get an answer to your research question. You will have produced new knowledge that will add to a body of knowledge.

- *Engage in, or facilitate, evidence-based decision making* – It is a really good feeling to know that commonsense, practical decisions are being influenced by data you generate. If well managed from conception through to dissemination, your research project might just have the ability to influence change.

- *Offer a pathway for gaining academic qualifications or getting a raise* – Perhaps these goals are not as noble as the learning objectives above, but let's face it, this kind of stuff is often important to us.

NAVIGATING THE PROCESS

Research is a process that simultaneously demands imagination, creativity, discipline, and structure, and needs to be navigated strategically from start to finish. So right from the start it is worth considering a number of practicalities related to the process. In order to hit the ground running it is a good idea to (1) familiarize yourself with your institution/programme's resources and requirements; (2) get appropriately set up; (3) negotiate the advisory process; and (4) manage your workload in ways that will see you complete on time and still manage to maintain a life!

Understanding your programme

In order to move strategically through the research process, you need to become familiar with the requirements and resources of your university. If you do not, you might just end up wasting a lot of time undertaking and producing research that falls outside set guidelines and/or not taking full advantage of the resources available to you.

Requirements

One of the greatest frustrations for students and lecturers alike is when good work does not meet set requirements. The best way to ensure that university protocols are met is to find out what they are early on, and to keep them in mind throughout the research project. Common research requirements include:

- *Meeting deadlines* – Perhaps one of the biggest hurdles you will face, but extremely important to manage. Late submissions might not be accepted, or may be subject to penalties. It is well worth knowing your deadlines and familiarizing yourself with policies for late submission and extensions before you even start the journey.
- *Staying within word limits* – Word limits vary with level of study, discipline, and university. But whatever the limit is, it is generally expected that it will take close to this to produce a quality research paper/thesis. As a lecturer, seeing a very 'thin' paper is almost (but not quite) as disappointing as seeing one you will have to get home with a trolley. Try not to go too far under or over the prescribed word count. Some lecturers/institutions can be quite strict with works that fall outside set limits.
- *Gaining ethics approval* – This is essential for most research that involves human (or animal) participants and is discussed fully in the next chapter. Each university will have its own requirements, committees, and deadlines for gaining such approval.
- *Progress reports/seminars* – For longer projects, universities often require reports to be submitted by students, supervisors, or both, on an annual or biannual basis. Students might also be expected to present in regularly scheduled seminars.
- *An examination process* – This too varies by level of study and university. Some research write-ups will be given a grade or level, while others are simply deemed satisfactory/unsatisfactory. For higher degrees, the examination process often involves external examiners that the student may or may not have a say in determining. It may also involve an oral defence of the work. It is highly advisable to discuss the issue of examination/examiners with your supervisor quite early in the process. There can be great benefit in knowing what to expect.
- *Originality and avoidance of plagiarism* – Virtually all universities have clear policies on originality and plagiarism. Familiarizing yourself with what constitutes plagiarism can help you avoid some deadly grey areas.

Resources

When it comes to resources, many students do not bother to ask, therefore they do not receive. Finding out what your university/programme offers research students should be high on the list of initial priorities. As highlighted in Box 2.1, nothing is more frustrating than finding out about an excellent service or facility just a bit too late.

BOX 2.1   DAMN! I WISH I KNEW THAT SIX MONTHS AGO

SCENARIO 1

'$1,300! You got $1,300 for your field trip? How in the world did you get that?'
'All research students are entitled to $2,500 a year to help cover costs; you just have to put in a form.'
   'You're kidding me. How come I wasn't told?'

SCENARIO 2

'Hey, how did you get an access number for the photocopier?'
   'Debbie in main office. The school provides them for all research students.'
   'Aw, that's just great; do you know how much I have spent on photocopying over the past six months?!'

SCENARIO 3

'So where are you headed?'
   'Can you believe I have to go halfway across town to Nelson Library to pick up a book? They don't have it on this campus.'
   'Oh … Why didn't you do an inter-campus loan on the Internet? They send it right to you.'
   'You are joking … since when?'

Some of the resources you may want to check on are:

- *Accommodation* – Is dedicated or shared office space available?
- *Equipment* – Will you have access to telephone, computer, printer, and/or photocopier?
- *Software* – What software is supported by the university? Is it willing to acquire any software you might need?
- *Funds* – Is there any money available to help with costs such as university fees, books, photocopying, postage, consumables (paper, ink cartridges, cassette tapes), travel costs (site visits, conference attendance), and equipment (tape recorder, transcription machine, PC, laptop, software, etc.)?
- *Library facilities* – What databases are available? Is there a system of inter-library loans? Will you have Internet access?
- *Workshops* – Does the university offer any methods workshops or writing circles?

- *Methods assistance* – Is there any assistance available for questionnaire design, transcription, data entry? Is statistics advice available?
- *Writing assistance* – Is there anyone who can help you put together a proposal, or structure a final draft? Is there anyone to help with editing?

Getting set up

Researching is an activity that requires more independence and autonomy than most types of learning you are likely to have attempted, and requires that you spend a fair amount of time reading or working at a computer. Getting set up therefore requires access to a quiet place to work, a good reliable computer, and proficiency in the use of that computer and its software:

- *The study/office* – Having a comfortable place to lock yourself away is essential. Researching can be an alienating activity and creating or finding a space where you can work comfortably is well worth the effort.
- *The computer* – Most students find it impossible to do research without an up-to-date word processing program and reliable Internet access. You may also need to run statistical and/or qualitative data management programs that can be demanding on the system. It is well worth investing in a computer that can not only meet your current needs, but also needs that might arise with use as the research process gets underway.
- *Proficiency* – With the computer/Internet age well upon us, most of you will have pretty good skills when it comes to basic word processing and Internet searching. Nonetheless, a bit of upskilling won't go astray. Whether it be managing large documents, working with graphics, advanced searching, and just working on your touch typing, there is a lot to be gained from feeling competent in these areas.

Getting the right advice

Doing a research project usually involves working with the guidance and support of a mentor or supervisor. For many this is a new and somewhat daunting experience. Now I would like to be able to say that this experience will be highly rewarding – and more often than not it is. But at times, it can be tumultuous, frustrating, aggravating, and just plain unsatisfactory. Supervisors can be busy, dismissive, muddled, and sometimes even arrogant. So it is extremely important to negotiate expectations right from the onset and work towards open, clear, and comfortable communication.

If you are new to supervisory relationships, you may not be aware of just how varied they can be. Some relationships are based on student autonomy and independence, while others are much more collaborative and dependent. The only way to know where you stand is to negotiate both student and supervisor expectations. Keep in mind that if you do not do this early, you may be setting yourself up for a tremendous amount of frustration and angst. Box 2.2 highlights some of the expectations you may want to openly negotiate with your supervisor.

BOX 2.2   NEGOTIATING EXPECTATIONS

Expectations that need to be clarified in student/supervisor relationships include:

Autonomy

- Who is responsible for orienting the student to university resources/requirements?
- Who sets the timelines?
- How much advice/direction can/will the supervisor provide on the selection of topic, question, methodological and theoretical frameworks?
- Will the student be expected to submit all drafts for review/comment?
- Do all new directions need to be cleared with the supervisor?
- Will writing/editing assistance be provided by the supervisor?
- Who makes the final decision on acceptability?

The Programme

- How regularly will you meet?
- What is the expected turnaround time for getting and responding to feedback?
- Are seminar presentations required?

The Nature of the Relationship

- Will the relationship be purely professional or professional/personal?
- Will emotional support be provided?
- Is open and frank discussion on progress expected/welcomed?

Your supervisor–student relationship is likely to be closer than any other relationship previously experienced with an academic. One reason this can be a bit nerve racking is that it is a relationship of very unequal power. On one side you have the professor and expert, while on the other you have the student and novice. Yes, the goal should be mentoring, growth, and mutual respect but, as highlighted in Box 2.3, it is a relationship that can easily leave students feeling patronized or even a bit intimidated.

BOX 2.3   THE POWER OF THE RED PEN – KATE'S STORY

When I switched universities, I was assigned to a supervisor who had just received her PhD and had research interests similar to my own. We met a few times, and I can't say it went very well. While her PhD was in an area similar to mine, our approaches seemed worlds apart, and I got the distinct feeling that she thought my approach was not just different, but wrong. No one wants to be 'judged', so it was with much trepidation that I handed her an early chapter of my thesis. I hated the thought of her passing judgement as she read, and dreaded receiving her feedback.

I got the chapter back a few weeks later and it was even worse than I thought. The paper was literally covered in red ink. Angry, vile, 'I have power over you', 'you are wrong', red ink. Well I went from feeling apprehensive to angry. There was no need to exercise that type of power trip on me. I did not need hypercritical judgement, what I needed was support, guidance, advice, and perspective. In the end, what I actually needed was a new supervisor.

This does not mean that you and your supervisor need to be on the same 'wavelength'. A lot can be learned from a supervisor whose style pushes your boundaries and helps you grow in ways you might not have even considered. The thesis acknowledgement below sums this up quite well:

> My thanks to Dr Sherman who was a great supervisor for the way my mind works. And my thanks to Dr Hakim who was an equally great supervisor for the way it doesn't.

In sum, I would recommend three strategies for facilitating a positive supervisor–student relationship: (1) know what your supervisor expects of you and what you can expect from your supervisor right from the start of your relationship; (2) be open – do not bottle up concerns and frustration. Share them with your supervisor in as non-threatening a way as possible as soon as issues arise; (3) if you cannot see a way to make the relationship work, talk to someone about it, i.e. a course coordinator, the research office, an academic you trust. Not every relationship is destined for success, and your progress needs to be your priority. It is important to remember that if you can develop a healthy rapport with your supervisor, you will make your journey that much easier.

Managing the workload

One word that I stress in all student research projects, regardless of level or discipline, is 'doability'. Is it doable? Well, assessing doability involves more than just looking at the quality of the research design. It also involves looking at the full gamut of pressures

TABLE 2.1   GANTT CHART

	Jan.	Feb.	Mar.	Apr.	May	June	July	Aug.	Sept.	Oct.	Nov.	Dec.
Groundwork	xx	xx										
Literature review		xx	xx	xx	xx	xx						
Defining methods			xx	xx								
Data collection					xx	xx	xx					
Progress seminar						12th						
Data analysis							xx	xx	xx			
Write first draft		xx	xx	xx	xx	xx	xx	xx				
Write second draft									xx	xx	xx	
Final seminar											27th	
Write final draft										xx	xx	xx
Thesis due												15th

and responsibilities that you as an individual need to manage. Realistically assessing and managing your workload is essential. If you don't, time will simply slip away.

There are no set rules for time management. You might be a night owl, an early bird, someone who can multi-task, someone who can only tackle one task at a time, someone who feels anxious without a defined schedule, or someone who is more spontaneous. Recognizing your own approach and working its strengths and addressing its shortcomings will be important to timely completion. If you can work your own style into a plan, it can help you manage what is likely to end up a very complex and, at times, seemingly unending task.

One useful tool is a Gantt chart. As shown in Table 2.1, a Gantt chart can be used to map out a project from start to finish. Now keep in mind that researching is often a fluid and flexible exercise likely to incorporate the unexpected, and your chart will invariably need to shift in order to reflect the dynamic nature of your project. However, having a document that can be negotiated and modified is more likely to keep you true to deadlines than not having one at all.

For some, the discipline it takes to stick to a Gantt chart comes naturally. These amazing individuals are able to get up at a pre-defined time, work diligently to a plan, and take only minimal food and toilet breaks. *And* they manage to do this five days a week. For us ordinary humans, however, the procrastination skills we have developed over many years of formal schooling are much too sophisticated to see us succumb to that level of discipline. Instead, we wait for inspiration. Which is fine if inspiration strikes with enough frequency and regularity – but what if it doesn't? Well then, you may have to 'trick' yourself into some sort of pseudo-inspirational state. Some things you might want to try are:

- *Working on/reading over your research journal* – An invaluable tool for any researcher is a good journal that can capture creative inspiration and help you manage the process. Your journal might include observations, notes on method and theory, lists of relevant contacts, notes/reminders to yourself, and any other ideas, doodles, concept maps, etc, that come to mind. Adding to your journal, or simply reading it over, may get the creative juices flowing.
- *Forcing yourself to get on the computer* – Engaging in some menial task can be a catalyst for doing richer work. Try starting with relatively mindless editorial work, data cleaning, or referencing, and then try to move to whatever you are procrastinating over. If you don't approach the computer at all, then nothing gets done. But if you sit down to a task, not only is the task accomplished, but the real work might get going as well.
- *Writing a letter to a real or fictional friend* – If you are feeling stuck, try writing an informal letter that tells 'whoever' what you are trying to do. Freeing yourself from academic writing can often help liberate ideas.
- *Go for a walk* – Sometimes a good head-clearing walk can be a trigger for a flood of fresh ideas. Having a small tape recorder handy (which if kept by the bed can also capture early morning inspiration) can capture those thoughts you are bound to forget.

STAYING ON COURSE

> ❝ Patience and tenacity are worth more than twice their weight of cleverness. ❞
> *Thomas Henry Huxley*

I don't think I've been involved in the supervision of one student who has not agonized over the research journey. For most, their research project is likely to be the biggest academic project ever undertaken. Knowing a field, being responsible for the production of 'new knowledge', designing methods, collecting and analysing data, and writing it all up can be an intimidating challenge – particularly for those whose roles and responsibilities in the real world extend beyond those of student. But rest assured, feelings of frustration, confusion, and even incompetence are both commonplace and surmountable. Being able to find a balance and deal with a crisis are part and parcel of researching.

Finding a balance

Student, employee, parent, child, partner – no student is a student alone. We all have a variety of roles to play. Yet sometimes those around us, ourselves included, forget that we need to manage and balance all of these simultaneously, even if they are sometimes incompatible. Balance is essential. No one can reach or work to their potential if they are neglecting important areas of their life.

So how do you find balance when you know you need to focus on your studies, yet you are feeling pressure at work, and you realize that you must reprioritize family? Well, as highlighted in Box 2.4, whether at work, home, or university, being honest and open about your needs is a good start. That, combined with the ability to say 'no', can go a long way in staying on top of it:

- *At work* – Try taking the time to discuss the demands of study with your managers. Hopefully they will be supportive. If not, at least you know where you stand. If your research is work related, it may be possible to negotiate time and resources for your project, particularly if you explain the significance and potential benefits of your research to the workplace.
- *At home* – Having the support of family is essential, not only for the practical support that can come from assistance with domestic duties, child care, etc., but also for the emotional support that can be quite crucial during the process. Unfortunately, some partners can be threatened by, or envious of, your achievements. Working through this dilemma, or again at least knowing where you stand, can put you in a stronger position of power.
- *At university* – I think the best advice is to be professional, but put your concerns on the table for legitimization. Being open and honest with your supervisor is crucial to your ability to set realistic and, most importantly, achievable goals.

BOX 2.4   NO TIME FOR GUILT! DAKOTA'S STORY

I spent much of my time doing my Masters degree thinking about what I wasn't doing. When I was studying, I often wasted hours daydreaming about being with friends, family, going out. I was quite good at making myself miserable and unproductive. When I was with friends and family, things weren't necessarily better. I spent a fair portion of that time feeling guilty about the work I knew was waiting for me.

I decided to start my PhD when my youngest daughter turned 1, so I knew I had to get my act together. I now had two small children at home, and I could not afford to waste time agonizing over what I thought I should be doing. So I made a conscious decision to 'give up guilt'. I put the kids in high-quality part-time day care, and simply let it go. And you know what? It worked. When the kids were in care I simply focused on my work and did not allow myself the luxury of worrying about them. When I was with the family, however, I was really with the family. I was fully there and simply enjoyed. In the end, I finished my thesis on time. I have come to realize that there is simply no productivity in angst and guilt.

Dealing with 'crisis'

It may sound a bit dramatic, but it would be unusual to undertake a major research project without it intersecting with some sort of 'crisis'. Unfortunately, our lives are full of them. If you are finding it all too much, starting to doubt yourself, or doubt what you are doing, it is important to know that you're not alone. Knowing what to expect, knowing how others cope, and developing and using a support system can help you get through inevitable rough patches:

- *Crisis of motivation* – It can be awfully hard to stay motivated for an extended period of time. What starts as an exciting and interesting project can quickly end up being one you just want to finish. In fact a colleague of mine told me he regularly advises his students only to research the things they are *not* interested in, because if they are really interested in it, they will be sick to death of it before they finish! Now I am not sure if *I* agree with that advice, but it does highlight how universal the problem is. Developing a supportive research culture can go a long way in keeping up motivation. Whether it be an attentive/sympathetic ear at home, interested work colleagues, a peer support network, or a relevant Internet chat group, engaging with others can help keep your interest up. It might also be worth reminding yourself to 'enjoy the process' and that 'the end will come'.

- *Crisis of confidence* – There are a lot of people who start their 'research' careers at the end of very successful 'learning' careers. These are people who are used to competence and success. Well, research students generally set their own agenda, work independently, and attempt to work to their potential; and herein lies the problem. Working to your potential pushes at your own personal limits, often in ways prior learning has not. Feeling like an impostor, thinking that it is beyond your intellectual capabilities, and believing that your work is not good enough are, believe it or not, fears widely shared. Getting a more objective sense of how you are going can help put things in perspective. If you talk to your supervisor and your peers, you will often find that others have more faith in you than you have in yourself. I often tell students who are facing a crisis of confidence to remember that 'your first project is generally the worst'. You are in the midst of a learning process; your skills and confidence will grow with time.

- *Lack of direction* – Research often starts with broad-ranging exploration that can take you down many tangents. The up side is that this exploration will undeniably increase your learning and often lead to new insights. The down side, however, is that you risk feeling lost. It is pretty easy to get yourself off course and feel like you have no idea where you are going. Finding direction can come from reflecting on what it is that you really want to know, having open and candid discussions with your supervisor, and in the end remembering that the answers may not simply appear. You may need to make some hard decisions about the direction you will take.

- *Feeling disorganized* – It is too easy to say 'you need to be organized'. You probably knew that before you got yourself in a mess. The need for self-discipline may be obvious, but the ability to exercise it is much harder. If physical disorganization is your downfall, take a week or two off from 'doing' research and just clean up your work space and organize yourself. If, however, disorganization is more in your mind and you feel as though you cannot think straight, you can (1) try the above – an organized desk and office can pave the way for an organized mind – or (2) get away from it all. Sometimes a good weekend away is all you need to refresh the mental batteries.

- *Personal crisis* — I think it was John Lennon who said 'life is what happens while you are making other plans'. It would be nice if the world stopped while you got on with your research, but that is simply not going to happen. Whether it is difficulties with finances, partners, parents, children, in fact any variety of drama, the research process necessarily coincides with life's inevitable ups and downs. Reach out to your support network and speak openly with your supervisor. My experience is that people are generally supportive. Perhaps most important of all, don't put too much pressure on yourself. Get support and then make a guilt-free decision to press on, take it slower, or have a hiatus until the crisis subsides.

FURTHER READING

There are quite a few project survival guides out there. The following might be worth a look.

Cryer, P. (2006) *The Research Student's Guide to Success*. Buckingham: Open University Press.

Hall, G. and Longman, J. (2008) *The Postgraduate's Companion*. London: Sage.

Moore, N. (2006) *How to Do Research: A Practical Guide to Designing And Managing Research Projects*. London: Facet.

Phelps, R., Fisher, K., and Ellis, A. H. (2007) *Organizing and Managing Your Research: A Practical Guide for Postgraduates*. London: Sage.

Rudestam, K. E. and Newton, R. R. (2007) *Surviving Your Dissertation: A Comprehensive Guide to Content and Process*. London: Sage.

Tarling, R. (2005) *Managing Social Research: A Practical Guide*. London: Routledge.

CHAPTER SUMMARY

- Research is a process that needs to be actively managed. Being strategic in your preliminary planning, being organized and prepared, and creating the mental space necessary for research are important parts of the process.
- Conducting a research project offers tremendous opportunity for professional development in areas including, but not limited to, problem-based learning, action learning, communication, evidence-based decision making, and academic qualifications.
- In order to produce research that falls within university guidelines, you will need to familiarize yourself with your institution's requirements. Similarly, taking advantage of all possible resources involves knowing what they are.
- Navigating a path through the research process should begin by making sure you have access to an adequate work space and computer system/ programs.

- Supervisory relationships can be difficult to negotiate. Working towards good communication with clear expectations, as well as striving for a sense of comfort in power relations, can help ensure a positive and productive relationship.
- Researching can present real challenges in terms of workloads and timelines. Using Gantt charts and working with both discipline and inspiration can help you manage the process.
- Most students carry the burden of having a variety of roles. Finding a balance is essential to personal well-being and hence success in all endeavours, including research.
- The research process is rarely an easy and straightforward journey. It often involves crises of confidence and motivation, and coincides with life's ups and downs. Knowing that you are not alone and that there is support can help get you through.

3
STRIVING FOR INTEGRITY IN THE RESEARCH PROCESS

CHAPTER PREVIEW

- Power, politics, ethics, and research integrity
- Credibility: integrity in the production of knowledge
- Ethics: integrity and the 'researched'
- Integrity indicators and checklist

POWER, POLITICS, ETHICS, AND RESEARCH INTEGRITY

> **"** All our science, measured against reality, is primitive and childlike – and yet it is the most precious thing we have. **"**
> *Albert Einstein*

Science is 'primitive and childlike', yet it is 'precious'. What did Einstein mean by this and what implication does it have for researchers? Well, science is primitive and childlike simply because the quest to capture reality is a challenge we have not fully met, and probably never will. But it is precious because it is so central to our ability to learn, to grow, to shift, to change – to make a difference. And this means research needs to be handled with the utmost care. At every stage, the goal needs to be responsibility and integrity. The challenge demands nothing less.

Integrity in research plays out in two broad arenas in which power and politics both play a role. The first is in your quest to produce knowledge – your responsibility here is to make sure you have captured 'truth'; reached conclusions not tainted by error and unrecognized bias; and have conducted your research with professional integrity. The second is in working with others – your responsibility here is an ethical one that ensures the rights and well-being of those involved with your study are protected at all times.

TABLE 3.1   POWER, PRIVILEGE, AND SELF

Power and privilege	Disadvantage and marginalization
White	Person of colour
From a developed country	From a developing country
Christian	Muslim, Hindu, Buddhist
University educated	Secondary education or less
Middle class	Working class
Midlife	Young/old
Male	Female
English as first language	No English skills

Understanding the power game

Research as a purely objective activity removed from all aspects of politics and power is a myth no longer accepted in the research world. As early as the turn of the twentieth century, Max Weber recognized that 'the existence of a scientific problem coincides personally with ... specifically oriented motives and values' ([1904] 1949). It is now recognized that research, and therefore researchers, are responsible for shaping the character of knowledge. The responsibilities associated with this knowledge production have led to a growing recognition and acceptance of the need for ethical and political awareness to be a mainstream consideration in research. Researchers must actively manage power, politics, and ethics. As Jacob Bronowski (1971) said, '[n]o science is immune to the infection of politics and the corruption of power'.

I must admit that when I began 'doing' research I did not feel powerful. I was just a student and didn't see how power might impact on my ability to conduct credible research. But of course I should have, because I did have power. It was power derived from being well educated and middle class, power derived from being in a position to conduct research, power that comes from being in a position of control and authority.

Now it would be nice if gender, age, ethnicity, religion, social class, etc., no longer caused or created prejudice. But they do. Attributes affect both how others see you and how you see the world. And as inequitable as it might be, certain traits are associated with power and privilege, while others are not. This fact is likely to be self-evident to anyone who has been the victim of discrimination. But for those whose attributes place them in the dominant position (see Table 3.1), potential power can go unrecognized.

The impact of unrecognized power can be profound. For years, anthropologists conducted research without this reflexive awareness of self, and for years their findings were imprinted with the biases and assumptions of white, patriarchal, Western society. Both the integrity of the knowledge produced and the well-being of the researched are dependent on the ethical negotiation of power and power relationships.

CREDIBILITY: INTEGRITY IN THE PRODUCTION OF KNOWLEDGE

CREDIBILITY
The quality, capability, or power to elicit belief.

If the goal of conducting research is to produce new knowledge, knowledge that others will come to trust and rely on, then the production of this knowledge needs to be credible. It must have the 'power to elicit belief'.

But this is easier said than done. Social science research generally involves working with people – and research that involves people provides a host of challenges to research integrity. In fact people are extremely difficult. Bacteria, cells, DNA, etc., generally behave in the laboratory – you know what to expect, and the little bacteria are not attempting to consciously or subconsciously throw you.

But people are tough. They have hidden agendas, fallible memories, and a need to present themselves in certain ways. They can be helpful, defensive, and/or deferential – and there will be plenty of times when you won't know when they are being what. And then there is the researcher. Also a fallible, biased, or subjective human entity, faced with the challenge of producing 'unbiased', trustworthy results. Now when you combine a subjective researcher with an unpredictable 'researched' it makes the production of credible knowledge no easy feat.

Outside the research world credibility can come from that which is believable, plausible, likely, probable, or realistic. But within the research world, credibility takes on a more specialized meaning and is demonstrated by a range of indicators such as reliability, validity, authenticity, neutrality, and auditability. Such indicators point to research that has been approached as disciplined rigorous enquiry and is therefore likely to be accepted as a valued contribution to knowledge.

Working with appropriate indicators

Knowing what indicators are relevant and appropriate for a particular research project is not without ambiguity. As the assumptions that underpin research expand beyond the realms of positivist knowing (see Chapter 1), debate over how research should be critically evaluated intensifies. For traditional researchers, indicators of good research are premised around a world that can be: quantifiably measured through defined rules of enquiry; approached with objectivity; and is, in fact, knowable. These assumptions, however, have been called into question by those critiquing the positivist paradigm. It is now recognized that an alternative set of indicators is more appropriate for research premised around a post-positivist/postmodern world – a world that is recognized as infinitely complex and without a defined 'truth'; recognizes and values subjectivities; and is unlikely to be captured by statistics alone.

The difficulty for many researchers is that the assumptions that underpin their research may not fit neatly into one paradigmatic way of knowing. To pigeonhole themselves and their research into either positivist or post-positivist frameworks limits their ability to think and act reflexively. Designing studies that can cross the constructed boundaries dividing these two camps is difficult when researchers adopt frameworks derived from within the paradigms.

So in the face of such complexity, how do you begin to work towards indicators of credibility? Well, rather than use a paradigmatic base, I suggest you look at the underlying challenges that need to be met in order to ensure good research, namely:

- Have subjectivities been acknowledged and managed?
- Has 'true essence' been captured?
- Are methods approached with consistency?
- Are arguments relevant and appropriate?
- Can the research be verified?

These questions can act as a framework for evaluating the credibility of your own work as well as the work of others. It is then up to you as a researcher to determine the appropriate indicators for each of these questions through an examination of your own worldview and assumptions; the aims and objectives of the research; and the methodological approaches adopted (see Table 3.2 at the end of the chapter).

Managing subjectivities

The question here is not whether researchers are subjective entities (everyone is), but (1) whether we recognize ourselves as subjective, and (2) whether we can manage our personal biases.

There is no doubt that we make sense of the world through the rules we are given to interpret it. But because we are immersed in these rules and surrounded by them, they can be very hard to see. For example, those born into a religious faith do not often remember when they first heard about God; he or she simply is. Our sense of patriotism, our understandings of family, our belief in justice and equity – our morals and most core beliefs – are established within us before we have the ability to recognize or reflect on them as constructs. These beliefs are embedded within us. They are a part of how we understand and make sense of the world – and how we might research it. Working towards credible research therefore demands reflexive awareness of our worldviews and a conscious effort for us to take them into account as we enter into the research journey.

Now for traditional scientists, e.g. those working in a laboratory, this means putting aside any preconceived notions and aiming for pure *objectivity*. Strict methodological protocols and a 'researched' that is outside the self generally make striving for this indicator a manageable task. For social science researchers, however, the challenge is somewhat more difficult. It is society itself that is being researched, and as products of society, social science researchers need to recognize that their own worldview makes them value bound. If who we are colours what we see and how we interpret it, then the need to hear, see, and appreciate multiple perspectives or realities is essential to rigorous research. Feminists, for example, have long critiqued the social sciences for their tendency to analyse and interpret the world from a privileged, white, male perspective.

Objectivity is never a given. If you as a researcher don't take subjectivities into account and actively work towards the criteria of *neutrality*, you can readily fall into the trap of judging the reality of others in relation to your own. In fact, researchers who do not act to consciously manage their own positioning run the risk of conducting 'self-centric' analysis; that is, being insensitive to issues of race, class, or gender; hearing only the dominant voice; and disregarding the power of language.

Being insensitive to issues of race, class, or gender

Insensitivity to issues of race, class, gender, etc., refers to the practice of ignoring these constructs as important factors or variables in a study, and can be a by-product of 'self-centric' analysis. Researchers need to recognize and appreciate the reality of the researched, otherwise they run the risk of ignoring unique and significant attributes. For example, a study of student motivation in a multicultural setting would not be very meaningful without ethnicity as one significant variable. Yes, career ambitions, study enjoyment, perceived relevance, etc., can be important predictors of motivation, but all of these factors can be motivated by family and culture. For example, in many Anglo-Asian households, student success and failure is seen as parental success and failure, and this can be a huge student weight and/or motivator.

Insensitivity to issues of race, class, and gender can also lead to dichotomization, or the tendency to put groups at two separate ends of the spectrum without recognition of overlapping characteristics. We do this when we talk in absolute terms about 'men' and 'women' or 'blacks' and 'whites'. Research that dichotomizes is often research that has fallen prey to stereotypes.

Finally, insensitivity to race, class, and gender can lead to double standards where the same behaviours, situations, or characteristics are analysed using different criteria depending on whether respondents are black or white, male or female, rich or poor, etc. For example, let's say you wanted to explore reasons for marital infidelity. If you were to use different sets of responses for males and females in which your preconceived notions about men being 'easily bored' and women being 'quite needy' came through, you would have a double standard. Remember that in the conduct of research, there is an essential need to guard against the assumptions and biases inherent within our society.

Hearing only the dominant voice

It is very easy to listen to those who are speaking the loudest or to those who are speaking your 'language'. But when you do this – you're likely to end up missing an important undercurrent, a whole other voice. I have struggled with this in my own teaching.

When I give a workshop, I try very hard to relate to my students – to communicate with them rather than lecture at them. I try to engage 'dialogue' and get a two-way conversation going. And I think I do this fairly well. In every class a core group of students makes this easy for me.

But who is in this core group? Well, it can be a mixed bag, but I can tell you who it isn't. It is not generally the international students; they tend to stay in the background. Now there are a number of reasons for this. For one, many come from an educational system where they are not invited to participate. Others struggle with English as a second language. But another factor could be me and my reality. The examples I use, the personal anecdotes I share, my 'in your face' American style, can all conspire so that those with demographic characteristics similar to mine are the ones who speak up the most. So it is the Asian and Indian students in my class who can go unheard (as they are likely to do throughout their Western university careers).

When I am teaching, my challenge is to find a way to engage all of my class and to make sure I am reaching every student – and that they are reaching me. The challenge when researching is similar (see Box 3.1). If you do not consciously work on strategies for appreciating diversity and hearing the marginalized, you run the risk of gathering data and reaching conclusions that ignore those in society who often go unheard. Attempting to empower traditionally marginalized voices is essential in responsible research. Indigenous peoples, minorities, children, women, gays, and lesbians are often not heard, yet their voices are essential to any full understanding.

BOX 3.1   THE PEOPLE IN MY SHIRE – KEITH'S STORY

I was conducting research with a local council and had already interviewed the mayor and a few of the local councillors about the community, when I attended my first council meeting. The meeting was a real eye-opener. The ethnic background for the region I was studying was about 45% Anglo, 25% Asian, 20% Indian, and 10% Greek, with at least seven different religions. Yet, when I walked into the meeting I was asked to give my 'Christian' name, and the meeting started with a prayer from the Protestant minister. At that stage, I took a good look around and realized that *all* of the councillors looked to be of Anglo descent. In fact, almost everyone present at the meeting was Anglo.

I then thought of all the times the mayor and councillors had spoken of their 'community'. I was left wondering what their 'community' was. Was their frame of reference the range of constituents in their jurisdiction, or was their frame of reference individuals with the same demographic background as themselves – in other words, 'community' as the white Christians who came to the council meetings? From that point on I was committed to ensuring that my research reflected the 'real' community, not just those with the ability/propensity to be heard.

Disregard for the power of language

Research is coloured by our use of language in a number of ways. First, there is the subtle yet formidable power of words themselves. The words we use to speak to respondents and them to us can be easily misunderstood and misrepresented. For example, language that might be 'shocking' for one group might be quite 'everyday' for another. It is worth remembering that analysis of words needs to come from the perspective and reality of the researched, not the researcher.

Working with respondents with whom you do not share a common language presents an added level of difficulty. There isn't a single computer program that can accurately translate one language to another; and that is because languages are highly metaphorical, mythical, poetic, and full of hidden meanings, riddles, and assumptions. Accurate interpretations, let alone the nuances of language and speech, are often lost through interpreters or in the process of translation. The researcher who assumes that English can capture thoughts processed in a different language with any sophistica tion risks reducing the richness and complexity of a respondent's ideas and views. Researchers working outside their first language need to find ways to confirm that their data's accuracy and richness are not lost in the process of interpretation and translation.

Strategies for managing subjectivities

Managing subjectivities is more than something you should do. It is, in fact, a task which is crucial to the production of credible data and trustworthy results. Strategies you can adopt include:

- *Appreciating your own worldview* – Your ability to manage subjectivities is dependent on being able to recognize and articulate them. In fact, the first chapter of many theses now includes a section on researcher positioning.
- *Appreciating alternative realities* – Actively explore the personal and societal assumptions that underpin the understandings of the researcher and the researched, and accept that these might be quite distinct.
- *Suspending initial judgements* – We live in a society where it is common to judge what we do not understand. Yet as researchers, not understanding is precisely why it is important not to judge.
- *Checking your interpretation of events, situations, and phenomena with 'insiders'* – This is particularly relevant in cross-cultural research. Finding out how someone from within a cultural reality understands a situation can help illuminate your own biases.
- *Getting the full story* – Those we seek out and those willing to participate are often those with the strongest voices. Your research design should seek representation from all those you wish your research to speak for or about, including those often silenced.
- *Seeking out and incorporating alternative and pluralistic points of view* – Even when crystallizing interpretations, hold on to the richness and complexity that can come from outside viewpoints.

Capturing 'truth'

It could be said that research is all about the elusive concept of 'truth' and our desire to capture it. Traditionally, we are talking here about a knowable world in which a singular truth can be assessed by the indicator of *validity*. In other words, we assess whether our findings are 'correct'. For example, say you were exploring whether 'gender identification causes girls to relate better to their mothers than do boys'. Validity would rest on: (1) showing that how you measured 'relate' truly reflected 'relating'; (2) showing that you had a sample size large enough and representative enough to make the claim about girls and boys in general; (3) showing that it truly is gender identification that is affecting the ability to relate, and not any other factors.

In a world where we accept the possibility of multiple realties, however, *authenticity* is more likely to be an appropriate indicator. Authenticity indicates that rigour and reflexive practice has assured that conclusions are justified, credible, and trustworthy even when truth is dependent on perspective (see Box 3.2).

BOX 3.2   WHOSE REALITY ANYWAY?

I once took a group of humanities students to a local school to look at the layout of the fifth-grade classroom. There were 42 10-year-old children sitting down in seven rows of six, all facing forward. The teacher was standing in the middle of the front of the classroom, facing the children. I broke my students up into two groups and asked them to find out why the classroom was set up in this manner.

The eventual responses were quite distinct. The first group attempted to answer the question from the perspective of the teacher. They interviewed her and found that this was the best set-up, and that there is no other logical way the room could be arranged. The children need to face both the teacher and the blackboard. My students also found that this set-up minimized the propensity for the children to distract or be distracted by each other, and allowed them to direct their focus on the teacher.

The analysis of the second group was completely different. They answered the question from the perspective of critical literature, and claimed that the structure was typical of how most classrooms are set up, which is a clear mechanism of control. The seating arrangement exists because it facilitates a relationship of power between teacher and student that is all one way. There is no respect for what peers can give to each other. This structure alienates the children from each other, making them unable to act as a collective and therefore rendering them powerless. It also limits learning because it tends to facilitate rote memorization, rather than hands-on engagement.

Which group were right? I guess this is the point – it is not a matter of right or wrong. It is simply a matter of reality and perspective. You need to be cognizant of the realities you are presenting as well as those you are not.

Building trust

Your ability to capture truth, whether you understand it as a single valid truth or an authentic truth that may sit alongside other interpretations, will be highly dependent on your ability to get your respondents to talk to you with openness and honesty. And while there are no techniques that can guarantee candour, building trust is essential. It is therefore absolutely crucial to minimize any real or perceived power differential between you and the 'researched'. If you can't do this, the 'researched' are likely to feel alienated, intimidated, and/or uninterested by the research process.

There are any number of factors that can influence your ability to build rapport and trust including:

- *Gender* As drawn out in Box 3.3, the rapport and trust you build, the slant on stories you hear, and the memories you draw out can be very dependent on gender. For example, some women might only feel comfortable talking about the loss of a child with another woman. Or imagine conducting an interview on promiscuity; the answers you might elicit could be highly dependent on your own gender. Now there are no hard and fast rules here. What is important is to consciously think through the issue of gender and whether it is likely to be a factor in building trust.

- *Age* – Trust is often dependent on your ability to relate to your respondents and their ability to relate to you, and age can certainly be a factor. For example, there are very few parents who can ask their teenagers 'What did you do this weekend?' and get the full story – especially if the weekend was any good! Like it or not, age can be a critical factor in credible data collection. And again there are no hard and fast rules, just a mandate that you consider how age might influence researcher–researched relationships.

- *Ethnicity* – The ethnic and cultural background of the researcher can certainly influence the research process. It is sad to say we still have much inequity, suspicion, and mistrust running across ethnic and racial lines. But that is a reality – and it is a reality that can affect your ability to gain trust. Say, for example, you wanted to research attitudes towards education in a Hispanic community. While a 'white' outsider might struggle to gain trust, a Hispanic insider might have an easier time opening up honest and open lines of communication.

- *Socio-economic status/education* – Societal position can also have great bearing on the research process. Researchers often come from a position of privilege so you need to think about breaking down barriers, and convince the 'researched' that you are not sitting in judgement. Being aware of your own socio-economic status and educational background, as well as that of the researched, puts you in a position to manage any potential power-related issue that might influence your study.

- *Position of power and privilege within a culture or subculture* – An imbalance of power can be a common difficulty for researchers working within a culture where they are cast as a 'scientist' or 'expert'. Gary Larson once drew a cartoon showing 'natives' in a hut frantically hiding their VCRs and TVs while yelling out 'Anthropologists!' He very insightfully illustrates how deference to the expert changes the researched. A major dilemma when understanding cross-cultural studies is knowing how you can conduct 'authentic' research when you are immersed in a culture where your position of power and privilege finds those you are researching acting in ways that may not be 'natural'.

> ### BOX 3.3   GENDER, SEXUALITY, AND ROLLER COASTERS – ANNE'S STORY
>
> There was supposed to be a group of us going to the amusement park from graduate school, but it ended up just being John, his male partner, and me. Being the 'third wheel' to an in-love couple is bad enough, but to be the third wheel to a gay couple was really strange. All the little acts of chivalry that I never really noticed before were suddenly conspicuous by their absence. No one offered to pay for anything, no one let me go first, no one tried to win me anything. I even had to ride the roller coaster by myself. Two men together in the front carriage, me by myself behind them. You couldn't help but stop and reflect on that. In fact, until that day, I had no idea how much I related to men as a 'woman'. I was shocked by the realization that my interactions with men were so coloured by my sexuality.
>
> I reflected on this experience in relation to my own research, and realized just how important the role of gender and sexuality might be, particularly when collecting data. I realized that if I wanted to really understand what I was studying, my own practice as a researcher needed to take into account who I was.

Listening without judgement

I was recently reminded how hard it can be to withhold judgement. I often give workshops in Hong Kong and one of my students flew from there to Australia (where I now work and live) for a visit. Over lunch, he and his wife told me that their youngest son, who is 10 and has just gone off to boarding school in the UK, has been crying on the phone every day saying that he hates it, is being picked on and racially abused, and really wants to go home. Now I was raised, and still live, in a cultural reality where I could not even contemplate sending any 10-year-old of mine that far away from home. Yet in no way do I question that this family's decision was made out of love and a desire to give their child the best. It's just that it is so far from my own reality and the way I have been socialized.

I had to make a conscious effort to suspend judgement and not snarl 'What were you thinking, sending him there in the first place?' People can sniff out judgement from a mile off, and if you do not make an effort to suspend or withhold it, you won't stand a chance at building trust and getting to the heart of an issue. Be conscious of both verbal and non-verbal cues here – what you say, how you say it, your facial expressions, and your body language can all work to build trust or alienate the other.

Now it may seem as though issues of trust are more likely to be a factor in research that involves close interaction with the researched, e.g. when conducting an interview. And while this is true, it is also worth thinking about how trust can be undermined or built in a survey. The words you use, the concepts you call on, and the assumptions you premise can all conspire to put respondents at ease or cause them to feel alienated.

Approaching methods with consistency

Once you have worked through issues related to the management of subjectivities and the building of trust to capture 'truth', the quest for integrity in knowledge production turns to questions of method. It is important to remember that regardless of approach, researching is not a haphazard activity. Rather, it is an activity that needs to be approached with discipline, rigour, and a level of standardization. If the goal is to have your research stand up to scrutiny and be taken as credible, it is important that readers are confident that your methods have been implemented in ways that best assure consistency.

Often consistency in methods is referred to as *reliability* or the extent to which a measure, procedure, or instrument provides the same result on repeated trials. A good example here is bathroom scales. If you were to jump on your scales 10 times in a row and got the same results each time, the scales would be reliable. The scales could be wrong – it might always be 10 pounds heavy or 10 pounds light (personally, I prefer the light variety), but it would be reliable. A more complicated example might be trying to measure job satisfaction with a questionnaire. The questionnaire would only be reliable if results were not dependent on things like who administered the questionnaire, what kind of day the respondent was having, or whether or not it was a weekend.

The flipside of this is that people are complex and multi-faceted. At any given time, for any given reason, they may only reveal part of themselves. Say, for example, you wanted to ask about stress – this is something that can, and often does, vary from day to day. So developing methodological tools that are 'reliable' might not be straightforward. Nevertheless, the process of data collection needs to be more than haphazard. In fact, it should meet the criteria of *dependability*. Methods need to be designed and developed in ways that are consistent, logical, systematic, well documented, and designed to account for research subjectivities.

Making relevant and appropriate arguments

Assume you have gotten to the point where you have some great data. You're pretty sure you have been able to manage your biases, got your respondents to open up, and employed data collection tools and analysis strategies capable of holding up to a good level of scrutiny. The next step is to put forward some credible arguments. Now this will involve a few challenges we have already discussed, i.e. keeping a check on subjectivities and exploring multiple interpretations. But as discussed below, it will also involve weighing up your findings in light of your study's limitations, and being confident that you are speaking for an appropriate group of people.

Being true to your study's limitations

Very few researchers get to conduct their studies in a way they consider ideal: there is rarely enough time or money; the cooperation of others might be less than ideal;

and there could be a whole list of things you would have done differently with the benefit of hindsight. So what do you do?

Well, making appropriate arguments is about being able to attest to the credibility of your data and the trustworthiness of your results – in spite of any limitations. Now it can be tempting to downplay difficulties and write up your research as though everything went smoothly in a study that was optimally designed. But if you are challenged here, your ethics and credibility can come into question. As outlined in Box 3.4, a much better approach is to take it in three steps. The first step is to honestly outline the study's limitations or shortcomings. The second step is to outline the strategies that you have employed to gather credible data and generate trustworthy results because of, or in spite of, any limitations. The third step follows from the second and is a 'therefore' type of statement that offers justification or rationalization for the data and findings of your study.

BOX 3.4   BEING TRUE TO YOUR STUDY'S LIMITATIONS

The following student excerpt is a good example of the three-step approach to outlining your study's limitations:

> While the original data collection protocol was to survey a random sample of the population, preliminary investigation showed that the extent of this population is unknown. A directory of men who have experienced domestic abuse simply does not exist. It also became clear that many men who had experienced this type of abuse did not want to be approached **[Step 1]**. It was therefore decided to ask for volunteers through the use of flyers in counsellors' offices, and combine that with snowball sampling that asked the volunteers to pass on the request to anyone else they might know of who has experienced a similar situation **[Step 2]**. While there is no guarantee that the results from this sample will be representative of the greater population, this study, through the use of willing and open volunteers, does offer valuable insights to the phenomenon, and sheds much light on an under-explored area of domestic violence **[Step 3]**.

Speaking for an appropriate group of people

Conclusions relevant to only a particular sample or only within a certain research setting can provide important knowledge for key stakeholders, but they do not allow findings to be applied to a broader population and thereby limit broader generation of new knowledge.

Broad applicability of findings is therefore a goal of many researchers. There is a desire to argue that findings extend beyond a particular sample or setting. But to do this researchers need to ensure they are speaking for an appropriate group of people. Any sample used should be (1) representative of a wider population and (2) large enough that they can be confident that their findings do reflect larger trends.

Meeting these criteria means that your findings are *generalizable*. The key (as discussed in Chapter 10) is ensuring both adequate and broad representation. And this is certainly possible in medium- to large-scale survey research. But what if your research project is centred on a particular case, or is designed to collect more in-depth qualitative data that will limit your sample size? Under these circumstances, you may not be able to argue *generalizability*. Yet broader applicability may still be a goal. If this is the case, your goal will be the indicator of *transferability* or highlighting 'lessons learned' that are likely to be applicable in alternative settings or populations. For example, the results of an in-depth case study in any one school will not be representative of all schools – but there will definitely be lessons learned that can illuminate relevant issues and provide rich learning within other school contexts. The key here is providing a detailed description of the research setting and methods so that applicability can be determined by those reading the research account.

Providing accurate and verifiable research accounts

Conducting research is a highly complex process. Without a doubt, it is hard to get it right. So it is the responsibility of the researcher to consciously minimize the possibility that results are false or misleading. To that end, research approaches are expected to be open and accountable. Physicist Richard Feynman argues the need to 'report everything that you think might make it (your study) invalid – not only what you think is right about it ... Details that could throw doubt on your interpretation must be given, if you know them' (1997). The admission of shortcomings and limitations is encouraged and research is expected to be reproducible. In fact, codes of ethics often require researchers to keep their raw data for a period of five to seven years thereby protecting themselves from accusations of fraud or misrepresentation.

Even though the price of fraudulence can be quite high (students shown to be acting fraudulently are often forced to withdraw from their degree programmes), misrepresentation and fraud are quite rampant. Researchers (and not just students) have been known to:

- blatantly fabricate data or falsify results
- omit cases or fiddle with numbers in order to show 'significance'
- plagiarize passages from articles or books without crediting the original author(s)
- misrepresent authorship by: (1) using a ghost writer; (2) taking full credit for authorship when more than one author was involved; (3) naming a co-author who had no involvement with the study.

Verifiable accounts are therefore considered essential. As well as allowing others to attempt to replicate or reproduce findings, verifiable accounts help establish a study's credibility by making them 'auditable' (others can see exactly how findings were generated). It is difficult to blatantly fabricate data; falsify results; omit cases; fiddle with numbers; plagiarize; and even misrepresent authorship, if your methods are out there for all to see.

ETHICS: INTEGRITY AND THE 'RESEARCHED'

Absolutely central to research integrity is ethics. With power comes responsibility. As a researcher you have an explicit and fundamental responsibility towards the 'researched'. The dignity and well-being of respondents, both mentally and physically, is absolutely crucial. Understanding how this responsibility is best negotiated at legal, moral, and ethical levels is a prerequisite for any potential researcher.

Legal obligations

In a nutshell, researchers are not above the law. Some might like to be – but clearly they are not. The laws of society stand in the world of research. If it is illegal for the general public, then it is illegal for researchers and research participants. Now for most researchers, the criterion of non-engagement in illegal activities is not too difficult to appreciate or meet. Most recognize the logic here. But a more common legal dilemma is faced by researchers who: (1) wish to study illegal activities; or (2) come across illegal activities in the course of their investigations. For example, I have had students with interests in everything from cockfighting, to abuse of patients by hospital staff, to corporal punishment in private schools. And a dilemma that faces these student researchers is knowing whether they have an obligation to report any illegal activities they may come to know of in the course of their study. For example, say you were interviewing parents about stress and you discovered a case of child abuse. Do you maintain confidentiality, or are you obligated to report the abuse?

Well, the law here is quite ambiguous and can vary by both country and case. You may or may not be obligated to report illegal activities, but in most countries, the courts can subpoena your data and files. Legal precedents suggest that researcher assurances of confidentiality do not hold up in court. As a researcher, you are not afforded the same rights as a lawyer, doctor, or priest.

Moral obligations

When we talk about morals, we are talking about rights and wrongs, societal norms, and values. In research, this boils down to responsibility for the dignity and welfare of both individuals and cultural groups. Put simply, research should not be offensive, degrading, humiliating, or dangerous. In fact, it should not be psychologically or physically damaging in any way.

Some moral considerations in the conduct of research include:

- *Conscientiousness* – This refers to a need to keep the interests of respondents or participants at the forefront in any decision-making processes related to the conduct of research. It is important to remember that researchers hold a certain position of power, and being conscious of this power is essential in ensuring the well-being of those involved in your research project.

- *Equity* – Equitable research is concerned with the practice of asking only some segments of the population to participate in research, while other segments are immune from such requests. For example, prisoners, students, children, minorities, etc., may have characteristics that make them targets for research studies. It is important that particular groups of individuals are not treated as, or made to feel like, 'guinea pigs'.
- *Honesty* – Gone are the days when researchers could 'dupe' respondents and lie to them about what was going to happen, or why a research study was being done in the first place. There is an expectation that researchers are open and honest and that details of the research process are made transparent.

Ethical obligations

Ethics tend to be based on moral obligations, but put a professional spin on what is fair, just, right, or wrong. Ethics refer to principles or rules of behaviour that act to dictate what is actually acceptable or allowed within a profession. Ethical guidelines for the conduct of research will vary by professional code, discipline area, and institution, but generally cover the following areas:

- *Ensuring respondents have given informed consent* – Participants can only give 'informed consent' to be involved in a research study if they have full understanding of their requested involvement – including time commitment, type of activity, topics that will be covered, and all physical and emotional risks potentially involved. Informed consent implies that participants are: *competent* – they have reasonable intellectual capacity and psychological maturity; *autonomous* – they are making self-directed and self-determined choices; *involved voluntarily* – they are not unaware, forced, pressured, or duped; *aware of the right to discontinue* – they are under no obligation (or pressure) to continue involvement; *not deceived* – the nature of the study, any affiliations or professional standing, and the intended use of the study should be honest and open; *not coerced* – positions of power should not be used to get individuals to participate; *not induced* – while it may be acceptable to compensate individuals for their time and effort, an inducement should not compromise a potential participant's judgement.
- *Ensuring no harm comes to respondents* – This includes emotional or psychological harm as well as physical harm. Now physical harm is relatively easy to recognize, but risks of psychological harm can be hard to identify and difficult to predict. Whether it be resentment, anxiety, embarrassment, or reliving unpleasant memories, psychological 'harm' can be unplanned and unintentional, yet commonplace. Keep in mind that as well as being ethically and morally unacceptable, risks of harm can give rise to legal issues. We are talking about lawsuits here. So even if your conscience or your professional ethics can justify your decisions, the potential for legal action may be enough to make you reassess your approach.
- *Ensuring confidentiality and, if appropriate, anonymity* – Confidentiality involves protecting the identity of those providing research data; all identifying data remains

solely with the researcher. Keep in mind that pseudonyms may not be enough to hide identity. If others can figure out who you are speaking about, or who is doing the speaking, you need to further mask identity or seek approval for disclosure. Anonymity goes a step beyond confidentiality and refers to protection against identification even from the researcher. Information, data, and responses collected anonymously should not be identifiable with any particular respondent. A good example of this is 'anonymous' class evaluations where students should feel confident that there is no chance of damning feedback coming back to bite them. As well as masking identity, protection of confidentiality and anonymity should involve: secure storage of raw data; restricting access to the data; the need for permission for subsequent use of the data; and eventual destruction of raw data.

While such guidelines may seem straightforward, there's likely to be a tradeoff between following such guidelines and the data you want to collect. Ethics, however, must always take precedence, even if this means your design needs to go through a process of modification. Luckily, ethics committees have approval processes that can help you identify and work within the boundaries that define the conduct of ethical research.

Ethics approval processes

Commitment to the conduct of ethical research is simply not enough. Most universities and large bureaucratic institutions, such as hospitals or some government departments, require you to obtain official approval that will involve the development of an ethics proposal (see Chapter 5) in order to undertake a study. This will require you to carefully examine all aspects of your study for ethical implications and work through all the logistics.

Now there are quite a few researchers who believe that getting ethics approval is simply a bureaucratic hurdle-jumping process designed to take up limited and precious time. But there are actually some good reasons to take the process seriously. An ethics committee is there to: (1) ensure integrity in knowledge production; (2) promote responsibility towards participants; and (3) protect both the researcher and the granting institution from any potential legal ramifications that might arise from unethical research.

Most universities will have their own ethics protocols, but there is a move for greater standardization. The Economic and Social Research Council in the UK, for example, is in the process of developing a national framework for social science research ethics. Australia has taken this a step further with the development of a national ethics approval form (NEAF) designed to assist researchers complete standardized proposals for submission to various research committees (now adopted by most Australian universities). The goal is to increase the consistency, efficiency, and quality of the review processes.

TABLE 3.2   CREDIBILITY INDICATORS BY ISSUES AND PARADIGM

'Positivist' indicators	'Post-positivist' indicators
Have subjectivities been acknowledged and managed?	
Objectivity – conclusions based on observable phenomena; not influenced by emotions, personal prejudices, or subjectivities	*Neutrality* – subjectivities recognized and negotiated in a manner that attempts to avoid biasing results/conclusions *Subjectivity with transparency* – acceptance and disclosure of subjective positioning and how it might impact on the research process, including conclusions drawn
Has 'true essence' been captured?	
Validity – concerned with truth value, i.e. whether conclusions are 'correct'. Also considers whether methods, approaches, and techniques actually relate to what is being explored	*Authenticity* – concerned with truth value while recognizing that multiple truths may exist. Also concerned with describing the deep structure of experience/phenomenon in a manner that is 'true' to the experience
Are methods approached with consistency?	
Reliability – concerned with internal consistency, i.e. whether data/results collected, measured, or generated are the same under repeated trials	*Dependability* – accepts that reliability in studies of the social may not be possible, but attests that methods are systematic, well documented, and designed to account for research subjectivities
Are arguments relevant and appropriate?	
Generalizability – whether findings and/or conclusions from a sample, setting, or group are directly applicable to a larger population, a different setting, or to another group	*Transferability* – whether findings and/or conclusions from a sample, setting, or group lead to lessons learned that may be germane to a larger population, a different setting, or to another group
Can the research be verified?	
Reproducibility – concerned with whether results/conclusions would be supported if the same methodology was used in a different study with the same/similar context	*Auditability* – accepts the importance of the research context and therefore seeks full explication of methods to allow others to see how and why the researchers arrived at their conclusions
Have research participants been treated with integrity?	
Legality – concerned that the research process is not in breach of the law, including any obligation to report illegal activities that researchers may come to know of in the course of their research *Morality* – centres on the societal norms that should act to protect research participants. These norms include conscientious decision making, equity, and honesty through full disclosure *Ethicality* – refers to a professional 'code of practice' designed to protect the researched from an unethical process, and in turn protect the researcher from legal liabilities. Key ethical considerations include informed consent, causing no harm, and a right to privacy	

INTEGRITY INDICATORS AND CHECKLIST

A challenge for all research students is to become conversant with indicators of research integrity. Not only will you need to work towards such indicators in your own research, your ability to critically engage with relevant literature will be enhanced if you can assess the work of others in relation to relevant indicators. Table 3.2 provides a summary of the key issues covered in this chapter and offers a range of associated 'indicators' appropriate to different modes of research.

FURTHER READING

Integrity in knowledge production and integrity in working with the 'researched' are both essential to research credibility. It is well worth reading a bit more in these crucial areas.

Integrity in knowledge production

Hood, S., Mayall, B., and Oliver, S. (eds) (1999) *Critical Issues in Social Research: Power and Prejudice*. Buckingham: Open University Press.

IMNRC (2002) *Integrity in Scientific Research: Creating an Environment That Promotes Responsible Conduct*. Washington, DC: National Academies Press.

Macfarlane, B. (2008) *Researching with Integrity: The ethics of academic research*. London: Routledge.

Macrina, F. L. (2005) *Scientific Integrity: Text and Cases in Responsible Conduct of Research*. Herndon, VA: ASM Press.

Ethics

Israel, M. and Hay, I. (2006) *Research Ethics for Social Scientists*. London: Sage.

Mertens, D. M. and Ginsberg, P. E. (2008) *The Handbook of Social Research Ethics*. London: Sage.

Oliver, P. (2003) *The Students' Guide to Research Ethics*. Buckingham: Open University Press.

CHAPTER SUMMARY

- Responsibility and integrity should be paramount research considerations. This includes integrity in the production of knowledge, and integrity in dealing with research participants.
- Ethical and political awareness need to be a mainstream consideration in the research. Power, politics, and ethics must now be actively managed.
- Integrity in the production of knowledge can be complicated by the human element. Idiosyncrasies of both researcher and researched alike make striving for integrity a challenge.

- Rather than selecting indicators strictly by paradigm, researchers are encouraged to consider underlying challenges and determine appropriate indicators by critically examining their methodological approaches.
- Recognizing and balancing subjectivities is central to integrity in knowledge production. If this is not done, researchers risk conducting 'self-centric' analysis; being insensitive to issues of race, class, or gender; and hearing only the dominant voice.
- Building trust is essential in capturing truth. Trust can be impacted by researcher attributes as well as a researcher's ability to listen without judging.
- Integrity in knowledge production without consistency in methods is difficult to achieve. Methods need to be developed in a consistent, logical, systematic, and well-documented manner that can account for researcher subjectivities.
- The ability to make relevant and appropriate arguments is crucial. Researchers need to make arguments that acknowledge and take limitations into account. It is also imperative that an appropriate group of people are being spoken for or about.
- Providing accurate and verifiable accounts of the research process is essential to a study's credibility.
- Integrity and the 'researched' refers to responsibility for the dignity and welfare of research participants.
- Legal obligations include the design of studies not in breach of the law. Researchers must also consider their obligation to report illegal activities.
- Moral obligations relate to societal norms that protect research participants. These include conscientious decision making, equity, and honesty through full disclosure.
- Ethical obligations refer to professional 'codes of practice' designed to protect the researched from an unethical process, and in turn protect the researcher from legal liabilities. Key issues include informed consent, causing no harm, and a right to privacy.
- Official ethics approval will ensure integrity, promote responsibility towards participants, and protect both the researcher and the granting institution from legal ramifications.
- A checklist for exploring integrity can help researchers critically review relevant literature and design sound methodologies.

4
DEVELOPING YOUR RESEARCH QUESTION

CHAPTER PREVIEW

- The importance of good questions
- Defining your topic
- From interesting topics to researchable questions
- The hypothesis dilemma
- Characteristics of good questions

THE IMPORTANCE OF GOOD QUESTIONS

> **The scientific mind does not so much provide the right answers as ask the right questions.**
> *Claude Lévi-Strauss*

You're ready. You have got yourself set up and have a pretty good idea of what you are in for. You even have a few research ideas. Next step? To develop and articulate a clear research question.

Now you may be thinking, "I have a pretty good idea about what I want to research. Is working on my actual question so important?" Well, the answer is an unequivocal '*Yes*'. There are a lot of students who want to jump right into their research project without taking the time to really think through and develop their research question. Some have ideas about their topic, but they are not clear on the aspects they want to explore. Others will have their ideas pretty much narrowed down, but have not clearly articulated this in a researchable question.

I have to say that I am a real stickler for good research questions. I believe they are absolutely fundamental to good research; and your ability to articulate one is essential.

After all, how will you know when you have found the answer to your question, if you can't say what your question is?

Remember: research is a decision-making journey. The process, in fact, demands that you constantly engage in decision making that is logical, consistent, and coherent. And what do you think is the benchmark for logical, consistent, and coherent decision making? It's that the choices you make take you one step closer to being able to answer your research question credibly. So without clear articulation of your question you are really travelling blind.

Research questions are essential because they:

- *Define an investigation* – A well-articulated research question can provide both you and your eventual readers with information about your project. It can: *define the topic* – youth suicide, environmental degradation, secularization, etc.; *define the nature of the research endeavour* – to discover, explore, explain, describe, or compare, *define the questions you are interested in* – what, where, how, when, why; *define your constructs and variables* – income, age, education, gender, self-esteem, pollution, etc.; and *indicate whether you foresee a relationship between variables* – impacts, increases, decreases, relationships, correlations, causes, etc.

- *Set boundaries* – Along your research journey you are likely to find yourself facing plenty of tangents, detours, and diversions, and a well-defined question can help you set boundaries. When faced with an interesting tangent, ask yourself: 'What does this have to do with my question?' I would suggest that there are three potential answers: (1) actually nothing – I will have to leave it and maybe pick it up in my next project; (2) actually it is quite relevant – if you think about it, it really does relate to … (this can be exciting and add new dimensions to your work); and (3) well nothing really, but I actually think this is at the heart of what I want to know – perhaps I need to rethink my question.

- *Provide direction* – A well-defined, well-articulated research question will act as a blueprint for your project. It will point you towards the theory you need to explore; the literature you need to review; the data you need to gather; and the methods you need to call on. In fact, I would suggest that it is nearly impossible to define a clear methodology for an ill-defined research question. If you do not know what you want to know, you will not be in a position to know how to find it out.

- *Act as a frame of reference for assessing your work* – Not only does your question provide continuity and set the agenda for your entire study, but it also acts as a benchmark for assessing decision making. The criteria for all decisions related to your project will be whether or not choices lead you closer to credible answers to your research question.

Now I don't want to make it sound like research questions are reductionist devices that take all exploration, creativity, and fluidity out of the research process. Not at all. Research questions themselves can be designed so that they are open and exploratory. As well, research questions can, and often do, change, shift, and evolve during the early stages of a project. Not only is this fine, it is appropriate as your engagement in the literature evolves both your knowledge and thinking. Yes, research questions define an investigation and provide direction, but it is up to the researcher to define and redefine questions so that they can most appropriately accomplish these tasks.

DEFINING YOUR TOPIC

All this talk about the importance of research questions is fine, but what if you're not even sure what interests to pursue? Well, you are not alone. Yes, there are plenty of students who are quite clear about what they want to research, but there are also a lot who really struggle with the idea of generating a research topic. In fact, many feel that coming up with something worthy of research is beyond them.

So how do you focus in on a topic? Well, as highlighted below and in Box 4.1, you work on generating ideas by homing in on your curiosity and creativity; looking for inspiration; and exploring your options with an eye towards practicalities.

Curiosity and creativity

> **Discovery** consists in seeing what everyone else has seen, and thinking what no one else has thought.
> *Albert Szent-Györgyi*

Ideas for research are generated any time curiosity or passion is aroused. Every day we are surrounded by events, situations, and interactions that make us wonder, stop, and think, or bring joy, frustration, relief, or anger bubbling to the surface. This is the rich and fertile ground from which research ideas are born. Think about what stirs you, what you argue about with your friends, family, and peers, and what issues are topical in the world, at home, or in your workplace. You will soon find that research topics abound. If you can learn to catch yourself thinking, 'Gee, I wonder ...', you will have an unending supply of ideas.

An option worth trying here is a concept map. Mapping allows you the freedom to think laterally as well as linearly. It uses free association to encourage the mind to jump from one idea to another, thereby enhancing creative processes. Concept mapping can facilitate brainstorming, drawing out connections, and building themes; and can also be a great tool for overcoming writer's block. Figure 4.1 shows a simple concept map used to draw out potential research topics.

Looking for inspiration

Another approach for narrowing in on your topic (see Box 4.1) is to be highly attuned to the world around you. Inspiration might be drawn from:

- *Personal insights and experiences* – Everyone has experience and insight they can draw on. Take the workplace, for example. Just about anyone who has ever had a job will tell you that workplaces are rife with issues: for example, red-tape, inefficiencies, ineptitude, incompetence, decision makers not in touch with the coal-face, corruption, profit before service, morale, and motivation. Your own frustrations are often tied to the frustrations of many – and if they can also be tied to the goals, aims, objectives, and vision of the organization, community, or

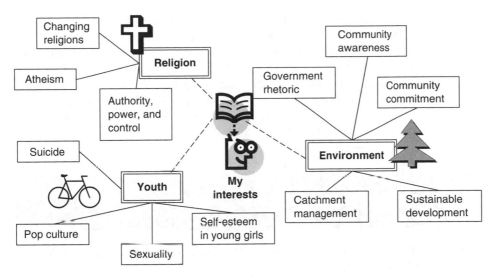

FIGURE 4.1   CONCEPT MAP OF POTENTIAL RESEARCH TOPICS

institution in which they sit, then there is a good chance those very frustrations will have 'research' potential.

- *An observation* – It can be quite hard to see what surrounds us, so viewing the world through fresh eyes can provide powerful research insights. This happened to a student of mine who was on a train when he suddenly became fascinated by the unwritten rules of personal space. He found himself intrigued by the rules that governed who sat where, how close they sat, who moved away from whom, and under what circumstances. He watched with fascination as people jockeyed for seats as the number of carriage occupants changed with each stop, and decided that he wanted to study the rules that govern such behaviour.

- *Contemporary/timely issues* – Sometimes an old topic can take on fresh life. A topic might suddenly become an agenda at the workplace, or may even become the focus of global attention. The Western world's interest, fascination, and judgement of Islamic faith is a case in point. 'Angles' become easy to find and questions such as 'How are the media covering the topic?', 'What is the policy, practice, and rhetoric of government?', 'What impact is this having on school yard racism?', become quite easy to generate.

- *Identifying stakeholder needs* – Stakeholder needs can be extremely broad and can range from the need for an equitable health care system, to a need for remediation of blue–green algae blooms in the local catchment, to a need to motivate students to stay in school. Identifying needs can come from following media coverage, reading letters to the editor, or listening to stakeholders at various forums including town council meetings, workplace meetings, or any other place where stakeholders may gather to express their concerns.

- *Exploring the literature* – The importance of reading for research cannot be overemphasized. When you are conversant with topical literature it becomes quite easy to find researchable issues. You can explore whether an important aspect of a problem has been ignored; whether assumptions underpinning an investigation need to be re-examined; or whether further questions related to a particular issue have been posed by researchers at the end of their research papers.

- *Theory* – Theoretical inspiration is most likely to happen when you find yourself relating theory to a real-world situation. The theory resonates and you think 'Aha', maybe that is why a particular situation is the way it is, or perhaps that is why they do what they do. A student of mine had such a moment when he read a work by Althusser that highlights the role of institutions such as the family, schools, and the Church, in embedding government ideology into individual consciousness. The student began to view the role of the Church in a new light and decided to investigate if and how the Irish Catholic Church operates as an arm of the government in the socialization of its citizens.

BOX 4.1   SELECTING ISSUES SUITABLE FOR RESEARCH

Below is a list of research topics some of my students are working on and how/why these issues were selected:

- *The inclusion of climate change risk as a factor in fire management planning* – Selected by a manager in the NSW Rural Fire Service who recognized the need for currency in planning processes.
- *A large percentage of non-recyclable materials in household recycle bins* – Selected by a frustrated council officer in charge of waste management who was undertaking a higher degree.
- *Decision making in a health promotion centre without any evidence base* – Selected by the new centre director who was unsure how to prioritize issues.
- *Violence towards nursing staff in emergency wards* – Selected by an ex-nurse undertaking an occupational health and safety postgraduate degree after being forced into a career change due to a patient attack.
- *Bastardization in university residential halls* – Selected by a student who went through such practices in her first year at university.
- *Subcontractors in the construction industry with poor safety records* – Selected by an occupational health and safety student because of current media coverage related to the topic.
- *Underutilization of experiential learning in the classroom* – Selected by an education student through the literature she came across in the course of her degree.
- *The motivations of individuals adopting strategies to mitigate climate change* – Selected by a student as fascinated by apathy in spite of individuals' knowledge of a threat.
- *Disregard of fire alarms in Hong Kong high-rises* – Selected by a fire safety officer undertaking a higher degree, who was in charge of an investigation where seven people died because they ignored an alarm.

Practicalities

As limiting as it may seem, all budding topics need to be checked by practicalities. No matter how interesting a topic appears, in the end your project must be 'doable'. Now doability is something we will talk about quite extensively when we look at the potential methods you might use to carry out your study, but even at the point of topic identification it is worth keeping practicalities like appropriateness, supervision, and funding requirements in mind:

- *Appropriateness* – There are many students who come up with ideas that are not relevant to the degree they are undertaking. I once had an industrial design student who wanted to undertake a research project in extraterrestrial abduction (which I suspect was based on rich personal experience). As a topic, maybe there was some potential, but the requirements of the subject clearly stated that research needed to be related to developing professional practice, and I am not sure what the career options are in AA (Alien Abduction, of course). Now, granted this may be an extreme example, but there are plenty of research students who, after a period of time, feel that they are not in the right department or school. Fitting in and finding a cohort you can relate to can be crucial to success.
- *Supervision* – Not many students manage to readily negotiate a major research project without a great deal of supervisory support. Finding out whether appropriate supervision for your topic is available before you lock yourself into a project is well advised.
- *Funding body/employer requirements* – If a funding body or employer has sponsored you to conduct research in a particular area, you may not be able to shift topics. Even within a defined project, however, there can be scope to concentrate on particular aspects or bring a fresh perspective to an issue. Open negotiation and even a 'sales pitch' covering the relevance and potential benefits of your proposed research can give you more creative potential.

FROM INTERESTING TOPICS TO RESEARCHABLE QUESTIONS

OK, hopefully you now recognize the importance of developing a clear research question and have an interesting topic in mind. Time to begin narrowing in on your question.

Narrowing in

While expansive questions can be the focus of good research, ambiguity can arise when questions are broad and unwieldy. Being bounded and precise makes the research task easier to accomplish. If you are worried about being too limited, keep in mind that each question can be likened to a window that can be used to explore rich theory and depth in understanding. 'Focused' is not a synonym for 'superficial'. There are two strategies I recommend for narrowing in. The first is to revisit your concept map, while the second is to work through the four-step question generation process outlined below.

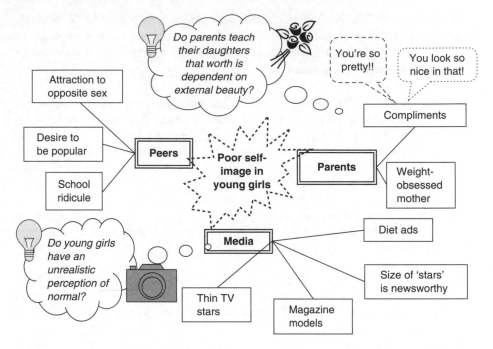

FIGURE 4.2   MAPPING YOUR QUESTIONS

The concept map revisited

Just as a concept map can be used to brainstorm research topics, it can also be used for question clarification. The map in Figure 4.2 explores 'why young girls have poor self-image'. The student has mapped out some major influences – peers, parents, and the media – and has begun to think about causes of the 'problem'. This leads to some interesting ideas that might all be researchable. The student then takes this further by asking two things: (1) what aspects am I most interested in; and (2) do I have any insights that I might be able to add? From this, the student has two 'Aha' moments and research questions begin to come into focus. The first looks at the role of the media as a whole and asks: 'What do young girls consider normal in terms of body image?' The second comes from an interesting reflection on the compliments parents give to daughters, and how often they relate to how 'pretty they are'. The student begins to wonder whether parents are subconsciously teaching their daughters that worth is determined by external beauty.

Four-step question generation process

A more linear process than concept mapping is to work through the following four steps:

1   Using only one- or two-word responses, write down the answers to the following questions:

   (a)   *What is your topic?* That is, back pain, recycling, independent learning ...
   (b)   *What is the context for your research?* That is, a school, local authority, hospital, community ...
   (c)   *What do you want to achieve?* That is, to discover, to describe, to change, to explore, to explain, to develop, to understand ...
   (d)   *What is the nature of your question?* That is, a what, who, where, how, when, or why question.
   (e)   *Are there any potential relationships you want to explore?* That is, impacts, increases, decreases, relationships, correlations, causes ...

2   Starting with the nature of the question, i.e. who, what, where, how, when, begin to piece together the answers generated in step 1 until you feel comfortable with the eventual question or questions. For example, say your problem was the large percentage of non-recyclable materials in household recycle bins (as discussed in Box 4.1). The answers from step 1 might lead to a number of questions:

   (a)   Topic: recycling. Context: domestic/community. Goal: to explore why there is a lack of efficiency. Nature of your question: who and why. Relationship: correlation between demographic characteristics and inefficient recycling.
         Question: Is there a relationship between household recycling behaviours and demographic characteristics?
   (b)   Topic: recycling. Context: domestic/households. Goal: to understand how individuals go about the task of recycling. Nature of your question: how. Relationship: N/A.
         Question: How do individuals engage in decision-making processes related to household domestic waste management?
   (c)   Topic: recycling. Context: domestic/community. Goal: to describe the nature of recycling inefficiencies so that an effective community awareness campaign can be developed. Nature of your question: what. Relationship: N/A.
         Question: What are the most common non-recyclable items found in household recycle bins?

3   If you have developed more than one question (remember: any one problem can lead to a multitude of research questions), decide on your main question based on interest and practicalities as well as the advice of your supervisor.

4   Narrow and clarify until your question is as concise and well articulated as possible. Remember: the first articulation of any research question is unlikely to be as clear, helpful, and unambiguous as the third, fourth, or even fifth attempt.

The need to redefine

You now have the perfect research question. You are on track and ready to set that question in stone. Well maybe not – research questions can, and often do, change, shift, and evolve during the early stages of a project; and not only is this fine, it is actually appropriate as your engagement in the research process evolves both your knowledge

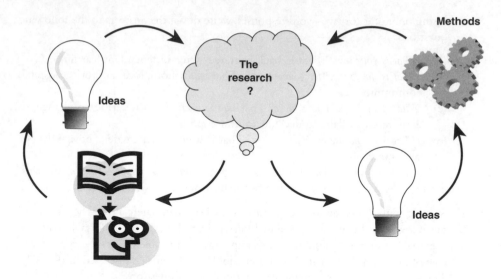

FIGURE 4.3   CYCLES OF RESEARCH QUESTION DEVELOPMENT

and thinking. Developing a clear question is essential for direction setting, but it is important to remember that the research journey is rarely linear. It is a process that generates as many questions as it answers, and is bound to take you in unexpected directions.

Consider the following. In order to do research you need to:

1   Define your research question so that you can identify the body of literature you need to become conversant with and eventually review.
2   Read and review a body of literature so that you are in a position to form appropriate, researchable questions.

So what comes first, the chicken or the egg? In the case of reading and question setting, one does not necessarily precede the other. They should, in fact, be intertwined. Research generally starts with an idea, which might come from any number of sources. The idea should then lead to reading, this reading should lead to the development of a potentially researchable question, the potential question should lead to more specific reading, and the specific reading should modify the question. As shown in Figure 4.3, forming a question is an iterative process, one that needs to be informed by reading at all stages.

A similar situation can occur when you begin to explore your methodology. Delving into 'how' your research might unfold can peak your interest in aspects of your topic not reflected in your currently defined question. Yet without that defined question, you might not have gone as far in exploring potential methods.

In fact, as you get going with your research, you may come across any number of factors that can lead you to: query your aims and objectives; see you modify your question; add questions; or even find new questions. The challenge is assessing whether these factors are sending you off the track, or whether they represent developments and refinements that are positive for your work. Discussing the issues with your supervisor can provide invaluable support in making such determinations.

THE HYPOTHESIS DILEMMA

'Do I need a hypothesis?' This must be one of the most common questions asked by students, and there seems to be two clearly defined paradigmatic schools of thought driving the answers. Positivists (see Chapter 1) believe that the hypothesis is the cornerstone of scientific method and that it is an absolutely necessary component of the research process. Post-positivists, however, often view the hypothesis as a reductionist device designed to constrain social research and take all life force from it.

Unfortunately, this tendency for dichotomization offers little assistance to students struggling to figure out if a hypothesis should drive their research. To answer this question, students need to know two things: (1) what a hypothesis actually does; and (2) whether a hypothesis is appropriate given their research question.

Hypothesis defined

> **HYPOTHESIS**
> Logical conjecture (hunch or educated guess) about the nature of relationships between two or more variables expressed in the form of a testable statement.

In other words, a hypothesis takes your research question a step further by offering a clear and concise statement of what you think you will find in relation to your variables, and what you are going to test. It is a tentative proposition that is subject to verification through subsequent investigation.

For example, say you are interested in research on divorce. Your research question is 'What factors contribute to a couple's decision to divorce?' Your hunch is that it has a lot to do with money – financial problems lead to divorce. Here you have all the factors needed for a hypothesis: logical conjecture (your hunch); variables (divorce and financial problems); and a relationship that can be tested (leads to). It is therefore a perfect question for a hypothesis – maybe something like 'Financial problems increase the likelihood of divorce.'

A question like 'Is there a relationship between household recycling behaviours and demographic characteristics?' is also a good candidate for hypothesis development. Your hunch here may be that age has a large impact on recycling behaviour – basically, you suspect that young people put anything in the recycle bin. Here you again have all the factors needed for a hypothesis: logical conjecture (your hunch); variables (recycling behaviours and age); and a relationship that can be tested (recycling behaviours depend on age). Your hypothesis might end up as 'Children and teenagers are more likely than adults to put inappropriate materials in recycle bins.'

Basically, if you have (1) a clearly defined research question, (2) variables to explore and (3) a hunch about the relationship between those variables that (4) can be tested, a hypothesis is quite easy to formulate.

Appropriateness

Now not all research questions will lend themselves to hypothesis development. For example, take the question 'How do high school students engage in decision-making processes related to career/further study options?' Remember: a hypothesis is designed to express 'relationships between variables'. This question, however, does not aim to look at variables and their relationships. The goal of this question is to uncover and describe a process, so a hypothesis would not be appropriate.

Generally, a hypothesis will not be appropriate if:

- *You do not have a hunch or educated guess about a particular situation* – For example, you may want to study alcoholism in the South Pacific, but you do not feel you are in a position to hypothesize because you are without an appropriate cultural context for educated guessing.
- *You do not have a set of defined variables* – Your research may be explorative in a bid to name the contributing factors to a particular situation. In the case of alcoholism in the Pacific Islands, your research aim may be to identify the factors or variables involved.
- *Your question centres on phenomenological description* (see Chapter 8) – For example, you may be interested in the question, 'What is the experience of drinking like for Pacific Islanders?' A relationship between variables does not come into play.
- *Your question centres on an ethnographic study of a cultural group* (see Chapter 8) – For example, you might want to ask, 'What is the cultural response to a defined problem of alcoholism in a South Pacific village?' In this situation, force fitting a hypothesis can limit the potential for rich description.
- *Your aim is to engage in, and research, the process of collaborative change* (see Chapter 9) – In 'action research', methodology is both collaborative and emergent, making predetermined hypotheses impractical to use.

In short, whether a hypothesis is appropriate for your question depends on the nature of your enquiry. If your question boils down to a 'relationship between variables', then a hypothesis can clarify your study to an extent even beyond a well-defined research question. If your question, however, does not explore such a relationship, then force fitting a hypothesis simply won't work.

CHARACTERISTICS OF GOOD QUESTIONS

Once you come up with a research question, you need to assess if it is going to be researchable at a practical level. Try running through the following checklist (summarized in Box 4.2). If you find yourself feeling uncomfortable with the answers, it may indicate a need to rethink your question.

Is the question right for me?

Common wisdom suggests that setting a realistic research plan involves assessing (1) your level of commitment and (2) the hours you think you will need to dedicate to the task – then double both. You need to consider whether your question has the potential to hold your interest for the duration. As discussed in Chapter 2, it is very easy to lose motivation, and you are likely to need a genuine interest to stay on track.

There is, however, a flipside. Questions that can truly sustain your interest are usually the ones that best bring out your biases and subjectivities. As discussed in Chapter 3, these subjectivities need to be carefully explored and managed in ways that will ensure the integrity of the research process. You may want to give careful consideration to:

- Researching questions where you know you have an axe to grind. Deep-seated prejudices do not generally lend themselves to credible research.
- Researching issues that are too close to home, for example something like domestic violence or sexual abuse. While researching such issues can be healing and cathartic, mixing personal and professional motivations in an intense fashion can be potentially detrimental to both agendas.

Is the question right for the field?

The role of research is to do one or more of the following: advance knowledge in a particular area/field; improve professional practice; impact on policy; or aid individuals. Research questions need to be significant – not only to you, but to a wider academic or professional audience as well.

I often ask my students to imagine they are applying for competitive funds that will cover the cost of their research. Before they can even begin to make arguments that will convince a funding body they are competent to do the research and that their approach is likely to give meaningful and credible results, they will need to convince the body that the topic itself is worth funding. They need to be able to articulate:

- Why the knowledge is important.
- What the societal significance is.
- How the findings will lead to societal advances.
- What improvements to professional practice and/or policy may come from their research.

An early task in the research process is to be able to clearly articulate a rationale for your study that outlines the significance of the project. Your question needs to be informed by the literature and be seen as significant.

Is the question well articulated?

A research question not only indicates the theory and literature you need to explore and review, but also points to the data you will need to gather, and the methods you will need to adopt. This makes clear articulation of research questions particularly important. Terms need to be unambiguous and clearly defined.

Take the question, 'Is health care a problem in the USA?' As a question for general debate, it is probably fine. As a research question, however, it needs a fair bit of clarification. How are you defining 'health care'? What boundaries are you putting on the term? How are you defining 'problem'? Social, moral, economic, legal, or all of the above? And who are you speaking for? A problem for whom? The more clarity in the question, the more work the question can do, making the direction of the study that much more defined.

Another point to consider is whether your question rests on unfounded assumptions. Take the question, 'How can women in Fijian villages overthrow the patriarchal structures that oppress them?' There are a few assumptions here that need to be checked:

1   That there are patriarchal structures. This information might exist and be found in literature. Assuming this is true …
2   That these patriarchal structures are indeed oppressive to the women concerned.
3   That there is a desire on the part of Fijian women to change these patriarchal structures.
4   That 'overthrowing' is the only option mentioned for change. It is a loaded term that alludes to strong personal subjectivities.

Is the question doable?

Perhaps the main criterion of any good research question is that you will be able to undertake the research necessary to answer the question. Now that may sound incredibly obvious, but there are many questions that cannot be answered through the research process. Take, for example, the question, 'Does a difficult labour impact on a newborn's ability to love its mother?' Not researchable. For one, how do you define love? And even if you could define it, you would need to find a way to measure a newborn's ability to love. And even if you could do that, you are left with the dilemma of correlating that ability to love to a difficult labour. Interesting question, but not researchable.

Other questions might be researchable in theory, but not in practice. Student research projects are often constrained by:

- a lack of time
- a lack of funds
- a lack of expertise

- a lack of access
- a lack of ethical clearance.

Making sure your question is feasible and that it can lead to a completed project is worth doing early. Nothing is worse than realizing your project is not doable after investing a large amount of time and energy.

Does the question get the tick of approval from those in the know?

When it comes to articulating the final question it makes sense to ask the advice of those who know and do research. Most supervisors have a wealth of research and supervisory experience, and generally know what questions are 'researchable' and what questions will leave you with a massive headache. Run your question past lecturers in the field, your supervisor, and any 'experts' you may know.

BOX 4.2   THE GOOD QUESTION CHECKLIST

Is the question right for me?

- Will the question hold my interest?
- Can I manage any potential biases/subjectivities I may have?

Is the question right for the field?

- Will the findings be considered significant?
- Will it make a contribution?

Is the question well articulated?

- Are the terms well defined?
- Are there any unchecked assumptions?

Is the question doable?

- Can information be collected in an attempt to answer the question?
- Do I have the skills and expertise necessary to access this information? If not, can the skills be developed?
- Will I be able to get it all done within my time constraints?
- Are costs likely to exceed my budget?
- Are their any potential ethics problems?

Does the question get the tick of approval from those in the know?

- Does my supervisor think I am on the right track?
- Do 'experts' in the field think my question is relevant/important/doable?

FURTHER READING

Most research methods texts give some coverage to developing research questions. Texts with particularly good chapters on question development include:

Booth, W. C., Colomb, G. C., and Williams, J. M. (2008) *The Craft of Research.* Chicago: University of Chicago Press.
Bryman, A. (2008) *Social Research Methods.* Oxford: Oxford University Press.
Punch, K. (2005) *Introduction to Social Research.* London: Sage.
Robson, C. (2002) *Real World Research.* Oxford: Blackwell.

There are, however, two excellent works that are solely dedicated to the challenge of research question development:

Andrews, R. (2003) *Research Questions.* London: Continuum International.
White, P. (2009) *Developing Research Questions: A Guide for Social Scientists.* Basingstoke: Palgrave Macmillan.

CHAPTER SUMMARY

- Developing a well-articulated research question is essential because it defines the project, sets boundaries, gives direction, and acts as a frame of reference for assessing your work.
- The ability to generate topics for research can be a real challenge. Tuning into your own curiosity and using creativity tools such as concept mapping can help you focus.
- Research inspiration can come from any number of areas including personal insights and experiences; observations; contemporary/timely issues; stakeholder needs; literature; and theory.
- Research directions are not always at the full discretion of the researcher. Practicalities you need to be mindful of include: appropriateness of the topic; your ability to get supervisory support; and funding opportunities and commitments.
- Moving from topics to researchable question can be daunting. Using a concept mapping process or following the more linear four-step process can aid you in the task.
- Redefining your questions is essential to the research process. Forming the right 'questions' should be seen as an iterative process that is informed by reading and doing at all stages.
- Hypotheses are designed to express relationships between variables. If this is the nature of your question, a hypothesis can add to your research. If your question is more descriptive or explorative, generating a hypothesis may not be appropriate.
- Good research questions need to be: right for you; right for the field; well articulated; doable; and get the tick of approval from those in the know.

5
CRAFTING A RESEARCH PROPOSAL

CHAPTER PREVIEW

- The role of the proposal
- Elements of the proposal
- Writing a winning proposal
- Obstacles and challenges

THE ROLE OF THE PROPOSAL

> **"Let us read with method, and propose to ourselves an end to which our studies may point."**
> *Edward Gibbon*

When it comes to research, very few projects get off the ground without some sort of approval. It may be as straightforward as verbal approval from your lecturer, but it is more likely to involve a formal approval process gained through an admissions board, an ethics committee, or a funding body. And of course you may need approval from more than one of these.

This means you will need to develop a research proposal. Now many see the proposal as an opportunity to clarify thinking, bed down ideas, and articulate thoughts in a way that will provide a study's outline as well as a blueprint for future action. And yes, a research proposal is all these things. *But* – and this is important – a proposal is not something you write for yourself. It is, without a doubt, a sales pitch. Your proposal is your opportunity, and sometimes your only opportunity, to sell your project and get your study off the ground.

So whether you are after admission to a university research programme, seeking ethics approval, or looking for funding, the role of the proposal is to convince the powers that be that what you are proposing meets their requirements. Namely, that the research question, the proposed methods, and the researcher all have merit. In other words, not only will a committee assess whether a project is useful and practicable, but the committee will also assess whether or not it thinks you as the proposer have the ability to carry the project out.

Now keep in mind that the weight given to various aspects of a proposal varies according to the type of committee you are addressing and the type of approval you are seeking. For example, a proposal written to get into a PhD programme really needs to sell your potential as a researcher. A proposal written for an ethics committee needs to focus on the relationship between methods and participants. A proposal to a funding body, however, would need to have a strong emphasis on practicalities of method and the benefits of potential outcomes.

Demonstrating merits of the research question

Essential to any successful proposal is your ability to sell the merit of your research question. Demonstrating merit will rely on two things. The first is that you are able to clearly and succinctly share your research topic and question (generally the work of the title, summary/abstract, aims/objectives, research question/hypothesis). The second thing is that you can demonstrate your research question is worth answering; that is, your question is significant enough to warrant support either at the level of admission to a program or via funding (generally the work of the introduction/background/rationale).

When it comes to a committee's assessment there are several possible scenarios:

1 The worth of the research question is self-evident, e.g. 'What are the most effective strategies for curbing binge drinking in under 18s?', and you are able to argue the importance and significance of your question to the satisfaction of the assessors. So far so good.

2 The worth of the research question is, as above, self-evident, but you do a lousy job arguing the case and do not convince the assessors that you are capable of mounting what should be a straightforward argument. Major problem.

3 The worth of the research question is not self-evident, e.g. 'Do residents of the UK enjoy watching *Big Brother* more than US residents?', but you are able to convincingly argue the case by citing evidence that attests to a real issue and what benefits there might be in conducting research into this area. If you can do this (particularly for this question) that's impressive!

4 The worth of the research question is, as above, not self-evident, and you do little to help your case. Your arguments are weak so assessors are left scratching their heads and quickly put your proposal into the reject pile.

The point here is that while the significance of the research question is important, what is actually being assessed is your ability to argue the significance. It is therefore crucial that your writing be tight, well structured, and well referenced.

Demonstrating merits of the proposed methods

Once your assessors are convinced that your research question has merit, their focus will turn to methods. Here they are looking for several things:

1   Are the proposed methods clearly articulated? If your assessors cannot make sense of what you are proposing, your proposal has little chance of getting off the ground.
2   Are the proposed methods logical? In other words, do they make sense and do the assessors believe your approach can lead to credible data (generally the work of the methods section)?
3   Has the candidate considered the study's boundaries as well as any potential hurdles to effective data collection and analysis? Established assessors know that all research is constrained; your job here is to acknowledge this and show the credibility of your methods in spite of any limitations (generally the work of the methods and limitations/delimitations sections).
4   Are the proposed methods ethical? As discussed in Chapter 3, ethics are central to all research processes (and of course the main focus of an ethics proposal). Your proposal needs to show that the dignity and well-being of respondents, both mentally and physically, are fully protected (the work of the methods and ethical considerations sections).
5   Are the proposed methods practical/doable? It doesn't matter how logical and well considered your methods are if your assessors do not believe their implementation can be achieved. You need to show that you have or can develop the necessary expertise; that you can gain access to required data; that your timeline is realistic; and that you will come within budget (the work of the methods section as well as, if required, the timeline and budget).

Basically, your methods section needs to convince readers that your approach is an efficient, effective, and ethical way to get credible answers to your questions and that you are capable of pulling this off.

Demonstrating merits of the researcher

OK, assume the assessors are happy with both your questions and your methods. The final question is 'are they happy with you?' Do they think you are the right person for the job? Do they trust that you can pull this off? Do they believe you have the necessary background knowledge, at least some familiarity with the literature, and writing skill commensurate to the task?

Now that's a lot of questions, and it would be great if your assessors could get to know you and get a real feel for what you are capable of. But that's not likely to happen. In fact there is a good chance your proposal will be reviewed by people you have never met. So what do they use to assess your potential? Simply your proposal. Assessors will judge your ability to engage with the literature through your proposal's short literature review. They will assess your ability to carry out method, based on the knowledge you show and how well you argue your methodological case. And they will assess your potential to write by the quality of writing in your proposal. It therefore pays to give amazing attention to detail and make your proposal one of the tightest pieces of writing you have ever attempted.

ELEMENTS OF THE PROPOSAL

Proposal requirements vary according to the role of the proposal and by institution. But generally, you will be required to include some combination of the following:

- *Title* – Go for clear, concise, and unambiguous. Your title should indicate the specific content and context of the problem you wish to explore in as succinct a way as possible.
- *Summary/abstract* – Proposals often require a project summary, usually with a very tight word count. The trick here is to briefly state the what, why, and how of your project in a way that sells it in just a few sentences – and trust me, this can take quite a few drafts to get right.
- *Aims/objectives* – Most proposals have one overarching aim that captures what you hope to achieve through your project. A set of objectives, which are more specific goals, supports that aim. Aims and objectives are often articulated in bullet points and are generally 'to' statements: for example, to develop …; to identify …; to explore …; to measure …; to explain …; to describe …; to compare …; to determine …; etc. In management literature you are likely to come across 'SMART' objectives – SMART being an acronym for **S**pecific, **M**easurable, **A**chievable, **R**elevant/results-focused/realistic, and **T**ime-bound. The goal is to keep objectives from being airy-fairy or waffly; clearly articulating what you want to achieve aids your ability to work towards your goal.
- *Research question/hypothesis* – As discussed in Chapter 4, a well-articulated research question (or hypothesis) should define your investigation, set boundaries, provide direction, and act as a frame of reference for assessing your work. Any committee reviewing your proposal will turn to your question in order to get an overall sense of your project. Take time to make sure your question/hypothesis is as well defined and as clearly articulated as possible.
- *Introduction/background/rationale* – The main job of this section is to introduce your topic and convince readers that the problem you want to address is significant and worth exploring and even funding. It should give some context to the problem and lead your readers to the conclusion, that, yes, research into this area is absolutely essential if we really want to work towards situation improvement or problem resolution.
- *Literature review* – A formal 'literature review' (discussed in more depth in Chapter 6) is a specific piece of argumentative writing that engages with relevant scientific and academic research in order to create a space for your project. The role of the literature review is to inform readers of developments in the field while establishing your own credibility as a 'player' capable of adding to this body of knowledge. This is a tough piece of writing with a very tight word count so be prepared to run through a few drafts.

- *Theoretical perspectives* – This section asks you to situate your study in a conceptual or theoretical framework. The idea here is to articulate the theoretical perspective(s) that underpin and inform your ideas, and, in particular, to discuss how 'theory' relates to and/or directs your study.
- *Methods* – Some form of 'methods' will be required in all proposals. The goal here is to articulate your plan with enough clarity and detail to convince readers that your approach is practical and will lead to credible answers to the questions posed (see Chapter 7). Under the heading of methods you would generally articulate:

  o the approach/methodology – for example, if you are doing ethnography, action research, or maybe a random control trial (see Chapters 8 and 9)
  o how you will find respondents – this includes articulation of population and sample/sampling procedures (see Chapter 10)
  o data collection method(s) – for example, surveying, interviewing, document analysis, etc. (see Chapters 11 and 12)
  o methods of analysis – whether you will be doing statistical or thematic analysis and perhaps variants thereof (see Chapters 13 and 14).

- *Limitations/delimitations* – Limitations refer to conditions or design characteristics that may impact on the generalizability and utility of findings, e.g. small sample size, or restricted access to records. Keep in mind that most projects are limited by constraints such as time, resources, access, or organizational issues. So it is much better to be open about 'flaws' than leave it to assessors who might be much more critical. Delimitations refer to a study's boundaries or how your study was deliberately narrowed by conscious exclusions and inclusions, e.g. delimiting your study to children of a certain age only, or schools from one particular region. Now remember that your overarching goal here is to convince readers that your findings will be credible in spite of any limitations or delimitations. So the trick is to be open about your study's parameters without sounding defensive or apologetic. It is also worth articulating any strategies you will be using to ensure credibility despite limitations.
- *Ethical considerations* – Whenever you are working with human participants there will be ethical issues you need to consider (see Chapter 3). Now if this were an application for an ethics committee you would need to focus much of your proposal on ethical issues. But even if this were a proposal for admission or funding, your readers would still need to be convinced that you have considered issues related to integrity in the production of knowledge and responsibility for the emotional, physical, and intellectual well-being of your study participants.
- *Timeline* – This is simply superimposing a timeline on your methods, and is often done in a tabular or chart form. The committee reading your proposal will be looking to see that your plan is realistic and can conform to any overarching timeframes or deadlines.
- *Budget/funding* – This is a full account of costs and who will bear them. While not always a required section for ethics proposals or proposals for academic student research, it will certainly be a requirement for a funding body. Now it is definitely worth being realistic – it's easy to underestimate costs. Wages, software, hardware, equipment, travel, transcription, administrative support, etc., can add

up quite quickly and running short of money mid-project is not a good option. But also keep in mind that if you are tendering for a commissioned project, it's a good idea to get a ballpark figure of the funding body's budget. This will put you in a position to design your methods accordingly and hopefully make you competitive.

- *References* – This can refer to two things. The first is citing references in the same way as you would in any other type of academic/professional writing. Believe it or not, it's often missed. The second is that some committees want a list of, say, 10 or 15 primary references that will inform your work. This information can help a committee assess your knowledge and give its member a clearer indication of the direction your study may take.

WRITING A WINNING PROPOSAL

In my experience, when a person or a committee has the power to make major decisions about someone else's work/future, they like to wield that power, and they often like to wield it in very pedantic ways. When it comes to assessing research proposals, this translates to committees wanting what they want, the way they want it, when they want it. If you are the person writing the proposal this means you need to be just as pedantic and make sure you follow all guidelines, write purposively, and be prepared to work through several drafts.

Following guidelines

So how many words can you get away with when the application says the title needs to be no more than 20 words or that the abstract must be less that 150 words? Well, it is certainly not uncommon for applicants to try to stretch these limits – but I would advise against it. Some assessors cannot get a bit bent out of shape when they think applicants cannot follow simple directions. Control freaks? Maybe. But you need to realize that assessors often see the application as a test of whether you will be able to meet requirements when you actually start working on your project. It may seem a bit parochial, but if you cannot follow guidelines in a short application, your assessors might just ask what that says about your potential to complete.

The best advice here is to follow guidelines as close to the letter as possible. This means:

- constructing your proposal according to, or as close to, the recommended section/ headings as possible
- keeping to all word limits
- being absolutely meticulous about spelling and grammar
- strictly adhering to deadlines.

Writing purposively

It is important to recognize that a proposal should never be sloppy, rushed, or thrown together at the last minute. It needs to be a highly polished and well-constructed piece of writing. Remember: the clarity of your thoughts, the voracity of your arguments, and the quality of your writing will be used to judge your potential as a researcher.

The following tips should help you craft a winning proposal:

- *See if you can get access to a few successful proposals* – If possible, seek out those that have gone through the committee you are applying to, or to as similar a committee as possible. If you cannot gain access, the books cited at the end of the chapter contain more generic examples you can refer to.
- *Find a voice* – The convention here is third person; however, using 'I' to state what you will do is now more commonly accepted. Also remember to write in the future tense. A proposal is about what you will do, not what you are doing now, or have done in the past.
- *Write tight* – Your writing needs to be concise and succinct, direct and straightforward. Avoid rambling and/or trying to show off by using unnecessary jargon.
- *Write enough* – Somewhat paradoxical to the above, you also need to make sure you write a sufficient amount for assessors to make judgements.
- *Write to the 'non-expert'* – Your proposal needs to be 'stand-alone' and be comprehensible to someone potentially outside your field.
- *Do your homework* – The last thing you want in a short formal proposal is 'mistakes'. Get your facts right, make sure you don't have gaping holes in your literature, and make sure any references to theory and/or methods are accurate.
- *Don't overquote* – Generally the writing expected is so tight that you probably won't have enough room for too many direct quotes. Keep the words and ideas yours, *supported* by the literature.
- *Don't let the deadline sneak up on you* – Plan on finishing early so that you have time to review and redraft. Remember: deadlines are often inflexible and this is a case where you do not want to have to rush and let quality suffer.
- *As discussed below, be prepared to draft and redraft.*

Drafting and redrafting

The best advice here is to leave yourself enough time to get feedback and redraft, if possible, more than once. Remember: even if your reader does not understand the details, the overarching arguments should make sense to the non-expert – so don't hesitate to ask a peer, parent, friend, etc., if they can follow the proposal and if it makes sense. But if you have access, I certainly recommend seeking the advice of someone who has experience in research/research proposals.

Chapter 15 offers a detailed checklist for working towards final drafts, but to summarize here, your final draft should: follow set criteria; be logical; make your point with convincing arguments; contain sufficient information; use a consistent voice; avoid being repetitious; be clear and fluent; avoid waffling; avoid paragraph-long sentences; limit acronyms and jargon; strictly adhere to word counts; have exemplarily spelling and grammar; avoid all typos; and be well formatted.

OBSTACLES AND CHALLENGES

So if you do all of the above, surely you are bound to impress? It should all be smooth sailing, shouldn't it? Well hopefully that will be the case. But there are a couple of sticky situations you may need to negotiate.

When your design does not fit proposal requirements

If you have read this far, you know how important I think it is to give a committee what it asks for. But what if your research design simply does not fit in with the committee's requirements? Now this is likely to be the case in 'qualitative' research where terms like hypothesis, variables, validity, and reliability may not be appropriate to your study, but may nonetheless be required 'sections' in your proposal.

Unfortunately, there can still be a bias towards the quantitative paradigm, the legacy of which can be reflected in proposal proforma and even committee expectations. If this is the case, I would suggest seeking the advice of someone who has worked with the committee to see how it tends to handle such dilemmas – each committee will have a different approach. If, however, you cannot get this insider information, or are told 'just do the best you can', I would suggest remembering the bigger agenda of the proposal: that is, to demonstrate the merits of the research question, the merits of the proposed methods, and the merits of the researcher. So regardless of paradigm, you will need to show you are confident with the theoretical, conceptual, and methodological landscape you are proposing to enter. To that end, write confidently, not aggressively nor apologetically. If the committee wants a hypothesis, yet it is not appropriate, you have the option of saying N/A and giving justification for inappropriateness (see Chapter 4). If the committee wants you to list variables but your study is more exploratory, say so. If validity, reliability, or generalizability is inappropriate, confidently talk about credibility indicators that are more appropriate (see Chapter 3). Any committee worth its weight will be able to spot a researcher who knows what he or she is talking about, even when it doesn't fit with the committee's expectations/jargon.

When your design is emergent

Another major dilemma is when you are proposing a study that will have evolving methods that cannot be fully articulated at the time proposal applications are required.

This is particularly problematic for ethics proposals, which are used to protect the dignity and welfare of the 'researched' as well as protect the researcher and home institution from legal liability. These proposals often demand a full account of methods, which often includes appending things like surveys and interview schedules.

Once again 'qualitative' researchers who wish to use conversational/unstructured data gathering techniques that are not fully predetermined will face a dilemma. Those undertaking action research can also struggle as their methodological protocols are based on stakeholder collaboration in multiple cycles (see Chapter 9). In fact, there are many research projects (including quantitative studies) in which methods are conducted in multiple phases, with each phase determined by what has happened previously. For example, key informant interviews may be used to inform survey design, or survey results may determine the questions used in in-depth interviewing.

The best strategy here is to be open and knowledgeable about your approach. Show that your design is not haphazard or ill considered. Show that even if you cannot articulate all the specifics, your required flexibility is planned and you have a defined framework. Show the committee forethought. Offer, if possible, indicative questions. And finally, show that you can link your approach back to accepted methodological literature. If you can manage to make such arguments your chances of success will be greatly enhanced.

Of course, even if you are able to make such arguments there is the possibility that the committee will require further information. If this is the case, you can attempt to add more definition to your methodological plan. But if your overarching design makes this impossible and your committee is immovable, you will need (1) to see if it is possible to put in a supplementary application as your methods evolve; or (2) to talk to your supervisor about required methodological modifications.

When want to or need to change direction/method

OK, say you are all set to interview 15 CEOs, but try as you might, you just can't get more than 3 to participate. Or say you plan on spending $500 surveying 1,000 homeless people, but after spending $378 you only have 36 surveys returned. Or imagine that you have undertaken a much more comprehensive literature review than included in your proposal and you realize that the survey questions you originally proposed are way off target.

What do you do? Well from a methodological standpoint, you improvise. You think about your question, talk to your supervisor, and determine the most 'doable' way to get some credible data. But disappointingly, most students who do this simply charge ahead and change their study protocols without further committee consultation. And while this may be the path of least resistance, it is not recommended. If your application represents a 'contract' to do a job, say, for example, to a funding body, you need to inform it of shifts in your approach. Updating ethics applications is equally important. Not only do you want an outside committee to oversee that you will not threaten the dignity and well-being of the researched, but you also want to ensure that you have protected yourself and your institution from potential lawsuits.

FURTHER READING

There are quite a few books that can help you navigate your way through proposal development, most of which give good examples. Have a look at:

Coley, S. M. and Scheinberg, C. A. (2000) *Proposal Writing*. London: Sage.

Locke, L. F., Spirduso, W. W., and Silverman, S. J. (2007) *Proposals That Work: A Guide for Planning Dissertations and Grant Proposals*. London: Sage.

Marshall, C. and Rossman, G. (2006) *Designing Qualitative Research*. London: Sage.

Munhall, P. L. and Chenail, R. J. (2007) *Qualitative Research Proposals and Reports: A Guide*. Sudbury, MA: Jones & Bartlett.

Ogden, T. E. and Goldberg, I. A. (eds) (2002) *Research Proposals: A Guide to Success*. New York: Academic Press.

Punch, K. (2006) *Developing Effective Research Proposals*. London: Sage.

CHAPTER SUMMARY

- A research proposal offers an opportunity to clarify your thinking, bed down ideas, and articulate thoughts in a way that will provide a blueprint for future action. It is also a means for 'selling' your project and getting it off the ground.
- Your proposal should convince assessors of the merits of the research question; that is, you have clearly articulated the question and successfully argued that it is worth exploring.
- Your proposal should convince assessors of the merits of the proposed methods; that is, you have clearly proposed a logical, practical, ethical means for answering your research question.
- Your proposal should convince assessors of the merits of the researcher; that is, you have shown a requisite level of skill, knowledge, and potential.
- Proposals differ in requirements, but most will ask you to articulate some combination of the following: title; summary/abstract; aims/objectives; research question/hypothesis; introduction/background/rationale; literature review; theoretical perspectives; methods; limitations/delimitations; ethical considerations; timelines; budget/funding; and references.
- Writing a winning proposal requires you to follow guidelines as close to the letter as possible.
- Writing purposively involves good planning, knowing your subject, finding a voice, writing tightly yet sufficiently, writing for the non-expert, and being prepared to redraft.
- Obstacles you may face include proposals that do not fit a committee's requirements and proposals with emergent designs. In both cases, being knowledgeable, confident, and open will enhance chances of success.
- Even though it may seem painful, if you want or need to change direction/ method you are well advised to keep your approval body informed.

6
WORKING WITH LITERATURE

CHAPTER PREVIEW

- The importance of literature
- The role of literature
- Sourcing relevant literature
- Managing the literature
- Writing the formal 'literature review'

THE IMPORTANCE OF LITERATURE

> " I not only use all the brains that
> I have, but all that I can borrow. "
> *Woodrow Wilson*

There really is no way around it – reading is an essential part of the research process. Why? Because you cannot really engage in research from a platform of ignorance. When you are learning and your goal is to take on board knowledge that is already out there, it does not really matter if you know a little or a lot. The goal is self-education, which needs to, and should, start from wherever you are and attempt to take you to the next level.

Conducting research is a bit different. When you are conducting research, you are attempting to produce knowledge, knowledge that you hope others will learn from, act on, and use towards situation improvement. And this demands responsibility. You need to know what you are talking about. The production of new knowledge is fundamentally dependent on past knowledge. Knowledge builds, and it is impossible for researchers to add to a body of literature if they are not conversant with it.

Yes, a lot of knowledge can come from experience – and I strongly advocate drawing on this. But even rich experience is likely to be seen as anecdotal if it

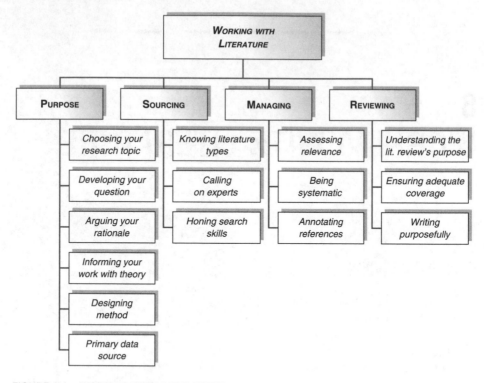

FIGURE 6.1   WORKING WITH LITERATURE

is not set within a broader context. Reading is what gives you that broader context. It inspires, informs, educates, and enlightens. It generates ideas, helps form significant questions, and is instrumental in the process of research design. It is also central to writing up; a clear rationale supported by literature is essential, while a well-constructed literature review is an important criterion in establishing researcher credibility.

Working with literature, however, is often seen as an onerous task. The multiple purposes, the volume and variety, the difficulty in finding it and managing it, dealing with its inconsistencies, the need to formally review it, and perhaps underpinning all of this, your own lack of knowledge, experience, and proficiency can make working with literature somewhat daunting.

Figure 6.1 outlines the variety of tasks involved in working with literature, and explores processes that will help you understand it, source it, manage it, and review it.

THE ROLE OF LITERATURE

Research requires engagement with literature at each and every stage of the process. As highlighted in Figure 6.2, literature can help you:

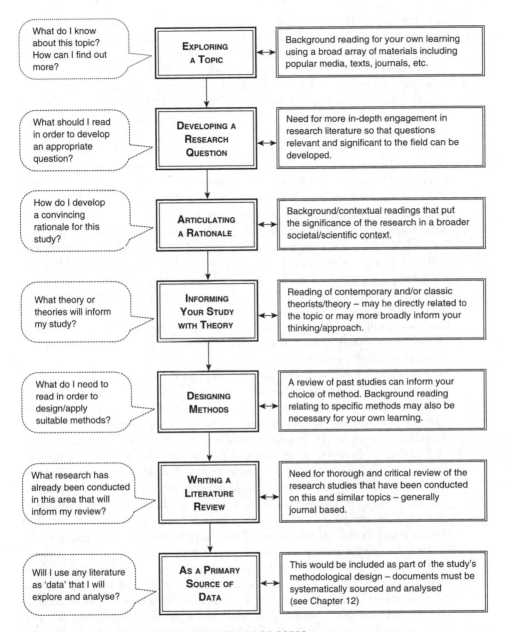

FIGURE 6.2 LITERATURE AND THE RESEARCH PROCESS

- *Explore a topic* – Not many students, or even experienced researchers, know all they need to know about a particular topic, and reading can certainly help you get up to speed. This might involve delving into texts and media reports, as well as journal-based research studies that make up an area's scientific literature.
- *Develop a research question* – As discussed in Chapter 4, a good place to look for guidance on the development of your research question is in literature. Popular media that covers current debates, controversy, and disputes around a particular

issue can help generate questions of societal significance. Engagement with scientific literature can also be instrumental in the development of questions. Finding 'gaps', exploring questions that have not been adequately addressed, or attempting to ask questions within a new context, are all dependent on 'reading'.

- *Articulate a rationale* – A well-articulated rationale is part and parcel of any research proposal, and needs to suggest why time and money should be invested in addressing your particular research question. In order to do this, you need to draw on literature that can argue the societal and scientific significance of your study.

- *Inform your study with theory* – Theoretical reading can be difficult for students who perceive a large gap between research and theory – something not uncommon. For years, social 'scientists' engaged in research without strong links to theory, while social 'theorists' theorized without doing much research. This tendency to dichotomize, however, is diminishing and we are beginning to recognize the value of exploring quite tangible issues in relation to theory. For example, research that touches on issues of power, class, and religion generally demand the exploration of theorists such as Weber, Marx, or Durkheim. In fact, every discipline area, i.e. nursing, education, management, etc., as well as broader areas of sociology and philosophy, rest on rich theory that can add both depth and credibility to your study. Now for some, theoretical reading is a passion and joy – and therefore not problematic. But for others, it can be a laborious task. If you fall into the second category, it is important to discuss the issue of theory with your supervisor and clearly negotiate the extent to which it is expected to inform your work.

- *Design methods* – Reading can support the design of methods in a number of ways. It can: (1) support learning related to relevant methodologies and methods; (2) allow you to critically evaluate, and possibly adopt, methods considered 'standard' for exploring your particular research question; (3) help you in assessing the need for alternative methodological approaches; and (4) support you in the design of a study that might overcome methodological shortcomings prevalent in the literature. To appropriately design a study, collect the data, and conduct analysis, you will need to engage with broadranging methods texts such as this one; books focusing on particular research approaches you plan to adopt, i.e. ethnography, action research, or statistics; research articles on methods themselves; and journal articles that report on studies that use methods similar to those you plan to use. The recommended readings, references, and bibliography of this book can be a great starting point for finding a range of relevant literature.

- *Write a literature review* – A formal 'literature review' is a very specific piece of argumentative writing that acts to create a 'space' for your research study. It is a critical review of past research that relies on articles published in well-established research journals and is usually a distinct and required section of any research write-up, including grant applications, research reports, and journal articles. Virtually all student theses require a literature review that should be relevant, critical, and comprehensive; in fact, the review should represent a level of engagement in the literature that indicates a readiness to contribute to the literature itself. The ins and outs of writing a good literature review are covered later in this chapter.

- *As a primary source of data* – We generally think of data as something we purposefully generate, i.e. transcripts from interviews or the results of surveys. But as covered in Chapter 12, all types of literature can be used as primary sources of data. From meta-analysis of past studies, to content analysis of the media, to in-depth analysis of historical documents, literature can be used to do more than provide context, inform your study, and argue the case. It can, in fact, be central to your analysis.

SOURCING RELEVANT LITERATURE

Unfortunately, recognizing the importance of literature and understanding its varied uses will not put it in your hands. You still need to find and access it. To do this efficiently, you need to be familiar with various categories of literature; be ready to call on experts and ask for help; and hone your search skills so that you are in a position to best utilize the library and Internet.

Types of literature

The array of literature you might find yourself delving into may be a fair bit broader than you first imagine. Because reading for research is something that informs all aspects of the research journey, almost any type of reading is fair game. For example, you are likely to call on:

- *Discipline-based reference materials* – It is easy for those who know the jargon of a particular discipline to forget that many of its terms are not a part of everyday language. If you are relatively new to a particular discipline, subject-specific dictionaries and encyclopedias can help you navigate your way through the area's central terms, constructs, and theories.
- *Books* – These might include introductory and advanced texts, anthologies, research reports, popular non-fiction, and even fictional works that can provide background and context, or inform theory and method. When it comes to the formal literature review, however, the lengthy production time of books means that the most contemporary research is unlikely to be found in this format.
- *Journal articles* – These take you beyond background readings to readings providing rigorous research accounts. They are central to literature reviews because they (1) are often targeted for 'academic' audiences; (2) are generally peer reviewed, which means they have met at least some benchmark for credibility; and (3) have specific areas of content and regularity of production, which means articles are likely to be both relevant and current. The array, specialization, and the accessibility of journal titles are ever increasing and the advent of online journals and computer-based inter-library loan schemes has made them highly accessible.
- *Grey literature* – This refers to both published and unpublished materials that do not have an International Standard Book Number (ISBN) or an International Standard Serial Number (ISSN), including conference papers, unpublished research theses, newspaper articles, and pamphlets/brochures. Most researchers utilize some type of grey literature in the course of their study. Recent theses and conference papers can be a valuable source of contemporary original work, while newspaper articles, pamphlets, and brochures can be used for background and context – or in the process of document analysis (see Chapter 12).
- *Official publications, statistics, and archives* – These materials can be a valuable source of background and contextual information, and often help shape a study's rationale. They can also be a terrific source of primary data in document analysis (see Chapter 12) or a good source of secondary data in statistical analysis (see Chapter 13).

- *Writing aids* – These include bibliographic reference works, dictionaries, encyclopedias, and thesauruses, almanacs, yearbooks, books of quotes, etc. Such resources can offer significant support during the writing-up process, and can be used: (1) to improve the linguistic style of your work; (2) to add points of interest to the text; (3) to check facts; and (4) to reference those facts.

Calling on 'experts'

If there was one piece of advice that I could give in regard to searching for and finding appropriate literature, it would be 'Don't go it alone!' There are some amazingly knowledgeable experts out there who can give you the advice you need to make a start.

One resource you do not want to overlook is your university librarian. My first-year university students often grumble about the need for library orientations. But information technology is changing so fast that students and professional researchers alike need to update their skills on a regular basis. See your librarian! Not only are librarians experts on the latest computer/Internet searching facilities, but also they can often provide you with the training necessary to have you searching for books/articles in libraries all over the world. Many university librarians are designated to a particular academic area, e.g. social science, nursing, education, environment, etc. These 'specialists' can introduce you to relevant databases, journals (both hardcopy and electronic), bibliographies, abstracts, reviews, etc., specific to your area.

'Academics' can also be quite helpful in your search for relevant literature. Talk to supervisors, professors, and lecturers. They often know the literature and are able to point you in the right direction; or can at least direct you to someone better acquainted with your topic who can give you the advice you need to make a start. Also, see if you can browse through their book shelves. While any one academic's library is unlikely to cover all perspectives or be completely up to date, academics often hold key readings that can kick-start your search.

Finally, think about calling on experts in the field. Those working in your area have often had to source relevant literature. I have had any number of students tell me that they are having difficulty finding literature and can only find one or two recent studies that relate to their research question. I ask them, 'Well, who did these people cite? Who is in their reference list?' One relevant journal article should lead to several relevant readings. As well as relevant journal articles, have a look at Masters and PhD theses. These works require comprehensive literature reviews and thorough bibliographies that can give you a huge head start when it comes to sourcing your readings. And don't forget that you can also turn to practitioners – those who actually work in the area often know the literature. Finally, try attending relevant conferences. It is quite likely that this will lead to a wealth of leads in your literature search.

Honing your search skills

The tools for literature searching are changing at a rate of knots. Literature abounds and library search facilities now allow you to explore way beyond the confines of local holdings. And, of course, an amazing amount of research literature is now accessible on the Internet using commonly available search engines. In fact, the popular search engine Google now offers Google Scholar (scholar.google.com), which allows you to specifically search for abstracts, peer–reviewed articles, books, theses, and technical reports across a variety of disciplines.

Now the downside of this incredible availability is the need to develop skills to navigate your way through it. If you're a regular Internet user, you have an advantage because the skills you need to negotiate the Web are the same as those you need to find literature. Basically, you need to be able to run a search engine using key words and 'Boolean operators', i.e. words such as AND, OR, and NOT. It is, therefore, essential to be able to identify your topic, subtopics, variables, theories, theorists, methods, key concepts, etc., in the form of key words. You can then search for works by both single and combined key word searches.

For example, say you were interested in body piercing, and were particularly interested in teenagers. Your first key words might be:

- body piercing (earrings, nose rings, etc.)
- teenagers (girls) (boys).

You would start your literature hunt by running a search using an amalgam of these key words. This is likely to lead you to a mass of relevant literature that can be culled by adding additional variables you find particularly relevant or interesting. For example:

- rebellion
- rites of passage.

Using this process you can add additional key words, i.e. family background, or a particular theorist, e.g. Foucault, in order to narrow your search. You can also remove key words to capture more literature – or swap key words around to see what you come up with.

Figure 6.3 highlights the relevance of the generated literature based on key concepts and their interrelationships. Some areas of intersection may not yield much literature, but if you keep playing around with ideas, concepts, and variables, you are bound to build a solid literature base.

MANAGING THE LITERATURE

Students are often shocked at just how much literature might be relevant to a research project. In your searching, you are bound to gather a mound of readings, and finding a way to manage it will be essential. If you don't, it may just end up gathering dust in a corner. Making it manageable involves being able to quickly and efficiently assess relevance; systematically keep track of sources; and make relevant notes.

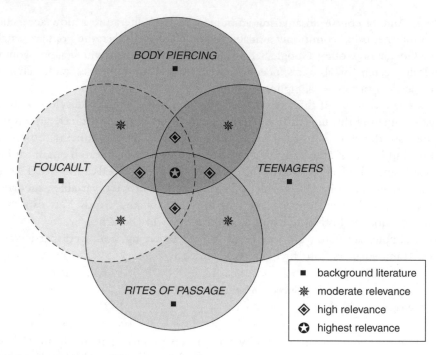

FIGURE 6.3   INTERSECTING AREAS OF LITERATURE

Assessing relevance

You probably won't be able to read every word of every piece of relevant literature you have located, so being able to quickly and efficiently wade through your literature in order to assess relevance and 'get the gist' will save you a lot of time and frustration. If you are reading a journal article, look at the abstract or executive summary. This should give you a good sense of relevance. In a book, peruse the table of contents, the back cover blurb, and the introduction. Also have a look at the conclusion offered at chapter ends, as well as the overall conclusion. Within a few minutes you should be able to assess if a work is likely to be of value to your own research process.

One simple suggestion is to rank the relevance of readings using 'Post-it' notes. For example, if you are looking at literature related to three distinct concepts, you could use three different colour Post-its, one for each concept, and then rank the overall work, or chapters within a work, with a 1 (minimally relevant), 2 (somewhat relevant), or 3 (highly relevant). It is amazing how much time this can save when you begin a more rigorous review of materials.

Being systematic

Nothing is worse than looking for a lost reference that you really need. It could be a quote with a missing page number, or a fact with no citation, or a perfect point that needs to go right there – if only you could remember where you read it. If you can incorporate each of your resources into a management system you will be saving yourself a lot of future heartache.

Keep and file copies of relevant books, articles, etc., and avoid lending out your 'only copies'. It's amazing how many books and articles never get returned, even when the borrower swears he or she will get it back to you by the end of the week. You also need to keep good citations. Now as common as it may be to see bad referencing, I refuse to believe that proper referencing is an intellectually difficult task. A pain in the neck and lower – yes, but it really is not that hard to do right. You just need to be organized and diligent. Find out right from the start what your recommended referencing style is, get a style guide, and just get on with it. Rigorous referencing and appropriate filing can save you much grief in the future.

You may also want to consider using bibliographic file management software such as ProCite, EndNote, or Reference Manager. These programs can automatically format references in any number of styles, i.e. Harvard, APA, Vancouver, etc., once basic bibliographic details are entered. Just one final point: be sure to back up anything and everything related to your project, including references. If there is one thing you can rely on, it's that computers cannot be relied on.

Annotating references

> **Reading furnishes the mind only with materials of knowledge; it is thinking that makes what we read ours.**
> *John Locke*

It is definitely worth developing a systematic approach to note taking that allows for a methodical and organized review of materials from first read. There are a lot of students who read materials without such a systematic approach, and later find they need to go back and reread the material – often when they are short of time and hard pressed to meet deadlines.

A good strategy here is to keep an annotated bibliography or a systematic review of all your significant literature that can remind you of the relevance, accuracy, and quality of sources cited (see Box 6.1). Now this does not mean you need to take huge amounts of formal notes. Annotations are generally for your eyes only and are jotted down in order to minimize the time it takes to incorporate these works into your own. So while 'annotating' every single relevant reference may seem like a highly onerous task, you will be grateful for the annotations when you undertake a formal literature review, or when you need to call on the references while writing up.

Annotations vary in both content and length depending on the relevance of the reviewed work, but things I would suggest incorporating include:

- *Author and audience* – The ability to retrieve vast amounts of literature has increased the need to assess the quality of that literature. The Internet is full of propaganda, uninformed opinion, and less than credible research. Ask yourself: Who is doing the writing? What are their qualifications? Are they professionals, politicians, researchers, unknown? And who is the work written for? Is it for an academic audience, general public, constituents, clients? If the answers to these questions leave you feeling less than comfortable with the source, it is probably best to move on to more credible literature.

- *Summary* – I often get asked how long a summary should be. The answer is, 'it depends'. The aim is to jot down key points that will help you research and write. You may be able to summarize a less relevant work in a sentence or two, while others will be much more instrumental to your own thinking and researching and require more in-depth coverage. Write what you think you will want to know later on, and try not to fall into the trap of trusting your memory. What you think you will remember today is likely to be forgotten, if not tomorrow, then certainly in a few months. Keep in mind that you can write annotations in any manner/style you want; you don't have to be formal. Doodles, mind maps, quotes, page numbers, etc., are all fair game.

- *Critical comment* – Students generally don't have a problem summarizing information. Where they often struggle, however, is in their ability to be critical. Now I know the word 'critical' has a tendency to imply negativity, but in academic reviewing the word 'critical' means informed and considered evaluation. As a potential researcher you need to be able to ask and answer the question, 'What did I really think of that and why?' Ask yourself: Is this new? Is this old? Is this cutting edge? Is this just a rehash? Are there fundamental flaws in the methodology? Are author biases coming through? Do you believe the results are credible? Also consider comparing and contrasting this work with others you have read. How does this work 'sit' with the general literature?

- *Notes on relevance* – This is where you try to make the connection between what others have done and what you propose to do. Ask yourself how this work sits in relation to the study you plan to conduct. Is there anything in the work that turn a light bulb on in your head? How does the theory or ideology compare? What about the methods? Is there some flaw in the thinking/methods that makes you want to explore this area/topic/question from a different angle? Is there a quote, passage, or section that really gets to the heart of what you are trying to do or say? Look to be inspired. Look to be surprised. Look to be appalled. Use this section to get the creative juices flowing.

BOX 6.1   BRIEF SAMPLE ANNOTATION

O'Leary, Z. (2001) 'Conversations in the kitchen', in A. Bartlett and G. Mercer (eds), *Postgraduate Research Supervision: Transforming (R)elations.* New York: Peter Lang.
Citation (Harvard reference)

The author is a senior lecturer at the University of Western Sydney who has written a chapter in a book targeting postgraduate research students and supervisors.
Author/audience

This is basically an anecdote that discusses, and attempts to normalize, the emotional and intellectual
Summary

hardships many research students can go through when trying to juggle family obligations and study. The anecdote is quite short and written in a warm and personal style that makes it very easy to relate to. It is not, however, a research study backed up by any data/rigour and therefore does not allow one to assess the extent of the issues raised to whether the concerns she raises are widespread. That said, it does seem to relate well to the more rigorous research studies conducted by Field and Howard (2002) and Dreicker (2003).

Critical comment

This relates quite well to my chapter on 'coping mechanisms and strategies for managing roles and workloads' and may be good for a quote or two, especially if I feel my text is too dry.

Relevance

WRITING THE FORMAL 'LITERATURE REVIEW'

As discussed at the beginning of the chapter, a literature review is a very specific piece of argumentative writing, based largely on critical review of relevant journal articles, that acts to create a 'space' for your research. It is generally required in research projects, proposals, reports, journal articles, and student theses. So it needs to be tackled – even if it is seen as a somewhat overwhelming task.

Now the tendency to feel overwhelmed by the concept of doing a literature review is pretty commonplace. In fact, I would go as far to say that the need to write a literature review can strike fear into the heart of even the most confident student. Not only do you need to engage with a body of literature, you also need to be able to compare, contrast, synthesize, and make arguments with that literature in ways that indicate a readiness to contribute to the literature itself. And that is a big task, especially if it is your first rigorous attempt.

Just knowing how to start can be difficult – and not all supervisors know how to get you on your way. Most will know a good literature review when they read one, but more than a few will have difficulty articulating exactly how to go about constructing one. Understanding the literature review's purpose, coming to grips with the potential ways you can handle coverage, and approaching the task methodically can go a long way in making the task manageable.

Purpose

You'd think that the purpose of a formal literature review should be simply to review the literature. But expectations of what a literature review is meant to achieve go far

TABLE 6.1   REVIEWING THE LITERATURE VS 'THE LITERATURE REVIEW'

Self-educative reasons for reviewing the literature	What the formal 'literature review' attempts to achieve
• Inform yourself of what is happening in the field	• Inform your audience of what is happening in the field
• Form a foundation of topical and methodological knowledge and expertise	• Establish your credibility as a knowledgeable and capable researcher
• Develop skills in critical thinking/analysis	
• Find potential gaps in the literature that may point to potential research questions	• Argue the relevance and the significance of your research question
• Critically evaluate common/typical methods	• Provide the context for your own methodological approach
• Facilitate the development of your own methodological approaches	• Argue the relevance and appropriateness of your approach

beyond a simple articulation of what previous researchers have done and found. The formal literature review is a purposeful argument that needs to:

- *Inform readers of developments in the field* – Not only should a research study inform readers of your particular research question, but it should also inform them of the general topic. The inclusion of a strong literature review should provide readers with contextual learning through an up-to-date account and discussion of relevant theories, methods, and research studies that make up a particular topic's body of literature.
- *Establish researcher credibility* – Because researchers are responsible for the production of new knowledge, it is essential they show they are abreast of the field; are aware of relevant new developments; and are conversant with academic and scientific discourse and debate within their research area. The literature review allows researchers to establish credibility through rigorous and critical evaluation of relevant research works; a demonstrated understanding of key issues; and the ability to outline the relationship of their own work to the rest of the field.
- *Argue the need for, and relevance of, their study* – The literature review needs to make an argument for a researcher's own research agenda. It needs to set the current study within the context of past research. The literature review has the potential to identify 'gaps' that show the appropriate and significant nature of a study's research questions. It can also justify methodological approaches by critically evaluating methods generally accepted/typical for this type of research; highlighting the limitations that might be common to past studies; and uncovering the possibly unwarranted assumptions that can underpin method.

Table 6.1 attempts to break this down a bit further by highlighting the broader, more self-educative reasons for reviewing the literature, and the corresponding purposes of the formal 'literature review'.

Coverage

Once you understand propose, the question you are likely to ask is 'what exactly needs to go into my lit review?' Well, the coverage in your literature review should be broad enough to: inform your readers of the nature of the discourse and debate current to your topic; establish your own credibility as a researcher abreast of the field; and demonstrate the need for, and relevance of, your own research. But the depth of the general body of literature, the arguments you are trying to make, and the level of the project/thesis will also determine what is both suitable and required. A one-semester undergraduate project may only demand engagement with 20 or so of the most relevant and recent articles, while a PhD thesis may require in excess of 250 or more articles and require you to dig into both theory and seminal works.

Options for coverage include:

- exhaustive coverage that cites all relevant literature
- exhaustive coverage with only selective citation
- representative coverage that discusses works that typify particular areas within the literature
- coverage of seminal/pivotal works
- a combination of the above.

The writing process

There are students who are able to pull together an impressive literature review without too much guidance. They have a sense of the task and tackle it admirably. But I have to say this is the exception. Most students struggle and are looking for a clear way forward. So while the following is not the only process you can follow, it is one that will get you from A to B and help you go well beyond a 'he said'/'she said' report. Remember: the goal here is to inform, establish, and argue. To do this, I suggest the following steps:

1 *Make doing the literature review an ongoing process* – Your literature review will inform your question, theory, and methods, and your question, theory, and methods will help set the parameters of your literature review. This is a cyclical process. A literature review is often a moving target that should evolve in both thinking and writing as your study develops.

2 *Read quite a few good, relevant reviews* – You need to have a sense of what a good literature review is, before you are in a position to construct your own.

3 *Identify the variables in your study* – For instance:

   (a) body piercing
   (b) teenagers
   (c) rites of passage.

4 *Develop a list of synonyms or alternatives – That is:*

   (a) piercing, earrings, nose rings, body art, etc.
   (b) teenagers, girls, boys, adolescents, young adults
   (c) rites of passage, initiation, induction, observance.

5 *Place in a Venn diagram* – As shown earlier in Figure 6.3.

6 *Use a search engine* – Ask your librarian for guidance or try using Google Scholar as shown in Figure 6.4. Search using all variables and their synonyms/alternatives.

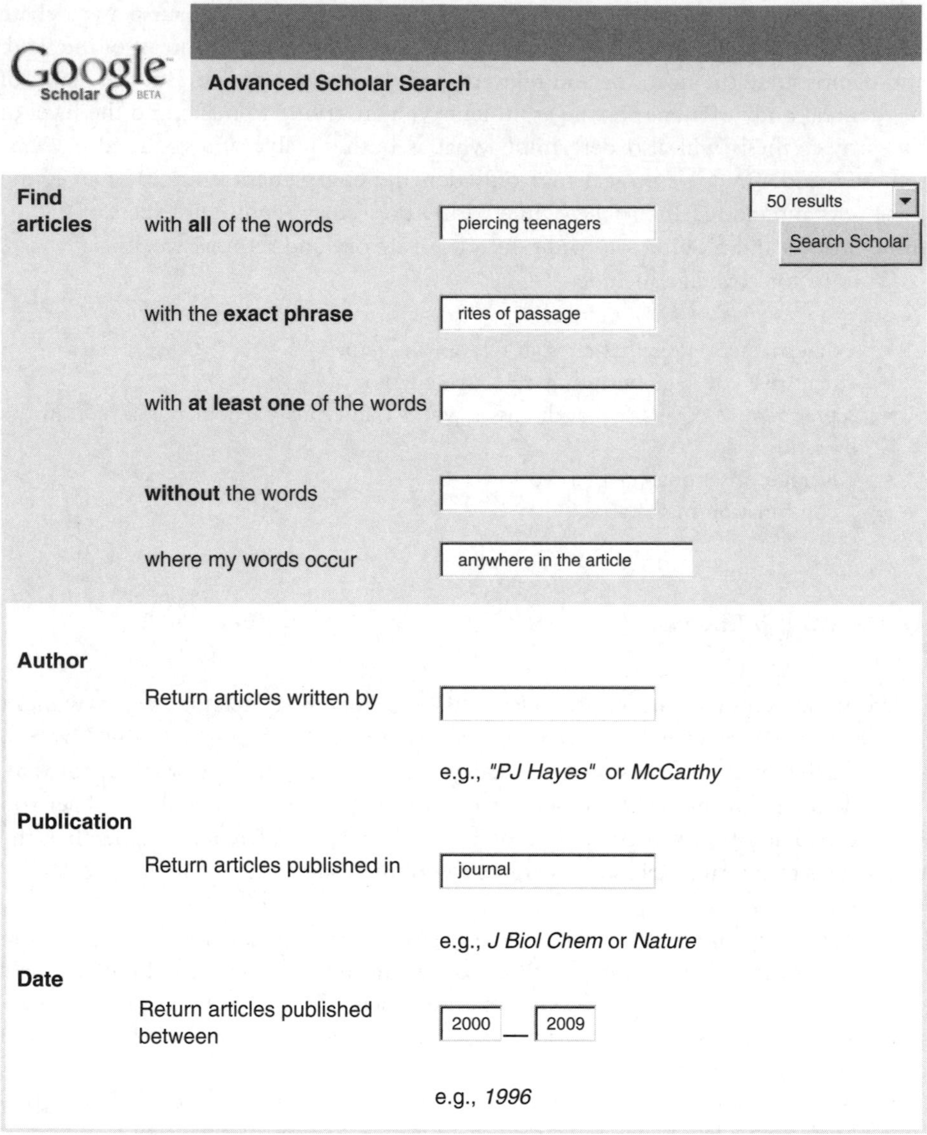

FIGURE 6.4   GOOGLE SCHOLAR ADVANCED SEARCH

Note that if using Google Scholar, the advanced search option allows you to identify the names of journals you might be interested in. A good tip is to put the word 'journal' in this box. This will limit your search to all journals with the word journal in the title (which is a good percentage) thereby cutting out a lot of extraneous hits.

7   *Compile citations with abstracts* – Many of these will be available electronically.

8   *Read abstracts and cull all irrelevant articles* – Get rid of anything obviously off topic, and rank remaining readings by relevance.

9   *Assess whether you need to dig deeper or focus your review* – To focus in, you can add relevant variables (see Figure 6.3) and/or look at studies conducted in the past, say, five or seven years. You can also think about limiting your review to selective or representative coverage. Expanding may mean limiting/modifying variables and/or increasing time span. Remember that studies do not have to directly explore your particular research questions to be relevant, informative, and highly useful.

10   *Systematically log your relevant readings* – Choices here are to manually construct a comprehensive bibliography or use bibliographic software such as ProCite, EndNote, or Reference Manager.

11   *Read and annotate each relevant article* – As suggested earlier in the chapter, comment on author/audience, key points, critical comment, and relevance.

12   *Sort and organize your annotations* – Look for themes, issues of concern, common shortcomings, etc. You may find that patterns begin to emerge, which can go a long way towards the development of your own arguments.

13   *Develop a potential outline for your literature review* – Consider what arguments will best convince readers you are fully engaged with the relevant body of literature. Your structure can always be modified as your thinking evolves, but your main argument should relate to the need for your research study to be undertaken in the way you are proposing.

14   *Write purposefully* – You cannot write a formal 'literature review' without an agenda. Your audience should be able to readily identify the 'point' of each section of your review. If your audience do not know why you are telling them what you are telling them, you need to reconsider your approach.

15   *Use the literature to back up your arguments* – Rather than review, report, or borrow the arguments of others, use the literature to help generate, and then support, your own arguments. That means each paragraph should make a point that is backed up by the literature. For instance:

> Within the context of climate change, the relationship between knowledge and behavioral change is contentious [THE POINT YOU ARE TRYING TO MAKE]. While several studies have shown that knowledge of climate change affects behavior (Jones 2008; Wong 2002; Smith 2007), a new study conducted by Burnie and Powis (2009) argues that knowledge has minimal impact on change and that practices of peers and neighbors are much more influential [THE EVIDENCE THAT SUPPORTS YOUR POINT].

This is a much more sophisticated approach than leading each paragraph by author, i.e. starting paragraphs with 'Jones (2008) states'; 'Wong (2002) found'; 'Smith (2007) argues'.

16   *Adopt an appropriate style and tone* – The trick here is to avoid being too deferential, but also avoid being overcritical. Keep in mind that your goal is to engage, debate, argue, evolve your own ideas, and contribute. If you think of yourself as a mere student, you might find it hard to be critical. On the other hand, if you attempt to establish credibility by showing you are able to pick holes in the work of others, you run the risk of being judgemental, hypercritical, and unable to draw relevance and significance from the works reviewed.

17   *Get plenty of feedback* – Writing a literature review is not an easy task, and supervisors' expectations can vary widely. Don't wait until the last minute to

begin the writing process or to get feedback. Be sure to pass a draft to your supervisor, or anyone else willing to read it, early on.

18 *Be prepared to redraft* – Whether you are a student or professional researcher, you are not likely to get away without a redraft or two (or three or four).

FURTHER READING

There are quite a few readings that can help you navigate your way through the complexities of working with research literature. You may find the following sources a good place to start:

Fink, A. (2004) *Conducting Research Literature Reviews: From the Internet to Paper.* Thousand Oaks, CA: Sage.

Galvan, J. L. (2005) *Writing Literature Reviews: A Guide for Students of the Social and Behavioral Sciences.* Glendale, CA: Pyrczak.

Hart, C. (2000) *Doing a Literature Review.* London: Sage.

Hart, C. (2001) *Doing a Literature Search.* London: Sage.

Machi, L. A. (2008) *The Literature Review: Six Steps to Success.* Thousand Oaks, CA: Corwin Press.

Pan, M. L. (2007) *Preparing Literature Reviews: Qualitative and Quantitative Approaches.* Glendale, CA: Pyrczak.

Ridley, D. (2008) *The Literature Review: A Step by step Guide for Students.* London: Sage.

CHAPTER SUMMARY

- Reading is an essential part of the research process. The quest to add to a body of knowledge demands engagement with topical, methodological, and theoretical literature.
- Literature is used for disparate purposes throughout the research process including exploring your topic, defining questions, articulating a rationale, theoretically informing your study, developing appropriate design, writing a formal literature review, and potentially as a source of primary data.
- Literature types include reference materials, books, journals, grey literature, official publications, archives, and writing aids.
- In finding relevant literature it is worth calling on the expertise of librarians, supervisors, and other researchers.
- The ever-increasing availability of literature requires students to develop proficient key word search skills that can be used to access a variety of electronic databases and search engines.
- Managing the literature requires efficient reading skills that allow you to cull vast amounts of written work. You also need to develop a system for diligently managing references.

- Annotating your sources provides you with a record of relevant literature. It should include the citation, articulation of the author and audience, a short summary, critical commentary, and notes on relevance that can remind you of the significance, accuracy, and quality of the sources cited.
- The formal literature review is a very specific piece of writing designed to inform your readers of your topic, establish your credibility as a researcher, and argue the need for, and relevance of, your work. Most find it a difficult task that takes patience, practice, drafts, and redrafts.
- Students are often unsure of what needs to be included in the literature review. Some have difficulty finding relevant literature, while others have difficulty focusing their reading. Organizing and searching for the literature according to various concepts/variables can help manage the task.
- A good literature review is an argument that is more purposeful than a simple review of relevant literature. Being systematic can help you build a review that argues the case for the conduct of your research project.
- A good literature review builds your credibility by obliging you to engage, learn, debate, argue, contribute, and evolve ideas, without being hypercritical or sycophantic.

7
DESIGNING A RESEARCH PLAN

CHAPTER PREVIEW

- Methodology, methods, and tools
- Moving from questions to answers
- Getting down to the nitty-gritty

METHODOLOGY, METHODS, AND TOOLS

You've now gotten through the preliminaries. You understand the major constructs related to research; you believe you are ready for the demands of the process; you understand what constitutes credibility; you are prepared to meet ethical obligations; you have managed to develop a first-class question; you know what is expected in a convincing proposal; and you have even managed to engage with some literature. At long last you are ready to develop your research design – you are ready to figure out how you will move from questions to answers. Who would have ever thought it would take so much just to get here?

Now if you have done all of the above, you should be well on your way to a sound design that incorporates both appropriate methodology and logical/feasible methods. But what exactly is the difference between research methodologies and research methods? And how are they related to the design – of a study?

There's no doubt that 'methods' terminology can be hazy, so I thought I would start this chapter by offering a few definitions that should help you differentiate key terms.

METHODOLOGY
Overarching, macro-level *frameworks* that offer principles of reasoning associated with particular paradigmatic assumptions that legitimate various schools of research. Methodologies provide both the strategies and grounding for the conduct of a study.

Examples here include scientific method, ethnography, and action research (see Chapters 8 and 9).

METHODS
The actual micro-level *techniques* used to collect and analyse data. Methods of data collection include interviewing, surveying, observation, and unobtrusive methods (see Chapters 11 and 12), while methods of analyses comprise quantitative strategies (i.e. statistics) and qualitative strategies (i.e. thematic exploration) (see Chapters 13 and 14).

TOOLS
The *devices* used in the collection of research data, e.g. questionnaires, observation checklists, and interview schedules (see Chapters 11 and 12).

METHODOLOGICAL DESIGN
The *plan* for conducting your research project that includes all of the above.

The relationship between methodology and methods

Your methodological design is basically your study's blueprint and as such will comprise elements that are as broad as questions related to paradigm, and as specific as questions dealing with the nuts and bolts of who, where, when, how, and what.

Now it is not uncommon for students to want to jump straight into the details of their research *methods* without engaging at the level of research *methodology*. They want to fast-forward to designing strategies for data collection and cannot understand why it's important to grasp, adopt, and apply frameworks that sit at a higher macro level.

But methodologies are crucial to the research process and, in fact, provide us with much more than just research strategies. They actually provide us, as researchers, with legitimization for knowledge production. They are our means of showing the outside world that we are not just random people with an opinion, but that we are researchers who are engaging with well-considered, rigorous processes. The adopting of various methodological positions shows that we have grappled with the responsibilities and controversies associated with the production of knowledge.

Credible research design therefore requires more than just the adoption of data collection and data analysis methods. It requires that such methods are nested within more macro-level frameworks, or methodologies, that work in concert with methods to provide researchers with a voracious design that can stand up to the highest level of scrutiny.

MOVING FROM QUESTIONS TO ANSWERS

> "Methods and means cannot be separated from the ultimate aim."
> *Emma Goldman*

FIGURE 7.1   THE PATH

When it comes to methodological design, it may sound incredibly obvious, but your goal is to come up with a plan that will allow you either to answer your well-articulated research question, or to test your skilfully constructed hypothesis. Now this clearly implies that methodological design requires a well-articulated research question or a skilfully constructed hypothesis, and this is true. A well-articulated question defines an investigation, sets boundaries, provides direction, and acts as a frame of reference for assessing your work. In this way, your question acts as a blueprint for decision making related to method. So if you think you are ready to move to methodological design, but you are still struggling to articulate your question clearly, you really need to go back and work on the question itself (see Chapter 4). If you don't know where you want to go, you simply can't determine a path for getting there.

Finding a path

So let's talk about paths for a minute. Assuming you are pretty happy with your research question, the next step is figuring out how to best go about getting the answers; in other words, defining the elements of your methodological design. Have a look at Figure 7.1. It represents a common conception of how we move from questions to answers. The arrow represents the methodological design that will best get you from Q to A. The assumption here is that there is a correct or best design.

Figure 7.2 offers an alternative representation of methodological possibilities. Here the assumption is that there might be numerous ways to move from questions to answers. Paths are varied and diverse, but they all have the potential to generate the data that can lead to credible answers. The trick is to travel down a methodological path that is appropriate for the question, the researcher, and the context.

Figure 7.3 works on the same 'multiple path' assumption as Figure 7.2, but reminds us that both who we are and what we do can influence how we see and what we find. Each methodological design has the potential to draw out answers from a somewhat different perspective. I think Werner Heisenberg, one of the twentieth-century physicists who founded the area of quantum mechanics, said it best: 'It is worth remembering that what we observe is not nature itself, but nature exposed to our method of questioning' (in Shulman and Asimov 1988: 324).

The significance of the progression of these models is in the increased responsibility they represent for the researcher. As you move from finding the path, to choosing from a range of potential paths, to reflexively considering the implications of the paths themselves, your need to consider issues associated with credibility increases. If you view the development of method in a manner similar to that in Figure 7.3, design becomes a real thinking game that requires you to make well-considered decisions

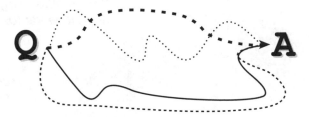

FIGURE 7.2   MULTIPLE PATHS

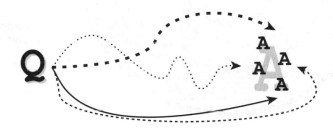

FIGURE 7.3   PATHS AND PERSPECTIVE

that best ensure you are approaching your study in a manner that will lead to highly credible data and trustworthy results.

Hitting the target

So what do you need to consider in your methodological decision making? Well, as depicted in Figure 7.4, getting your methodological design on target requires that: (1) your methodological design addresses your question; (2) you have, or are willing to develop, the skills and interests needed to undertake your plan; and (3) all the elements of your methodological design are doable.

Addressing your question

Unfortunately, there can be a real tendency for researchers, both new and established, to be quite wedded to particular methodological approaches. They might have it in their minds that they will do an ethnography or a population study, do a survey or a series of interviews, even before they have really engaged in a critical examination of what their question logically demands. But keep in mind that the goal in developing methodological approaches is working towards what is most appropriate for answering your question. It is important that you do not fall prey to the belief that

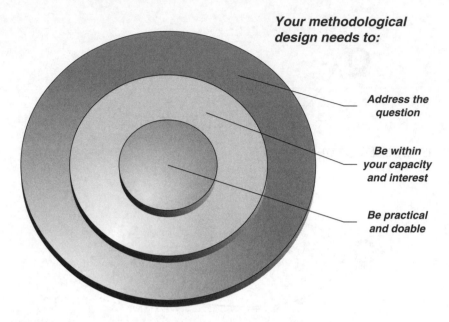

Your methodological design needs to:

Address the question

Be within your capacity and interest

Be practical and doable

FIGURE 7.4   GETTING YOUR METHODOLOGICAL DESIGN ON TARGET

one way of doing things is inherently better than another, or to think that it's OK to stay within your comfort zone. Methods need to fall from questions.

Now, as discussed in Chapter 4, this does not mean your question must be set in stone from its first articulation. Research is generally an ongoing and iterative process of development and redevelopment that may see questions shift at various stages throughout the research process. What needs to be stressed, however, is that in the end, there needs to be a goodness of fit between your final question and your methodological design. One, the other, or both may evolve, but in the end, your question and your design (which will incorporate decision making at both the level of methodology and methods) will need to have the tightest of relationships.

Working at the level of methodology

One of the most crucial factors involved in the selection of methodology is familiarization. You need to be aware of what is out there. As covered in Chapter 8, you can explore traditional quantitative strategies based on scientific, hypothetico-deductive methods, as well as any number of qualitative strategies designed to get you delving at a deeper level. You might also consider mixed methodological approaches that will have you working across more than one strategy. There are also more purposive strategies that allow you to work simultaneously towards both knowledge and change, such as action research, as well as methodologies designed for both front and back end evaluation. While the ideal would be for you to have in-depth knowledge of all these approaches, what is crucial in undertaking a research project is familiarity with what's out there and the ability to reflexively consider these strategies in relation to the aims and objectives of your study.

Now when it comes to your project, you are generally trying to do one or more of the following: (1) understand a problem or an issue; (2) find workable solutions; (3) work towards a solution; or (4) evaluate success and/or failure. As discussed below, each of these distinct goals tends to be aligned with particular methodological approaches:

- *Understanding a problem* – Attempting to develop a better understanding of a problem situation might involve looking outwards towards broad societal attitudes and opinions, or inwards into the intricacies and complexities of your problem situation. Take, for example, the issue of workplace stress. You might want to know, 'How common is stress in the workplace?' If this were your question, outward exploration, say a population study using a survey approach, might be called for. If, however, your interest was in understanding how a particular staff group react to stress, or what it feels like to live with workplace stress, you might look at more inwardly focused strategies that allow you to delve deeper into complexity, e.g. ethnography or phenomenology (see Chapter 8).

- *Finding workable solutions* – The quest to find workable solutions might involve: assessing needs and visioning futures; locating potential programmes, interventions, and/or services; or exploring the feasibility of particular change initiatives. For example, sticking with the issue of workplace stress, your goal might be to understand what can be done to reduce such stress. Specific questions might be: 'Is workplace stress a priority issue for employees?', 'What vision do employees have for a different workplace culture?', 'What programmes have been introduced in other settings to reduce stress?', or 'Will programme X be suitable/cost effective for my workplace?' Now these types of question are sometimes referred to as 'front end analysis' and are common approaches in evaluative research. So if this is where your aims/objectives are pointing, you need to explore this area of literature (see Chapter 9).

- *Working towards solutions* – I am referring here to research goals that go beyond the production of knowledge, i.e. research that has the goal of change directly embedded in its research agenda. Now this might refer to improving practice, shifting systems, or even working towards some level of fundamental or radical change. For example, let's say your goal was to collaborate with staff on a co-learning project that developed and implemented a stress reduction strategy. Whether you want to work on changing employee behaviours, workplace practices, or the broader corporate culture, your desire to produce knowledge while actioning change is likely to lead you towards the literature related to 'action research' (see Chapter 9).

- *Evaluating change* – The goal here is to answer the question, 'Has a change initiative/programme been successful?' Now your interest in evaluation might be related to outcomes, i.e. 'Did programme X meet its objectives?' But it might also be related to a process, i.e. 'How and how well is programme X being implemented?' So, for example, if you wanted to evaluate a recently introduced stress reduction programme you might ask, 'Has programme X reduced stress?' This question would lead you to literature related to 'outcome' or 'summative' evaluation. If, however, you wanted to ask, 'What are the strengths, weaknesses, opportunities, and threats related to the implementation of this programme?', you would need to explore 'process' or 'formative' evaluation literature (see Chapter 9).

Figure 7.5 attempts to logically work you through the links between aims, questions, and methodology. While neither definitive nor exhaustive, it will give you examples of sound connections and point you to areas that you may want to explore further. But also keep in mind that you always have the option of using a mixed approach – which may just help you answer your question in a holistic fashion (see Chapter 8).

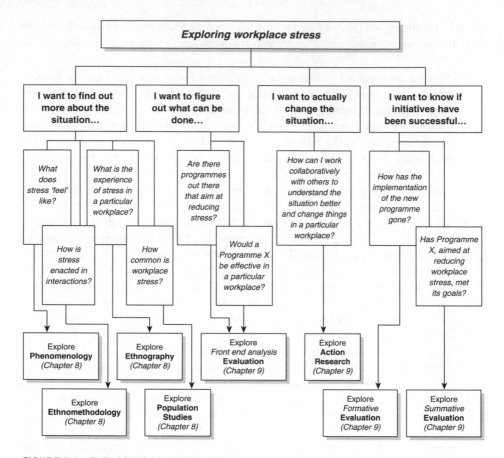

FIGURE 7.5   EXPLORING METHODOLOGIES

Working at the level of method

Once your broader methodological approaches are in line with your aims and objectives, you will need to go a step further and think about the actual methods best suited for collecting and analysing your data.

Now decision making related to methods is clearly question driven. A well-articulated question should lead you to who you need to talk to and what you need to ask – and as an extension of this, what data collection methods/tools you might use. For example, imagine you want to research the self-image of teenage girls. You can do one of two things. You can jump in and begin to design your study – after all, you have it in your mind that you will conduct 'interviews'. Or you can really think about what you want to know, go through some of the more relevant literature, work on the process of narrowing and clarifying, and maybe even work through a further articulation of your question before you attack the issue of methods.

In my experience, students who go for the jump-in approach and work from a topic rather than a question can really struggle. They often end up getting lost and confused. Things take a long time to fall into place (and sometimes never do), and students can end up with data they don't know how to use. Believe me, trying to retrofit a question to your data is not easy and rarely works!

On the other hand, say you have been able to narrow your question to, 'Do parents somehow teach their daughters that worth is dependent on external beauty?' Because you know what you want to know, deciding on the methods is only one small logical step away. For example, you can consider whether you want to get the perspective of parents, children, or maybe counsellors. This then clearly points you to both the population and sample you will need to target in your data collection (see Chapter 10).

You can then consider the scale of research you wish to do, perhaps a large-scale survey that compares various socio-economic or cultural groups, or perhaps you think conducting interviews or focus groups will draw out richer descriptions (see Chapter 11). You might also consider a less unobtrusive measure like observation that will allow you to witness first hand parent/daughter interactions (see Chapter 12). Perhaps you will consider doing a variety of the above.

No matter what the case, familiarity with the expectations related to methodology, as well as clarity and precision in your question, can readily lead to a range of methods that can be explored and considered on the basis of both their logic and practicality.

Making it right for the researcher

There is often a desire to stay with what you know. But as discussed above, questions should drive choice of both methodology and method. So it is important to check your own assumptions, biases, and, dare I say, narrow-mindedness. Too many researchers are dismissive of what is outside their comfort zone and do not take the time to understand what each approach has to offer holistic knowledge production.

But even given this treatise on the importance of being open and willing to push at the boundaries of your comfort zone, it can be difficult to work with an approach that conflicts with your own epistemological framework. In fact, there is no sense undertaking a traditional 'quantitative' study if you hold a well-considered, strong critique of positivism/scientific method. Similarly, you will not be comfortable delving into the qualitative paradigm if you have a problem with the value of data not supported by statistics. You need to give real consideration to your own belief systems, as well as your willingness (1) to develop new skills/interests and (2) to take on particular research 'roles'.

Skills and interests

Are you a people person, or do you like sitting behind a computer? Are you comfortable having intimate chats with strangers, or are you better at more distant and formal communication? Do you like working with words or would you rather play with numbers? Can you handle a level of emotional investment or do you want to be removed and always 'objective'? Can you be objective or will you struggle to keep your opinions to yourself? Do you loathe statistics, or is loathe not a strong enough word?!

Yes, you can develop new skills, and of course this is a worthwhile goal, but you really need to keep your timeline in mind. New skills are not always easy to master, and the number of new skills you would need to develop to be able to do it all is probably not practical. Have a good think about where your skills and interests lie. It would be kind of silly to go down the path of large-scale surveys if you know you hate stats and the thought of having to do it makes you break out in hives. On the other hand, even if you see the value of in-depth interviewing, without the right communication skills it might be a torturous route that ends up not doing justice to your research process. Not only do you also need to consider your own comfort zone, you also need to think about how your skills, or lack thereof, might affect the quality of the data you collect. Remember that competence is not a luxury – it is a requirement.

Research roles

There is no shortage of metaphors for the role of the researcher. From theorist to scientist, choreographer to change agent, the range of metaphors used to depict the researcher points to the diversity of possibilities for approaching your research project. Have a look at the following metaphors and consider which best suits you and your research process. Perhaps just as important, consider what roles might be uncomfortable or inappropriate for you and your methodological design. Also keep in mind that there is no need for these roles to be mutually exclusive, and of course there is nothing keeping you from creatively and strategically creating your own researcher role.

- *Theorist* – The 'philosopher' or 'thinker'. The theorist metaphor suggests a researcher who can analyse critically and think abstractly. Theorists are likely to draw on the work of other theorists and are interested in new ways of seeing. In explaining a particular phenomenon or situation, theorists often attempt to develop understandings that lie outside the dominant paradigm. Can be comfortable with various methodological/methods approaches.
- *Scientist* – The 'objective expert'. The scientist metaphor suggests a researcher who works to a formula; is removed, precise, methodical, logical, highly trained; and is in control of the research process. Objectivity ensures that scientists do not have an undue influence on the research process. Most comfortable with the 'quantitative' paradigm.
- *Change agent* – The 'emancipator'. The change agent metaphor suggests a researcher who not only acknowledges subjectivities, but is working to better a situation based precisely on these subjectivities. There is often devotion to the research/change process and sensitivity to the words and actions of respondents. Change agents often work in participatory and collaborative ways. Most suited to action research strategies.
- *Bricoleur* – The 'jack of all trades' or 'professional do-it-yourself person'. The bricoleur metaphor suggests a researcher who sees methods as emergent and dependent upon both question and context. The bricoleur will employ a variety of methodological tools and even create new ones as needed to solve a puzzle or find a solution (Denzin and Lincoln 2007). Comfortable with a variety of methodological/methods options.
- *Choreographer* – The 'coordinator of a dance'. The choreographer metaphor suggests a researcher who begins with a foundation of key principles, has vision, and tries not to have a limited view. The choreographer works by warming up or preparation, exploration, and exercise, and finally illumination and formulation (Janesick 2007). Usually comfortable with 'qualitative' approaches.

Pragmatics: making it doable

Assume your intended design addresses your research question. In fact, you are quite comfortable with the approach, and believe you have or can develop the skills and adopt the roles necessary to carry off your project. There is just one more question. Is it doable? Regardless of how appropriate your methodological design might be for you and your question, if you do not have ethics approval, or the resources, time, or access necessary to accomplish the task, you will need to rethink your approach. The 'best' design is simply worthless if you are going to come up against impermeable barriers to implementation.

The following questions can help you assess the practicality of your methodological plan:

- ☑ **Is your method ethical?/Is it likely to get required ethics approval?** A clear criterion of any research design is that it is ethical; and ethicality is likely to be audited by an ethics committee. If a study calls for interaction with people, it will often require formal workplace and/or university approval. Chapter 3 talks about ethics in some detail, but to summarize, an ethical study takes responsibility for integrity in the production of knowledge and ensures that the mental, emotional, and physical welfare of respondents is protected.

- ☑ **Do you have required access to data?** A major challenge for researchers is gaining access to data. Whether you plan to explore documents, conduct interviews or surveys, or engage in observation, the best-laid plans are worthless if you cannot find a way to access people, places, and/or records. It is about being realistic. Ask yourself how you will go about gaining access and whether your methods are truly feasible.

- ☑ **Is your timeframe realistic?** Yes, ambitious is good, but ambitious yet realistic is much better. If you have not given yourself enough time to do what your methodological design demands, you are likely to be headed down a very frustrating and stressful path that might include missing deadlines; compromising your study by changing your methods mid-stream; doing a shoddy job with your original methods; compromising time that should be dedicated to other aspects of your job/life; or not completing your project at all.

- ☑ **Do you have access to adequate resources?** Doing research is not cheap, and university funding for student research projects generally ranges from non-existent to highly limited. It is therefore extremely important to develop a realistic budget for your study. You are likely to be surprised at just how expensive your design might be. Take surveys, for example. Say you wanted to gather 300 surveys. You might need to distribute over 2,000 surveys to get that number of respondents. By the time you add up the cost of producing that many surveys, plus the cost of envelopes and postage (both to send and return), your costs can be up in the thousands. But on the other hand, a smaller number of in-depth interviews can also be expensive. A transcript for a one-hour interview can be over 50 pages long. If you plan on paying someone to type up a few of those, costs will add up really quickly. Books, computers, computer programs, equipment, interpreters, translators, training, etc., all need to be realistically considered. Any project, no matter how worthy, will not be practicable, or in fact possible, if you cannot cover costs.

GETTING DOWN TO THE NITTY-GRITTY

Once you feel comfortable with your general research plan, it is time to get down to the nuts and bolts of that plan. This involves being able to answer fundamental questions related to the who, where, when, how, and what of your approach. If you can answer these questions, you are well on your way to articulating a clearly defined research design.

Fundamental questions

As they say, it's all in the details. It is amazing how well defined a methodological plan can become once you work through the basic questions outlined below.

Who

- *Who do you want to be able to speak about?* In other words, what is your 'population', or the realm of applicability for your results? Are your findings limited to only those you spoke to, or do you want to be able to speak for a broader group? For example, are your findings applicable to the children you interviewed, children from Philadelphia, children from the USA, or children from the Western world? Or do your findings represent one rural community in Kent, all rural communities in England, or all rural communities in the UK?
- *Who do you plan to speak to/observe?* It is quite rare to be able to speak to every single person you wish to speak about. If who you wish to speak about is your 'population', then those you will actually speak to are your 'sample'. The key is that your sample is either intrinsically interesting or representative of a broader population. Chapter 10 discusses the issue of sampling and population in depth.

Where

- *What is the physical domain of your sample?* This relates to working out how far afield you need to go in order to carry out your methods. Will you need to travel to different geographic areas? Are there various sites you need to visit?
- *Are settings relevant to the credibility of your methods?* This involves considering how place can impact on method. For example, if you wanted to conduct job satisfaction interviews with construction workers, you would need to consider if an informal chat at the Friday night watering hole will generate data distinct from that gathered through informal on-site interviews.

When

- *How do your methods fit into your timeframe?* There are plenty of students who under-estimate just how long it takes to collect data, let alone analyse it, draw conclusions from it, and finally produce a report. The question of when needs to be framed in relation to your overall timeline.
- *Is timing relevant to the credibility of your methods?* If you were to conduct a survey or interview when it is most convenient to you, without considering how 'when' can affect your data, you could put your study's credibility at risk. For example, a face-to-face community survey conducted from 9 to 5 is likely to lead to a large under-representation of workers. And if you conduct university subject evaluations on the same day that results are released, it is sure to affect your data.

How

- *How will I collect my data?* This involves deciding on the methods and tools you will use to collect, gather, and/or generate your data. Chapters 11 and 12 cover a range of fundamental methods such as observation, interviews, surveys, and document analysis.
- *How will I conduct my methods?* Once you decide on your methods, thinking about how you will conduct those methods is an even deeper level of 'nitty-gritty'. For example, you will need to consider whether you will record your interviews or take notes; or whether your observations will involve living in a community for a year, or making a defined number of visits.

What

- *What will you look for/what will you ask?* Depending on your methods, this might involve developing questionnaires, observation checklists, and frameworks for doc-ument analysis. Do not do this alone; make sure you get advice and support. These tools are difficult things to get right, and it may take a few trials or pilots to really develop them to a point where you are comfortable with the data they generate (see Chapters 11 and 12).

Table 7.1 provides an example of this who, where, when, how, what framework for developing the nitty-gritty of your methodological design. It embeds the 'prerequi-sites' discussed at the start of the chapter (true to the question, right for the researcher, and doable) to assess the appropriateness of those elements.

In this example, the use of the framework has led to significant modifications in the second draft that should make the quest for credibility much more achievable. Note that even in the second draft, there are a couple of question marks remaining. This highlights that beyond mere reflection, there is a need to pilot or trial certain aspects of your design before you can fully assess its appropriateness.

TABLE 7.1   CHECKLIST FOR METHODOLOGICAL DESIGN

**'Do parents (mothers) teach their daughters
that worth is dependent upon external beauty?'**

A one-year research project

Methods – 1st draft	Methods – 2nd draft
WHO	*WHO*
Speaking about: parents of girls in Australia	**Speaking about:** mothers of young girls in Australia
Speaking to/observing: 30 mothers of 2–5-year-old girls in Western Sydney	**Speaking to/observing**: observe 30 mothers of 2–5-year-old girls in W. Sydney, interview 10 mothers in two focus groups
✗ True to the question (not a tight match – parents/mothers Australia/Western Sydney – need to modify)	✓ True to the question (I will modify question to mother and try to make a case of Australian applicability through the literature)
✓ Right for the researcher (I will enjoy working with the group)	✓ Right for the researcher (I will enjoy working with the group)
? Doable (I have access, but 30 interviews may be too many)	✓ Doable (10 in two groups is more realistic)
WHERE	*WHERE*
Domain: Western Sydney	**Domain:** Western Sydney
Setting: book room at university for interviews/observations	**Setting:** observe and conduct focus group at playgroup
? True to the question (maybe I need a more natural setting)	✓ True to the question (more naturalistic observation)
✓ Right for the researcher (convenient)	✓ Right for the researcher (mothers live locally)
✓ Doable (can book room)	✓ Doable (I have checked with playgroup coordinator)
WHEN	*WHEN*
Timing: midday, midweek	**Timing:** during playgroup (4 weeks)
Timeframe: early May	**Timeframe:** March
? True to the question (mothers may be rushed/stressed – effect nap times etc.)	✓ True to the question (already in mothers' weekly schedule)
✓ Right for the researcher (convenient)	✓ Right for the researcher (convenient)
? Doable (midday fine, May might not leave enough me time)	✓ Doable (March should fit the overall timeline)
HOW	*HOW*
Method: observation and individual interviews	**Method:** observation and focus group interviews
Use of method: will videotape mothers and children on four occasions and also videotape the interviews	**Use of method:** will use an observation checklist at playgroup and tape record focus groups
? True to the question (lots of detail with videotape, but mothers may act different if they feel surveilled)	? True to the question (I think the checklist and tape will work, but I will need to trial the method before I really know – will pilot – may need to modify depending on pilot results)
? Right for the researcher (I have made videos before, but not analysed them – will need skill development)	✓ Right for the researcher (I have done some observation and group facilitating – but will work on developing skills)
✗ Doable (too many cameras needed to capture it all, a few mothers have said they do not feel comfortable being videotaped, 30 interviews may generate too much data)	✓ Doable (should be able to manage the data generated)

TABLE 7.1 *(Continued)*

Methods – 1st draft	Methods – 2nd draft
WHAT	**WHAT**
Questions: develop observation checklist and interview questions	**Questions:** develop observation checklist and focus group discussion topics
? Answers the question (I will need to get support in development and pilot the tools)	**?** Answers the question (I will need to get support in development and pilot the tools)
✓ Right for the researcher (these are skills I would like to build)	✓ Right for the researcher (these are skills I would like to build)
✓ Doable (I have support of supervisor/ methods lecturer in developing tools)	✓ Doable (I have support of supervisor/ methods lecturer in developing tools)

Emergent methodological design

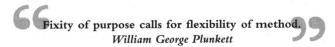

> **Fixity of purpose calls for flexibility of method.**
> *William George Plunkett*

Before leaving the nuts and bolts of method, I want to briefly touch on issues related to emergent methodological design – or a particular type of research design in which researchers do not predetermine all of the details of their methodological protocols in advance of going into the field. Now I am a strong believer in having a plan and thinking your way through the best possible approach for conducting your study. And most of the time this will mean being able to define and articulate the details that make up your approach. There are, however, several situations where you will need to have flexibility embedded in your plan. In the case of both grounded theory and action research, for example, emergence itself is a well-considered and planned part of the process.

Grounded theory

Emergent methodological design is often central to grounded theory methodology. In grounded theory, researchers work inductively to generate theories strictly from the data. In the first phase of a grounded theory study a research question or topic is defined, a methodological protocol for initial data collection is implemented, data is coded and analysed, and theories subsequently generated. Any successive phases of the study are then emergent based on generated theories. This can involve re-examination of existing data, or the development and implementation of new methodological protocols for generating, coding, and analysing additional data. In both cases, grounded theory researchers know that from the planning phase of their study, much of their methodological protocol cannot be developed in advance, and is in fact dependent on what emerges from initial data. This, however, is not meant to imply that grounded theory should be used as an excuse for qualitative studies conducted without a well-defined methodological plan. Grounded theory may be flexible, iterative, and emergent, but it is never ill defined, haphazard, or ad hoc.

Action research

Action research methodology (see Chapter 9) is also highly emergent. The goal of action research is to work with stakeholders to generate knowledge in order to action change. Because this process works towards significant change for the stakeholders, they take on the role of co-researchers. The main 'researcher' becomes a facilitator of a team that will develop the methodological protocols necessary for the action research process. This is a highly participative and collaborative type of research for which defined methodological approaches are outside the full control of the lead researcher. Rather, the process is emergent and cyclical, and is based on collaborative input from the stakeholder/researcher team.

The unexpected

Life is unpredictable, and research is not any different. You can have a plan – but that won't stop circumstances from arising that you will need to be responsive to. Whether it is surveys that are not returned, a workplace that suddenly won't give you access, or a key informant who drops out of the picture, hurdles will arise, and if you want to get over them you will need to be flexible and ready to redesign at a moment's notice.

FURTHER READING

There are quite a few readings that can help you navigate your way through the complexities of designing methods. You may find the following sources a good place to start:

Bickman, L. (ed.) (2000) *Research Design.* London: Sage.
Creswell, J. W. (2008) *Research Design: Qualitative, Quantitative and Mixed Methods Approaches.* London: Sage.
de Vaus, D. (2009) *Research Design in Social Research.* London: Sage.
Hakim, C. (2000) *Research Design.* London: Routledge.
Leedy, P. D. and Ormond, J. E. (2004) *Practical Research: Planning and Design.* Englewood Cliffs, NJ: Prentice Hall.
Mitchell, M. L. and Jolley, J. M. (2006) *Research Design Explained.* Belmont, CA: Wadsworth.

CHAPTER SUMMARY

- Before designing a research plan it is important to understand the distinction between *methodology* – macro-level research frameworks; *methods* – micro-level techniques used to collect and analyse data; *tools* – devices used in data collection; and *methodological design* – the plan that includes all of these.

- A good research plan will comprise paradigmatic considerations, methodology, methods, and details related to methods execution.
- There are often a number of ways to credibly move from questions to answers with each path giving a different perspective.
- Getting your methodological design on target requires that your design addresses your question; you have/can develop necessary skills and interests; and that your approach is doable.
- A strong methodological plan has logical links between aims, questions, and eventuating methodology.
- Clarity and precision in your question can readily lead to a range of method possibilities that should be considered on the basis of both their logic and practicality.
- As a researcher you need to design methods that sit well with your own epistemological frameworks, interests, and skills.
- Various researcher roles, e.g. the theorist, scientist, change agent, bricoleur, or choreographer, can be adopted as appropriate to your study.
- The 'best' possible design is worthless if you cannot gain ethics approval; cannot access required data; cannot finish on time; or run out of funds.
- Getting down to the nuts and bolts of design involves being able to reflexively answer questions related to who, where, when, what, and how.
- While forward planning is essential, there will be times when you will want to have flexibility. This is likely to be the case when working collaboratively with stakeholders, using a grounded theory approach, or the unexpected arises.

8
UNDERSTANDING METHODOLOGIES: QUANTITATIVE, QUALITATIVE, AND 'MIXED' APPROACHES

CHAPTER PREVIEW

- Understanding the quantitative/qualitative divide
- The quantitative tradition
- The qualitative tradition
- 'Mixed' methodology

UNDERSTANDING THE QUANTITATIVE/QUALITATIVE DIVIDE

It would certainly be more straightforward if the production of knowledge was without contention, but what fun would that be? Engaging in debates around how we can best understand our world is the favourite pastime of many social scientists, with one of the most contentious debates being that which exists between what is labelled 'qualitative' and what is labelled 'quantitative'.

Now for my money, 'quantitative' and 'qualitative' are two of the most confusing words in methods language. I must get asked a couple of times a semester if I am a quantitative or qualitative sociologist, which to my mind makes little sense. I do not believe these terms are appropriate descriptors of a researcher, or for that matter a methodology or method. It is much more useful to see these terms as simply adjectives for types of data and their corresponding modes of analysis: that is, qualitative data – data represented through words, pictures, or icons analysed using thematic

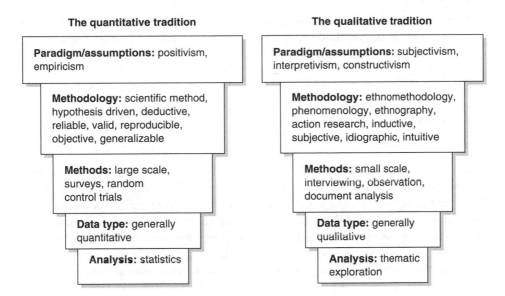

FIGURE 8.1   ASSUMPTIONS RELATED TO THE QUANTITATIVE AND QUALITATIVE

exploration; and quantitative data – data represented through numbers and analysed using statistics.

'Quantitative' and 'qualitative', however, have come to represent a whole set of assumptions that can unfortunately dichotomize methods and limit the potential of researchers to build holistic understandings. Quantitative research, for example, is often characterized as an objective positivist search for singular truths that relies on hypotheses, variables, and statistics, is generally large scale, but without much depth. Qualitative research, on the other hand, rejects positivist 'rules' and works at accepting multiple realities through the study of a small number of in-depth cases. Such processes, however, can be accused of being subjective, value laden, biased, and sometimes ad hoc (Cavana et al. 2001, Creswell 2008, Neuman 2005) (see Figure 8.1).

While there's no doubt that quantitative and qualitative traditions represent a fundamental and important debate in the production of knowledge (see Chapter 1), there's also no doubt that the use of the terms 'quantitative' and 'qualitative', particularly in relation to methodology, can be confusing, divisive, and highly limiting. In fact, these terms imply that designs that sit under the quantitative banner simply dismiss 'words', while those designs that sit under the qualitative banner do not have the time or space to deal with 'numbers'. This is simply untrue. After all, isn't quantitative data simply a coding system for qualitative concepts? And to think that you need to avoid counting or tallying in a 'qualitative' study is ludicrous.

But it is these descriptors that define the social science research landscape, so there is no question that understanding these traditions, the assumptions that underlie them, and the well-established and highly valuable research strategies they offer, is extremely important. But it is also important to understand the potential for traversing the divide and working across what has traditionally been quite disparate ways of knowing.

This chapter takes up the challenge by not only exploring each tradition, but also by delving into mixed methodologies that work to both blur and traverse what many now argue is an overworked dichotomy.

THE QUANTITATIVE TRADITION

The quantitative tradition is based on a belief that the study of society is no different than the scientific study of any other element of our world – from particles to animals. The social sciences (note the word 'sciences') are subject to the same rules of engagement as, say, physics or biology. There is a strong belief in the scientific method, the need to test hypotheses, deductive logic, the need for objectivity, and, as the name suggests, the value of quantification. There is an underlying belief in the power of numbers and their ability to represent the world with both vigour and accuracy.

Scientific/hypothetico-deductive methods

The scientific standard for conduct of research goes something like this:

1   Engage with and adopt, adapt, or generate a theory.
2   Drawing from the theory and using processes of deductive reasoning (the process of working down from theories to more specific examples), generate specific propositions or hypotheses.
3   Gather quantitative data, often through experimental design or, in the case of social science research, large-scale survey research.
4   Analyse the data using statistical processes.
5   Draw conclusions that may or may not support your hypothesis.

This process acts as a scientific control mechanism and gives us the right to produce 'real' knowledge. It differentiates researchers from 'crackpots' who might say, 'trust me, I just know', 'it came to me in a dream', or 'it was revealed to me by an angel'. By setting a standard, it also offers us protection from those who, in theory, accept the premise of scientific method, but might practise shoddy science tainted with personal biases, political agendas, sloppy procedures, and/or flawed logic.

In the social sciences, this methodological approach also allows us to step away from our object of study, the societies we are necessarily a part of, and therefore maintain scientific objectivity. This then allows us to work towards traditional indicators of credibility such as validity, reliability, generalizability, and reproducibility (see Chapter 3). In addition, the process of quantification allows us to tackle large populations and offers validity of results through the use of statistics and probability.

In the social sciences, the quantitative tradition goes back to the roots of the discipline and generally manifests in the methodologies of experimentation and population exploration through larger scale, survey-based research.

Experimental design

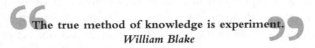

The true method of knowledge is experiment.
William Blake

> **EXPERIMENT**
> A rigorous and controlled search for cause and effect. Researchers vary an independent variable (something they believe is a key determinant in their study) in order to see if it has an impact on their dependent variable (the main object of your inquiry). In other words, you manipulate *X* to see if it has an effect on *Y*.

Now you might not have been able to define 'experiment' before you read the above, but it is probably a term you are at least familiar with. After all, it's the mainstay of medical researchers, crime scene investigators, and mad scientists alike – and would be a method of choice if your goals included: evaluating the effects of pharmaceutical drugs on disease; looking at the connection between suspect heights and bullet trajectories; or creating the perfect human–monster hybrid.

In the social sciences, you are unlikely to be working with cells, DNA, inanimate objects, or laboratory animals. The likely object of your enquiry will be people in all their complexity. It's also unlikely that your experiments will take place in the controlled confines of a laboratory. Your research is likely to take place in less controlled settings, with all the challenges thereof.

But even in the face of such challenges, experimentation offers tremendous potential in the social sciences. For example, say you were interested in exploring students who had difficulty engaging in learning. An experimental design would allow you to test a hypothesis, something like, *student attentiveness can be enhanced by group-oriented classroom layout*, by manipulating classroom layout (the independent variable) to see how it affects student attentiveness (the dependent variable).

Or say you were interested in understanding the factors that affect sick leave. You might hypothesize that *a lack of general fitness increases sick leave* and design an experimental study that introduces a workplace exercise programme (independent variable) to see if the number of sick days taken decreases (dependent variable). Or if you were interested in high levels of domestic waste in a particular county or municipality, and hypothesize that *there is a desire in the community to recycle, but implementation is difficult*, you might 'experiment' by introducing free household recycle bins (independent variable) to see if this leads to a reduction in household waste levels (dependent variable).

Conducting an experiment

On the radio a while back, I heard that 'eating fish increases your IQ'. The story reported on the latest research that found that children who eat fish at least once a week have higher IQs than their non-fish-eating peers. Hence, the 'eat fish and get smart' headlines that led the story. But as I listened, I found out that the study looked at children's IQs and explored it in relation to a number of factors including diet, education, socio-economic status, age of the parents, parental marital status, parental education level, etc. And *one* of the correlations they found was between eating fish and IQ. As fish consumption rose, so too did intelligence – but then again you could also say that as IQ rose so did fish consumption. Does eating fish make you smart or do smart people eat more fish? Correlation is simply *not* cause and effect.

An intervening or confounding variable might also come into play. Maybe it's not the fish that makes you smart – maybe what is going on is that smart parents feed their children fish, and their child's IQ is determined by genetics.

OK, let's say you really want to get to the bottom of the great fish debate and you decide you want to determine cause and effect by conducting an experiment (after all, you've read that experiments really are the best way to work through this type of research problem). So how do you go about it?

Well, initial planning will involve lots of decision making. As you work through your methodological design you will need to decide on your:

1   *Dependent and independent variables* – You will need to identify the main focus of your study or what you are trying to assess (the dependent variable), as well as the variable(s) you will manipulate in order to cause an effect (the independent variable(s)). In this case, you are hypothesizing that IQ depends on fish consumption, thereby making IQ the dependent variable and fish consumption the independent variable. This identification of variables by type is central to moving from correlation to cause and effect.

2   *Assessment of change* – In order to determine whether the manipulation of your independent variable has affected your dependent variable, you will need to be able to assess change. The most effective way to do this is through pre- and post-testing, which means collecting or having access to good baseline data and being able to collect comparable data after the experimental intervention. In this case, assessing change is relatively straightforward and would involve administering standardized IQ tests.

3   *Research setting* – Consider whether you will be conducting your study in a controlled environment such as a laboratory or if you will use a natural setting. In this case a lab may give you total control, but as is the case for many social science questions, it may not be practicable. In our scenario, other options include asking parents to vary diets at home, or to make arrangements with a day care centre to change its weekly menu.

4   *Number of participants* – The number of participants you will use is also crucial. Think about how many participants will be necessary for you to make any conclusive or statistically significant judgements. For example, if you find a pattern in five children, is it enough? (Chapter 10 covers the basics of determining sample size.)

5   *Number of groups* – You will also have to decide if you will use a control group. In our fish example, using a single group would involve testing the IQ of all the children, feeding all of them fish a set number of times a week, and testing them at some period thereafter to see what happens. With a control group you would test all of the children at the start, put half the children in a control group and the other half in a target group, and only give fish to the children in the target group. You would then test both groups again at a later date and compare findings.

6   *Assignment strategy* – If you are using a control group you will need to determine how you will assign your groups. Will children be randomly selected for fish consumption or will you use different criteria for selection? While randomization will provide you with stronger cause and effect arguments, you might find it more practical to select children based, for example, on the days of the week they are in a day care centre.

7   *Number of variables* – Will you test just one independent variable or will you test for others as well? For example, will you simply look at fish consumption or are there other aspects of the children's diet you will explore, such as vegetable intake?

8   *Ethics* – Consider whether you will need informed consent. In our fish consumption case, you will need parental consent. You will also need to consider if there are any advantages or potential threats to group members based on their inclusion in either a control or a target group. Now while there may not be high risks associated in eating or not eating fish, issues of equity represent a huge ethical dilemma in drug trials, treatment programmes, and educational initiatives.

9   *Control of the environment* – Finally, you will need to consider how you will negotiate the balance between the practicalities of working in real-world situations and the need to control the environment. In other words, you need to consider how you can ensure your findings can be attributed to a true cause and effect relationship between your independent and dependent variables. Now the more controls you embed into your experimental design, the more convincing your arguments will be. But without such controls, arguments can be spurious. For example:

(a)   without a controlled environment it can be hard to ensure that the only variable that has been changed, shifted, manipulated, or introduced is your particular independent variable, e.g. other dietary changes, changes in sleep patterns, personal stress, etc., may be happening outside your experimental design;

(b)   without adequate numbers it will be hard to show statistical significance or that results are more than coincidence;

(c)   without a control group it is hard to ensure that there is not some other factor that might account for changes in your target or dependent variable, e.g. that improvements in IQ scores cannot be attributed to things like additional attention that the children might be receiving, practice in taking IQ tests, or the coincidental commencement of a new educational programme;

(d)   without a random assignment strategy (which is often impractical in field-based research) you will need to argue that differences between the two groups are non-existent or at least minimal. In our case, if there is an innate difference in the learning abilities of the two groups, it will be impossible to attribute increased IQ to dietary habits.

The decisions you make will determine the 'type' of experiment you will conduct. The gold-medal standard is the 'true' experimental design (often called a *random control trial*). In this type of design, independent variables are manipulated by the researcher; experiments are conducted under controlled circumstances; control groups are used; and there is random assignment to both control and target groups.

Unfortunately, random assignment may not always be possible in field situations. For example, say you did get agreement from a local preschool to trial a food program. The school, however, will not allow random assignment (the school predicts chaos when some kids get chicken nuggets and others have to eat grilled flounder), so it asks you to run your trial on Mondays and Wednesdays. There is therefore a control group (which is good), but there is no random assignment (which is a problem if the groups are qualitatively different from each other, i.e. brighter children on these days, different teachers/carers, different cooks, etc.). When you have a control group but no random assignment, you have a *quasi-experimental design* and while this is less than ideal, it is often a reality in social science field research.

Even more problematic is when you do not have access to any control group (*a single group design*). For example, say the preschool wants an all-or-nothing approach. Your only measure of success will be pre/post-testing, which will not allow you to assure that any change in the class is due to your programme and not any other factors.

Strengths and challenges associated with experiments

There is definitely something appealing about saying, 'I wonder what would happen if I were to ...?', and then be able to set up and assess the effects of that exact scenario. You would get to see it unfold for yourself. You would get to manipulate the environment and both witness and record the results. You would be in control.

Experiments, if well conducted, allow you to: assess cause and effect; compare groups; explore real actions and reactions and, if so designed, in real contexts; avoid reliance on respondents' memory or reactions to hypothetical situations; and generate both standardized quantifiable data and in-depth qualitative data.

Sounds pretty good. But as you might already suspect, there is no guarantee of smooth sailing. When studying individuals, often in a social context, it is hard to control for all influences that sit outside your experimental design. In social science experimentation you will need to consider: (1) if there is equity in your design (e.g. will the manipulation of your independent variable advantage or disadvantage any individuals/or groups?); (2) if your design will allow you to get informed consent from participants; (3) if participants will stay involved for the duration of the experiment; (4) if you can control for your own biases; and (5) if your design can control for extraneous, confounding, or intervening variables (the things that effect your study that are not a part of your methodological design).

The Hawthorne studies, a series of workplace-based experiments conducted in the 1920s (Mayo 1933, Roethlisberger and Dickson 1939), offer an excellent example of social science experimentation and the challenges posed by real-world settings (see Box 8.6 later in this chapter).

Exploring a population

A central objective in social science research is to understand the make-up, or demographics, of a particular population and build an understanding of that population's knowledge, attitudes, and practices (KAP) on a particular topic or issue. In fact, this is one of the most common objectives in social science research.

Now without a doubt, the population that a social scientist might want to explore can be quite small and certainly studied in depth, often at a cultural level (see ethnography later in the chapter) but what is more often referred to is larger scale studies that attempt to understand broad populations – and it is precisely this scale that leads to the need for quantification and places this type of research squarely under the quantitative umbrella.

Conducting studies of populations

In the quantitative tradition, there are actually two broad methodological strategies that can help you understand a population; that is to capitalize on existing data or to generate your own primary data.

Capitalizing on existing data

To my mind, it makes a lot of sense to at least consider/explore the possibility of working with existing data. Data is truly everywhere, with any number of organizations, individuals, students, research teams, professors, government and non-government agencies alike collecting, re-collecting, and replicating data collection processes. Resist falling into the trap of thinking that the only data you can use is data you generate. The data you find may not be in a form that directly answers your question, but therein lays the challenge. Remember: refining the wheel will often get you further than reinventing it. Box 8.1 gives an example of this type of study.

BOX 8.1   USING EXISTING DATA TO EXPLORING THE INCIDENCE OF FOOD POISONING IN PALAU

In 2001, I was asked to be part of a team working on the development of Palau's *National Environmental Health Action Plan* and I have to admit that before this invitation I had never even heard of Palau. As it turns out, Palau is a speck in the middle of the Pacific Ocean, somewhere near Guam. It is made up of over 300 limestone rock islands and has a population of about 19,000. Up until 1994 it was an American Protectorate, but it is now a new nation trying to stand on its own two feet. With its unparalleled snorkelling and diving, its economic future relies on building its tourism sector.

Quite early in our orientation, my colleague and I were told that food safety was one of the greatest challenges facing the Palauan Division of Environmental Health (DEH). There was a lot of anecdotal evidence suggesting high rates of food poisoning, particularly among tourists. But there was no real 'data' to support these concerns. We

(Continued)

(Continued)

decided to prioritize designing a method for finding out more. We grappled with how we could find out about number of cases, severity of cases, who is affected, if there are seasonal variations, and potential causes.

After working through a number of options (including surveying tourists), we decided to capitalize on existing records. The team was to go to every hospital, doctor, and medical facility in the country and identify and explore records for all reported cases of food poisoning (which might sound bigger than it was – remember this is a nation whose total population is less than that of a small town). We did understand that this review of records would have its limitations: that is, it would be a review of reported cases, not all cases; it would be reliant on getting access to records; and it was reliant on the accuracy and thoroughness of the records reviewed. Nonetheless, we believed that this was the most effective and cost-efficient method for collecting data that would allow the DEH to (1) generate a 'reported' food poisoning figure; (2) look at distribution by season, race, tourist vs local, etc.; (3) begin to look at recorded causes; (4) write more effective food safety policy; and finally (5) produce recommendations about systematic data collection within the medical sector.

Gathering primary data

Existing data and records directly related to your specific topic are not always available, or perhaps not available to you. So there will be plenty of times when the best strategy for exploring a population is to gather primary data; that is, generating data from a population for the express purposes of your study. For the most part this involves survey processes, which are summarized here but discussed in much more depth in Chapter 11. Gathering this type of primary data involves:

- *Defining the population from which you wish to ascertain information* – For example, all people living in a particular community, state, country, cultural group, workplace, school district, or who have a common interest/trait, i.e. casual tennis players, those with muscular dystrophy, etc.
- *Assessing whether it is possible to gather information from every element of that population* – This is rarely possible due to the difficulty of identifying all population elements. For example, think of the difficulties associated with generating a list of all homeless people in the USA or all Australian mothers suffering from postnatal depression. Additionally, even if all members of a population can be accounted for, the time and resources needed to access each element are almost always beyond our capability. One exception here is National Censuses, which do invest the resources necessary to gather information from all members of their populations. If a census, however, is impractical you will need to move to the next step.
- *Developing a sampling strategy with a goal of representativeness and generalizability* – Your aim here is to gather information from enough people who represent the greater population so that statistically significant conclusions about that population can be drawn.

- *Adopting, adapting, or generating a standardized instrument* – Most often a survey questionnaire that can gather the information you require.
- *Thoughtfully piloting and fine tuning that instrument* – This is essential in all survey processes.
- *Implementing* – Distributing and collecting the completed instrument.
- *Using statistics to analyse the data* – You will probably call on both descriptive and inferential statistics.

(See Chapter 10 for more information on populations/sampling, Chapter 11 for surveying, and Chapter 13 for quantitative analysis.)

Strengths and challenges associated with studying populations

While the desire to work with both pre-existing and generated data can offer much to the production of knowledge, there are always tradeoffs between opportunities and challenges.

On the plus side, survey data is generally derived from a large number of respondents, represents an even larger population, is confidential and anonymous, can generate standardized, quantifiable, empirical data, enables you to show statistical significance, and allows you to mathematically establish reliability, validity, and generalizability.

There are, however, limitations inherent to the process. For example, it can be difficult to get an adequate response rate, the eventuating sample can be skewed and not representative, you are limited to what you (or someone else) has thought to ask, you do not have the opportunity to offer additional question clarification, it can be hard to assess respondent candour and honesty, and finally you cannot dig for more depth.

THE QUALITATIVE TRADITION

> **It's really about doing science differently ...**
> **We're talking about a paradigm shift.**
> *A. Johnson*

If the quantitative tradition represents the study of the social premised on the tenets of positivism, particularly tried and true scientific, hypothetico-deductive methods, then the qualitative tradition might best be described as (1) a critique of positivism as the reigning epistemology, and (2) recognition of the need for alternative ways to produce knowledge. The qualitative tradition therefore calls on inductive as well as deductive logic, appreciates subjectivities, accepts multiple perspectives and realities, recognizes the power of research on both participants and researchers, and does not necessarily shy away from political agendas. It also strongly argues the value of depth over quantity and works at delving into social complexities in order to truly explore and understand the interactions, processes, lived experiences, and belief systems that are a part of individuals, institutions, cultural groups, and even the everyday.

Delving into qualitative methodologies therefore means working in a world that accepts and even values: the search for holistic meaning; research conducted in natural settings; emergent methodological design; small numbers; non-random sampling strategies; rich qualitative data; inductive analysis; idiographic interpretation; and even the possibility of negotiated outcomes that recognize the need for the researched to be party to a researcher's constructed meanings. The goal is to gain an intimate understanding of people, places, cultures, and situations through rich engagement and even immersion into the reality being studied.

Credibility in qualitative studies

Because the 'rules' of science were born of the positivist/quantitative tradition, methodologies that sit under the qualitative umbrella are sometimes maligned for not reaching standards of credibility (see Chapter 3). But that does not mean that standards for credibility do not exist in the qualitative world. On the contrary, the rigour required of such studies is of the highest standard, and criteria appropriate to the task, as discussed in Chapter 3, have certainly been developed.

Debates over credibility, however, can arise when qualitative studies are inappropriately assessed according to positivist/quantitative criteria and, as might be expected, fall short of expectation. But this is simply a matter of using the wrong criteria for the job. As discussed in Chapter 3, all studies, regardless of goals or even their paradigmatic positioning, need to consider whether: subjectivities have been managed; methods are approached with consistency; 'true essence' has been captured; findings have broad applicability; and, finally, whether research processes can be verified. Criteria for such assessment, however, are likely to be neutrality or transparent subjectivity rather than objectivity; dependability over reliability; authenticity over validity; transferability over generalizability; and auditability rather than reproducibility (see Chapter 3). Box 8.2 covers some of the strategies that 'qualitative' researchers use to reach appropriate standards of credibility.

BOX 8.2   STRATEGIES FOR ACHIEVING CREDIBILITY IN QUALITATIVE STUDIES

Techniques that can be used to ensure thoroughness and rigor include:

- **Saturation** – To finish collecting data only when additional data no longer adds richness to understanding or aids in building theories.
- **Crystallization** – Building a rich and diverse understanding of one single situation or phenomenon by seeing the world as multi-faceted, and accepting that what we see depends on where we look, where the light is, etc.

- **Prolonged engagement** – Investment of time sufficient to learn the culture, understand context, and/or build trust and rapport.
- **Persistent observation** – To look for readings of a situation beyond an initial, possibly superficial, level.
- **Broad representation** – Representation wide enough to ensure that an institution, cultural group, or phenomenon can be spoken about confidently.
- **Peer review** – External check on the research process in which a colleague is asked to act as a 'devil's advocate' in regards to all aspects of methodology.

Techniques that can be used to obtain confirmation or verification include:

- **Triangulation** – Using more than one source of data to confirm the authenticity of each source.
- **Member checking** – Checking that interpretation of events, situations, and phenomena gels with the interpretations of 'insiders'.
- **Full explication of method** – Providing readers with sufficient methodological detail so that studies are auditable and/or reproducible.

Ethnography

> ❝The pure and simple truth is rarely pure and never simple.❞
> *Oscar Wilde*

If you were to come to my house for dinner and you were to reflect on that experience, you would probably do so in relation to what happens in your own home, i.e. 'we do that', 'that's different', 'how bizarre'. You would judge my family in relation to your own family or your own frame of reference.

Well, when it comes to studying cultural groups this is precisely what ethnography tries to avoid. Ethnography explores a way of life from the point of view of its participants and tries to avoid assessing a culture using pre-existing frames of reference or from a particular worldview. The goal is to 'see' things the way group members do, and grasp the meanings they use to understand and make sense of the world. In other words, ethnographers attempt to suspend judgement and understand the symbolic world in which people live in order to interpret meaning from within a culture.

To build this type of rich understanding, ethnographers tend to immerse themselves within a culture for a significant period of time. They participate, and then reflect on their lived conversations and observations. Whether it be foreign cultures, marginal cultures closer to home, or even their own culture, ethnographers attempt to delve into cultural complexities in order to understand the world from the perspective of participants. Ethnographers attempt to explore how cultural understandings are shaped, and how group members make sense of their experiences. The goal is to go beyond an exploration of simply what is, and begin to explore why it is (see Box 8.3).

ETHNOGRAPHY

To 'write a culture'. Involves exploration of a cultural group in a bid to understand, discover, describe, and interpret a way of life from the point of view of its participants. Its roots stem from cultural anthropology, particularly the work of Clifford Geertz, who argued that building 'thick descriptions' is the only way we can uncover the underlying frameworks that produce both behaviour and meaning ([1973] 2000).

Now on the surface this may seem fairly straightforward, but a number of complexities become clear as you unpack the definition:

1   *Ethnography is the study of cultural groups.* This is significant because the term 'cultural' suggests that what binds the group is more than, say, genetics, biology, or geography. 'Cultural' groups are bound together by social traditions and common patterns of beliefs and behaviours, e.g. ethnic groups, community groups, or even workplace groups. Ethnographic studies are premised on the belief that how an individual processes the world is constructed and constrained by cultural experience. The study of cultural groups is thereby the study of shared understandings as well as the symbolic aspects of behaviour that can uncover cultural or normative patterns. In other words, ethnography explores the methods, rules, roles, and expectations that structure any given situation.

2   *Ethnography explores a way of life from the point of view of its participants.* Ethnography attempts to understand the symbolic world in which people live. The goal is to 'see' things the way group members do, and grasp the meanings that they use to understand and make sense of the world. In other words, ethnographers attempt to interpret meanings from within a culture, or build what Geertz ([1973] 2000) refers to as 'thick descriptions'. This is significant because ethnography accepts multiple realities and requires cultural empathy. Rather than set understandings against a sometimes unrecognized Western worldview, ethnographers attempt to suspend judgement and understand from the perspective of the researched.

3   *Ethnography exploration involves a bid to understand, discover, describe, and interpret.* Now a somewhat common critique of ethnography is that it is merely descriptive. But generating 'thick descriptions' that build an understanding of the underlying frameworks that produce both behaviour and meaning is an act of discovery and interpretation as much as it is an act of description.

BOX 8.3   ETHNOGRAPHIC EXEMPLAR – WOMEN ON THE LINE

In the late 1970s and early 1980s a woman going by the name Ruth Cavendish (Miriam Glucksmann) (Glucksmann 2009) conducted an ethnographic study of female factory workers exploring their lives within the factory walls, how they juggled work/home responsibilities, and their views of life from the factory floor.

'Ruth', as a participant observer, not only empathetically engaged with the women she studied, but actually made an attempt to live their reality. Through this experience she offered an insightful, vivid, empathetic, and intimate narrative portrayal of the realities of the lives of women in an industrial world, a portrayal that could not have been painted through traditional social science techniques such as experimentation, surveys, or interviews. For these, and a host of other reasons, Cavendish's study is now considered not only a classic/pioneering ethnographic study, but also a classic study in economic sociology, the sociology of gender, and sociology of work.

Conducting an ethnographic study

Because ethnographic studies attempt to understand the reality of the researched, they generally rely on multiple data collection strategies, involve the exploration of cultural groups within natural settings, and often require 'immersion' through prolonged engagement and persistent observation. The research process is flexible and emergent, and likely to evolve as lived realities within the cultural group are revealed. While ethnography is a methodology commonly used in anthropological studies, its principles can be used in a wide range of contexts.

The range of potential cultural groups

As discussed, a cultural group is defined by more than biology or geography. A cultural group needs to meet the prerequisite of a shared culture. It may be an exotic foreign culture (e.g. a native 'tribe'), or a culture closer to home (e.g. a migrant community or a boarding school). It is also possible to study a 'dominant' cultural group, which can be quite revealing because it is often dominance itself that causes privileged knowledge and governing ideologies to go unseen.

The selection of any particular cultural group will be driven by pragmatics, intrinsic interest, theory, or any combination thereof. Pragmatics might involve research commitments, timely opportunities, or accessibility. Cultural groups can also be selected to increase idiographic understanding, i.e. selecting groups that are: unique and unfamiliar; misunderstood or misrepresented; marginal and unheard; or dominant, yet not reflexively explored. Finally, cultural groups can be selected on the basis of theory. For example, if the goal of a study is to understand how meaning is constructed, or to explore the interpretative and/or symbolic practices that define 'cultures', then the selection of a particular group might, on the judgement of the researcher, be made on the basis of being typical, atypical, extreme, or rare.

Regardless of how a cultural group is selected, it is essential that an ethnographic researcher has a very high level of access within the group. The researcher must believe that it will be possible to build rapport and trust. Credible ethnographic studies require that researchers are able to get below the surface, break through the pleasantries, and observe cultural actors and actions that are not performed solely for the benefit of the researcher.

The range of potential data collection/analysis methods

The goal of the ethnographer is thick description and rich and reflexive interpretation, and few ethnographers would want to limit themselves to only one method of data collection. Data collection is therefore multi-method and often continues until saturation. While the data generated can include the quantitative, the preponderance of ethnographic data is likely to be qualitative so that the richness of the symbolic world can be fully described. Data collection methods include:

- *Observation* – Participant observation is common to most ethnographic studies and tends to involve deep cultural immersion. Ethnographers attempt to build cultural empathy and 'live' the reality of the other. Ethnographers can also engage in non-participant techniques in order to generate more structured observations.
- *Interviews* – These are generally in depth and unstructured, and, in line with participant observation, often take the form of 'conversations'. Such 'interviews' can involve key informants and/or individuals who represent cross-sections of the cultural group, i.e. men, women, children, the elderly, new members, foundational members, etc.
- *Document analysis* – Sometimes a good way to understand the reality of the researched is to examine the texts that they themselves produce. Depending on the nature of the cultural group being explored, this might involve an examination of local newspapers, locally produced television, and/or radio broadcasts. Or it may involve analysis of local art, the poetry and essays of schoolchildren, journals and diaries, and/or doctrine and dogma.
- *Surveys* – While surveys are often critiqued by those conducting ethnographies for being too reductionist, I do not believe they should be unilaterally dismissed as a potential data gathering tool. While studies based solely on survey research would not qualify as ethnography, a survey instrument, such as a questionnaire, may be the best way to canvas widely within a particular cultural group.

Strengths and challenges associated with ethnography

Researchers are willing to immerse themselves in ethnographic studies because they believe they offer rich and in-depth exploration of the values, norms, symbols, beliefs, and practices of cultural groups. This allows them to enter into a dialogue with existing theory and/or develop insights that can lead to the development of new theory. Ethnographers also recognize the importance of multiple worldviews as well as the value of building understandings from the perspective of the researched.

Some of the difficulties associated with ethnography are shared by a range of studies that involve 'immersion'. These include: gaining access and building trust; emotional costs; the potential for the researcher to have an effect on the researched; and the demands placed on those being studied.

But there are also concerns more specific to ethnography that need to be seriously considered and skilfully negotiated. First, ethnographers need to guard against 'homogenization' that can give minimal recognition to divergence within a particular group. Ethnographers also need to be aware of a somewhat paradoxical dilemma in representing the reality of others. Ethnography has an explicit goal of building and interpreting understandings from the perspective of the researched. However, it also accepts that descriptions are necessarily interpretative, and that the basis of interpretation is the filtering of observations and inputs through theoretical and analytic frameworks that are, of course, imbued with a researcher's own worldview. This then begs the question, 'Can an outsider (particularly one from a very divergent culture) ever truly know, describe, and interpret the reality of being an insider?'

How you manage this 'paradox' will depend on how you reflect on the above question, as well as your ability to mount arguments that will satisfy a sceptic's concerns over credibility. This will require you to reflexively consider and articulate: how you as a researcher have had an impact on the interpretative practices within your research; what strategies you have employed to seek thoroughness and confirmation (see Box 8.2); and the significance of your research findings to a particular body of knowledge.

Phenomenology

Is it worth knowing what it feels like to win – or to lose? Is it worth understanding the lived experience of struggling with breast cancer? Is it worth knowing what it feels like to be at the bottom of the class? Now I'm not talking about cause and effect. I'm not asking why someone won or lost, or the implications of cancer, or why someone might struggle at school. I am strictly talking about 'phenomenon' or 'lived experience' – what it feels like for those subject to the experience.

Well I think understanding lived experience is absolutely vital. Let me try to explain. One of the key premises of adult education is that you need to start where people are. And I have certainly found this to be the case – not only in my own teaching, but in conflict mediation, change agency, situation improvement, and problem resolution. If you want to be truly effective in getting people to move from A to B you need to start at A, and you can only do that if you understand and appreciate A. And not just intellectually, but emotionally as well.

If you want to know why athletes are willing to take steroids – you need to understand their lived reality of winning and losing. If you want to help someone through breast cancer – you need to know how they feel about their body, their self-esteem, their future. If you want to understand how you can help motivate struggling students – you need to know what it is really like for them at the bottom of the class.

This is the goal of a phenomenological study. Rather than ask what causes X, or what is X, phenomenology explores the lived experience of X. In fact, phenomenologists would argue that 'objective' knowing or truth should be 'bracketed' or put aside so that the focus can be on internal processes of consciousness. There is no need to worry about causes, truth value, reality, or appearances. In a socially constructed, intersubjective world, our direct awareness is the only thing we can really know, since all knowing depends on individual perceptions (see Box 8.4).

PHENOMENOLOGY
Study of phenomena as they present themselves in individuals' direct awareness and experience. Perception, rather than socio-historic context or even the supposed 'reality' of an object, is the focus of investigation.

Phenomena as an object of study may be somewhat new to you, so let's break down the basic elements in a phenomenological study and highlight the role each element plays in defining, understanding, and researching phenomena:

1   *Phenomenological studies are highly dependent on individuals.* Individuals, either through interviews or their cultural products, i.e. what they write, paint, etc., are used to draw out the experiences of a particular phenomenon. For example, refugees, athletes, or leaders might be called upon to provide descriptions of the experience of displacement, victory, and power, respectively. Individuals are therefore central to the conduct of phenomenological studies. But it is their descriptions of lived experience, rather than they themselves, that are the focus of phenomenology.

2   *Phenomenological studies are also highly dependent on constructs.* Constructs such as displacement, victory, and power are central to the phenomenological experience being explored. In phenomenological studies, however, the 'reality' of the construct is not of concern and should, in fact, be 'bracketed', i.e. it should be explored as free as possible from what the world says it is supposed to be, or supposed to mean. In phenomenology, a construct freed from its constructed meaning is often referred to as an 'object'.

3   *Phenomena, which are the focus of phenomenology, actually sit at the intersection of people and 'objects', and centre on an individual's lived experience of these 'objects'.* Rather than ask what causes X, or what is X, phenomenology explores the experience of X. In other words, phenomenology is the study of the experience of the relationship between the individual and the object. It is the study of a phenomenon as it presents itself in an individual's direct awareness.

Conducting a phenomenological study

There are three basic elements in most methodological approaches in the social sciences. These are your participants, your data collection methods, and intended modes of analysis. And of course, the end product is your 'report'. Well, it does not quite work that way in phenomenology. The product of phenomenological studies is phenomenological descriptions; and gathering descriptions, making sense of those descriptions, and writing up those descriptions are not necessarily discrete activities.

Producing phenomenological descriptions

The key outcome of phenomenological studies is rich phenomenological descriptions. In fact, the goal is to produce descriptions so full of lush imagery that it allows others to share in how a particular phenomenon is experienced.

The process of generating such descriptions generally involves sourcing people who have experienced a particular phenomenon and conducting one or more in-depth interviews with each participant. The number of respondents can vary – but given that there is likely to be more than one way to experience any particular phenomenon, you generally need to conduct a sufficient number of interviews for drawing out variation. Interviewers often look for 'saturation': that is, additional interviews no longer add new perspective.

The goal of the interviews, most often conducted as a 'conversation', is to draw out rich descriptions of lived experience. In other words, you want your respondents to tell you what a phenomenon feels like, what it reminds them of, and how they would describe it. Respondents are then encouraged to further reflect on various aspects of their descriptions. This often involves digging below the surface of words to understand the meaning behind them. For example, the phenomenon of 'winning', first described as 'fantastic', might be further described as 'like being on top of the world' or 'I know I have worth'. In this way, the researcher and the researched create a narrative that is both descriptive and interpretive, and is often rich, poetic, and full of metaphor.

In addition to, or instead of, conducting interviews, researchers can also explore pre-produced texts. Beautiful, rich phenomenological descriptions abound in letters, journals, books, movies, poetry, and music. Take, for example, the phenomenon of 'going into battle'. Imagine the rich, candid, and chilling descriptions you might be able to gather just from reading letters home.

A second cycle

Once you have generated (or located) your descriptions and you feel you have reached a point of saturation, the next step is synthesis. The goal here is to explore commonalities and divergences in the experience of the same phenomenon. You are looking for the range of experiences related to the phenomenon itself. This is generally done by cycling between the texts and eventuating themes in a bid to reduce unimportant dissimilarities and integrate the essential nature of various descriptions. In some of my own research, for example, I found that giving up God showed itself in three 'types' of lived experiences: angry and resentful reaction; gloomy and melancholic introspection'; and 'open spiritual exploration' (O'Leary 2001).

BOX 8.4   PHENOMENOLOGICAL EXEMPLAR – WOMEN WITH AIDS

The aim of the study 'Women with Aids' (Sinfield 1995) was to understand the perspectives of *nurses* (the individuals the study was dependent on as referred to

(Continued)

(Continued)

point 1 above) on *the experience of making sense* (the lived experience referred to in point 3 above) of the *needs of women with AIDS* (the construct as referred to in point 2 above). Far from an academic exercise, objectives of this study included the ability to influence clinical nursing practice; nurse education; and nursing research.

In order to accomplish this, Sinfield used a phenomenological approach that involved *in-depth conversations* (phenomenological descriptions) with eight registered nurses who were employed in a 90-bed acute hospital in NSW, Australia. Each conversation was *iteratively explored* (the second cycle of synthesis) with five themes (indentifying a learning gap; focusing; normalizing; bracketing; and working within the system) eventually emerging from the data.

Strengths and challenges associated with phenomenology

I think the main strength of phenomenology is that it offers a way of exploring this thing called 'phenomena', something highly important in understanding our social world, yet often ignored in studies of the social. We tend to explore demographics, opinions, attitudes, beliefs, and behaviours of people, and we study the ideas, ideologies, and constructs that make up the social world, but the study of phenomena is marginalized and often goes undiscussed as a potential research strategy available to student researchers.

But just think about the value of being able to understand and describe lived experience. How much more insightful could change initiatives or problem resolution strategies be if we had this level of understanding? Take, for example, understanding and describing the lived experience of critical illness. This would be essential reading for anyone wishing to develop appropriate protocols for mental health workers dedicated to the critically ill. Or what about capturing the essence of what it is like to grow up in a war-torn country, a description that could be invaluable to building cultural empathy? And any study that explored stress would not be complete without understanding what it actually feels like.

As with anything worth doing, however, it is not necessarily easy. Literature on phenomenology tends to be thick and philosophical, and does not offer a lot of clear guidance on actual 'methods'. You probably won't get much advice from research texts either. Few texts cover the topic at all, and those that do, don't do it very well. The same goes for teaching and learning. In my 'training' as a social scientist, phenomenology was not a method that was discussed, and when it was covered in my philosophy classes, it was not done in a way that would help me in conducting a phenomenological study. The implication is that unless you have a supervisor or mentor experienced in phenomenology, 'doing' a phenomenological study will require you to get into the literature (some suggestions are offered at the end of the chapter).

Ethnomethodology

Throughout our day we interact – with our parents, friends, the checkout person at the grocery store. And we make judgements, sometimes consciously but mainly subconsciously, about how we should act and what we should say. And we generally do this without too much stress because we are socialized with appropriate 'methods', i.e. rules, norms, and patterns, that help us wade through such interactions.

Well, ethnomethodology is the study of everyday interactions and argues that individuals engage in interpretative work every time they interact with the world. In order to do this in a way that makes sense, they engage in what Garfinkel (1967) refers to as 'documentary method'. This involves 'indexicality' – or selecting cues from a social interaction that conforms to a recognizable pattern – and then making sense of that interaction in terms of that pattern. I know this sounds confusing, but in practice it is pretty simple because it is something you do automatically everyday. For example, if someone said, 'I couldn't help but notice you', you would take cues from the social interaction to find the likely pattern, and formulate an appropriate response. So if you were in a nightclub and the person speaking to you was of the opposite sex, the pattern might be 'the pick-up' and you might reply with a disgusted, 'get lost, you loser' or a seductive, 'yeah … I noticed you too'. The other party then has to subconsciously find the right pattern, in this case let's say 'rejection' or 'flirtation', and form the appropriate response. Through the use of 'reflexivity' you then use that response to generate your next response and so on and so forth until the interaction ends. In this way the pattern is emergent, but is consistently used in its most recent formulation to interpret new elements of the interaction (see Box 8.5).

ETHNOMETHODOLOGY

Study of the methods that individuals use to accomplish their daily actions and make sense of their social world. Ethnomethodological focus is on uncovering the 'rules' that direct ordinary life. It is not interested in whether what is said or done is right or wrong, true or false. In fact, ethnomethodology ignores the question of 'what' altogether and concentrates on 'how' interactions are performed.

Ethnomethodology can be traced to the work of Harold Garfinkel in the 1960s. But there is actually an even more famous 'ethnomethodologist' – the comedian Jerry Seinfeld, a man who makes his living by exploring and deconstructing the minutiae of the everyday. *Seinfeld*, the 'show about nothing', is actually a show about what we take for granted as we manage the interactions that make up everyday life – but more on Seinfeld later.

> **BOX 8.5   ETHNOMETHODOLOGY EXEMPLAR – GARFINKEL'S 'AGNES'**
>
> In his 1967 seminal work, *Studies in Ethnomethodology*. Garfinkel attempted to capture the socially situated work whereby Agnes, a 19-year-old who presented herself as a female, but was raised as a boy until 17 and had male genitalia, accomplished the daily task of being a traditional female. Garfinkel's goal was to unmask the taken-for-granted familiarity and everyday occurrence of being a woman. Having been raised as a male for the first 17 years of her life, Agnes offered a unique window for unmasking (and adopting) the generally taken-for-granted and unseen tasks associated with the daily work of being a female. As such, Garfinkel's study is considered an exemplar that highlights the power of ethnomethodology in showing how people produce the interactions that make up their everyday lives.

Conducting an ethnomethodological study

The goal of doing an ethnomethodological study is to draw out how individuals go about the interpretative work necessary to make sense and make meaning in everyday interactions. Approaches for drawing out meaning include 'breaching experiments', exploring the building of shared interpretation, and exploring interpretative miscues. Now remember I mentioned *Seinfeld*? Well, the show provides some very insightful examples of all of these approaches. As it turns out, there is something very funny about exposing the taken-for-granted rules that we use to structure our everyday interactions.

Breaching experiments

In breaching experiments (something Garfinkel often had his students attempt), the goal is to expose the rules of the everyday by breaking them and taking note of your own reactions as well as the reactions of others. In this way, what is taken for granted can become apparent, e.g. facing the back of a full elevator, or speaking to your family as though you just met them. Not only are you able to document the confusion, frustration, uncomfortableness, etc., of those around you, but you can also reflect on how it feels to break taken-for-granted rules. Logically, facing the back of a full elevator should not be an exceedingly stressful task, but it can make some 'experimenters' exceptionally uncomfortable.

As for *Seinfeld*, one of my favourite breaching experiments is undertaken by George. George, a self-confessed 'loser', has decided that every instinct he has ever had has been wrong, so as an experiment he decides to become 'Mr Opposite'. He decides to breach as many of the 'rules' he has traditionally used to conduct his interactions as possible. So instead of saying yes, he says no; instead of hiding the truth, he exposes himself. But of course the joke here is that rather than alienate the other, George's interactions with others, including women, suddenly go right.

Exploring the building of shared interpretations

George and Jerry (back to *Seinfeld*) often do this at the coffee shop. They make explicit and deconstruct the 'rules' of interpretative practice. For example, they discuss the 'rules' for breaking up: how many dates constitute the need for the face-to-face break-up (I think they actually come up with a number), or when can you get away with a telephone message or letter; what excuses (e.g. 'It's not you, it's me') can be used to break up in the most gracious manner; and why and when you might end with, 'let's stay friends'?

As a strategy of ethnomethodology, exploring the building of shared interpretations involves collecting raw naturalistic data that captures everyday interactions. These interactions are often specifically defined, i.e. interactions between doctor and patient, family members, friends, members of a particular cultural group, etc. Data is then captured by audio recording, or if analysis will go beyond speech, video recording. This data is then faithfully transcribed, often including hesitations, comments on tone, attitude, use of sarcastic pitch, non-verbal cues, etc. Analysis then turns to a search for the collaborative and constantly emerging nature of the interaction or conversation. The goal is to identify the 'rules' that underpin the interactions or how individuals manage action or conversation. Ethnomethodologists attempt to uncover the methodical, structured ways in which order in interactions is built. Because interpretative practices are indexical, i.e. indexed and dependent on a particular context or situation, the analysis will often include an exploration of the context-related or situational categories, classifications, and typifications used by individuals as they engage in interpretative practice.

Exploring interpretative miscues

A final method that can be used to uncover the taken-for-granted nature of communication and interaction is the exploration of conflicts or miscues – essentially, when it simply doesn't go right. It is often easier to spot, deconstruct, and understand the 'taken for granted' when it is exposed by 'conflict'. I will turn to *Seinfeld*'s Elaine for a final example. In one episode, the 'rules' for interacting with mothers of newborns is exposed through Elaine's internal conflict over the matter. While she well knows that the 'rules' mean that she has 'gotta see the baby' (always said in a whiney New York accent), she has absolutely no desire to do so. And when she finally submits, she struggles to follow the 'rules' that demand she say just how cute this hideous creature is, even though she recognizes that this a 'must lie' situation. Through this inner conflict over building an acceptable interpretative practice, cultural expectations are exposed.

Strengths and challenges associated with ethnomethodology

Ethnomethodology offers quite a bit to the study of the social, including recognition of the interpretative work of individuals, as well as methods for exploring that work. It explores how individuals make sense of, and make sense in, the social world, and recognizes that individuals are not passive in making meaning and establishing social order. Ethnomethodology also recognizes that the actual process of interacting ('how' questions) is a worthy topic of investigation, and that the topic of verbal interactions ('what' questions) and the reason for interactions ('why' questions) are not the only types of question a social scientist can ask. It is also another way to study culture. Ethnomethodology can be used to explore how members of a particular cultural group make meaning and engage in interpretative work. This can offer much to our understanding of the nature of communication and social structure within a culture. Finally, ethnomethodology offers a way of investigating how particular types of interactions are performed. For example, how juries deliberate and draw conclusions, or how medical practitioners can best deliver bad news in ways that minimize negative reactions.

As with any methodological approach that sits outside the mainstream, there are a number of issues that can make using its methods quite difficult. This includes the difficulty of getting experienced support, and having to explain and justify your choice of methodology to those who may not know much about it.

Some also argue that because ethnomethodology does not explore the 'meaning' of utterances or actions, it does not help us understand fundamental social issues or important constructs such as race, class, gender. Some even say that the 'rules' ethnomethodology draws out are obvious and not very interesting. Others, however, argue that ethnomethodology's interpretive work can help us understand how individuals produce, for example, racism or sexism.

Another misconception is that the analysis of interpretative works is limited to conversation analysis, or, in other words, the intricate exploration of transcribed verbal data (see Chapter 14). This mode of analysis can mean that ethnomethodological studies do not give much consideration to non-verbal aspects of communication and interaction. Now while conversation analysis is the most well-defined and frequently used method for the analysis of ethnomethodological data, it is important to remember that this is but one of its potential methods. Interpretation of the non-verbal is, arguably, as important to ethnomethodological understandings as is interpretation of the spoken word.

Understanding feminist approaches

First things first. Is there such as a thing as feminist methodology? Well, if there was, it would be almost impossible to define, since feminist researchers call on any variety of methodological frameworks and methods to conduct their research. What is easier to define, however, is a feminist perspective on research. The premise here is that traditional 'rules' of research have embedded within them an unconscious patriarchal bias. In fact, feminist researchers argue that what we accept as general knowledge is actually 'male' knowledge, which is knowledge underscored by patriarchal values and beliefs that shape what research is and how it should be done. This male bias pervades all aspects of the process from question development to the collection, interpretation, and presentation of data. Most significant is that this bias tends to go unaddressed in mainstream research. So research protocols derived from one particular reality (male) are accepted as the standard, proper, and credible way to produce knowledge.

Now while interpretations of what feminist research is/should be abound, feminist researchers agree that hidden male bias demands a critical stance towards existing methodological approaches. There is a need to unmask male bias and work towards research that is free from patriarchal influences and is informed by feminist theory/principles throughout all stages of the research process. Some feminist researchers even argue that women are better suited to capture diverse social reality than their male counterpoints who are not in a position to see patriarchal legacies.

The feminist perspective argues that research:

- is always politically motivated
- should be committed to the empowerment of women
- should work towards changing social inequality
- needs to represent human diversity including marginalized voices
- needs to recognize important differences between women and men, as well as among women themselves (according to race, class, ethnicity, religion, culture, sexual orientation, etc.)
- needs to acknowledge the power and position of the researcher
- should lessen the distinction between researcher and researched
- should accept and search for multiple, subjective, and partial truths.

The feminist critique of traditional social science method, however, is not without its own critique. For one, many argue that the premises above are not unique to feminist methodology and are central to many, if not most, qualitative frameworks. Second, feminist researchers have been accused of their own middle-class, white bias, which sets its own research boundaries. Finally, given the diversity of women's experiences, to claim that gender alone allows for more authentic interpretation, in itself marginalizes the rich rubric that makes up an individual's life world.

MIXED METHODOLOGY

So far this chapter has explored quantitative and qualitative traditions by focusing on the premises of each tradition, as well as their tried and true approaches. But it is time to mix things up. It is time to ask if, why, and when it is appropriate to traverse this traditional divide and employ quantitative and qualitative approaches in a single study, as well as how to go about it.

Arguments for mixed methodology

There are several reasons why mixed approaches are growing evermore common in social science research. Mixed approaches can: help you capitalize on the best of both traditions and overcome many of their shortcomings; allow for the use of both inductive and deductive reasoning; build a broader picture by adding depth and insights to 'numbers' through inclusion of dialogue, narratives, and pictures; add precision to 'words' though inclusion of numbers tallying, and statistics (which can make results more generalizable); allow you to develop research protocols in stages; offer more than one way of looking at a situation; facilitate capturing varied perspectives; and allow for triangulation.

So there is real potential here. But is it for you? Well, as covered in Chapter 7, the main prerequisites in any research design are: that (1) your approach answers your question; (2) that it is right for you as a researcher; and (3) that your design is doable. So deciding on the potential of a mixed methodological approach should come down to the exploration of these criteria. Ask yourself:

1   *Do I believe that the best way to answer my research question is through a mixed approach?* This is the most crucial question. If the answer is yes, then ask …
2   *Am I open to both traditions and willing to develop the skills necessary to carry off more than one approach?* Belief and dedication are both important to research, so you need to be honest in your assessment. Talk to your supervisor about the challenges of working across two traditions. If you think you are up for it, then ask …
3   *Will a mixed approach be impractical due to supervisory, time, and/or financial constraints?* Practicality must always be taken into account, otherwise you could be in for a very hard ride.

There are definitely traditionalists out there who argue that the assumptions underlying quantitative and qualitative traditions do not allow for a mixed approach. The paradigms are at a crossroads and cannot work in concert. Others, however, suggest that the logic that underpins various research paradigms is compatible and that methodological choice should always be based on what is useful in answering your question, regardless of any philosophical or paradigmatic assumptions.

The idea of the three questions above is to work between these two positions by allowing you to assess the ability of a mixed approach to answer your question, as well as to honestly assess how a mixed approach sits with your perspective on research – while always minding practicalities. After all, what we are after is the most appropriate approach in a real-world situation.

Perspectives and strategies

There are three main positions that researchers who wish to engage in mixed approaches can take. Each of these perspectives will lead you to quite varied research strategies and research designs.

Quantitative perspective with acceptance of qualitative data

I was once told that mixed methodology was all about adding a bit of qualitative flesh to the quantitative bones. The underlying premise here is that the heart of a mixed approach is quantitative. Researchers who think this way tend to accept the underlying assumptions of the quantitative tradition, but also accept that some qualitative data might help 'flesh out' their study.

This is likely to manifest in:

- designing surveys that ask open ended as well as closed questions
- conducting a few key informant interviews at the start of a project in order to facilitate survey development
- conducting key informant interviews after a survey to add depth to survey findings.

Whether strategies for qualitative data collection are embedded, as in the first example, or conducting in multiple phases, the point of commonality is the use of qualitative data as an "added extra" in a study that accepts the quantitative paradigm and relies, in the main, on quantitative data.

Qualitative perspective with acceptance of quantitative data

Believe it or not, there are more than a few qualitative researchers who are extremely nervous around numbers. Their belief in quality over quantity has left them questioning whether working with quantities means a lack of quality. Luckily this position is softening with more and more qualitative researchers accepting the power of numbers and recognizing that they can be capitalized on, even given the underlying assumptions of the qualitative tradition.

Research designs that stem from this tradition might include:

- an ethnographic study that embeds a small community survey
- conducting a series of in-depth interviews and coding some of the data for tallying/ statistical analysis
- complementing a case study with an examination of existing data.

The basic premise here is that in-depth exploration under a qualitative framework will best answer the research question. Quantification whether in the form of an embedded survey, quantifying what is traditionally seen as qualitative data, or exploring existing data, however, can add breath to a study and may even work towards making it more representative.

Question-driven perspective

This position involves putting questions before paradigm and premises neither the quantitative nor the qualitative tradition. It simply asks what strategies are most likely to get the credible data needed to answer the research question and sees you adopting whatever array of strategies can accomplish the task regardless of paradigm.

Some possibilities here are:

- any of the options listed for the quantitative and qualitative perspective as required by the research question
- studies with the express goal of in-depth understanding and broader representation, i.e. a project that asks what does it feel like (suited to phenomenological approaches) and how common it is (suited to survey research)
- studies which target two groups of people that require different approaches, i.e. a study exploring occupational health and safety compliance that targets employees (suited to survey research) and upper level management (suited to key informant interviews).

I have to say that I am an advocate of the question-driven perspective. Because I value both the quantitative and qualitative traditions and understand the strengths and shortcomings of each, I am open to anything from classic quantitative and qualitative approaches to quite eclectic multi-method approaches, my criteria being the most credible data possible (see Box 8.6).

BOX 8.6   MIXED METHODOLOGY EXEMPLAR – THE HAWTHORNE STUDIES

Between 1924 and 1932 a series of experiments were conducted at the Hawthorne Plant of the Western Electric Company on factors (such as lighting, breaks, hours of work) that might impact on productivity (Mayo 1933, Roethlisberger and Dickson 1939). To the surprise of the researchers, outputs generally increased any time a variable was manipulated even when this was counterintuitive or the manipulation was simply to change the variable back to how it was originally.

Such confounded findings (now known as the Hawthorne effect or the phenomena of behaviour changing simply by being observed) led to the development of a mixed methodological approach designed to offer a more holistic understanding of factors related to productivity. The experimental methods were thus complemented by more qualitative strategies. From 1928 to 1932, researchers interviewed about 21,000 employees at the Hawthorne Plant on issues such as worker attitudes, morale, home life, upbringing, diet, and other habits. They also engaged in observation, closely monitoring the daily activities of one particular work group.

Challenges and obstacles

Mixed methodologies certainly make sense. Why not take advantage of both traditions and build as rich a picture as possible? Well this goal is certainly admirable and worth pursuing, but there are quite a few challenges you will need to work through. First you need to understand two paradigms: the assumptions that underpin both; and the appropriate criteria for credibility, i.e. understanding the difference between validity and authenticity, reliability and dependability, generalizability and transferability, etc. (see Chapter 3). You will also need to develop the skills necessary to rigorously collect and analyse both quantitative and qualitative data. Open-ended questions, for example, are often asked in 'quantitative' surveys, but rarely analysed to their full potential. Similarly, students who do a qualitative work and wish to quantify some of their data can let a fear of statistics limit their analysis.

You also need to watch out for overambitious design and the possibility that you are trying to do two projects instead of one. Keep in mind that while building a rich picture is an admirable goal, you may not be able to do it all – you may need to set limits on the sub-questions you are asking and the population you wish to seek perspectives from. And of course you need to make sure you have the time, resources, and supervisory support for a multiple, mixed method approach.

Your ability to negotiate the above is a prerequisite for success. A mixed approach can offer great rewards, but developing the skills and rigour required to do it well will be a true challenge.

FURTHER READING

As you begin to narrow in on your approach, you will probably want to go a bit further in your reading. The following list is not comprehensive, but it does offer you a few good starting points.

The quantitative tradition

Gorard, S. (2003) *Quantitative Methods in Social Science*. London: Continuum International.
Maxim, P. S. (1999) *Quantitative Research Methods in the Social Sciences*. Oxford: Oxford University Press.

Hypothetico-deductive methods

Gauch Jr, H. G. (2002) *Scientific Method in Practice*. Cambridge: Cambridge University Press.
Lehmann, E. L. and Romano, J. P. (2005) *Testing Statistical Hypotheses*. New York: Springer.

Experimental design

Orr, L. L. (1998) *Social Experiments: Evaluating Public Programs with Experimental Methods*. London: Sage.
Trochim, W. M. (2009) *The Research Methods Knowledge Base*. Web page at www.socialresearchmethods.net/kb/index.htm.

(Continued)

(Continued)

Webster, M. and Sell, J. (eds) (2007) *Laboratory Experiments in the Social Sciences*. Boston: Academic Press.

Willer, D. and Walker, H. (2007) *Building Experiments: Testing Social Theory*. Stanford, CA: Stanford University Press.

Exploring a population

See readings related to sampling in Chapter 10, surveys in Chapter 11, and working with secondary data in Chapter 13.

The 'qualitative' tradition

Denzin, N. and Lincoln, Y. (2005) *The Sage Handbook of Qualitative Research*. Thousand Oaks, CA: Sage.

Marshall, C. and Rossman, G. B. (2006) *Designing Qualitative Research*. London: Sage.

Ethnography

Atkinson, P., Coffey, A., Delamont, S., Lofland, J., and Lofland, L. (eds) (2007) *Handbook of Ethnography*. London: Sage.

Geertz, C. ([1973] 2000) *The Interpretation of Cultures*. New York: Basic Books.

Glucksmann, M. (aka Ruth Cavendish) (2009) *Women on the Line*. London: Routledge.

Troman, G., Jeffrey, B., and Walford, G. (eds) (2005) *Methodological Issues and Practices in Ethnography*. Greenwich, CT: JAI Press.

Wolcott, H. F. (2008) *Ethnography: A Way of Seeing*. Lanham, MD: AltaMira Press.

Phenomenology

Berger, P. and Luckmann, T. (1967) *The Social Construction of Reality: A Treatise in the Sociology of Knowledge*. New York: Anchor.

Moustakas, C. (2000) *Phenomenological Research Methods*. London: Sage.

Seebohm, T. M. (2005) *Hermeneutics. Method and Methodology*. New York: Springer.

Sinfield, M. (1995) 'Women with AIDS: a phenomenological study', *Australasian Annual Conference, Society for HIV Medicine*, 16–19 November, 7: 61.

Van Manen, M. (1997) *Researching Lived Experience: Human Science for an Action Sensitive Pedagogy*. Albany, NY: State University of New York Press.

Ethnomethodology

Coulon, A. (2000) *Ethnomethodology*. London: Sage.
Francis, D. and Hester, S. (2004) *An Invitation to Ethnomethodology*. London: Sage.
Garfinkel, H. (1967) *Studies in Ethnomethodology*. Englewood Cliffs, NJ: Prentice Hall.
Ten Have, P. (2004) *Understanding Qualitative Research and Ethno-methodology*. London: Sage.

Feminist Perspectives

Hesse-Biber, S. N. and Yaiser, M. L. (2004) *Feminist Perspectives on Social Research*. New York: Oxford University Press.
Ramazanoğlu, C. with Holland, J. (2002) *Feminist Methodology: Challenges and Choices*. Thousand Oaks, CA: Sage.
Reinharz, S. (1992) *Feminist Methods in Social Research*. New York: Oxford University Press.

Mixed Methodology

Creswell, J. W. (2008) *Research Design: Qualitative, Quantitative and Mixed Methods Approaches*. London: Sage.
Creswell, J. W. and Plano Clark, V. L. (2006) *Designing and Conducting Mixed Methods Research*. London: Sage.
Greene, J. C. (2007) *Mixed Methods in Social Inquiry*. Hoboken, NJ: Jossey-Bass.
Mayo, E. (1933) *The Human Problems of an Industrial Civilization*. New York: Viking Press.
Roethlisberger, F. J. and Dickson, W. J. (1939) *Management and the Worker: An Account of a Research Program Conducted by the Western Electric Company, Hawthorne Works*. New York: John Wiley & Sons.
Tashakkori, A. and Teddlie, C. (eds) (2002) *Handbook of Mixed Methods in Social and Behavioral Research*. Thousand Oaks, CA: Sage.

CHAPTER SUMMARY

- Quantitative and qualitative research traditions represent a fundamental debate in the production of knowledge, but the use of the terms 'quantitative' and 'qualitative', particularly in relation to methodology, can be confusing, divisive, and limiting.
- The quantitative tradition is based on a belief that the study of society is no different than the scientific study of any other element of our world and

premises scientific method, hypothesis testing, deductive logic, objectivity, and quantification.

- Hypothetico-deductive method in the social sciences generally involves hypothesis testing through collection and analysis of quantitative data gathered through experimental design or survey research.

- Experimentation explores cause and effect relationships by manipulating independent variables in order to see if there is a corresponding effect on a dependent variable.

- Pure experimentation requires controlled environments and randomly assigned control groups. But this is not always possible in social science experiments which are often conducted in the field rather than in the lab.

- Exploring a population involves building an understanding of that population's knowledge, attitudes, and practices (KAP) on a particular topic or issue.

- There are two broad methodological strategies that can help you understand a population: to capitalize on existing data or to generate primary data – primarily through survey research.

- The qualitative tradition critiques the assumptions that underpin the quantitative tradition and premises inductive logic, subjectivity, multiple truths, the political nature of research, and the value of depth over quantity.

- Qualitative research strategies for achieving credibility include thoroughness, i.e. saturation, crystallization, prolonged engagement, persistent observation, broad representation, and peer review, and confirmation, i.e. triangulation, member checking, and full explication of method.

- Ethnography involves discovering, understanding, describing, and interpreting a way of life from the point of view of its participants and is reliant on prolonged engagement, persistent observation, and analysis that demands a high level of reflexivity.

- Because ethnographic studies involve 'immersion', ethnographers need to carefully manage their own subjectivities and thoughtfully negotiate their relationship with the 'researched'.

- Exploring phenomena (phenomenology) involves generating descriptions of lived phenomena as they present themselves in direct experience. Descriptions emerge through a dialogic process, and are synthesized to offer a range of distinct possibilities for the experience of a particular phenomenon.

- While phenomenology offers a way to study phenomena, something often neglected in the social science, literature on phenomenology can be thick, divergent, and not 'methods' oriented.

- Ethnomethodology explores the methods individuals use to make sense of their social world and accomplish their daily actions. Ethnomethodological studies involve a search for the collaborative and constantly emerging nature of interaction through exploration of breaching experiments, building of shared interpretations, and interpretative miscues.

- Ethnomethodology recognizes the interpretative work of the individual; offers a method for exploring 'how' questions; allows comparisons of divergent cultural norms; and allows exploration of specific forms of interaction.

However, it can be critiqued for not addressing 'significant' questions, and being too focused on verbal aspects of communication.

- While not a distinct methodology, feminist research is premised on the belief that traditional 'rules' of research are imbued with unacknowledged and unaddressed male bias and argue the need to unmask this bias so that research can be free from patriarchal influences.
- Feminist researchers argue that research is always political and should be committed to: the empowerment of women; overcoming inequity; diverse representation of humanity; empowerment of marginalized voices; lessening the distinction between researcher and researched; searching for multiple, subjective, and partial truths.
- Studies with mixed methodologies traverse traditional divides and employ quantitative and qualitative approaches in a single study and can help you capitalize on the best of both traditions while overcoming their shortcomings.
- A mixed approach would be appropriate if you believe it will help you in your quest for credible data and you have the dedication, time, and resources to take it on.
- Mixed approaches can be premised in the quantitative tradition with acceptance of qualitative data, the qualitative tradition with acceptance of quantitative data, or be driven by the questions themselves.
- Challenges associated with mixed approaches include: needing to be familiar with and skilled in two traditions; being mindful of overambitious design; and not having the necessary time, resources, or supervisory support for a multiple, mixed method approach.

9

UNDERSTANDING METHODOLOGIES: EVALUATIVE, ACTION-ORIENTED, AND EMANCIPATORY STRATEGIES

CHAPTER PREVIEW

- Research that attempts to drive change
- Evaluation research
- Action research
- Emancipatory research

RESEARCH THAT ATTEMPTS TO DRIVE CHANGE

> **A thought which does not result in an action is nothing much, and an action which does not proceed from a thought is nothing at all.**
> *Georges Bernanos*

Chapter 8 explored methodology paradigmatically – that is, it explored approaches to research according to various traditions. But the structure of Chapter 9 is somewhat different. In this chapter, methodologies are discussed by goals rather than a particular paradigmatic positioning. We look at methodologies according to objectives, in particular change-oriented objectives.

Now you may be thinking, all research is about the potential for change, isn't it? Shouldn't research lead to problem resolution, situation improvement, or progress? Well, as shown in Figure 9.1, the goals of research can be placed on a continuum

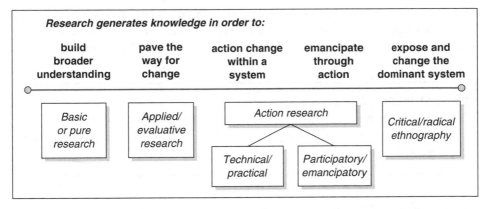

FIGURE 9.1 FROM KNOWLEDGE TO CHANGE – THE GOALS OF RESEARCH

from knowledge to change. At one end is basic or 'pure' research that attempts to produce knowledge in order to better understand the world. At the other end of the continuum is research that is conducted for the purpose of radical change to dominant structures. Now I realize these two ends of the continuum may seem worlds apart, but I would argue they are not diametrically opposed.

As far as the pursuit of pure research, I cannot think of too many 'ivory tower' researchers who conduct their research without some practical purpose in mind. In fact, all research proposals demand a rationale that highlights the scientific/ social significance of the research questions posed. In this type of research, however, applying findings is not part of the researcher's agenda. For those involved in applied/evaluative research, change is more closely tied to a project's objectives. Knowledge production is, in fact, driven by the immediate need for information that can facilitate practical, effective, decision making. Action research takes this a step further and rather than expect change *because* of research, it actually demands change *through* research processes. Finally, emancipatory research attacks change at the most fundamental levels, and includes liberation and self-determination in its agenda.

All researchers want their research to be useful, at least at some level in the real world. The question is whether that usefulness involves the production of knowledge that may some day lead to change, or whether change itself will be a direct product of the research process.

EVALUATION RESEARCH

If there is one thing we are not short of it is initiatives. In order to improve a situation, we are willing to try new things: new products, new practices, new policies, new legislation, new interventions, new programmes, new strategies, new structures, new routines, new procedures, new curriculum, etc. But how successful are our endeavours?

Did whatever we try do whatever it was supposed to do? Have we been able to make some contribution towards positive change? Have we been able to alleviate a problem situation? Well, answering these types of questions is the goal of evaluation research.

EVALUATION RESEARCH
Research that attempts to determine the value of some initiative. Evaluative research identifies an initiative's consequences as well as opportunities for modification and improvement.

The need for evaluative studies is ever increasing. A well-conducted evaluation is now a key strategy for supplying decision makers with the data they need for rational, informed, evidence-based decision making. In fact, change intervention proposals increasingly require evaluative components so that assessment is embedded into the management of change from conception.

Evaluative studies basically attempt to determine whether an initiative should be continued as is, modified, expanded, or scrapped and do this by asking various stakeholder groups two types of questions. The first is related to outcomes, i.e. did a particular initiative meet its objectives? The second is related to process, i.e. how successful was a particular initiative's implementation and how might it be improved?

Summative/outcome evaluation

Summative evaluation, also referred to as outcome evaluation, aims to provide data and information related to the effectiveness of the change strategy in question (that goals, aims, and objectives have been met) and its efficiency (that the effects justify the costs). The idea here is to investigate whether an initiative is responsible for outcomes that would not have occurred if it were not for the initiative, and this should include both intended and unintended effects. Now in the real world, the financial bottom line is almost always a factor, so many outcome evaluations also include data related to cost-effectiveness, often in the form of a cost–benefit analysis.

The results of outcome evaluations are expected to inform decision making related to programme funding, continuation, termination, expansion, and reduction. While findings are often case specific, results can be of interest to any number of stakeholder groups and, depending on the nature of the change intervention, might be of interest to the wider population as well.

Methods appropriate to summative evaluation

So what exactly is involved in the conduct of an evaluative study? Well, rather than be defined by any particular methods, an evaluative study is distinguished by its

TABLE 9.1   EVALUATIVE METHODS

	Provider perspective	Recipient perspective	Wider perspective
Outcome Did it work?	Was it cost effective/ beneficial to the provider? Potential methods: • Document review • Key informant • Interviews • Focus groups	Was there a real change in the target group? Potential methods: • Experimentation/ quasi-experimentation using control groups or before/after data • Exploration of post group only by survey/interview	Did it meet a wider community need? Potential methods: • Surveys • Focus groups
Process How could it be improved?	What were the strengths/ weaknesses; how could the process be made more efficient/effective for the organization? Potential methods: • Interviews with key organizational stakeholders • Focus groups • Observation • Document review	What were the strengths/ weaknesses; how could the process be made more efficient/effective for those it is intended to benefit? Potential methods: • Surveys • Focus groups • Interviews	What were the strengths/ weaknesses; how could the process be made more efficient/effective for the community? Potential methods: • Surveys • Focus groups • Interviews (often key informants/ stakeholders)

evaluative goals, and it is these goals that determine the appropriate approach. In summative evaluation, the main goal is to find out if an initiative worked. In other words, did it meet its objectives? Now, as shown in Table 9.1, initiatives often have multiple objectives that are likely to vary for each stakeholder group. As an evaluator exploring outcomes, you will need to determine whether success is to be measured from the perspective of the provider, the recipients, the wider community, or all of these. You need to determine which outcome objectives are to be explored and whose perspectives you seek. Your methods will then vary accordingly.

- **Provider perspective** – When designing methods, there are two general ways to find out if providers believe an initiative is a success. This first is to ask. Interviews and focus groups (see Chapter 11) allow you to talk to those responsible for design, delivery, implementation, as well as those with a higher level of organizational responsibility. The second method is to look at documentary evidence (see Chapter 12). This is particularly relevant for questions that focus on cost-effectiveness, or anywhere that evidence of success is likely to be in 'records'.
- **Recipient perspective** – This is where you really get down to brass tacks and see if the initiative's change-oriented outcome objectives have been met. Now many (including myself) would argue that the best way to do this is through experimental or quasi-experimental designs (see Chapter 8) that allow for comparison across groups and time. There are three possibilities here:

1 *Case/control design* – To see whether an initiative has made a difference for a target group, you can use a control group to compare those who have undergone an initiative with those who have not.
2 *Before/after design* – Sometimes called 'time series analysis', this approach allows for comparison of the same group of individuals before and after an initiative is implemented.
3 *Case/control – before/after design* – This allows for even more definitive results by combining the two methods above.

All three of these approaches require forward planning and, as discussed at the end of this section, this is not always possible. The alternative is to evaluate perceptions of change, rather than change itself, by surveying or interviewing recipients after implementation (see Chapter 11). The goal here is to see if recipients believe that change has occurred.

- **Wider community perspective** – Initiatives often include objectives related to stakeholder groups which are not direct recipients. For example, a school initiative to curtail bullying may include an objective related to decreasing parent/community anxiety. Or a health care initiative may include an objective related to improving an organization's reputation in the community. The methods of choice here are surveys and focus groups (Chapter 11). And while such approaches generally ask community members to report on their perceptions and recent changes in those perceptions, the collection of similar data prior to the initiative will allow you to engage in direct comparison.

Formative/process evaluation

Formative evaluation, also referred to as process evaluation, aims to provide data and information that will aid further development of a particular change initiative. Such studies investigate an initiative's delivery and ask how, and how well, it is being implemented. These studies can assess strengths, weaknesses, opportunities, and threats, and often work to assess the factors acting to facilitate and/or block successful implementation.

The results derived from process evaluations are expected to inform decision making related to programme improvement, modification, and management. And while these studies also tend to be case specific, 'transferable' findings will allow other organizations interested in the use of any similar initiatives to apply 'lessons learned' (see Chapter 3).

Methods appropriate to formative evaluation

As highlighted in Table 9.1, the main objective in formative or process evaluation is assessing an initiative's strengths and weaknesses and asking how the process could be made more efficient and effective. Stakeholder perspectives again play an important role here since providers, recipients, and the wider community are likely to have quite varied opinions on what did and did not work so well. Design of methods is, therefore, highly dependent on working out precisely what you want to know and whose perspective you seek:

- **Provider perspective** – The methods you use here will be highly dependent on the complexity and diversity of the groups responsible for provision. For example, at one end of the spectrum you might be asked to evaluate a classroom initiative driven by a particular teacher. In this case, an in-depth interview would make most sense (see Chapter 11). At the other end of the spectrum, you may be evaluating a new government health care policy whose design, development, and implementation might have involved individuals working at various levels of government and private industry. With this level of complexity you may need to call on multiple methods, e.g. interviews, focus groups, and even surveys, to gather the data you require (see Chapter 11). There may also be value in direct observation of the process or in a document review that finds you trolling through and examining records and minutes related to the process being explored (see Chapter 12).
- **Recipient perspective** – Just because management thinks something went well doesn't mean recipients will think the same. So good process evaluations will go beyond provider perspective and seek recipient opinions on strengths, weaknesses, and potential modifications. As with providers, target groups also vary in size and complexity, and you may find yourself calling on a variety of methods, including interviews, focus groups, and surveys, to gather the data you require (see Chapter 11).
- **Wider community perspective** – The first question you need to ask here is, 'Do you or your "client" want wider community opinion?' You may not feel that the wider community is a relevant stakeholder, or that broader community groups have the prerequisite knowledge for providing an informed opinion. On the other hand, the initiative under review might have far-reaching implications that affect the community or might be related to a problem where the community sees itself as a key stakeholder; say, for example, an initiative aimed to stop neighbourhood graffiti. In this situation, canvassing wider opinion on an initiative's strengths and weaknesses may be of value. The methods most likely to be called upon here are surveys, focus groups, and possibly key informant interviews (see Chapter 11).

The politics of evaluative research

> " In criticism I will be bold, and as sternly, absolutely just with friend and foe. From this purpose nothing shall turn me. "
> *Edgar Allan Poe*

It's said that all research is political, but none more so than evaluative research. It would be naive to pretend otherwise. Vested interests are everywhere and the pressure for researchers to find 'success' can be high.

So how do you begin to negotiate and balance the sometimes divergent political and scientific goals of evaluative research? Well, the first step is to understand researcher/ researched realities and relationships. For example, those seeking to have initiatives evaluated do not always have the same goals. Yes, some want honest and open feedback, but others might be after validation of what they have done, while others might just be doing what they need to do to meet funding requirements. And of course, some may be after a combination of these.

The same is true of researchers, whether insiders or outsiders; not all evaluative researchers operate with the same style, skills, or goals. For example, some see themselves as objective researchers whose clear and unwavering objective is credible findings regardless of political context. Others do operate at a more political level and are highly in tune with government/organization/political funding realities, and perhaps their own ongoing consultancy opportunities. There are others who tend to be overcritical and need to show their intelligence by picking holes in the work of others. Finally, there are those who see themselves as facilitators or even mentors who are there to help.

When I first began doing evaluative research I came across and learnt from all of these styles and assumed that my way forward would be as an objective researcher. But I soon realized that the political end of evaluative research cannot be ignored and that the key to real-world evaluation is flexibility. Now my main grounding objective, which is tied to my own professional ethics, is to produce credible and useful findings. But how those findings are presented, what is emphasized, and what is sometimes best left unsaid, are undeniably influenced by both politics and context.

Table 9.2 looks at the intersection of researcher/researched goals in terms of researcher credibility and researcher/researched relationships. While the matrix does not capture all possibilities, it does provide some insights into the realities of evaluative research and the skills required to work effectively in such a politically charged environment.

I have worked with quite a few evaluators and I think the best ones are politically astute but always work under a code of professional ethics and integrity. Some will adapt their style depending on the client and context, while others will stay true to a certain way of working. But almost all good evaluators understand the need to negotiate clear expectations that meet both client and researcher needs and goals with integrity.

Negotiating real-world challenges of evaluative research

Political realities are not the only challenge to the production of credible data in evaluative research. Evaluations tend to be conducted within messy and chaotic real-world settings, and you will need to skilfully negotiate this level of complexity if you want to produce solid, valuable results.

Now if it were up to me, all initiatives to be evaluated would be well established with clear and measurable aims and objectives. But rarely is this the case. You often need to find ways to work around circumstances that are less than ideal. Such situations include the following.

When the decision to evaluate comes after initial implementation

It would be terrific if the need to evaluate was a recognized part of project planning from conception. You would then have all the options. Early planning would allow you to design comparative studies such as randomized control trials, quasi-experiments

TABLE 9.2   RELATIONSHIPS IN EVALUATIVE RESEARCH

'Clients' who seek ... Evaluators whose style tends to be that of ...	Honest feedback	Validation	To meet funding requirements
The critic Credibility: can be difficult to build trust, thereby influencing data/ findings. Findings tend to overemphasize the negative and not point out the positive	While the clients may appreciate knowing their initiative's shortcomings, they can be left feeling deflated and undervalued by the critic	This relationship spells trouble. Clients are likely to be demoralized, disheartened, and even angry. Critics are likely to burn their bridges here	Those who do not appreciate the value of evaluation are likely to be further put off by the critic. There is a good chance here of weakening trust and building resentment
The unbiased scientist Credibility: best odds of credible data/findings, particularly if the approach is one that attempts to build trust while collecting unbiased data	A **good match,** but still no harm in the 'scientist' honing political skills. Even those who want honest feedback appreciate diplomacy	While findings might be fair, how they are accepted and acted upon by those seeking validation often depends on a researcher's sensitivity and communication skills	Relationships tend to be enhanced by supportive findings and a researcher's interpersonal skills – communication skills can be instrumental in 'selling' the value of evaluation
The facilitator/mentor Credibility: likely to result in credible findings if the initiative is a success. There can be a tendency to gloss over shortcomings and emphasize the positive. Can lead to thorough process-related recommendations	While relationships are generally positive, clients can be frustrated if they feel they are not getting the feedback/hard data they need for effective decision making	This is actually a **good match** that can leave clients feeling their work is valued. Good chance that process-related recommendations will be taken up	Mentors might be able to build trust and instil the value of evaluation. But if clients remain cynical, they may not put high value on the mentor's recommendations
The politician Credibility: findings need to be explored in light of the political context – there is a need to read between the lines. Findings may support the agenda of those commissioning the research	Generally not too problematic as long as expectations are clear. Researcher and client objectives should be made explicit and negotiated so that they are not at cross-purposes	If politician and client goals are the same, i.e. validation, the relationship is likely to be good, even if feedback is uncritical. If, however, goals are at cross-purposes, client satisfaction can be low	This tends to be a **good match** because goals are usually aligned with a particular agenda. Levels of critical feedback should be discussed and negotiated

with control groups, or before and after designs (see Chapter 8). But there are plenty of circumstances where you will need to undertake evaluations where the evaluative planning was but an after-thought – thereby limiting your methodological options.

The key here is remembering that evaluative studies, particularly those studies related to outcomes, are all about comparison. And by far the best way to compare is by using at least two data sets. Effective evaluations are based on either before and after data (data collected before the initiative that can be compared with data collected after the initiative), or case/control data (data collected from two groups, one that has undergone the initiative and one that has not).

Without the aid of forward planning you will need to consider if either of these options is available to you. In other words, you will need to determine whether you will be able to collect solid relevant baseline data, or whether you will be able to find a comparable control group. If you can, rigorous evaluation is not too problematic. But if baseline data or a comparable control group is not available, you are left with the following methodological options:

- Do a 'post group only' study in which you ask stakeholders about the effects (on knowledge, attitude, and/or practice) of the initiative under review. While generally not as strong as truly comparative methods, this approach can still have value. The key here is clear expectations. Your clients need to be aware of your methodological constraints and how they might affect findings.
- Limit your study to process evaluation that centres on stakeholders' reflections on an initiative's design, delivery, and implementation.

When objectives are not clearly articulated or are not readily measurable

If you want to know if an initiative has achieved its goals, then you clearly need to know two things: (1) what those goals were/are; and (2) how they might be measured. Now by far the best objectives are those that are 'SMART', which stands for Specific, Measurable, Achievable, Relevant, and Time-bound. If your initiative has been developed with such objectives in mind, in terms of methodological design, you are half-way there. By definition, your objectives are measurable – so you just need to go out and measure. But for initiatives where objectives are not clearly articulated, or are not measurable, you have to do a bit more work. Since you simply cannot evaluate non-existent or waffly objectives, you will need to:

- work with stakeholders to clearly draw out and articulate the initiative's objectives
- decide which objectives will be prioritized for evaluation
- determine and agree on how these objectives can be operationalized (e.g. designing a method that can measure 'the joy of reading in children' is much more difficult than designing a method that can measure 'an increase in recreational reading of third graders by 50% by the end of the year').

When the initiative has not been going long enough to expect results

It is not unusual for the timeframe given for evaluation to be shorter than that needed for an initiative to produce its intended results. For example, in health promotion campaigns, goals are often related to disease alleviation such as reducing the incidence of lung cancer, or decreasing the incidence of type 2 diabetes. But not only are such effects hard to attribute to a particular campaign, such effects might not be seen for several years.

A common strategy used by evaluators facing this situation is to negotiate short- to intermediate-term outcomes that can be (1) measured within the timeframe available, and (2) correlated to the expected long-term outcomes. For example, success might be measured by increased awareness, i.e. increased community knowledge about the dangers of smoking or increased awareness of the impact of carbohydrates on insulin. Success might also be measured by changes in behaviour, such as reducing the number of cigarettes smoked or decreasing levels of sugar consumption.

When effects are difficult to measure/difficult to attribute to the initiative

Say you were asked to evaluate a high school sex education programme that has a clear and central goal of increasing abstinence. To evaluate this programme, not only would you need to collect sensitive data from young people (who may not feel comfortable exposing themselves), but you would also need to design a research protocol that could control for any other factors that are known to have an effect on abstinence, such as parents, peers, media, etc. Remember: you are not just looking for a correlation here. You are actually trying to establish cause and effect, and your methods need to control for any other factors that might be causal to any perceived change or difference. Controlling for extraneous factors is the only way to be able to attribute results to the programme itself.

The lesson here is that before taking on an evaluative research study, you need to clearly consider, articulate, and negotiate what is, and what is not, possible. In the real world it can be difficult, if not impossible, to control for all extraneous variables that may affect change (see Table 9.3). Remember: it is much better to have critiques of your methodology come before you undertake a study, rather than after it has been completed!

ACTION RESEARCH

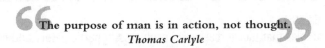

The purpose of man is in action, not thought.
Thomas Carlyle

In most research approaches, contributions are limited to the production of knowledge. Even in applied/evaluative research where the goal is to have research knowledge become key in evidence-based decision making, any actual change comes after the completion of research processes. But what if you want to do more than produce knowledge? What if your goals are to go beyond evidence and recommendations? What if your research goals include doing, shifting, changing, or implementing? Enter action research.

TABLE 9.3   EVALUATION IN AN IDEAL WORLD

Evaluation in an ideal world would mean ...	Unfortunately, in the real world ...
Politics	
• Full stakeholder cooperation	➢ Cooperation can be hard to obtain. Programme initiators may not want to invest time and resources, and they may resent feeling judged
• True desire for unbiased results	➢ Not everyone will want a candid assessment of their initiatives. Some will, but others will be looking to meet requirements, or simply receive validation
• No pressure from vested interests	➢ Whether overt or subtle, pressure to find success can come across loud and clear
Direction	
• Clear client directives	➢ A need to evaluate might be recognized, but there is often little consensus on the exact nature of the evaluation to be undertaken
• Realistic expectations	➢ Expectations are often unrealistic – especially when initiative effects can be: (1) difficult to measure; (2) difficult to attribute to the initiative under study
The initiative	
• Evaluation planned from the initiative's onset	➢ The decision to evaluate often comes after implementation, which means solid baseline data and/or comparable control groups can be hard to find
• Clear and measurable aims and objectives	➢ Objectives can be (1) implicit and not clearly articulated and/or (2) not measurable
• Well-established, mature initiatives	➢ Interventions rarely show immediate success, yet they can be subject to deadlines that might come before you would expect to see any real change
Resources	
• Adequate time and funding to undertake the study	➢ As in any study, time and resources can be in short supply
• Researchers with insider knowledge, political nous, and outsider objectivity	➢ There is almost always a need to balance political and research agendas

---

ACTION RESEARCH
Research strategies that tackle real-world problems in participatory and collaborative ways in order to produce action and knowledge in an integrated fashion through a cyclical process. In action research, process, outcome, and application are inextricably linked.

The term 'action research' was coined in 1946 by Kurt Lewin (1946) and represented quite a departure from 'objective' scientific method that viewed implementation as discrete from research processes. Under this traditional framework, responsibility for what happened as a consequence of the production of knowledge was not generally part of a researcher's agenda.

Researchers, however, began to recognize that: (1) the knowledge produced through research should be used for change; and (2) researching change should lead to knowledge. The appeal of a research strategy that could link these two goals while embedding elements of evaluation and learning was quite high, particularly in the fields of organizational behaviour and education, where continuous improvement was, and still is, a primary goal.

Action research also offered a departure from 'researcher' as expert and the 'researched' as passive recipients of scientific knowledge. It therefore had great appeal among community development workers who saw value in a collaborative research approach that could empower stakeholders to improve their own practice, circumstances, and environments (see Box 9.1 on p. 151).

The scope of action research

Action research, as it developed through the disciplines of organizational behaviour, education, and community development, has travelled down a number of divergent paths, each with its own priorities and emphases. Common across their divergences, however, is a desire for real and immediate change that involves engagement and involvement of stakeholders as collaborators or co-researchers; prolonged involvement in learning cycles; the production of rigorous, credible knowledge; and the actioning of tangible change.

The nature of the potential change can involve anything from improved practice to shifted programmes, policies, and systems as discussed below, through to more radical 'cultural' shifts that include empowering the marginalized (discussed under emancipatory research). While the goals of any one action research proposal may sit neatly in any one of these categories, it is not uncommon for action research studies to work simultaneously across a number of goals.

Improving practice

Action research can be an effective way of empowering stakeholders to improve their own professional practice. Rather than mandates that come down from on high, or knowledge that comes from outside experts, action research, which is expressly designed to improve professional practice, recognizes that various stakeholders can contribute to their own learning and development. Action research recognizes the professional nature of stakeholders and their ability to conduct meaningful research. In doing so, it helps break down the divide between stakeholders and the 'academic elite', and brings research into day-to-day professional practice.

Improving practice through action research is quite common in the educational sector where teachers are encouraged to work in ways that develop their own skills and practice. In recent years, however, there has been an increase in action research studies in health care and nursing, where the desire for professional recognition, autonomy, and respect for learned/local knowledge is high.

Shifting systems

Sometimes the action you want to pursue begins and ends with developing your own professional practice, but other times you may want to work at the organizational level. Beyond practice, you may be interested in working within an organizational setting to improve procedures or programmes. In fact, in the above example a higher level goal was to have the findings from an action research study aimed at developing professional practice contribute to the development of effective policy.

Personally, I cannot think of any organization that could not be improved in some way or another. Inefficient systems, ineffective management, and outdated policy provide action research opportunities for those working in and with businesses, government and non-government agencies, community groups, etc. But while action research has been around for the better part of 60 years and can offer much to the management of organizational change, it is not generally a core management strategy. Action research literature certainly addresses organizational change, but change management literature rarely tackles action research.

Nevertheless, terms such as learning, education, facilitation, participation, negotiation, and collaboration that are core in action research are also core in change-management-speak. This is particularly so in organizations that have recognized the value of on-the-ground knowledge, as well as the role of engagement and ownership in working towards effective and sustainable change. Action research as a strategy for driving workplace-based change can be highly effective in securing stakeholder support. It can also get a wide range of staff working together towards a common goal; provide a systematic and well-established approach to sustainable change; provide a framework for the conduct of research; and embed the concept of research into management practice. It can also be a step along the way in the development of a learning organization.

Key elements of action research

Because action research is quite distinct from traditional research strategies, working through its key elements is well worth the time. Understanding the benefits and challenges of this mode of research is an essential preliminary step in determining the appropriateness of action research for any particular context.

Addresses real-world problems

Action research is grounded in real problems and real-life situations. It generally begins with the identification of practical problems in a specific real-world context. It then attempts to understand those problems and to seek and implement solutions within that context. Action research is often used in workplaces and rural communities where the ownership of change is a high priority or where the goal is to improve professional practice. It is also considered an effective strategy when there is a strong desire to transform both theory and practice.

Pursues action and knowledge

Action research rejects the two-stage process of 'knowledge first – change second', and suggests that they are highly integrated. Action research practitioners believe that enacting change should not just be seen as the end product of knowledge; rather it should be valued as a source of knowledge itself. And we are not talking here about anecdotal knowledge. The knowledge produced from an action research study needs to be credible and must be collected and analysed with as much rigour as it would be in any other research strategy.

Action is also a clear and immediate goal in every action research project. Whether it be developing skills, changing programmes and policies, or working towards more radical change, action research works towards situation improvement based in practice, and avoids the problem of needing to work towards change after knowledge is produced.

Participation

The notion of research as the domain of the expert is rejected, with action research calling for participation of, and collaboration between, researchers, practitioners, and any other interested stakeholders. It minimizes the distinction between the researcher and the researched and places high value on local knowledge. The premise is that without key stakeholders as part of the research process, outsiders are limited in their ability to build rich and subtle understandings – or implement sustainable change. Contrary to many research paradigms, action research works *with*, rather than *on* or *for*, the 'researched', and is therefore often seen as embodying democratic principles. The key is that those who will be affected by the research and action are not acted upon.

The nature and level of participation and collaboration are varied and based on: the action research approach adopted; the particular context of the situation being studied; and the goals of the various stakeholders. This might find different stakeholders involved in any or all stages and cycles of the process. As for individuals driving the research process, in addition to taking on the role of lead researcher, at various points throughout the project, they might also have to act as planner, leader, catalyser, facilitator, teacher, designer, listener, observer, synthesizer, and/or reporter.

Cycles of learning and action

Action research is a cyclical process that takes shape as knowledge emerges. The premise here is that you learn, you do, you reflect, you learn how to do better, you

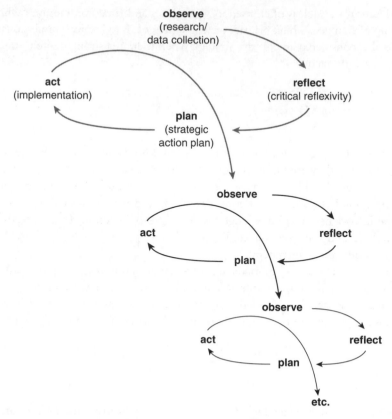

FIGURE 9.2 CYCLES IN ACTION RESEARCH

do it better, you learn from that, do it better still, and so on and so forth. You work through a series of continuous improvement cycles that converge towards better situation understanding and improved action. Action research can therefore be seen as an experiential learning approach to change. The goal is to continuously refine methods, data, and interpretation in light of the understanding developed in the earlier cycles.

The cycles themselves can be defined in numerous ways. But, as shown in Figure 9.2, they generally involve some variation on observation, reflection, planning, and action.

The exact nature of the steps in each part of the cycle is emergent and developed collaboratively with stakeholders who form the research team. Research for the 'observation' part of the cycle is likely to be set within a particular case, and is likely to involve a variety of approaches, methodologies, and methods in a bid to gather data and generate knowledge. The 'reflection' part of the cycle can be informal and introspective, or can be quite formal and share many elements with formative evaluations, as discussed earlier. The steps related to 'planning' and 'action', however, are likely to go beyond reflection and research, and may require practitioners to delve into literature on strategic planning and change management.

> **BOX 9.1   ACTION RESEARCH EXEMPLAR – IMPROVING INDIGENOUS STUDENT'S TAFE COMPLETION RATES**
>
> The empowerment of research participants is always paramount in action research and is therefore a highly effective methodology for the engagement of traditionally marginalized groups. In the action research study *Improving Indigenous Completion Rates in Mainstream TAFE* (Balatti et al. 2004), the authors attempt to address the practical problem of high indigenous student dropout rates in Australian TAFE (Technical And Further Education) through a participatory, cyclical process designed to generate knowledge and enact change. To that end, research processes involved the forming and facilitating of four teams of 7 to 10 people drawn from a range of stakeholder groups including students, administration, support officers, managers, and community members plus a facilitator and a cultural adviser. Each group then worked on a distinct problem recording their processes and attempting to both generate new knowledge and influence change (such as new organizational arrangements, new learning initiatives, and new forms of delivery) through their activities.

Challenges associated with action research

Yes, action research can produce knowledge and change in empowering ways. But anyone who has ever facilitated the process can tell you that it is far from easy. The participatory, cyclical, and multi-goaled nature of action research can make it a difficult process to navigate. And while a team approach means you will not have full control, you are still likely to be the one responsible for overall management. So you will be the one responsible for keeping the team to tight timelines and budgets. Being practical and realistic is, therefore, critical to the success of any action research project. In short, the project must be manageable.

Some of the issues you will need to negotiate as an action researcher include:

- *Facilitating rather than directing* – Because of its participatory nature, the ultimate direction of the project is not fully in your hands. Decisions made about the project's direction and its probable outcomes should be collective.
- *Managing the scope* – Action research projects can get very big, very quickly. New researchers can be surprised to find that a rigorously conducted needs assessment or the conduct of an evaluative study within just one action research cycle can be a large research project in its own right.
- *Assuring rigour in methods* – While continuous improvement strategies can rely on anecdotal evidence and general reflections, action research demands a higher degree of rigour. Perhaps the best advice is to identify the key research questions within each action research cycle and treat each of these as a small research study in its own right. While these studies will certainly need tight, realistic boundaries,

they still need to be conducted so that they meet indicators of good research, i.e. validity, authenticity, reliability, consistency, etc. (see Chapter 3).

- *Managing the pace* – Getting stakeholders together, getting consensus, and action-ing real change can be slow, particularly in multiple cycles. Action research takes time and tends to work best when embedded in day-to-day practice.
- *Keeping momentum* – In a long-term project, many things can go astray. Key stake-holders may come and go, change initiatives may not get off the ground, and the conduct of rigorous research may become overwhelming. And while this is the nature of action research, realistic planning, acceptance of the unexpected, and being prepared to be flexible can help keep momentum going.
- *Managing people* – Facilitating collaboration is not easy. Some stakeholders may feel unheard, ignored, and/or marginalized; some may be overbearing and pompous; others may be pushing their own agenda. As a facilitator, you will need to call on negotiation, facilitation, and, potentially, conflict resolution skills.
- *Acting ethically* – Researchers carry the burden of ethical responsibility for both the production of knowledge and for the welfare of the researched (see Chapter 3). In action research, the involvement of stakeholders in the research team, combined with the agenda of actioning change, make for very high levels of participant involvement. Protecting the welfare of these participants is paramount.
- *Needing a range of skills* – In addition to being a competent researcher, the action researcher must also be a consummate organizer, effective communicator, skilled negotiator, conflict resolution specialist, well-organized time manager, strategic plan-ner, efficient documenter, and willing to get his or her 'hands dirty' as an on-the-ground implementer – all of which might require the development of specialist skills.
- *Ownership* – Finally, the researcher needs to negotiate ownership of research out-comes, which may include rights to publish and issues of authorship.

When it comes to knowledge and change, action research attempts to let you have your cake and eat it too (which actually makes sense – after all, what good is a cake you can't eat?). It also allows you to work with others in empowering ways. And, while action research can be quite challenging, for individuals and organizations whose goals match those of action research, it can be a challenge well worth taking up.

EMANCIPATORY RESEARCH

> **The philosophers have only interpreted the world in various ways; the point, however, is to change it.**
> *Karl Marx*

It is one thing to want to improve skills and practice, or to endeavour to change how things are done in a workplace, a school, or a community, but what if you believe that the only path to sustainable change is through fundamental transformation of larger social systems? What if you believe that it will take more than working within the system, and that at the heart of the social issue or social problem is injustice or inequity in the system itself, i.e. the repressive school system, the authoritative nature of the workplace, or the hierarchical structures of the community? Or underpinning even this, the underlying ideologies of, say, capitalism, patriarchy, development, or globalization?

To strive for critical emancipation is to expose these underlying ideologies in a bid to liberate those oppressed by them. This requires:

CRITICALITY
Challenging taken-for-granted ways of knowing. Asking not only what it is, but why it is, who benefits, and what alternative possibilities there might be.

RADICAL VIEWS
Advocating fundamental or revolutionary changes in current practices, conditions, institutions, or ideologies.

EMANCIPATORY GOALS
To work towards transformative change.

Critical emancipation thus refers to fundamental or revolutionary changes in current thinking, practices, conditions, or institutions that can free people from the constraints of dominant social structures that often limit self-development and self-determination. For those whose research includes goals of critical emancipation, research is likely to proceed on the assumption that if social problems arise from a system, they are unlikely to be solved within that system. Critical emancipatory research necessarily delves into the underfelt of social systems. It is laden with political purpose and does not claim to be value free. It seeks transformation of society such that individuals are liberated and empowered towards action that opens up possibilities for improved situations.

Now in its radical extreme this might mean exploring the disempowerment and injustice created by industrialized societies; investigating the economic impacts of mass globalization; or exposing the patriarchal structures that act to disadvantage women. In terms of smaller scale research projects, however, the application might be as 'ordinary' as exploring workplace stress, bullying in the playground, or low self-esteem in young girls. The 'critical' end of such studies comes from exploring the ideologies that create systems in which: workplace stress becomes an expected product of well-entrenched practices of authority, power, and control; low self-esteem in girls can be seen as 'ordinary' given the cultural emphasis on the body image of women in the public eye; bullying in the playground can be seen as quite reasonable given the legitimization of power through other forms of aggression readily accessible to youth (movies, video games, sport, etc.). This criticality is then applied to emancipation through the production of knowledge that exposes repressive ideologies and opens up possibilities.

In the social sciences, these critical emancipatory goals have led to variations on ethnographic and action research. 'Participatory' action research has an explicit goal of emancipation through action, while 'critical' ethnography seeks to change existing social systems by exposing their dominant and repressive ideologies.

Participatory action research

Participatory action research (PAR), sometimes referred to as emancipatory action research or 'southern' participatory action research (which comes from the notion of working in developing countries often in the southern hemisphere), falls under the action research umbrella. It has goals of emancipation, but maintains the action research dedication to cycles of knowledge and action that produce on-the-ground change. Now action research can certainly have emancipatory goals, but PAR makes these goals much more explicit. It works in participatory ways that value local knowledge, and attempts to empower communities to expose and liberate themselves from repressive systems and ideologies. PAR is often found in international development research that strives towards social transformation of the 'marginalized' through advocacy and action.

The goal of PAR is to pursue action and knowledge in an integrated fashion through a cyclical and participatory process. It attempts to facilitate exploration and unmasking of the ways that dominant ideologies and systems shape and constrain thinking and action, and works towards interventions that can liberate the marginalized from those forces that contribute to poverty, oppression, repression, and/or injustice. PAR relies on the same basic tenants as action research, but with a more specific emancipatory agenda:

- *Addresses practical problems* – As with action research, PAR works with real problems in order to produce knowledge and action directly useful to stakeholders. In PAR, this often involves the empowerment of the 'marginalized' as they act to construct their own knowing, and attempt to create and action their own strategic plan for emancipation.
- *Generates knowledge* – PAR attempts to challenge not only things within the system, but the system itself. It attempts to unmask the political aspects of knowledge production that often sees knowledge as an instrument of power and control.
- *Enacts change* – As is common to all action research processes, PAR goes beyond knowledge generation and incorporates change into its immediate goals. In PAR, these goals are directly related to emancipation and liberation by changing inequitable power relations.
- *Is participatory* – PAR works *with* the researched, rather than *on* or *for* them. It recognizes that the knowledge and experience of the 'marginalized' should be respected and valued, and attempts to capitalize on capabilities and cultural practices that are often ignored. PAR also attempts to work towards 'conscientization' (Freire 1970) or 'enlightenment and awakening' (Fals Borda and Rahman 1991) of the oppressed, and acts to strengthen their capacity to generate knowledge and action from their own perspectives and in their own interests. Methods used to generate knowledge and action are broad, eclectic, and emergent, and need not be limited to traditional Western ways of researching. Song, poetry, art, drama, and storytelling might emerge as appropriate ways to draw out and generate knowledge.
- *Relies on a cyclical process* – As with all forms of action research, PAR converges towards better situation understanding and improved action implementation through cycles of observation, reflection, planning, and action.

Critical ethnography

Ethnography can be defined as 'the exploration of cultural groups in a bid to understand, describe, and interpret a way of life from the point of view of its participants' (see Chapter 8). Critical ethnography, also referred to as radical ethnography, adds a political agenda of exposing inequitable, unjust, or repressive influences that are acting on 'marginalized' cultural groups, in a bid to offer avenues for positive change.

There is thus an assumption that the dominant or existing system is indeed repressive or unjust and needs to be exposed. Critical ethnography attempts to expose the political nature of knowledge and unmask the dominant forces that shape our view of the world. By critical examination of worldviews, ideology, and power, critical ethnography attempts to contextualize the current situation in a larger socio-historic framework that offers, and encourages others to engage in, critical reflection. The goal is to work towards conscientization, empowerment, and liberation of the 'marginalized'.

While traditional ethnographic techniques can, and many would argue should, consider how interpretations are influenced by dominant paradigms, critical ethnographers have an express goal of understanding and interpreting situations from both within and outside the dominant. By naming and then distancing themselves from cultural assumptions in a bid to work through a series of alternative conceptions, critical ethnographers expose dominant paradigms. The goal is to present alternative and potentially more liberating realities (see Box 9.2).

Clearly, the highly political goals of critical ethnography link exposure of the dominant system to emancipation; to bring about change is a defined objective. According to Thomas (1993), ethnography as action can be seen in its ability to:

- change cognitive functioning of researchers
- offer a 'voice' to the marginalized
- instigate interactions with others that raise social awareness
- create networks of those with common goals
- become a starting point for legislative and/or policy reform.

BOX 9.2   A JOURNEY TOWARDS CRITICAL ETHNOGRAPHY

A student of mine conducted an ethnographic study of first-year university students who were subjected to hazing or bastardization. The study attempted to understand the reality of bastardization from the perspective of the 'victims'. Through observations, interview, and document analysis, the student wanted to be able to give a thick description and interpretation of both the phenomenon of bastardization and the culture in which it thrived. As she progressed in this work she realized that understanding the culture and how it might shift could not be done without a critical

(Continued)

(Continued)

examination of the forces that allow this culture to continue, and in fact flourish. She thus found herself immersed in exploration of the socio-historic context of the campus in a bid to expose and deconstruct notions of patriarchy, myth, aggression, mateship, cultures of silence, power, and control. In the end, her work had shifted to a strongly critical study that attempted to expose the broader social systems that had created a particular cultural reality.

Issues in emancipatory research

There is a level of debate around the intertwining of research goals and political agendas – basically this is because it flies in the face of one of the most well-entrenched 'positivist' rules of research, namely objectivity. It is easy to be accused of confusing social activism with research and an associated inability to manage subjectivities. And although both critical ethnography and PAR sit under a 'post-positivist' umbrella, they nevertheless suffer from this critique and are accused of confusing social activism with research. For those wanting to conduct such studies it will be important to clearly outline your methodological protocols, and call on literature that legitimizes, and acknowledges the importance of, critical agendas in research. Luckily, the proliferation and acceptance of post-positivist methodologies makes this task ever easier.

This said, there is still a need to manage subjectivities. It is one thing to have and work towards a political agenda, but it is another to have it bias the interpretation and analysis of your research. Political agendas may be acceptable, but to have them colour your perception in unrecognized ways will put a question mark over research credibility.

Another, perhaps more problematic critique is the risk of dedicated and motivated researchers imposing their political agenda on the 'marginalized'. Are problems necessarily problems if they are not recognized as such by the researched? Is it the researcher's right to stir this up, even if the goal is liberation and emancipation? Is 'conscientization' always justified? Within a particular culture, a problem identified by Western researchers might not be viewed as a problem by those supposedly affected by it. A huge responsibility in emancipatory research is thus negotiating political agendas that can 'arise from', be 'assigned to', or 'imposed on' the researched.

FURTHER READING

While most students determine their projects with the ultimate goal of change in mind, the majority do not give much consideration to research strategies that see change as a more instrumental goal of the research process itself. I hope this chapter has inspired you to consider at least some approaches that link knowledge and action. If so, have a look at some of the readings listed below. They represent a large range of possibilities for linking research and change.

Evaluation research

Fitzpatrick, J. L., Sanders, J. R., and Worthen, B. R. (2003) *Program Evaluation: Alternative Approaches and Practical Guidelines.* New York: Allyn & Bacon.

Patton, M. Q. (2001) *Qualitative Research and Evaluation Methods.* Thousand Oaks, CA: Sage.

Rossi, P. H., Freeman, H. E., and Lipsey, M. W. (2003) *Evaluation: A Systematic Approach.* Thousand Oaks, CA: Sage.

Royse, D., Thyer, B. A., Padgett, D. K., and Logan, T. K. (2005) *Program Evaluation: An Introduction.* Florence, KY: Brooks Cole.

Wholey, J. S., Hatry, H. P., and Newcomer, K. E. (eds) (2004) *Handbook of Practical Program Evaluation.* Hoboken, NJ: Jossey-Bass.

Action research

Balatti, J., Gargano, I., Goldman, M., Wood, G., and Woodlock, J. (2004) *Improving Indigenous Completion Rates in Mainstream TAFE – An Action Research Approach.* Leabrook, South Australia: NCEAR.

Coghlan, D. and Brannick, T. (2004) *Doing Action Research in Your Own Organization.* London: Sage.

Greenwood, D. and Levin, M. (2006) *Introduction to Action Research: Social Research for Social Change.* Thousand Oaks, CA: Sage.

Herr, K. G. and Anderson, G. L. (2005) *The Action Research Dissertation: A Guide for Students and Faculty.* London: Sage.

McNiff, J. (2002) *You and Your Action Research Project.* Oxford: Taylor & Francis.

McNiff, J. and Whitehead, J. (2002) *Action Research: Principles and Practice.* London: Routledge.

Reason, P. and Bradbury, H. (2006) *Handbook of Action Research.* London: Sage.

Stringer, E. (2007) *Action Research.* Thousand Oaks, CA: Corwin Press.

Emancipatory research

Brown, S. G. and Dobrin, S. I. (eds) (2004) *Ethnography Unbound: From Theory Shock to Critical Praxis.* Albany, NY: State University of New York Press.

(Continued)

(Continued)

Denzin, N. K. (2003) *Performance Ethnography: Critical Pedagogy and the Politics of Culture*. London: Sage.

Fals Borda, O. and Rahman, M. A. (1991) *Action and Knowledge: Breaking the Monopoly with Participatory Action Research*. New York: Intermediate Technology/Apex Press.

Freire, P. (1970) *Pedagogy of the Oppressed*. New York: Herder & Herder.

Kindon, S. (2008) *Participatory Action Research Approaches and Methods: Connecting People, Participation and Place*. London: Routledge.

Madison, D. S. (2005) *Critical Ethnography: Method, Ethics, and Performance*. London: Sage.

McIntyre, A. (2007) *Participatory Action Research*. London: Sage.

Thomas, J. (1993) *Doing Critical Ethnography*. Newbury Park, CA: Sage.

CHAPTER SUMMARY

- All researchers want their research to be useful; the question is whether that usefulness involves the production of knowledge that may some day lead to change, or whether change itself will be a direct product of the research process.
- Evaluative research is undertaken to determine the value of some initiative such as a programme or policy. Findings of evaluative studies are considered crucial to rational and informed decision making.
- Since change intervention strategies often require formal review, evaluation research has become increasingly common. Evaluative studies can relate to outcomes 'Did it work?', or process 'How can the design and implementation of the initiative be improved?'
- Rather than be defined by any particular methodological approach, evaluative goals and perspectives sought determine appropriate methodology.
- Methods that allow for direct comparison, such as experiments and quasi-experiments, can be highly useful when evaluating outcomes that affect target groups, while diverse methods such as interviews, surveys, focus groups, observation, and document review are often called on in process evaluation.
- Evaluative research is highly political, with both stakeholders and researchers having diverse goals and complex relationships. Navigating the politics of evaluation is easiest if client and researcher objectives/expectations are made clear and are openly negotiated.
- Evaluative research takes place in the real world with all its associated complexity. Challenges include: when the decision to evaluate comes after initial implementation; when objectives are not clearly

articulated or readily measurable; when the intervention has not been going long enough to expect results; and when effects of the initiative can be (1) difficult to measure or (2) difficult to attribute to the initiative.

- Action research is dedicated to the integrated production of knowledge and implementation of change. It addresses practical problems, generates knowledge, enacts change, is participatory, and relies on a cyclical self-reflective process.
- A common goal in action research is to empower stakeholders to improve practice by recognizing how they can make a contribution to their own learning and development. It is also utilized at the organizational level in order to improve programmes, policy, and even organizational culture.
- While the participatory and collaborative nature of action research can be highly rewarding and productive, it can also result in a number of management issues, including: facilitating rather than directing; researching with rigour; managing a project's scope, pace, and momentum; managing people; working ethically; being multi-skilled; and negotiating ownership.
- Striving for critical emancipation relates to goals that require more than just change within a 'system'; it requires radical change to the system itself. Two strategies for achieving such goals through research are participatory action research and critical ethnography.
- Participatory action research (PAR) is explicit in its agenda of empowerment. A central goal is to help community groups construct their own knowing in order to create and action their own plan for a better future.
- Critical ethnography also attempts to expose dominant systems in the interest of the 'marginalized'. Change comes from the voice offered to the oppressed, as well as the starting point it offers for action at individual, legislative, and policy levels.
- A common issue in emancipatory research is the intertwining of research and political agendas. In addition to managing subjectivities, researchers need to guard against imposing their own political agendas on the researched.

10
SEEKING 'RESPONDENTS'

CHAPTER PREVIEW

- Who holds the answer?
- Samples: selecting elements of a population
- Key informants: working with experts and insiders
- Cases: delving into detail

WHO HOLDS THE ANSWER?

If the research process is all about getting your research question answered, then it is probably a good idea to think about who might hold the answer to your question. So let's think about this for a minute. In most 'quantitative' models of social science research, what we are after is answers that are held by some population. We want to know what the 'masses' do, think, or feel. In this scenario, answers rest with a broad segment of society. In fact, one of the main reasons we work with quantitative data is because we want to reach such a broad sector of society that gathering qualitative data would not be feasible.

In 'qualitative' models of research, however, the opposite tends to be true. Because we want to preserve powerful text and rich narrative, what we tend to target is answers that are held by the 'few' rather than the 'many'. Yes, answers may still sit with a broad sector of society or within a population, but they might also be held by experts and insiders or even within the experiences of a particular individual. Equally, they might be held within the practices of a setting, say for example, a school or workplace.

No matter what the scenario, it is absolutely crucial to figure out who might hold the answer to your research question and how you will open up opportunities to gather information from those in the know. Respondent groups, however, can be quite diverse, so you may need to employ several strategies for finding those with the answers. Seeking broad societal representation (sampling a population), for example, may be most appropriate. But working with those in the know (by selecting key informants) and delving into the experiences of an individual or a setting (by defining an appropriate case) might be better suited to some qualitative approaches. And of course, as covered in the previous two chapters, there are plenty of research question and research designs that will require you to use more than one strategy.

There are, of course, plenty of challenges. Whether you decide to work with populations, key informants, cases, or a combination of these, locating and accessing respondents who are appropriate, representative, open, honest, knowledgeable, have good memories, are not afraid to expose themselves, and do not feel a need to present themselves in any particular light might be more difficult than you would expect. At times you will need to be systematic. You may decide that what is most appropriate is a defined sampling strategy that can generate a representative sample. At other times, you will need to be strategic. You may decide to turn to where you know you have an 'in' and can call on pre-existing relationships. At all times, you will need to be aware of the complexities of working with others in a bid to fulfil your own research agenda. Whether you decide to work with samples, informants, or cases, there will be plenty of issues and challenges you will need to work through.

SAMPLES: SELECTING ELEMENTS OF A POPULATION

Often the goal in social science research is to understand a population, to get a representative picture of what a particular group of people really do and really think.

POPULATION
The total membership of a defined class of people, objects, or events.

The ultimate in population research is to be able to ask everyone – in other words, to be able to gather data from every element within a population. But with the exception of in-depth research into very small, defined, and accessible populations, or the conduct of a 'census', which is a survey of every element within a population, the goal of asking everyone just isn't practical. Your study will probably involve a population that you cannot reach in its entirety; it will either be too large, or have elements that you simply cannot identify or access.

Yet our inability to access every element of a population does little to suppress our desire to understand and represent it. For example, in our day-to-day lives we might talk about a chain of restaurants or a race of people, but rarely do we do this on the basis of a 'full data set'. We are unlikely to have eaten at every McDonald's, or to have chatted with every Asian person. So what do we do? We gather information from a 'few' in order to capture the thoughts, knowledge, attitudes, feeling, and/or beliefs of the 'many'.

There are parallels in social science research. Rarely do we speak to everyone we wish to speak about, so we sample, investigate, conclude, and attempt to argue the broader applicability of our findings. The trick, however, is being able to apply our findings in a credible manner.

SAMPLING

The process of selecting elements of a population for inclusion in a research study. Many samples attempt to be representative: that is, the sample distribution and characteristics allow findings to be generalized back to the relevant population.

Opportunities in working with a 'sample'

So why would you choose to work with a sample? Well, samples can make the research process manageable. They allow you to explore groups of people, organizations, and events that you simply could not access in their totality. Whether your population is too large, too widely dispersed, too difficult to locate, or too hard to access, sampling can provide you with a window for exploring an unwieldy population.

Sampling can also be used to represent a population with some level of 'confidence'. Certain sampling strategies actually allow you to calculate the statistical probability that your findings are representative of a greater population. Sampling is therefore key to making research affordable and, if done with integrity, also credible.

Sample selection

In the real world, we would not taste a spoonful of spaghetti sauce to determine if the entire pot needs more salt without stirring first. Nor do we go and see the latest Angelina Jolie movie based solely on the comments made on her own website. We recognize that generalization requires appropriate, representative, and unbiased sampling.

The same is true in selecting a research sample. Far from a haphazard activity, sampling is a process that is always strategic, and sometimes mathematical. The goal is to select a sample that is: (1) broad enough to allow you to speak about a parent population; (2) large enough to allow you to conduct the desired analysis; and (3) small enough to be manageable. In studies with goals of generalizability, this will involve using the most practical procedures possible for gathering a sample that best 'represents' a larger population. At other times, however, the nature of the research question may find representativeness unable to be assessed or inappropriate. In these cases, researchers will still strategically select their samples, but in ways that best serve their stated research goals.

Meeting these goals will require you to think through a number of sampling issues including the need to: define your population; construct a sample frame; determine appropriate sample size; and select a suitable sampling strategy.

Defining your population

It is important to have a very clear and well-defined population in mind before you do any sampling. This means you will need to go into your study knowing the total class of 'elements' you want to be able to speak about. For example, say you want to present findings that will be representative of 13–18-year-olds in the UK. Your population here is made up of individuals (the most common type of population in social/applied science research) with a particular set of defining characteristics, in this case both age (13–18) and geography (in the UK). Keep in mind that in a study of individuals you might have used other defining characteristics, such as gender, marital status, race, etc.

And, of course, populations don't always need to be made up of individuals. Depending on the nature of your question, 'elements' of your population might be households, workplaces, or even events. For example, your population might be hospital emergency rooms across the USA. In this case, it is a particular type of organizational setting that makes up the population. Defining characteristics include both geography (across the USA) and type of setting (hospital emergency room). Other possibilities for defining 'organizations' might include number of employees, years of operation, public or private, etc. An example of a population made up of events might be professional soccer matches held in Sydney in 2009. Defining characteristics here are type of activity (professional soccer matches), geography (Sydney) and time period (2009).

Constructing a sample frame

A sample frame is a list that includes every member of the population from which a sample is to be taken, and is essential to all sampling processes. Now ideally, a sample frame would match your target population, but this is rarely the case. Being able to define your population does not guarantee you will have access to every element within it. There are plenty of times when you just cannot get the full 'list'. Listing all homeless people in Washington, DC, for example, would be impossible. That kind of list simply does not exist and cannot be generated with any accuracy.

The key here is to make strategic decisions that ensure your sampling frame is as close to the target population as possible, and to be ready to argue the relevance of your frame despite any discrepancies.

Determining sample size

Once you have come up with the best possible sampling frame, you will need to figure out how many elements from within that frame should be in your sample. And the answer to the question 'how many?' really is, 'it depends'. There are no hard and fast rules. Sample size is highly dependent on the shape and form of the data you wish to collect, and the goals of your analysis.

Statistical analysis of quantitative data, for example, will require a minimum number. Statistics and the ability to work with probabilities rest on adequate and appropriate sample size. On the other hand, the in-depth nature of qualitative data will generally limit sample size; you simply cannot collect that type of data from thousands. But fortunately you don't have to. Qualitative data analysis strategies are not generally dependent on large numbers.

The following guidelines might help you work through the intricacies of determining appropriate sample size:

- *Working with quantitative data/analysis* – When working with quantified data, the basic rule of thumb is to attempt to get as large a sample as possible within time and expense constraints. The larger the sample, the more likely it is to be representative, hence generalizable. Minimum numbers are determined by the level of statistical analysis you wish to do:

  o Minimal statistical analysis: Because statistical analysis is based on probability, the most basic statistical analysis requires a minimum of about 30 respondents; anything smaller and it can be difficult to show statistical significance, particularly if findings are widely distributed. Keep in mind that, with small samples, you will need to argue representativeness.

  o Intermediate statistical analysis: As you move to more sophisticated analysis, the use of any 'subdivisions' will require approximately 25 cases in each category. For example, you may have a sample of 500 members of a particular community, but only 263 females. Out of this, there are 62 mothers with children under 18, and only 20 mothers with children under 5. Statistical analysis of mothers with children under 5 would be difficult. Similarly, if you want to show significance in multivariate analysis (the analysis of simultaneous relationships among several variables), you will need at least 10 cases for each variable you wish to explore.

  o Advanced statistical analysis: If you want to represent a known population with a defined level of confidence, you can actually calculate the required size using the following formula:

$$n = [(K \times S)/E]^2$$
K = desired confidence level
S = sample standard deviation
E = required level of precision

Personally, I do not believe in working formulae unless I have to, so I tend to use a 'sample size calculator' where the only things I need to know are: the population size; the confidence interval (the range you will accept above and below the mean, say ±5%); and the confidence level (how sure you want to be that your findings are more than coincidental, generally 95% or 99%) (see Chapter 13). Table 10.1 was generated with a calculator from www.surveysystem.com/sscalc.htm and gives you some idea of the required sample size for more commonly used confidence levels. Note that as the population increases, shifts in sample size do not increase that dramatically. What does require a significantly increased sample size, however, is a desire for higher levels of confidence.

TABLE 10.1   REQUIRED SAMPLE SIZE

Population	95% ± 5% CI	99% ± 5% CI	99% ± 1% CI
30	28	29	Insufficient
100	80	87	99
500	217	286	485
1,000	278	400	943
5,000	357	588	3,845
10,000	370	624	6,247
50,000	381	657	12,486
100,000	383	661	14,267
1,000,000	384	665	16,369

- *Working with qualitative data* – Many researchers who collect qualitative data in order to understand populations are not looking for representativeness. Their goal is often rich understanding that may come from the few rather than the many. Such studies are reliant on the ability of the researcher to argue the 'relativeness' of any sample (even a single case) to a broader context. For those who want to collect qualitative data from a sample that *does* represent a target population, the challenge is being able to do this in-depth collection from a large enough sample size. There are two strategies you can call on here. The first is to 'handpick' a limited sample using criteria chosen to assure representativeness. For example, selecting your sample based on a clearly defined population profile, i.e. individuals with the average age, income, and education of the population you are studying. Rather than relying on numbers, you will need to logically argue that your sample captures all the various elements/characteristics of your population. The second strategy is to select a sample large enough to allow for minimal statistical analysis. This will give you the option of quantitatively summarizing some of your findings in order to make more mathematical generalizations about your population.

- *Working with both quantitative and qualitative data* – If you are working with both data types, you will find that the nature of collecting qualitative data will limit your sample size. However, any planned statistical analysis will require a minimum number of cases. The best advice is look above to determine the minimum size necessary for any statistical analysis you wish to do, then consider the practicalities of collecting and analysing qualitative data from this sample. Unless you have unlimited time and money, there will usually be some trade off between the collection of rich, in-depth qualitative data and the level of statistical analysis that might be possible.

Keep in mind that all the advice above needs to be checked against the criteria of 'do ability'. Yes, large samples are likely to mean less 'error', but they also mean more money and more time. But this does not mean you can simply cut sample size and forget about 'generalizability'. On the contrary, the credibility of your research needs to be paramount in all methodological considerations. What doability does highlight, however, is the need for credible research to be designed with practicalities firmly in mind.

Employing a sampling strategy

Once you have defined your population, constructed a sample frame, and determined appropriate sample size, it is time to adopt a strategy for gathering your sample. There are two main ways to go about this. The first is to use a strategy for random selection. The second is to use a strategy that aims to strategically select your sample in a non-random fashion. The best method will depend on a number of factors, including the nature of your question, the make-up of your population, the type of data you wish to collect, and your intended modes of analysis.

Random samples

Random samples rely on random selection, or the process by which each element in a population has an equal chance of being selected for inclusion in a sample, e.g. names drawn out of a hat, or computer-generated random numbers. The idea here is that if you have an adequate sample frame and a large enough sample size, random selection will allow you to: control for researcher bias; represent a population; and generalize findings to that population. An example is Nielsen Ratings, which monitor a small percentage of TV viewers' habits but generalize back to the entire population. Random samples are therefore seen as the gold-medal standard in social science research.

At the technical end, the logic of random samples is based on the central limit theorem (CLT). CLT posits that a random sample of observations for any distribution with a finite mean and finite variance will have a mean that follows a normal distribution. This allows researchers to conduct quite sophisticated analysis in the form of inferential statistics (see Chapter 13). Random sampling, however, demands that (1) all elements of a population are known and accessible and that (2) all elements are equally likely to agree to be part of a sample.

If this is not the case, two types of error can occur:

1 *Coverage error* – This is when your sample frame is deficient and does not adequately represent your target population. For example, while every name in the hat has an equal chance of being drawn, if your name belongs in the hat but wasn't put in there, you have a coverage error. This was once a common problem in telephone surveys of households. It was not long ago that many poorer homes did not have a phone, and of course there are still households where this is the case. Surveys reliant on e-mail addresses have a similar problem. Unless a population is defined by the fact that each individual within it has an e-mail address, coverage is likely to be lacking. It is therefore important to consider whether your sample frame is complete and how you can give a voice to any sector of the population that might miss inclusion.

2 *Non-response bias* – This is when those who agree to be in a sample are intrinsically different from those who decline. Non-response is not problematic if the characteristics of those who accept and those who decline are basically the same. But that is not often the case. For example, in customer satisfaction surveys, it might be that those who agree to participate have an axe to grind. Or you may want to offer an inducement that appeals to those with a particular need for, or interest in, what is being offered. In both cases your eventuating sample will not be representative of your population and you will need to come up with strategies that will ensure broad representation.

True (or simple) random samples are actually quite difficult to generate in real-world research, but as shown in Table 10.2, there are several sampling strategies that attempt to approximate a simple random sample.

TABLE 10.2   RANDOM SAMPLING

Simple random sampling

- Involves identifying all elements of a population, listing those elements, and randomly selecting from the list
- All elements have an equal chance of inclusion
- Considered 'fair', and allows for generalization
- Rarely used in practice because the process of identifying, listing, and randomly selecting elements is often unfeasible
- Resulting samples may not capture enough elements of particular subgroups you are interested in studying

Systematic sampling

- Involves selecting every *n*th case within a defined population. For example, going to every 10th house or selecting every 20th person on a list
- Easier to do than devising methods for random selection
- Offers a close approximation of random sampling as long as elements are not in a particular order, i.e. you would not have a random approximation if you were to go to every 10th house, which just happened to always be a detached home on the corner, in a neighbourhood with lots of duplexes

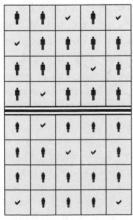

Stratified sampling

- Involves dividing your population into various subgroups and taking a random sample within each one
- Ensures your sample represents key subgroups of the population, i.e. males and females
- Representation of the subgroups can be *proportionate* or *disproportionate*, i.e. if you wanted to sample 100 nurses with a population of 80% females and 20% males, a proportionate stratified sample would be made up of 80 females and 20 males. In a disproportionate stratified sample you would use a ratio different to the population, e.g. 50 males and 50 females
- Stratification can be used in conjunction with systematic as well as random sampling

(Continued)

TABLE 10.2   *(Continued)*

Cluster sampling
- Involves surveying whole clusters of the population
- Clusters can include schools, hospitals, regions, etc.
- Clusters are sampled so that individuals within them can be surveyed/interviewed. The thinking here is that the best way to find high school students is through high schools; the best way to find hospital patients is through hospitals
- Often conducted in multiple stages, i.e. if your population is hospital patients in Australia you would use a random sampling strategy to select regions across Australia, then use a sampling strategy to select a number of hospitals within these regions, before employing another sampling strategy to select your final patients from these selected hospitals
- Full population lists are not required, and eventuating samples can be geographically contained

Non-random samples

Non-random samples are just that – they are samples that are not drawn in a random fashion. Now there are some quantitative researchers that view non-random samples as inferior because they cannot be statistically assessed for representativeness. For these researchers, 'non-random' implies samples that are gathered through strategies seen as second best or last resort.

There is growing recognition, however, that there is no longer a need to 'apologize' for these types of samples. Researchers using non-random samples may be involved in studies that are not working towards representativeness or generalizability. They may be selecting their sample for other defined purposes common in 'qualitative' research. For example, they may be looking to include deviant, extreme, unique, unfamiliar, misunderstood, misrepresented, marginalized, or unheard elements of a population. This is why non-random samples are sometimes called 'purposive' or 'theoretical' samples.

There is also growing recognition that non-random samples can credibly represent populations if: (1) selection is done with the goal of representativeness in mind; and (2) strategies are used to ensure samples match population characteristics. When working with populations that are hard to define and/or access (e.g. homeless women or sports people who have used steroids) non-random strategies may be the best option. There is, however, an added burden of responsibility in ensuring that eventuating samples are not biased. Specifically, researchers who are after representativeness need to be aware of unwitting bias and erroneous assumptions.

- *Unwitting bias* – This is the tendency to unwittingly act in ways that confirm what you might already suspect, something that can be quite easy to do when you are handpicking your sample. For example, you may want to conduct a focus group that can help evaluate an initiative you have started in your workplace; unless you make a conscious decision to do otherwise, it is just too easy to stack the deck in your favour. Or in a study of sexually active teenagers, you may be drawn to those whose experiences tend to re-enforce your belief that, say, parental conflict is related to sexual promiscuity. You unwittingly seek out teenagers whose history matches your preconceived notions. In both cases, any generalization will not be credible.

- *Erroneous assumptions* – This refers to sample selection premised on incorrect assumptions. For example, say you want to study Jewish women living in Detroit and you decide to go to Detroit's synagogues to look for volunteers. The problem is that you have assumed all Jewish women go to a synagogue. You might also make erroneous assumptions about the characteristics of 'elements' within your sample. Say, for example, you want to study teenage 'angst' and you select what you believe are extreme cases of angst. If your assumptions are incorrect and what you see as extreme is actually quite average, the generalizations you make will not be valid.

In order to control for such biases, it is worth brainstorming your assumptions and expectations as they relate to both your research questions and your sample. This will put you in a strong position to work towards the development of an appropriate sampling strategy.

Table 10.3 highlights a range of non-random sampling strategies. While they can be used to build representative samples, these strategies can also be called upon in studies that do not rely on representativeness, for example, when the goal is to build knowledge by working with cases and/or key informants.

KEY INFORMANTS: WORKING WITH EXPERTS AND INSIDERS

There is no doubt that social science research has a bias towards samples, particularly representative samples. Because we can make arguments about generalizability, we think this is where we need to go in order to gather credible data. But the goal in rigorous research is to determine the best possible means for credible data collection, and, depending on your question, this might just mean working with key informants rather than samples.

Working with key informants means attempting to gather some insider or expert knowledge that goes beyond the private experiences, beliefs, and knowledge base of the individual you are talking to. Your goal is to find out what this individual believes 'others' think, or how 'others' behave, or what this individual thinks the realities of a particular situation might be. Working with key informants means you believe the answers to your research questions lie with select individuals who have specialized knowledge and know what's going on.

But then again, who really knows what's going on? I will use my workplace as an example. If you were investigating my little academic world, I would not bother asking me anything, I am just not in the know. In fact, I try very hard to stay out of the loop. I would actually recommend talking to my Head of School or the Dean – but then again they may end up giving you the party line; when you work at that level, you are sometimes forced to call on rhetoric. Wait, here is an idea: you should talk to Joycee from administration. She is an institution unto herself, and if anyone knows

TABLE 10.3   NON-RANDOM SAMPLING

Handpicked sampling
- Involves the selection of a sample with a particular purpose in mind
- Representativeness will depend on the researcher's ability to select cases that meet particular criteria including typicality, wide variance, 'expertise', etc.
- Other options include the selection of critical, extreme, deviant, or politically important cases. While not likely to be representative, the selection of such cases allows researchers to study intrinsically interesting cases, or enhance learning by exploring the limits or boundaries of a situation or phenomenon

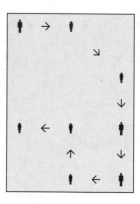

Snowball sampling
- Involves building a sample through referrals
- Once an initial respondent is identified, you ask him or her to identify others who meet the study criteria. Each of those individuals is then asked for further recommendations
- Often used when working with populations that are not easily identified or accessed, i.e. a population of homeless persons can be hard to identify, but by using referrals a sample can build quite quickly
- Snowballing does not guarantee representativeness. An option here is to develop a population profile from the literature, and assess representativeness by comparing your sample with your profile

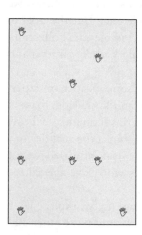

Volunteer sampling
- Involves selecting a sample by asking for volunteers. For example, putting an ad in the newspaper or going to local organizations such as schools or community groups
- While convenient, it is not likely to be representative. The characteristics of those who volunteer are likely to be quite distinct from those who do not
- Arguments for representativeness will rely on strategies used to minimize the difference between volunteers and the rest of the population

A note on 'convenience' sampling
In the course of your reading, you may have come across something referred to as 'convenience' sampling: that is, selecting a sample in a manner convenient to the researcher. In fact, non-random sampling is sometimes referred to in this way. But keep in mind that convenience sampling has no place in credible research

TABLE 10.3   *(Continued)*

There needs to be more to a sampling strategy than just convenience –
yes, limited time and resources may see convenience as *one* factor in
sample selection. But convenience should not be the main criterion or
descriptor of a sampling strategy. Regardless of type, all sampling
strategies need to work towards the ultimate goal of research credibility

what's going on, it's her. While she does not have official 'power', she does have
knowledge – which, of course, is a form of power in its own right.

This type of scenario tends to be the case in almost any institution, organization, or community group you might want to explore. There tend to be people
'in the know'. Whether through a position of power or some less official means,
some people have a knack for knowing what's really going on. So it is not unusual
for 'experts' or 'insiders' to be precisely the right people to help you answer your
research questions.

KEY INFORMANTS
Individuals whose role or experiences result in them having relevant information or
knowledge they are willing to share with a researcher.

Opportunities in working with key informants

There is nothing like having an inside track or having an expert at your fingertips.
In fact, key informants can be instrumental in giving you access to a world you might
have otherwise tried to understand while being locked on the outside. The insights
you can gather from one key informant can be instrumental not only to the data you
collect, but to how you process that data, and how you might make sense of your
own experiences as well as the experiences of others.

Now this does not mean that all your data should come from key informants.
Informants may end up being just one resource in your bid to build understandings –
but they can do this in several ways. Key informants can:

- *Be instrumental to preliminary phases of an investigation* – Key informants can be called
  upon by researchers to build their own contextual knowledge. They might also be
  used to help generate relevant interview questions, or be called on to aid in the
  construction or review of a survey instrument.
- *Be used to triangulate or confirm the accuracy of gathered/generated data* – Data from
  interviews with key informants can be used to confirm the authenticity of other
  data sources such as data gathered by survey, observation, or document review.
  Key informants might also be called upon in a less formal way to overview data
  to confirm credibility, or to explore researcher interpretations for misunderstandings,
  misinterpretations, or unrecognized bias.
- *Be used to generate primary data* – In-depth interviews with key informants can also
  be a primary source of qualitative data in its own right.

Informant selection

There are six distinct challenges you need to face before you can work with key informants. The first is to identify the type of informant you are after. Now it is important to recognize that key informants do not need to be foremost experts. There are a number of characteristics that might make someone useful to your research processes. Depending on your research question and context, any or all of the following might have something to offer:

- *Experts* – The well respected who sit at the top of their field.
- *Insiders* – Those who sit on the inside of an organization, culture, or community and who are willing to share the realities of that environment.
- *The highly experienced* – Perhaps not deemed an expert, but someone with a rich depth of experience related to what you are exploring.
- *A leader* – This might be at a formal or informal level.
- *The observant* – Individuals in an organization or community who have a reputation for knowing who's who and what's what.
- *The gossip* – Similar to the observant but enjoy passing on observations (and sometimes rumours); it will pay to make sure your information here is accurate.
- *Those with secondary experience* – For example, if exploring the problem of youth suicide, in addition to youth, you might look to certain counsellors, teachers, or parents to provide relevant insights.
- *Stool pigeons* – Individuals who want to be classic police-type 'informants'; you will need to be wary of both overt and hidden agendas!
- *The ex* – This might include someone who is disenfranchised, alienated, recovered, converted, retrenched, fired, or retired.

The second challenge is to identify individuals who have the characteristics associated with that type. It makes sense to ask around or try a snowball technique in which you generate a list of informants through a referral process (see Table 10.3). One person in the know is likely to lead you to a host of others.

The third challenge is to confirm the status of those identified. Do they really have the expertise, experiences, or insider knowledge that will inform your study in a credible way? The advice here is to seek confirmation by looking for things like a long record of involvement, direct personal experiences, and detailed comments from potential informants that show internal consistency. You are after more than just broad generalizations.

The fourth challenge is related to your ability to gather open and honest information from your informants. Key informants must be accessible and willing to share information. If they have the knowledge you are after, but are not willing to share it, they will not be of any use to your study. Building trust (see Chapter 3) will be essential.

The fifth challenge is to look for and recognize informant subjectivities. All respondents will have a particular worldview and some will have a real agenda operating. Some may want to be listened to, some may have an axe to grind, some may like the sound of their own voice, some think they know a lot more than they do, and some think their particular take on an experience is how the world should or

TABLE 10.4 KEY INFORMANTS: OPPORTUNITIES AND ETHICAL DILEMMAS

Opportunities	Ethical dilemmas
Building relationships of trust to enhance flow of information	• Having informants become too emotionally invested • Developing friendships that are one way • Making promises you cannot or do not intend to keep
Gaining the ability to avoid or skirt around official channels and protocols	• Putting informants in an unethical position • Acting unethically in regard to the organization you might be exploring
Being able to get your hands on confidential information	• Asking for, expecting, or accepting illegal/unethical conduct from your informants • Acting unethically, and possibly illegally, in regard to the organization you are exploring
Being able to really dig into the emotional aspects of a topic	• Asking your informant to make a large emotional investment • Having your informant relate private and personal details of others • Asking your informants to relive their own unpleasant memories

does respond to the same experience (sounds like a family reunion!). You will need to develop and build a strong relationship with your key informants, not only so they can open up to you, but so you are in a position to know how to best treat the data they provide.

The final challenge is related to ethics. If you look at the list of informant types above and think about their motivation, it should be pretty obvious that ethics and integrity need to come into play when selecting and working with key informants. In addition to the challenge of managing bias (both yours and theirs), you will need to think about your power as a researcher. You have to remember that key informants can be put, and can put themselves, in very vulnerable positions. It is your responsibility to respect their needs at all times.

Table 10.4 highlights some of the ethical issues you will need to negotiate when selecting and working with key informants.

CASES: DELVING INTO DETAIL

When it comes to respondents, how many is really enough: 100, 200, 1,500? Well, these are the kinds of numbers we think of when we think of samples/respondents. Even in 'qualitative' research we are looking at 10, 20, 30 interviews. But what about one or two? Can one or two ever be enough? Can it ever be more than thin? Well when I was a student, a professor once told me that if I were to do a PhD that surveyed 1,500 people, he might expect me to generate between 1,500 and 3,000 pages of data. He then asked me how much data I thought he would expect from a single case study. I really had no idea, and guessed 200–300 pages. He told me, 'No, 1,500–3,000 pages, same as the survey.'

In other words, he was telling me there is no shortcut. A case study is all about depth; it requires you to dig, and to dig deep. You need to delve into detail, dig into context, and really get a handle on the rich experiences of the individual, event, community group, or organization you want to explore. The goal is to get underneath what is generally possible in, for example, large-scale survey research.

If you think the answer to your research question might require this type of in-depth exploration, then legitimate, valid, and worthwhile answers might just be held by or within a particular 'case'.

CASE

A bounded system, or a particular instance or entity that can be defined by identifiable boundaries.

CASE STUDY

A method of studying elements of the social through comprehensive description and analysis of a single situation or case, e.g. a detailed study of an individual, setting, group, episode, or event. Case study research can refer to single and multiple case studies.

Opportunities in working with cases

The use of cases in social science project research is more common than you might realize. Researchers often limit their methodological design to a particular context in a bid to maximize both relevance and practicality. At the practical end, cases are often located in one site, which means travel is minimized, access is enhanced, and costs are reduced. But more importantly, it allows for the building of holistic understandings through prolonged engagement and the development of rapport and trust within a clearly defined and highly relevant context.

Prolonged engagement and immersion, however, can involve its own 'costs'. For one, the required level of access can be difficult to negotiate. Second, because case studies draw from only one or even a few, the demands on that one or few can be quite high. Third, researchers can come to have an effect on the researched and vice versa. Finally, immersion can come with emotional costs for all parties involved.

Now if you decide to tackle a case study, you may come across an individual who just won't give the time of day to any study not deemed to be representative or generalizable. But if you can clearly articulate your goals and show how your study contributes to a particular body of knowledge, you are more likely to establish credibility and worth. Cases can:

- *Have an intrinsic value* – Cases might be extremely relevant, politically 'hot', unique, interesting, or even misunderstood, e.g. exploring a cult undergoing high media scrutiny.
- *Be used to debunk a theory* – One case can show that what is commonly accepted might, in fact, be wrong; for example, societal assumptions related to violence in prison can be called into question through in-depth case exploration that attempts to understand the phenomenon from a prisoner's perspective.

- *Bring new variables to light* – Exploratory case studies can often bring new understandings to the fore; for example, in-depth exploration of a particular hospital emergency room might uncover new staff stressors yet to be identified in the literature.
- *Provide supportive evidence for a theory* – Case studies can be used to triangulate other data collection methods or to provide support for a theory; for example, a particular organization might be explored as a lived example of a twenty-first-century learning organization.
- *Be used collectively to form the basis of a theory* – A number of cases may be used to inductively generate new understandings; for example, finding empowerment as a common theme in the ability to recover from the stress of divorce might be the basis of new insights.

Case studies can also allow researchers to bust through the quantitative/qualitative divide. In a case study of an organization, for example, strategies for data collection could easily include both survey research and in-depth interviewing.

Case selection

If you think your research question can be illuminated by delving into cases, you will need to turn your attention to the process of case selection. Now there are two distinct processes involved here. The first is to define your case, or to set the boundaries that will give meaning and characterization to the class of 'elements' you wish to explore. The second involves selecting an individual case or series of cases that meet your definition and sit within your case boundaries.

To define a case, you need to set clear and distinctive characteristics. Perhaps the broadest and easiest distinction here is to decide if your cases will be made up of individuals, institutions, events, cultural groups, etc. Will you be looking at people, places, or things? Once this is determined, more specific criteria can be applied. For example, if your cases will be made up of individuals, you might turn to characteristics such as employment status, gender, or race to narrow the case description. If you are looking at institutions, you might look at function (factory, hospital, school, etc.), location, or size. Cultural groups (groups bound together by social traditions and common patterns of beliefs and behaviours) can be further defined by things like geography, social networks, or shared hardships. Finally, for events, defining characteristics will be the nature of the event as well as things like timeframe, geography, and size.

As shown in Figure 10.1, possibilities are wide open. The only criteria are that your boundaries are clear, and you are able to argue the importance of case exploration within those boundaries.

Once your class of cases has been defined, your boundaries are clear, and you know precisely what it is that you are trying to delve into, you will need to select the right case (or cases) from the range of possibilities. Now depending on your goals, you may decide to delve into only one case, or you may want to compare and contrast two or more cases. You might also decide to analyse a number of cases in order to make broader generalizations.

INDIVIDUALS	Defined by characteristics such as... • Gender, race, class • Education • Experiences • Employment • Geography i.e. inner city high school students or hospital patients with depression	**INSTITUTIONS**	Defined by characteristics such as... • Function • Public/private • Size • Location i.e. households in a rural area, local government offices, or large factories in Asia
CULTURAL GROUPS	Defined by characteristics such as... • Race, class, gender • Language • Experiences • Employment • Social networks • Geography i.e. students living in a boarding school or members of a cult	**EVENTS**	Defined by characteristics such as... • Nature • Size • Timeline/timeframe • Location i.e. anti-war protests in the USA or soccer riots in the UK

FIGURE 10.1   DEFINING A CASE

After determining the appropriate number of cases to be explored, the selection of any particular case or cases is generally done through a strategic process with researchers often handpicking cases with a particular purpose in mind. Factors that will influence case selection include:

- *Pragmatics* – There is nothing wrong with being practical. Pragmatics can involve commitments such as being commissioned/sponsored to study a particular case. They might also involve timely opportunities that see you take advantage of current events and work at being in the right place at the right time, e.g. studying a community recovering from a flood event, or exploring a recent sports-related riot. Pragmatics can also involve accessibility where you take advantage of access that might normally be hard to get, e.g. exploring a case that has connections to your own workplace, or delving into a case involving an individual with whom you have an existing relationship based on mutual trust and respect.
- *Purposiveness* – Researchers will often select cases they hope will enable them to make particular arguments. For example, if the purpose is to argue representativeness, you may select a case considered 'typical'. 'Extreme' or 'atypical' instances may be chosen in order to debunk a theory or highlight deviations from the norm, while wide variance in cases might be used to build new understandings and generate theory. The section on non-random sampling at the beginning of this chapter provides strategies that can be used in purposive case selection.
- *Intrinsic interest* – Researchers might also select a particular case because it is interesting in its own right. It might be relevant, unique, unfamiliar, misunderstood,

misrepresented, marginalized, unheard, politically hot, or the focus of current media attention. In this situation, the challenge is to argue the inherent worth and value of a particular case.

It is worth keeping in mind that a prerequisite to all case selection should be access. It is absolutely essential that researchers who wish to delve into cases will be able to reach required people and data. When working with individuals, your ability to generate rich data will depend on building high levels of trust and rapport. In an organizational setting, you may need to gain high-level access to relevant records and documents or be allowed broad access to an array of individuals associated with a case. In fact, organizational case studies may require you to seek respondents from within the case itself. This can see you searching for both key informants and samples as discussed earlier in the chapter. No matter what the situation, the holistic understanding and rich detail demanded in case studies will require you to have access to what is going on 'inside'.

FURTHER READING

While there is plenty of literature that can help you in your quest to work with both samples and cases, it is much more difficult to find literature that deals directly with key informants. You can, however, extrapolate quite a bit from readings on both 'non-random' sampling and case selection.

Samples/sampling

Dorofeev, S. and Grant, P. (2006) *Statistics for Real-Life Sample Surveys: Non-Simple-Random Samples and Weighted Data*. Cambridge: Cambridge University Press.

Levy, P. S. and Lemeshow, S. (2008) *Sampling of Populations: Methods and Applications*. New York: Wiley-Interscience.

Rao, P. S., Rao, R. S., Poduri, S. R. S., and Miller, W. (2000) *Sampling Methodologies with Applications*. New York: Lewis.

Schaeffer III, R. L. and Mendenhall, W. (2005) *Elementary Survey Sampling*. Belmont, CA: Duxbury.

Thompson, S. K. (2002) *Sampling*. New York: John Wiley & Sons.

Tortu, S., Goldsamt, L. A., and Hamid, R. (eds) (2001) *A Practical Guide to Research and Services with Hidden Populations*. Boston, MA: Allyn & Bacon.

Wainer, H. (2000) *Drawing Inferences from Self-selected Samples*. Mahwah, NJ: Lawrence Erlbaum.

(Continued)

(Continued)

Cases/case studies

Gerring, J. (2006) *Case Study Research: Principles and Practices.* Cambridge: Cambridge University Press.

Hammersley, M., Foster, R., and Gomm, R. (2000) *Case Study Method: Key Issues, Key Texts.* London: Sage.

Hancock, D. R. and Algozzine, R. (2006) *Doing Case Study Research: A Practical Guide for Beginning Researchers.* New York: Teachers College Press.

Tavers, M. (2001) *Qualitative Research through Case Studies.* London: Sage.

Yin, R. K. (2008) *Case Study Research: Design and Methods.* Thousand Oaks, CA: Sage.

CHAPTER SUMMARY

- Knowing who might hold the answer to your questions and how you will open up opportunities to gather information from them is fundamental to collecting credible data.
- Whether you decide to work with populations, key informants, cases, or a combination of these, locating and accessing respondents and being able to elicit credible information might be more difficult than you would expect.
- Sampling allows us to gather information from a 'few' in order to capture the thoughts, knowledge, attitudes, feeling, and/or beliefs of the 'many' and makes the research process manageable.
- Sample selection involves defining your population, constructing a sample frame, determining sample size, and employing an appropriate sampling strategy.
- In random sampling the aim is to generate a representative sample. In order to accomplish this, every element of a population has an equal chance of sample selection. Strategies include simple random sampling, systematic sampling, stratified random sampling, and cluster sampling.
- There are two common errors in random sampling: coverage error, where the list you draw your sample from is incomplete; and non-response bias, when the characteristics of those who accept and those who decline participation are distinct.
- In non-random sampling, respondents can be handpicked, they can be found through snowball techniques, or they may volunteer. To select a sample on the basis of convenience alone can threaten a study's credibility.
- Non-random sampling strategies are not always used to generate representative samples. Researchers with that goal, however, need to consider

the issues of: unwitting bias – drawing samples that confirm preconceived notions; and erroneous assumptions – sample selection premised on incorrect suppositions.

- Key informants can be a valuable source of information in project research. They can be used in preliminary phases of an investigation; to triangulate and confirm data; or as a primary source of data in its own right.
- Informant selection can involve individuals in any variety of roles, including experts, the experienced, leaders, the observant, gossips, those with secondary experience, insiders, stool pigeons, and 'ex's.
- Six challenges you will need to meet in selecting and working with key informants include: (1) indentifying various informant types; (2) identifying potential informants; (3) confirming the status of those identified; (4) building trust; (5) negotiating potential informant agendas; and (6) remembering ethical responsibilities.
- Studying elements of the social through comprehensive description and analysis of a single situation or case is called a case study. While not necessarily representative, cases can add to new knowledge through their ability to debunk theory, generate theory, and support existing theory.
- Case selection involves defining your case and selecting an individual case or series of cases that meet your definition and sit within your case boundaries.
- The selection of any particular case can be made on the basis of pragmatics (such as commitments, opportunities, and access); purposefulness (to facilitate the ability to make relevant arguments); and/or intrinsic interest.

11
DIRECT DATA COLLECTION: SURVEYS AND INTERVIEWS

CHAPTER PREVIEW

- The challenge of getting data directly from the source
- Surveying
- Interviewing

THE CHALLENGE OF GETTING DATA DIRECTLY FROM THE SOURCE

There is no doubt that surveys and interviews are methods of choice in social science data collection. After all, surveys and interviews put the researcher in charge. Not only do you get to ask what you want, you also get to ask it how you want, i.e. you get to choose the wording, the order, the prompts, the probes. And because your data collection can be directed to match your research question, hypothesis, aims, and objectives with some precision, this has real appeal. The data collected is not superfluous but is, in fact, custom built for your research project.

Sounds great – which is precisely why so many project students opt for these approaches. But they're not without stumbling blocks. If you want survey and interview data to be credible, you will need to put in the time and effort to learn all the ins and outs of these methods.

SURVEYING

You are probably all too familiar with surveys and surveying. I hate to admit it, but when I was an undergraduate at Rutgers University, I actually worked for a market research company. Yes, I was one of those highly annoying people who called in the middle of dinner and asked if you would mind 'answering just a few short questions that should only take a couple of moments of your time'. As the French author de Certeau said, 'surveys are everywhere' (2002). Market research, political polling, customer service feedback, evaluations, opinion polls, social science research – when we want to know what the masses are thinking, we survey.

SURVEYING
The process of collecting data by asking a range of individuals the same questions related to their characteristics, attributes, how they live, or their opinions through a questionnaire.

Options and possibilities

You may think all surveys are the same, but they're not. In fact, in order to determine which approach best suits you and your research agenda, you will need to work through several key issues. As shown in Table 11.1, the survey approach you adopt will

TABLE 11.1   SURVEY ISSUES AND TYPES

Do you plan to sample or ask everyone in your population?

Census: a survey that does not rely on a sample. In other words, a survey that covers every single person in a defined population	The US Census is a good example. A smaller scale census might be all the students in a particular school
Cross-sectional surveys: surveys that use a sample or cross-section of respondents. The goal is to be able to represent your target population and generalize findings back to that population	Most surveys fall under this category, e.g. a community survey that targets only 1 in 10 households but aims to represent the entire community

Will your survey simply describe or attempt to explain?

Descriptive surveys: the goal is to get a snapshot or to describe your respondents by gathering: demographic information, i.e. age, socio-economic status, and gender; personal information/behaviours, i.e. voting patterns or use of illegal drugs; and attitudinal information, i.e. attitudes towards multinational corporations, abortion, or health care costs	A classic example here is political polling, which attempts to describe voters and voter intentions
Explanatory surveys: the goal is to build complex understandings that go beyond description or even correlation. The aim is to figure out why things might be the way they are; in other words, determine cause and effect	An Australian newspaper recently conducted a survey that collected data describing attitudes to the Iraq conflict as well as data used to establish what might shape and form those attitudes, e.g. personal experience, familial attitudes, and political leanings

Will you survey over a period of time and, if so, do you want to explore changing times or changing people?

Trend surveys: a trend survey asks the same cross-section (similar groups of respondents)	An example here is a three-phase survey conducted over a 20-year period (1989, 1999,

(Continued)

TABLE 11.1   *(Continued)*

the same questions at two or more points in time. The goal here is to see if classifications of individuals change over time	2009) that asks newlyweds their attitudes towards marriage. The goal is to assess if attitudes of newlyweds now are the same as attitudes of newlyweds in the late 1980s and 1990s
Panel study: a panel study involves asking the same (not similar) sample of respondents the same questions at two or more points in time. The goal here is to see if individuals themselves change over time	Using the example above, if you had surveyed newlyweds in 1989, you would survey these same individuals in 1999 (10 years after their marriage) and again in 2009 in order to assess attitudinal shifts as individuals get older

How do you plan to administer your survey?

Face-to-face surveys *Pros:* good response rate, allows rapport and trust to be established, can motivate respondents, allows for clarification, prompting, probing, and the reading of non-verbal cues *Cons:* can be lengthy and expensive, limits geographical range, does not assure anonymity or confidentiality, and requires surveyor training	One example here is the mall or supermarket survey where you are stopped by someone with a clipboard ready to ask you a series of questions
Telephone surveys *Pros:* relatively inexpensive, allows wide geographic coverage, offers some assurance of anonymity and confidentiality, and allows for some clarification, prompting, probing *Cons:* response rate can be low, it is easy to catch people at a bad time, respondents can hang up on you if they've had enough, and you are limited to surveying only those with a telephone	In market research the telephone tends to be the mode of choice – but as more and more individuals get annoyed by this, it becomes harder for social science researchers to get individuals to participate over the phone
Self-administered surveys *Pros:* can offer confidentiality/anonymity, allows wide geographic coverage, and gives respondents the opportunity to answer in their own time *Cons:* response rates can be very low, does not allow for clarification, and can end up being costly	These can include both snail mail and e-mail. E-mail can save you thousands in printing and postage costs, but you are limited to surveying within online populations. Additionally, the proliferation of spam mail means that unless your respondents know you, your survey may not even get looked at

be dependent upon whether you want to: sample a range of respondents or target everyone in your population; describe or explain; capture a moment, changing times, or changing people; administer face-to-face, or by mail, e-mail or phone.

Issues and complexities

When it comes to the collection of credible data, there are no easy answers. There will always be tradeoffs between opportunities and challenges, and this is certainly true when it comes to surveying. While surveys can offer much to the production of knowledge, their reputation for being a relatively simple, straightforward, and inexpensive approach is not really deserved – they can be a thorny and exasperating process, particularly if you want to do it right.

On the plus side, surveys can:

- reach a large number of respondents
- represent an even larger population
- allow for comparisons
- generate standardized, quantifiable, empirical data
- generate qualitative data through the use of open-ended questions
- be confidential and even anonymous.

On the downside, constructing and administering a survey that has the potential to generate credible and generalizable data is truly difficult. As you probably realize, there are a lot of crappy surveys out there that aren't worth the paper they are printed on, yet the data they generate is reported as truth and used in all kinds of decision-making processes.

Challenges associated with surveying include:

- capturing the quantifiable data you require
- gathering in-depth data
- getting a representative sample to respond
- getting anyone at all to respond!
- needing proficiency in statistical analysis
- only getting answers to the questions you have thought to ask
- going back to your respondents if more data is required.

The survey process

Conducting a good survey is a process that involves a whole lot of steps. Surveys require you to: plan your attack; develop your survey instrument; pilot your approach; make necessary modifications; administer; and manage/analyse your data. Box 11.1 breaks this down and outlines the 29+ steps (some you will need to do more than once) involved in surveying. You should find this box helpful as both a guide and a checklist.

BOX 11.1   STEPS (AND THERE ARE A LOT) FOR CONDUCTING A 'GOOD' SURVEY

A: PLANNING – CONSIDERATION OF 'WHO', 'WHERE', 'WHEN', 'HOW', AND 'WHAT'

The success of your survey will hinge on the forethought you put into the planning process.

1 **Population and sample/respondent/participants** – who you plan to speak about (population), and gather data from (sample) (see Chapter 10).

(Continued)

(Continued)

2 **Access** – how you will reach your sample. This includes considering any language or cultural barriers that might limit access.

3 **Your biases** – recognizing and controlling for subjectivities in ways that can best ensure the credibility of any survey instrument you use.

4 **Your skills** – how you might develop the skills/resources needed to carry out your survey, i.e. statistics proficiency.

5 **Ethics/ethics approval** – consideration of any ethical dilemmas inherent in your project, and getting appropriate ethics approval.

6 **Data** – thinking through the aspects of your research question that can be answered through a questionnaire. Also considering if the shape and form of the data you will collect will be compatible with intended modes of analysis.

7 **Details** – distribution, reminders, response rates, and data management.

8 **Contingencies** – the unexpected, the unplanned, and the unfortunate. This means having a back-up plan ready to go if response rates are low.

B: DEVELOPING YOUR QUESTIONNAIRE

This is covered more fully in the following section, but, in short, involves the need to:

9 **Operationalize concepts** – this involves going from abstract concepts to variables that can be measured/assessed through your survey; for example, the exact measure of poverty or environmental citizenship that your survey will capture.

10 **Explore existing possibilities** – you don't need to reinvent the wheel. If an existing survey instrument has addressed your variables, see if you can adopt, adapt, and modify.

11 **Draft questions** – have a shot at drafting new questions as clearly as possible.

12 **Decide on response categories** – consider both the effect of response categories on responses themselves and how various response categories translate to different data types that demand quite distinct statistical treatment.

13 **Review** – carefully read each question and response choices and think about whether your questions might be considered ambiguous, leading, confronting, offensive, based on unwarranted assumptions, double-barrelled, or pretentious.

14 **Rewrite questions** – run them past a few peers/supervisors for assessment. Repeat this step as many times as necessary to get each question as right as possible.

15 **Order questions** – put questions in an order that will be logical and ease respondents into your survey.

16 **Write instructions** – make these as clear and unambiguous as possible.

17 **Lay out** – construct a clear, logical, professional, and aesthetically pleasing layout and design.

18 **Write a cover letter/introductory statement** – this generally includes information on who you are, your projects aims and objectives, assurances of confidentiality/anonymity, and whether results will be available to participants.

C: PILOTING – CONDUCTING A 'TRIAL'

Good planning and development is essential – but not sufficient. The only way really to know if something is going to work is to give it a try.

19 **Have a run-through** – pilot your process with a group of respondents whose background is similar to those in your 'sample'.
20 **Reflect** – reflect on the piloting process and note any difficulties you encounter. Also review your data and note any difficulties in making sense of your completed surveys.
21 **Seek feedback** – get feedback from the pilot group in relation to the effectiveness of the cover letter, the overall layout and design, the usefulness of the instructions, the question wording, and the length of time it took to complete the questionnaire.
22 **Trial your stats package** – attempt to create variables, code the pilot responses, and then enter them into a statistical program to see if you are likely to encounter any issues when you input your main data.

D: MODIFYING – REFINING YOUR APPROACH

Review and refine until you are comfortable with the process and data collected.

23 **Make modifications** – this will be based on your reflections, the feedback from your pilot group, as well as the quality of the data generated.
24 **Back to the start?** – if the need for modification is substantial, you may need to revisit your planning, development, and piloting process. This may involve a return to the ethics committee.

E: IMPLEMENTING – SURVEY ADMINISTRATION

Most researchers want to get to this point as quickly as possible, and some are willing to short-cut some of the steps above, but this is a sure-fire way to get into trouble.

25 **Administration** – time to distribute your questionnaires. Be sure to include instructions for return (address and return date) and possibly a self-addressed stamped envelope.
26 **Reminder letters** – send these out if response rates are low.
27 **Low-response-rate plan** – put this into action if not enough data has been gathered by your deadline.

F: MANAGING AND ANALYSING – KEEPING TRACK AND MAKING SENSE

Unless your data is effectively managed and thoughtfully analysed, all the hard work above will be wasted.

(Continued)

(Continued)

28 **Organize/collate your data as soon as possible** – when the time comes to work with your data, nothing is worse than a big mess. Be systematic and organized, use a database if appropriate, and enter data expediently.

29 **Analysis** – time to see what your data yields. Most survey data will be analysed statistically (see Chapter 13), but you will need to engage in thematic analysis for any open-ended questions (see Chapter 14).

The survey instrument

Students often underestimate the difficulty of constructing a good survey instrument. The best advice is to take it in steps, pilot, and get lots of feedback. It is almost impossible to get a questionnaire right the first time around. As discussed below, developing a questionnaire will require you to: (1) operationalize your concepts; (2) formulate your questions; (3) decide on response categories; (4) provide background information and clear instructions; (5) decide on organization and length: and finally (6) create aesthetically pleasing layout and design – all of which need to be done in conjunction with several stages of piloting and redevelopment.

Concept operationalization

Operationalizing concepts refers to turning abstract concepts into measurable variables. For example, say you wanted to conduct a survey that could help you determine if old-fashioned parenting was a cause of teenage rebellion. Your abstract concepts would be 'old-fashioned parenting' and 'teenage rebellion'. Operationalizing these concepts means not only defining them, but developing indicators so that you can determine whether your survey respondents are the products of some level of old-fashioned parenting and whether they should be considered rebellious and to what extent.

This is an area where a lot of projects fall short. Students want to capture concepts, but they don't put enough effort into exploring the literature and searching for measures that have proven to be both valid and reliable. Concepts such as self-esteem, anger, angst, and poverty, for example, have been studied by countless researchers who have developed various scales, items, and indicators that can capture these concepts with credibility. This is definitely a situation where you do not want to reinvent the wheel. Remember: your goal is to add to a body of knowledge, and drawing on what other researchers have done is an important part of the process.

Valid and reliable indicators for various concepts, however, cannot always be located in the literature. A student of mine, for example, wanted to determine levels of environmental citizenship in Australian adults. Standard, valid, reliable indicators of environmental citizenship, however, have yet to be established. Now if she manages to capture this, not only will she make a contribution to the literature by offering an understanding of Australians' levels of environmental citizenship, but she will also be offering a range of indicators that can be used in measuring this concept.

Box 11.2 briefly covers Likert, Guttman, and Thurstone scaling, three common methods for operationalizing concepts.

BOX 11.2   OPERATIONALIZING CONCEPTS – SCALING TECHNIQUES

One of the most common ways to operationalize a concept is to create a scale that allows you to place respondents along a continuum for some variable of interest. For example, say you wanted to understand high school students' attitudes towards gay peers – your goal might be to give them a rating that indicates where they fall from least to most comfortable. Three options are *Likert, Guttman,* and *Thurstone* scales.

For each type of scale, development begins by generating a large set of items (as many as 100) that reflect the concept you are interested in. A good idea is brainstorming with a knowledgeable group. If you were to do this for items related to high school students' attitudes towards gay peers, you might come up with the following:

1   I believe homosexuality is immoral.
2   I am comfortable having gay friends.
3   I am comfortable with gay students in my class.
4   I think gay students should stay in the closet.
5   I would not want to be in a locker room with a gay student.
6   And so on (up to 100 items).

For all three scales, the next step is to have experts give opinions on how relevant each statement is to the concept. Now it is important to realize that you are not interested in whether the experts personally agree with each statement – you just want to understand whether they think it is relevant.

Each scale has its own way of gathering expert opinion on relevance – which leads to the three distinct scales, as follows.

Likert: To rate relevance, experts use a 5-point scale such as 1 = strongly unfavourable to the concept, 2 = somewhat unfavourable to the concept, 3 = undecided, 4 = somewhat favourable to the concept, 5 = strongly favourable to the concept. The researcher then uses a statistics package to compute correlations between all pairs of items and keeps items with the highest correlations with the total score across all items (high levels of correlation show that experts are in agreement on these particular items). The goal is to come up with 10–15 reliable items.

(Continued)

(Continued)

Administering the scale involves asking respondents to rate each of the chosen 10–15 items on a 4- to 9-point response scale. A 5-point scale, for instance, might consist of 1 = strongly disagree, 2 = disagree, 3 = undecided, 4 = agree, 5 = strongly agree. Scales with an odd number of points offer a neutral midpoint, while even-number scales force a side. To get the overall rating, individual item scores are summed.

Guttman: Experts give a *yes* for each statement that is favourable towards the concept and a *no* for each that is not. The researcher then constructs a table that shows respondents' answers on all items and sorts this into a matrix so that respondents who agree with more statements are listed at the top and those agreeing with fewer are at the bottom. The goal is to come up with a set of items that are ordered so that a respondent who agrees with any specific question in the list will also agree with all previous questions. So if the respondent scores a 3, it should mean that he or she agreed with the first three statements. If the respondent scores a 7, it should mean he or she agreed with the first seven. The object is to find a set of items (done through scalogram analysis) that perfectly matches this pattern.

Administering the scale involves asking respondents to check items they agree with. Each item has a scale value associated with it (obtained from the scalogram analysis) and to get the overall rating you simply add the scale values of every item respondents checked.

Thurstone: Experts rate each item from 1 to 11 where 1 is extremely unfavourable towards the concept and 11 is extremely favourable towards the concept. The researcher then computes the median and the interquartile ranges for each item and selects the statements that are at equal intervals across the range of medians and have a small range (this shows most agreement between experts). The goal is to come up with a yardstick for measuring where people sit on a continuum. Items with higher medians should indicate a more favourable attitude towards the concept.

Administering the scale involves asking participants to agree or disagree with each statement. To get the overall rating you average the medians of all the items that the respondents agreed with.

While there are several resources that can help you develop your own scales, the classic work by McIver and Carmines (1981) cited at the end of the chapter is a good starting point.

Question formulation

There is certainly more than one way to ask the same question. In fact, the possibilities are almost endless. The dilemma here is that subtle (or not so subtle) differences can affect your data. Box 11.3 offers a distillation of the most fundamental 'rules' related to question wording. The aim is to help you avoid the pitfalls of leading, offending, or confusing your respondents.

BOX 11.3 QUESTIONS TO AVOID

Good questions should be unambiguous, inoffensive, and unbiased – something easier said than done. It is easy to fall into the trap of constructing questions that are:

POORLY WORDED

- **Complex terms and language** – there are plenty of people who are hippopo-tomonstrosesquippedaliophobic (scared of big words). If these words are not necessary, don't use them, i.e. *polysyllabic linguistic terminology can act to obscure connotations* vs *big words can be confusing*.
- **Ambiguous questions** – frames of reference can be highly divergent, so writing an ambiguous question is easy. For example, consider the questions, *'How big is your family?'* or *'Do you use drugs?'* Families can be nuclear or extended, or for children of separated parents, may include two households. Similarly, 'drugs' is an ambiguous term. Some respondents will only consider illegal drugs, while others may include prescription drugs. And, of course, it would be impossible to know whether alcohol or cigarettes were also considered.
- **Double negatives** – like many people, I have a hard time with double negatives. Take the following agree/disagree statement: *'You are not satisfied with your job.'* To state that you are satisfied, you would have to choose 'disagree', which can be quite confusing.
- **Double-barrelled questions** – this is when you ask for only one response to a question with more than one issue. For example, *'Do you consider the President to be an honest and effective leader?'* Respondents may think yes, effective – but definitely not honest.

BIASED/LEADING/OR LOADED

- **Ring true statements** – these are statements that are easy to agree with simply because they tend to 'ring true'. Some good examples here are agree/disagree statements like *'You really can't rely on people these days'* or *'Times may be tough, but there are generally people around you can count on.'* Both of these somewhat opposite statements are likely to get high percentage of 'agrees' because they tend to sound reasonable.
- **Hard to disagree with statements** – these are statements where your respondents are likely to think 'Yes that's true, BUT ...' They are not, however, given a chance to elaborate and are forced to agree or disagree. For example, *'It is good for young children if their mothers stay at home through the week.'*
- **Leading questions** – leading respondents in a particular direction can be done unintentionally, or intentionally for political purposes. Consider how the wording

(Continued)

(Continued)

of these agree/disagree statements might affect responses: *'Protecting defenceless endangered species from inhumane slaughter is something the government should take seriously'* vs *'The protection of biodiversity should be a government priority.'* *'Mothers have the right to murder an unborn child'* vs *'Women should be able to make choices about their own bodies.'*

PROBLEMATIC FOR THE RESPONDENT

- **Recall dependent questions** – these are questions that rely on memory. For example, *'How many relationships have you had?'* Without boundaries such as level of significance or timeframe, this question can be easy to answer 'incorrectly'.
- **Offensive questions** – if respondents take offence to a question or a series of questions, not only are they likely to skip them, but they may just throw out the entire survey. Offensive questions can range from *'What did you do to make your husband leave you?'* to *'How much money do you earn?'*
- **Questions with assumed knowledge** – don't assume your respondents know about, or are familiar with, the same things as you. Take for example the agree/disagree statement *'Marxist theory has no place in twenty-first-century politics.'* You should not be surprised when the response here is 'What kind of academic crap is this?!' – with your survey then taking a quick trip to the garbage.
- **Questions with unwarranted assumptions** – respondents are likely to be at a loss when it comes to answering a question that contains an assumption they do not agree with. For example, the question *'What was the most enjoyable part of your hospital stay?'* assumes that the respondents enjoyed something about their hospitalization.
- **Questions with socially desirable responses** – this is more likely to be an issue in face-to-face surveying. For example, a respondent may be uncomfortable disagreeing with the statement *'Do you think women serving in the armed forces should have the same rights and responsibilities as their male colleagues?'*, especially if the interviewer is female.

Working within these guidelines is a start, but unlikely to be enough. Once you have drafted your questions, run them past an experienced researcher. They are likely to pick up things you have missed. You can also trial your questions with your peers. They will certainly be able to tell you if you managed to confuse, offend, or lead them in any way. Finally, once you have made modifications based on feedback received, you will need to run a pilot study. The idea here is to distribute your survey to a small group of individuals whose characteristics match that of your sample and then thoroughly debrief with them. Remember – in the end it is not what you think, or even what your supervisor or peers think that counts. The only opinion that really matters will be that of your eventual respondents.

Response categories

As if getting your questions as precise and non-problematic as possible was not enough, a good survey and good survey data are equally dependent on the response categories you use. And there are a lot of things to consider here. For one, response categories will influence the data you collect. For example, if you add an 'I'm not sure' option to a controversial Yes/No question, it will affect your findings. Second, different types of response categories generate data with different types of measurement scales, and data with different measurement scales demand quite distinct statistical treatment. In fact, understanding the difference between nominal, ordinal, interval, and ratio data (as discussed in Chapter 13) will definitely facilitate the process of survey construction, particularly determining response categories. But until you actually have some data to play with, understanding the relationship between data types and survey construction is quite abstract.

This makes conducting your first survey a real challenge. So, again, I will turn to the need for a good pilot study. Not only will a pilot study allow you to assess your questions and response categories from the perspective of your respondents, but it will also allow you to generate a mini data set that you can enter into a database, and work with statistically. This really is the best way to see how your data collection protocols, including response category determination, will impact on your analysis. Box 11.4 covers response category options.

BOX 11.4   RESPONSE CATEGORIES

Responses to survey questions can be either open or closed:

OPEN RESPONSES

Respondents are asked to provide answers using their own words. They can offer any information or express any opinion they wish, although the amount of space provided for an answer will generally limit the response. The data provided can be rich and candid, but can also be difficult to code and analyse.

CLOSED RESPONSES

Respondents are asked to choose from a range of predetermined responses. The data here is generally easy to code and statistically analyse. Closed response categories come in many forms, each with their associated issues.

(Continued)

(Continued)

- Yes/No – Agree/Disagree:

  Do you drink alcohol?   Yes/No
  Drinking is bad for your health.   Agree/Disagree

  While it can be easy to work with 'binomial' data (or data with only two potential responses), you need to consider whether respondents will be comfortable with only two choices. For example, in the first question a respondent might be thinking 'Not really (I only drink when I go out, which is hardly ever)', or for the second question, 'It depends on how much you're talking about?' A potential strategy is to offer a *don't know/no opinion* option, but this allows for a lot of 'fence sitting'.

- Fill in the blank:

  How much do you weigh?   _____

  Even a simple question like this (assuming your respondents know the answer and are willing to tell you) can lead to messy data. Will respondents write 90 kg, 198 lb, or 14 stone? Of course you can convert these answers to one system, but that is not going to be possible if they just put 90.

- Choosing from a list:

  What would you drink most often?

  Beer   Wine   Spirits   Mixed drinks   Cocktails

  There is an assumption here that there will not be any 'ties'; you need to consider what you will do if more than one option is circled. You also need to make sure all options are covered (are exhaustive) and do not overlap (are mutually exclusive). A potential strategy is to offer an 'Other' or 'Other: _____' option.

- Ordering options:

  Please place the following drinks in order of preference

  Beer   Wine   Spirits   Mixed drinks   Cocktails

  These questions tend to be quite difficult for respondents, particularly if lists are long. It is worth remembering that if respondents get frustrated trying to answer, they are likely to leave the question blank, leave it half finished, or just write anything at all.

- Interval response scale:

  It is normal for teenagers to binge drink

1	2	3	4	5
Strongly disagree	Disagree	Unsure	Agree	Strongly agree

  Interval response scales (often referred to as Likert scales) offer a range of responses, generally ranging from something like 'Strongly disagree' to 'Strongly agree'. In this type of scale, you will need to consider: the number of points you will use; whether you will force a side by using an even number of responses; and whether you think your respondents are likely to 'get on a roll' and keep circling a particular number.

Information and instructions

A survey instrument is not complete without some level of background information that can give credibility to your study and make your respondents feel like they are a part of something. In your background information, it is a good idea to include: the sponsoring organization/university; the survey's purpose; assurances of anonymity/confidentiality; return information, including deadlines and return address; and a 'thank you' for time/assistance. This information can be included at the start of the survey, or as a cover letter.

Also crucial are instructions. What might be self-evident to you may not be so obvious to your respondents. Instructions should introduce each section of the survey, give clear and specific instructions for each question type, provide examples, and be easy to distinguish from actual survey questions. In fact, I would suggest using a distinct font – try changing the style, size, boldness, italics, underlining, etc. It may take a couple of drafts to get your instructions as clear and helpful as possible. Be sure you seek advice and feedback from other researchers, peers, and your pilot group.

Organization and length

Once you are comfortable with all the various elements of your survey, you will need to put it together in a logical format that is neither too long nor too short: too short, and you won't get all the data you need; too long, and your survey might be tossed away, returned incomplete, or filled in at random. People might not mind spending a few minutes answering your questions, but ask for much more and they may not be bothered to help you out. Appropriate length is another aspect of your survey you can assess in your pilot run. Be sure to ask your trial respondents what they thought of the overall length and the time it took to complete the survey.

In terms of logical organization, there are a few schools of thought. Some suggest that you start with demographics in order to 'warm up' your respondents. Others, however, suggest that you start with your topical questions and finish off with questions related to demographic information. What is right for your survey will depend a lot on the nature of both your questions and your respondents. In fact, you may want to pilot two different versions of your questionnaire if you are unsure how it should be laid out.

There is one consistent piece of advice, however, and that is to avoid starting your survey with questions that might be considered threatening, awkward, insulting, difficult, etc. It is really important to ease your respondents into your survey and save any sensitive questions for near the end.

Layout and design

You would think that all of the intense intellectual work that has gone into opera-tionalizing your concepts, writing clear and unambiguous questions with appropriate, well-thought-out response categories accompanied by clear instructions and organized into a sensitive, logical, and manageable form would be enough to ensure a 'good' survey. Not quite. Aesthetics counts!

If your survey looks unprofessional (poor photocopies, faint printing, messy and uninteresting layout, etc.), two things can happen. For one, respondents are less likely to complete a survey that is unprofessional and lacking an aesthetically pleasing layout and design. Second, the potential for mistakes increases dramatically if surveys are cluttered, cramped, or messy. So the effort here is well worthwhile.

INTERVIEWING

> "I like to listen. I have learned a great deal
> from listening carefully.
> Most people never listen."
> *Ernest Hemingway*

Interviewing: the 'Art of Asking' or the 'Art of Listening'?

There is no doubt that asking and listening are both crucial to the interview process, but we tend to spend a much greater proportion of our time working on getting our questions and questioning right. When it comes to the listening end of things, we barely give it a mention. Well, according to Hemingway, 'Most people never listen', and unfortunately, there are quite a few researchers who would rather talk than listen. Remember: your job is to talk only enough to facilitate someone else's ability to answer. It is your interviewees' voice that you are seeking, and it is their voice that needs to be drawn out.

INTERVIEWING
A method of data collection that involves researchers seeking open-ended answers related to a number of questions, topic areas, or themes.

Options and possibilities

What pops into your mind when you think 'interview'? Well, you are likely to conjure up an image of a job interview. You know, that formal scenario where the interviewee has to get dressed up, do the firm handshake, use a formal presentation of self – all the while feeling quite nervous. Meanwhile, the interviewer sits behind a big desk, holds all the cards, and is definitely the power person. So it is not surprising to find that it is this image that new researchers subconsciously take with them into the research world; they tend to think this is how research interviews should unfold. But they do not have to. Yes, research interviews can be formal – but, as covered in Table 11.2, there are actually quite a few options that might better suit your research agenda.

TABLE 11.2   INTERVIEW ISSUES AND TYPES

Will you conduct your interview in a formal manner or will it be more relaxed?

Formal: the interviewer attempts to be removed from the interviewee and maintains an objective stance. This is often done within a formal setting	This can be likened to the classic job interview. While it allows interviewers a high level of control, it can limit interviewee comfort and possibly free flow of information
Informal: bends or ignores rules and roles associated with formal interviewing in order to establish rapport, gain trust, and open up lines of communication. The style is casual and relaxed in order to minimize any gulf between the interviewer and the interviewee	Settings are not limited to an office and might occur over a beer at a bar or while having a cup of coffee at the local preschool. The idea is to do what you can to get your interviewee chatting comfortably. Informal interviews are often unstructured, but this varies with the style, comfort zone, and goals of the researcher

Will your interviews be highly structured or more free flowing?

Structured: use of pre-established questions, in a predetermined order, with a standard mode of delivery. Prompts and probes are also predetermined and used under defined circumstances. Interviewers often call on a formal style to help them stay on track	Best suited for interviews where standardized data is a goal. Inexperienced interviewers generally feel most comfortable with this high level of structure
Semi-structured: use of a flexible structure. Interviewers can start with a defined questioning plan, but will shift in order to follow the natural flow of conversation. Interviewers may also deviate from the plan to pursue interesting tangents	The advantage here is being able to come away with all the data you intended but also interesting and unexpected data that emerges. This style of interviewing can take a bit of practice
Unstructured: attempts to draw out information, attitudes, opinions, and beliefs around particular themes, ideas, and issues without predetermined questions. The goal is to draw out rich and informative conversation. Often used in conjunction with an informal structure	Most interviewees enjoy this type of interview because it allows them to talk and really express their ideas in a way not dictated by the interviewer. Interviewer challenges here are to avoid leading the conversation and to keep it focused enough to get the data needed

Will you interview one person at a time or will you attempt to tackle a group?

One on one: an interaction between an interviewer and a single interviewee. One on one allows the researcher control over the process and the interviewee the freedom to express his or her thoughts. One on one can also involve an additional person such as a translator or note taker	One-on-one interviews are generally face to face, but can also be done over the telephone in order to increase geographical range or capture a difficult-to-catch respondent. The lack of non-verbal cues in telephone interviews, however, can be a challenge
Multiple: interviewing more than one person at a time. This can be done in a formal structured way that attempts to capture the independent thoughts of each individual or may involve a more open process that allows	Not only can a group interview save time and money, but it can also really get people talking (which can influence data – something you will need to consider/manage). Group interviews can, however, leave some members feeling

(Continued)

TABLE 11.2   *(Continued)*

respondents to interact and influence each other's opinions	unheard or marginalized. Group interviews can be difficult to follow, so most interviewers attempt to preserve raw data by tape recording
Focus group: a type of group interview with approx 4–12 people. It is more a discussion than a strict question/answer process. The interviewer acts as a facilitator or moderator and there is an express goal of interaction within a nurturing environment	The goal is to use rich discussion to draw out depth of opinion that might not arise from direct questioning. Added bonuses are high efficiency and lower costs

Issues and complexities

What could be better than getting out there and actually talking to real people, asking them what they really think, finding out first hand how they genuinely feel? Well, interviews allow all of this, but like any other data collection method, its opportunities are balanced by a series of challenges. Interviews:

- allow you to develop rapport and trust
- provide you with rich, in-depth qualitative data
- allow for non-verbal as well as verbal data
- are flexible enough to allow you to explore tangents
- are structured enough to generate standardized, quantifiable data.

Now many of these 'pros' are the result of the human element in interviewing – but so too are the 'cons'. The closer you become to your respondents and the closer they become to you, the bigger the challenge you will face in managing the process. Such challenges include the following:

- Gaining access to interviewees in an ethical manner (see Table 11.3).
- A lack of respondent anonymity.
- Resisting the urge to lead your respondents.
- Making a good impression that will keep doors open (see Box 11.5).

TABLE 11.3   ACCESS AND ETHICS

Using power	Abusing power
✓ Using official channels and protocols	✗ Avoiding and skirting around official channels and protocols
✓ Establishing points of contact	✗ Going around or above the appropriate person's head
✓ Using gatekeepers and insiders	✗ Asking gatekeepers and insiders to act unethically or to go behind management's back
✓ Building rapport	✗ Ingratiating yourself to the point of becoming sycophantic
✓ Leaving doors open	✗ Becoming a nuisance
✓ Offering something back	✗ Making promises you cannot or do not intend to keep

BOX 11.5   FACILITATING A GOOD INTERVIEW

DO YOUR HOMEWORK

- **Be prepared to talk about your research** – the ability to clearly articulate the rationale, aims, objectives, and methods of your project can be instrumental in getting the right doors opened.
- **Prepare a brief outline of your project** – certain individuals or organizations may want to have a document they can consider and/or present to 'gatekeepers'.
- **Have a letter of introduction** – a letter of introduction from your supervisor can professionally answer questions like 'So who are you and where are you from?'
- **Find out about appropriate protocols** – sometimes the contacts that are most willing to help do not have the authority to authorize access. Finding out about appropriate protocols can help avoid awkward situations.

BE PROFESSIONAL

- **Be respectful** – choose the right time for your approach, be prompt, dress appropriately, and be modest in your initial requests.
- **Plan for the unexpected** – very rarely does the research process run smoothly, especially when you are dealing with individuals; be prepared for glitches.
- **Leave doors open** – many researchers swear they have collected all the data they are going to need, but later wish they could go back and ask just a few more questions.

OFFER SOMETHING BACK

- **Don't disappear** – let your contacts know how things are progressing and/or send a note of thanks.
- **Make results available** – it is quite natural to have a sense of curiosity about studies of which you are a part; the results of your study can be quite valued by those who have facilitated your research.

- Facilitating honest and open responses even though your interviewees may want to impress, be liked, or maintain privacy.
- Suspending all judgement – if respondents feel judged, ashamed, or offended, it is difficult to gather credible data.
- Figuring out how attributes such as race, gender, ethnicity, class, and age of interviewer and interviewee alike might affect the interview process.
- Communication miscues – as shown in Box 11.6, moving from questions to answers is anything but a straightforward process. Misunderstandings and misinterpretation are all too common.

BOX 11.6   IT'S JUST Q & A, ISN'T IT?

From A to K			Getting lost along the way ...

The Interviewer

A *formulates a question*

B *asks the question*

C *hears the question*

The Respondent

D *interprets the meaning*

E *considers a response*

F *articulates an answer*

G *hears the response*

The Interviewer

H *interprets the meaning*

I *takes notes*

J *synthesizes/analyses*

K *reports*

Getting lost along the way ...

A to B: Your thoughts and words do not always match up.

B to C: Respondents can simply mishear. Accents, language difficulties/interpreters can make this quite common.

C to D: Respondents don't always share the same understandings as the interviewer.

D to E: Respondents can intentionally filter/hide/lie or simply forget.

E to F: Again, words do not always capture thoughts.

F to G: Interviewers also have the potential to mishear. If taping, make sure audio is of adequate quality.

G to H: The more 'foreign' the culture, the more potential for divergent interpretation.

H to I: Note taking is not easy. You can miss significant information. You can also lose data in the transcription process.

I to J: Judgements/interpretations need to be made by the interviewer.

J to K: The interviewer reports back understandings as truth!

The interview process

As with surveying, conducting a 'good' interview is a process that requires a lot more steps than you may realize. Interviewing involves the need to: plan for all contingencies; prepare an interview schedule and data recording system; run a trial; modify the process as appropriate; conduct the interviews; and, finally, analyse the data. Box 11.7, which can be used as both a guide and a checklist, outlines the steps involved.

BOX 11.7 STEPS IN THE INTERVIEW PROCESS

A: PLANNING – CONSIDERATION OF 'WHO', 'WHERE', 'WHEN', 'HOW', AND 'WHAT'

The success of your interview will hinge upon the forethought you have put into the planning process.

1 **Population and sample/respondent/participants** – who you plan to speak about (population), and gather data from (sample) (see Chapter 10).
2 **Access** – the first step in an interview is access. Table 11.3 offers tips for gaining access.
3 **Your role** – how will you present yourself? How will you strike a balance between formality and rapport? Is your interview style/research goal better suited to officiousness or informality? What tone of voice will you use? Will you joke around? Also consider body language. Reading non-verbal cues (while your interviewee is reading yours) is worth thinking about. Are you both making eye contact, looking down, looking around, picking your nails, coming across aggressively, looking relaxed?
4 **Your biases** – recognizing and controlling for subjectivities in ways that can best ensure the credibility of any survey instrument you use.
5 **Ethics/ethics approval** – consideration of any ethical dilemmas inherent in your project, and getting appropriate ethics approval.
6 **Data** – exactly what it is you want to elicit from your respondents, i.e. memories, descriptions, feelings, thoughts, opinions, etc.
7 **Details** – appointments, timing (travel time, interview time, wait-around time), location, recording methods, etc.
8 **Potential cultural/language barriers** – familiarizing yourself with, and planning for, any potential language and/or cultural issues. Find and trial a good translator if necessary (see Box 11.8).
9 **Contingencies** – the unexpected, the unplanned, and the unfortunate. This means developing a contingency plan in case key interviews fall through.

(Continued)

(Continued)

B: DEVELOPING AN INTERVIEW SCHEDULE/RECORDING SYSTEM

No matter what style of interview you intend to conduct, you will need to have a game plan ready to go.

10 **Draft questions and/or themes** – for a structured interview this will involve drafting and redrafting your questions. For a less structured interview, you will need to think about the themes you want to cover and whether you will put any boundaries on potential conversation.

11 **Review** – carefully read each question and consider whether your questions might be confusing, leading, offensive, or problematic for your interviewees (see Box 11.3).

12 **Rewrite questions** – run them past a few peers/supervisors for their assessment. Repeat this step as many times as necessary to get each question as right as possible.

13 **Order questions** – put questions in an order that will be logical and ease respondents into your interview.

14 **Prepare additional information** – consider and develop any instructions, prompts, or probes you feel are appropriate to the interview.

15 **Decide on recording methods** – if note taking, consider/develop a form that can aid this process. If audio or videotaping, be sure to acquire and become familiar with the equipment.

16 **Train any note takers/translators** – if using note takers or translators you will want to work as a team, which is likely to involve some trial and error (see Box 11.8).

C: PILOTING – CONDUCTING A 'TRIAL'

Good planning and development is essential – but not sufficient. Interviewing is a skill that takes practice and giving your process a run-through can be invaluable.

17 **Have a run-through** – a mock interview can boost confidence and highlight potential issues.

18 **Reflect** – note any difficulties you encountered, i.e. access, time taken, question clarity, structure, introductory information, instructions, prompts, pacing, comfort zones, recording/note taking, roles, objectivity, conversational flow, ambiguities, cultural issues, etc.

19 **Seek feedback** – get feedback from the interviewees on the issues above and anything else they wish to discuss.

20 **Review notes/transcribe data** – make sure you can make sense of notes and that transcription (if a goal) is doable. You may be surprised at how labour/time intensive transcription tends to be.

D: MODIFYING – REFINING YOUR APPROACH

Review and refine until you are comfortable with the process and data collected.

21 **Make modifications** – this will be based on your own reflections, feedback from your interviewee, as well as the quality of the data generated.

22 **Back to the start?** – if the need for modification is substantial, you may need to revisit your planning, development, and piloting process. This may involve a return to the ethics committee.

E: IMPLEMENTING – CONDUCTING YOUR INTERVIEW

Finally, you get to talk to someone! While covered more fully in the next section, conducting your interview involves the need to:

23 **Take care of preliminaries** – make appointments early (people can put you off for months) and arrive early for your interview so that you have time to set up and check any equipment.
24 **Make your interviewee as comfortable as possible** – establish rapport, introduce the study, and discuss 'ethics'.
25 **Ease into main questions/themes** – it is easy to offend when you jump straight into controversial areas, so ease your way into things.
26 **Keep a balance** – manage the process and work between keeping on track and/or explore interesting tangents as appropriate to your interview goals.
27 **Wind down and close the interview** – make sure you show your gratitude and attempt to keep the door open for future interaction.

F: MANAGING AND ANALYSING – KEEPING TRACK AND MAKING SENSE

Unless your data is effectively managed and thoughtfully analysed, all the hard work above will be wasted.

28 **Organize/collate your data as soon as possible** – when the time comes to work with your data, nothing is worse than a partially forgotten conversation or illegible notes. Be systematic and organized.
29 **Thematic analysis** – it's time to see what your data yields. Most interview data will be analysed thematically (see Chapter 14), but if you have 30 or more interviews you may want to engage in some level of statistical analysis (see Chapter 13).

BOX 11.8   LOST IN TRANSLATION

If you require a translator, there are plenty of issues that can affect your ability to collect credible data. You will need to consider the following:

- Whether your translator is experienced – being bilingual does not guarantee the necessary skills, so be sure to trial and/or seek references.
- Whether your translator will translate for you and the interviewee on the spot or whether the translator will conduct the interview in the interviewee's native language and translate into English at a later time.

(Continued)

(Continued)

- If you would like to capture a literal translation or if you want your translator to use some discretion and judgement in conveying meaning.
- If you can (and how you can) manage the overall process, including establishing rapport, keeping on time, exploring tangents, keeping respondents focused, etc., all through a translator.

There are no rights and wrongs here. It is the context of your particular research question that will determine the best course of action, and you may need to trial a couple of processes before you know which way to go.

Conducting your interview

'Intimidating': I do not think there is a better word to describe what it feels like to conduct your first interview. No matter how prepared you think you are, you are still likely to feel nervous at the beginning, and wish you did things differently at the end.

Now when you start to prepare, you will probably spend a lot of time thinking about what to ask and how to say it, and this is important. But even more important are your listening skills. Perhaps the golden rule of interviewing is to:

Listen more than talk

The main game is facilitating an interviewee's ability to answer, and to do this with confidence you will need to: take care of preliminaries; ease respondents into the interview; ask questions that facilitate answers; effectively manage the process; and wind down at the right time – all the while being true to your role.

Take care of preliminaries

Quite a few things need to come together before you are in a position to ask your first question. Asking good questions is preceded by:

- *making appointments early* – allow for travel time, interview time, and wait-around time
- *arriving on time* – building rapport can be a real challenge if you keep someone waiting, and if you miss an appointment altogether you may not get a second chance
- *setting up and checking any recording equipment* – you can do this in advance or, if done efficiently, when you first arrive for your interview
- *establishing rapport* – this includes introductions, handshakes, small talk, and expressions of appreciation

- *introducing the study* – this includes reviewing who you are, the purpose of the study, why involvement is important, and approximately how long the interview will take
- *explaining ethics* – this can involve assurances of confidentiality, the right to decline to answer any particular questions, and the right to end the interview upon request.

Ease your respondents into the interview

As with surveying, it is important to ease your way into the main questions and themes. If you start off with a 'sensitive' question or one that might be considered threatening, you may find yourself facing an uphill battle for the remainder of the interview. In fact, it can be easy to get an interviewee off-side, so it is well worth considering how you might handle such a situation.

Ask questions that facilitate answers and be ready to capture those answers

If you ask a Yes/No question, you should expect a Yes/No answer. Try to ask questions that open up conversations and draw out rich responses. Questions should create possibilities, open up options, dig below the surface, and lower defences.

Capturing answers can be done in a number of ways and you may need to trial a couple of recording methods in order to assess what is best for you and your research process. In most cases you will be responsible for both conducting an interview and capturing responses. Under some circumstances, however, you may use a note taker, which can allow you to focus and engage more fully in listening and directing your interview. But as well as considering resource implications, you will need to carefully consider whether a third party is likely to have an affect on the respondent and the interview process:

- *Note taking* – This can range from highly structured to open and interpretative. Highly structured note taking often utilizes a form that can be filled in as the interviewee speaks. It may even include a list of codes for common responses (this can allow for statistical analysis if enough interviews are conducted). At the other end of the spectrum is unstructured note taking that may take the form of a concept map or involve jotting down interpretative ideas during or even after an interview. Remember that if you are going to take notes during an interview, be sure you practise talking, listening, and note taking simultaneously – and that you can read your own writing. You also need to keep in mind that note taking is actually a preliminary form of analysis (you are making decisions about what to record). You may want to consider taking notes in conjunction with audio/video recording.
- *Audio recording* – This allows you to preserve raw data for review at a later date. It therefore allows you to focus on the question/answer process at hand. The disadvantages of taping are: the unease it can cause for the interviewee; its inability to capture non-verbal cues; the fallibility of equipment (see Box 11.9); and the enormous time and financial cost of transcribing data (a half-hour interview can generate up to 30 transcription pages).

- *Videotaping* – This offers the added bonus of being able to record visual cues, but is more intrusive, is prone to more technical difficulties, and can generate data that is hard to analyse.

BOX 11.9   TAPE-RECORDING DILEMMAS

SOME THINGS YOU DON'T WANT TO FIND YOURSELF SAYING ...

To your interviewee:

- 'Oh jeez, wait – hold on. I don't think the silly thing's recording.'
- 'Sorry, I didn't realize the tape finished. Do you mind repeating everything you said for, let's see ... the last 43 minutes?'

To yourself:

- 'Damn – all I can hear is that stupid lawnmower.'
- 'I knew I should have stopped at the 7–11 for more batteries.'
- 'Oh nooo ... I think I recorded over the interview I did last week.'

AND ONE THING YOU MIGHT WANT TO CONSIDER SAYING ...

To your interviewee when you are sensing 'wariness':

- 'Would you feel more comfortable if I turned it off and just took notes?'

Manage the process

Conducting an interview is quite a complicated management task because you are actually doing three things at once. The first is questioning, prompting, and probing in ways that will help you gather the richest possible data. The second is actively listening to, and making sense of, what your interviewee is saying. The third is managing the overall process so that you know how much time has passed, how much time is left, how much you still need to cover, and how you might move it all forward.

Moving the interview forward might involve the use of prompts, i.e. giving the interviewee some ideas that might jog a response, and probes, which are comments and questions that help you dig for more, i.e. 'tell me more', 'really', or 'why?'. Sometimes probes can be an inquisitive look or a few moments of silence. You will also need to consider the balance between keeping on track vs exploring interesting tangents. If you are conducting a structured interview and have a limited amount of time, you will want to make sure you are keeping your interviewer on track and moving at a good pace. If your interview is less structured, you may find yourself wanting to explore interesting tangents as they develop. The trick here is to be mindful of the time, and be sure you end the interview with the full range of data you aimed to gather.

Wind down/close

Winding down involves questions that 'round off' an interview and asks respondents if there is anything else they would like to cover, contribute, or clarify. The interview then ends by thanking your interviewees for their contribution and their time, and asking them if it might be possible to contact them again if you need to ask any further questions, or need to clarify any points. It is also good practice to offer something back, e.g. a copy of your completed report.

Be true to your role

It is easy to get swept up in your interview – after all, you are probably highly interested in the topic and full of your own informed opinions. But this needs to stay in check. Remember: before anything else, and regardless of the style of interview you conduct, you are a researcher whose primary objective is credible data. Even if your goals are highly change oriented and even emancipatory (see Chapter 9), your desire for change should not leave a question mark over your interpretive work.

FURTHER READING

While this chapter offers quite a few insights into surveying and interviewing, there is a lot more reading you can do. The following list contains some of the latest and most accessible readings available.

Surveying

Aldridge, A. (2001) *Surveying the Social World: Principles and Practice in Survey Research*. Buckingham: Open University Press.

Bradburn, N. M., Sudman, S., and Wansink, B. (2004) *Asking Questions: The Definitive Guide to Questionnaire Design*. Hoboken, NJ: Jossey-Bass.

Dillman, D. A. (2006) *Mail and Internet Surveys: The Tailored Design Method*. Hoboken, NJ: John Wiley & Sons.

Fowler Jr, F. J. (2008) *Survey Research Methods*. London: Sage.

Groves, R. M., Fowler, F. J., Couper, M. J., Lepkowski, J. M., Singer, E., and Tourangeau, R. (2004) *Survey Methodology*. Hoboken, NJ: John Wiley & Sons.

McIver, J. P. and Carmines, E. G. (1981) *Unidimensional Scaling*. London: Sage.

Rea, L. M. and Parker, R. A. (2005) *Designing and Conducting Survey Research: A Comprehensive Guide*. Hoboken, NJ: Jossey-Bass.

(Continued)

(Continued)

Saris, W. E. and Gallhofer, I. N. (2007) *Design, Evaluation, and Analysis of Questionnaires for Survey Research.* New York: Wiley-Interscience.

Interviewing

Gillham, B. (2005) *Research Interviewing: The Range of Techniques.* Buckingham: Open University Press.
Gubrium, J. F. and Holstein, J. A. (2001) *Handbook of Interview Research: Context and Method.* London: Sage.
King, N. and Horrocks, S. (2009) *Interviews in Qualitative Research.* Thousand Oaks, CA: Sage.
Kvale, S. and Brinkman, S. (2008) *InterViews: Learning the Craft of Qualitative Research Interviewing.* London: Sage.
Rubin, H. J. and Rubin, I. S. (2004) *Qualitative Interviewing: The Art of Hearing Data.* Thousand Oaks, CA: Sage.
Seidman, U. (2006) *Interviewing as Qualitative Research: A Guide for Researchers in Education and the Social Sciences.* New York: Teachers College Press.
Wengraf, T. (2001) *Qualitative Research Interviewing: Semi-Structured, Biographical and Narrative Methods.* London: Sage.

CHAPTER SUMMARY

- Surveys and interviews are key in social science data collection because they allow researchers to directly ask what they want, the way they want to.
- Surveying involves gathering information from respondents related to their characteristics, attributes, how they live, opinions, etc., through administration of a questionnaire.
- Surveys can involve entire populations or samples of populations, be descriptive or explanatory, capture a moment or map trends, and be administered in a number of ways.
- A good survey has the potential to reach a large number of respondents, generate standardized, quantifiable, empirical data (as well as some qualitative data), and offers confidentiality/anonymity. Credible data, however, can be difficult to generate.
- Conducting a survey capable of generating credible data requires thorough planning, meticulous instrument construction, comprehensive piloting, reflexive redevelopment, deliberate execution, and appropriate analysis.
- Questionnaire development is often underestimated and should begin by turning to relevant literature to see if there are existing instruments that can be drawn upon.

- Questionnaire development begins with concept operationalization or turning abstract concepts into measurable variables. This often involves construction of various scales such as Likert, Guttman, and Thurstone.
- Good questions avoid leading, offending, or confusing respondents and are paired with response categories that best capture the data you are after.
- Questionnaires need to have clear background information and instruction, be highly organized, be an appropriate length, and have good layout and design.
- Interviewing involves researchers seeking open-ended answers to any number of questions, topic areas, or themes.
- Interviews can range from formal to informal; structured to unstructured; and can be one on one or involve groups.
- Interviews have the ability to generate standardized, quantifiable data, but are more often used to capture in-depth qualitative data. Digging for depth, however, can create many opportunities for miscommunication and misinterpretation.
- Conducting an interview that can generate relevant and credible data requires thorough planning, considered preparation of an interview schedule and recording system, sufficient piloting, reflexive modification, the actual interview, and appropriate analysis.
- Conducting an interview can be an intimidating experience that does get easier with practice. It is worth remembering that the main objective of any interview is to facilitate an interviewee's ability to answer.
- Before you are in a position to ask your first question you need to gain access in an ethical manner, make appointments, arrive on time, set up and check equipment, establish rapport, introduce your study, and explain ethics.
- Your interview should ease respondents into the main questions and themes with 'sensitive' questions only coming after the interview is in full swing.
- The questions you ask should be ones that facilitate rich answers. You will also need to consider what means you will use to capture these answers.
- Managing the interview involves questioning in ways that gather rich data; actively listening to, and making sense of, your respondent; and managing the overall process so that you are in a good position to move your interview forward and close when appropriate.
- As an interviewer you will need to be true to the researcher role and manage your subjectivities at all times.

12

INDIRECT DATA COLLECTION: WORKING WITH OBSERVATIONS AND EXISTING TEXT

CHAPTER PREVIEW

- The challenge of gathering indirect data
- Observation
- Working with existing 'texts'

THE CHALLENGE OF GATHERING INDIRECT DATA

Ask a question, get an answer. That is the advantage of surveys and interviews. The answers, whether or not they are tainted by the process, are right there on the table. You get to direct the process and collect only the data relevant to your research question.

Not so with indirect data. Indirect data is situational data, data that exists regardless of a researcher's questioning, prompting, and probing. It is data that can be found in social situations, documents, databases, and artefacts, none of which were created by the researcher for the express purpose of his or her research project. It is existing data that researchers simply gather and analyse.

The appeal here is that the collection of indirect data minimizes the relationship between the researcher and the researched. Interviewing and surveying, for example, are driven by the researcher who undoubtedly has an impact on the reality of the situations, events, or people being explored; researchers and researching have an influence on social environments. But with indirect data, primary interaction does not involve the researcher, so any need a respondent might have to impress, hide, or obscure is taken away. Researchers simply observe what participants actually do; read what they actually write; see what they actually produce; and take note of things they leave behind. Indirect data may not be custom built for the researcher, but at the same time it is not 'constructed', which represents a tradeoff worth exploring.

OBSERVATION

> ❝ He plies the slow, unhonored, and unpaid task of observation ... He is the world's eye. ❞
> *Ralph Waldo Emerson*

We sometimes overlook observation as a potential data collection method; surveying and interviewing tend to corner the social science research market. But I can give you three good reasons for thinking about conducting an observational study. The first is that there are times when you need to 'see it for yourself' – having it explained to you is just not the same. The second is that the gulf between what people say they do and what they actually do can be far and wide. Third, data collected through observation generally takes place in the real world, not a constructed research world. You are out there in the field, in the heart of the action.

Observation invites you to take it all in; to see, hear, smell, feel, and even taste your environment. It allows you to get a sense of a reality and work through the complexities of social interactions. In the words of Emerson, you become the 'world's eye'.

OBSERVATION
A systematic method of data collection that relies on a researcher's ability to gather data through his or her senses.

Options and possibilities

The options for observation are incredibly broad, and range from studies that are highly removed and structured to those that are highly involved and messy. For example, at the structured end, you might be talking about a psychologist holding a clipboard and watching a series of interactions from behind a one-way mirror. At the messy end, there might be an anthropologist who has lived in a remote village in Papua New Guinea for the past 15 years and is dedicated to understanding the reality of this village from the perspective of the observed.

On the surface, similarities between these types of observations may seem few and far between. In fact, these extremes are often treated as two distinct methods of data collection derived from diverse paradigms and disciplines. But when you get down to brass tacks you will find that these two extremes do sit on a continuum. Table 12.1 covers the key issues you will need to negotiate in order to determine how your own observation processes should best unfold.

While the observation types covered in Table 12.1 can be combined in any number of ways, Figure 12.1 delves into four major strands of observation that combine candid and covert strategies with varying levels of participation.

TABLE 12.1   OBSERVATION ISSUES AND TYPES

As an observer will you attempt to be removed or immersed? In other words, will you become a participant in the environment you are studying?

Non-participant: researchers do not become, nor aim to become, an integral part of the system or community they are observing. The observer is physically present but attempts to be unobtrusive. Non-participant observation tends to occur over a fixed time period and is often highly structured	Examples here include watching interactions through a one-way mirror, sitting in the corner of a room observing a meeting, or watching how pedestrians cross a dangerous intersection
Participant: researchers are, or become, part of the team, community, or cultural group they are observing. The goal is to preserve the natural setting and to gain cultural empathy by experiencing phenomena and events from the perspective of the observed. Participant observation is often aligned with a less structured, often ethnographic, process	Observers may be outsiders who attempt to become insiders (a researcher joins a cult) or they can be insiders who decide to study their own (a member of a workforce, community, or church). In both cases, participant observation can involve large emotional and time commitments

Note: Participant and non-participant roles are not necessarily discreet and often overlap, which can cause difficulties for the researcher. For example, when non-participant observers begin to participate, they can influence and contaminate their research settings. On the other hand, observation is still the goal of the 'participant', and the more immersed the participant becomes, the harder it may be to maintain the role of researcher.

Will you conduct your observations in a covert fashion, or will you offer full disclosure?

Candid: researchers offer full disclosure of the nature of their study; the role the observations will play in their research; and what they might expect to find through the observation process. Full disclosure is often an ethics requirement	It is hard to act natural when you know you are being watched – even more so when you know you are being 'studied', so building trust and making sure participants are comfortable with candid/open processes is essential
Covert: researchers do not disclose the nature of their study to those they are observing; they may not even disclose that they are undertaking a study at all. It can be difficult to get ethics approval for covert studies since they breach the core ethical principle of informed consent	Covert studies overcome the issue of participants struggling to act natural by allowing researchers to 'spy' and observe unfeigned behaviours – but this can be unethical

Will you use highly structured or unstructured observation techniques?

Structured: researchers use predetermined criteria related to people, events, practices, issues, behaviours, actions, situations, and phenomena to collect data in a highly systematic fashion	Checklists or observation schedules are prepared in advance, and researchers attempt to be objective, neutral, and removed in order to minimize personal interactions
Semi-structured: observers use, but are not limited to, predetermined criteria	Observation schedules or checklists are used to organize observations, but observers also attempt to record the unplanned and/or the unexpected
Unstructured: observers attempt to observe and record data without predetermined criteria	Observers can record all observations and later search for emergent patterns, or they make judgement calls on the relevance of initial observations and attempt to focus any subsequent observations

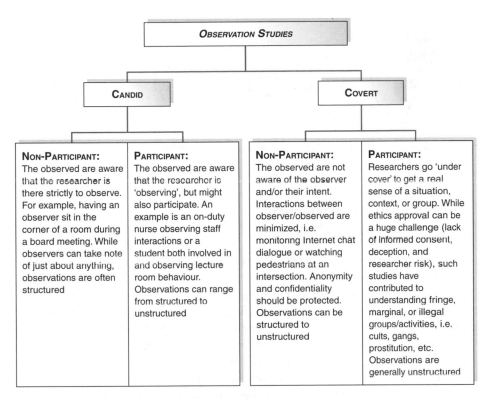

FIGURE 12.1   FOUR MAJOR STRANDS OF OBSERVATION STUDIES

Issues and complexities

It is easy to think that conducting an observation study will be straightforward – you just need to 'observe' and take note of what is happening in a given situation or context. But it is important to recognize observation as a systematic data collection method. It can be challenging to take something done on a daily basis and convert it into a rigorous research tool. But if done with rigour, observation allows you to:

- explore what people actually do, and not just what they say they do
- take it in for yourself, often in the field
- collect both rich, in-depth qualitative data and standardized, quantifiable data
- collect non-verbal as well as verbal data.

Observation studies, however, do require you to consider continually and negotiate how your inherent biases, i.e. your history, interests, experiences, and expectations, can colour observations. As highlighted in Figure 12.2, a world exists, but we cannot capture all of it – our understandings are narrowed by what we can manage to take in through our senses. Sensory input is then filtered and processed by a brain that has been socialized into thinking and understanding through very structured, defined, and

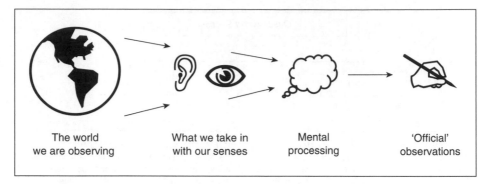

FIGURE 12.2   FILTERING OBSERVATIONS

indeed limited frameworks. Finally, our constructed understandings are condensed into our official observations.

This puts a lot of responsibility for the generation of credible data squarely on the thought processes of the researcher, and highlights the need for observational studies to be systematically planned and, if possible, confirmed through the use of other methods.

The other thing you need to consider is how you will manage your relationship with study participants. For example, people don't always act the same when they know they are being observed. You will need to consider whether you can expect natural behaviours from those who know they are being watched. But being covert in your observations has its own dilemmas, i.e. you will need to have a plan you can put into place if your covert study suddenly becomes exposed. And what if, as a non-participant, you cannot help yourself and start to participate? Or what if you get too immersed in the culture you are studying and begin to have second thoughts about your research role? These can be huge challenges and may require you to rethink your methodological design.

Of course the paradox here is that the more entwined you become with the researched, the richer and more meaningful the data you might generate. But this entwining can also make it a much more difficult process to navigate. The key will be your ability to think through such issues, to plan with care, and to exercise considered flexibility.

Box 12.1 gives an example of the difficulties researchers can face when they observe without reflexive consideration of their own impact and positioning.

BOX 12.1   COME FOR MILES, WILL THEY? TIMOTHY'S STORY

I remember a documentary I saw in an anthropology class where researchers were conducting an observational study of a small community somewhere in South America. They were filming an old woman who they described as a local 'guru', and decided to film her doing her 'Sunday ritual'. This was the first time the researchers had been to this event and talked about how far people were coming just to see this woman. I watched this film and thought, 'Hold on, what if these people are coming here to see you? You know … white people with cameras, lights, and sound booms.' My suspicions became even greater when the camera briefly panned to a couple of laughing children trying to pat the big fuzzy microphone. The researchers never mentioned the potential impact they had on what they were observing, and ended up attributing all they observed to the local context.

The observation process

Even though we make casual observations on a daily basis, observing as a social science method requires the need to: plan for all issues and contingencies; observe all aspects of the situation; record observations; review the process; refine as appropriate; and, finally, analyse the data. Box 12.2 outlines the steps involved in observation. As was the case for surveying and interviewing, you should find this box helpful as both a guide and a checklist.

BOX 12.2   STEPS FOR CONDUCTING OBSERVATION STUDIES

A: PLANNING – CONSIDERATION OF 'WHO', 'WHERE', 'WHEN', 'HOW', AND 'WHAT'

The success of your observation study will hinge on the forethought you put into the planning process.

1   **Consider type of observation study** – do your goals and context lend themselves to an observation study that is candid or covert, participant/non-participant, structured/unstructured, and of what duration?
2   **Population and sample/respondent/participants** – who you plan to speak about (population), and gather data from (sample) (see Chapter 10)?
3   **Access** – realistically consider access/acceptance to the group/situation/ activities you wish to observe. That is, are there any potential language and/or cultural issues likely to affect the process? Can you get past 'gatekeepers'? Will you be welcomed? Will you be able to build trust?
4   **Your biases** – recognizing and controlling for subjectivities in ways that can best ensure credibility. A good idea is to brainstorm preconceived ideas/expectations and also brainstorm alternatives.
5   **Your skills** – how you might develop the skills/resources needed to carry out your observations.
6   **Presentation of self** – the role you will take and how involved you will be.
7   **Credibility** – consider strategies for ensuring credibility (see Chapter 8, Box 8.2).

(Continued)

(Continued)

8   **Tools** – prepare an observation schedule/checklist or, if unstructured, consider any relevant themes to explore.

9   **Details** – what timeframe will you be working towards? Will you observe on one occasion, multiple occasions, or will your study involve prolonged engagement? How will you record your data?

10 **Ethics/ethics approval** – for participant studies, you will need to consider whether immersion will have a physical, mental, or emotional toll on the observed and/or the observer, i.e. observers may find themselves immersed in a dangerous situation; they may feel pressured to become involved in immoral/illegal activities; or they may feel stressed when they need to leave the setting and report findings. Issues related to covert studies include justifying and getting approval for a study where there is a lack of informed consent. While some ethics committees are loath to do this under any circumstances, others will consider such studies if the researcher can give convincing assurances related to the physical, mental, and emotional welfare of the observed and observer; protection of confidentiality; and perceived societal benefits.

11 **Contingencies** – the unexpected, the unplanned, and the unfortunate. This means having a back-up plan ready to go if your original plan does not pan out.

B: IMPLEMENTING – OBSERVING

12 **Ease into the observation situation** – if structured and candid, this will be similar to the opening stages of an interview where you need to be on time, set up and check any equipment, introduce the study, and establish rapport. If your study involves greater immersion into a culture, early stages will require you to sit back, listen, attempt to gain trust, and then establish rapport.

13 **Be ready for a range of sensory input** – use all your senses, and possibly your intuition, to gather data.

14 **Invest time** – because you will not be directing the process, you need to be prepared to invest significant time in your observations.

15 **Look for saturation** – try to ensure your observations no longer yield new knowledge before ending the process.

C: RECORDING – KEEPING TRACK

The ability to capture observations is as important as the act of observing.

16 **Record your observation as soon as possible** – observations need to be recorded in a timely manner. If using schedules, they should be filled in while observations occur. If you are more immersed in your research context, you may want to record your observations when removed from the situation either on data sheets or in a journal. Your record may also include photographs and video/audio recordings.

D: REVIEWING – REFLECTING AS YOU GO

17 **Review the process** – note any difficulties encountered, i.e. access, time taken, engagement, cultural 'ignorance', comfort zones, recording/note taking, roles, objectivity, etc.

18 **Review your observation records** – note any difficulties you might encounter in making sense of your record.

19 **Confirm** – check with an insider, ask another observer to compare notes, or triangulate your observational data with other data types.

E: REFINING – MODIFYING YOUR PROCESSES

20 **Make modifications** – based on your own review of the process; any confirmation strategies you have attempted; and the quality of the data generated.

21 **Keep reviewing and refining** – observation takes practice; keep refining until you are comfortable with the process and the data collected.

22 **Major issues?** – if there are major issues, you will need to openly discuss them with your supervisor and consider modifications.

F: ANALYSING DATA – MAKING SENSE

23 **Analysis** – data collected in observation can be quantitative (through the use of checklists) (see Chapter 13) or can be much more qualitative (through the use of journaling) (see Chapter 14). Remember: analysis should work towards addressing your research questions in insightful ways.

Receiving, reflecting, recording, authenticating

As highlighted above, a common feature of all observation studies is that they attempt to document what people actually do, rather than what they say they do; observational studies rely on actual behaviour. There are no tools used to generate particular responses from the observed. There are no 'questions'. It is simply the observed doing what they do, and observers taking that in, noting it, and making sense of it. While the perceived advantage here is genuineness, the disadvantage is how complicated it can be for researchers to work through the process of receiving, reflecting, recording, and authenticating their observations.

Receiving

When it is time to begin your observations, the exact protocol you will use will be highly dependent on the type of observation study you plan to conduct. Most observation processes, however, begin by attempting to build rapport and gain trust. The idea is to try to make the observed feel as comfortable as possible; in fact, comfortable enough to carry on as if you were not even there.

The next step is opening your eyes, ears, and mind to all that is going on around you. What do you see, what do you hear, what do you sense? We tend to be a visual society, so it is important to make sure you are taking it in through your full range of senses. And this can take time. Because you are not directing the process, you need to be prepared to make a significant investment in order to get the data you need. In fact, unless your design sees you observing for a predetermined period of time, it pays to look for saturation (your observations no longer yield new knowledge) before ending the process.

Now keep in mind that we do not all take in or perceive the world in the same way. Some of us are tuned into the bigger picture, while some of us concentrate on separate components. Some like to take in the world by looking around, some like to listen. Others understand best by moving, doing, and touching. So when it comes to observation, it is not only possible, but in fact probable, that two observers in the same situation will take things on board in quite different ways. Attempting to control for this is important. If your observations are structured, an observation schedule that requires information to be gathered through a variety of senses can ensure you miss any potential sources of data. In a less structured study, the key will be your ability to critically reflect on your data collection processes and make any necessary modifications.

Reflecting

While not always conducted as a 'pilot', there is still a need to review, reflect on, and modify your observation methods. Such modifications are generally based on difficulties you encountered in your initial observation work, e.g. difficulties with access, timing, cultural 'ignorance', comfort zones, recording/note taking, roles, and objectivity. It also pays to review your observation records and assess if they make sense, and are logical, rich, and complete.

Also look for 'bias'. It is exceptionally difficult for researchers, particularly those who choose to immerse themselves within the research setting, to be objective. Our worldviews are embedded within us. We carry with us the biases and prejudices of both our attributes and our socialization. They are a part of how we understand and make sense of the world, and how we might go about observing it. And as discussed in Chapter 3, if we do not recognize and attempt to negotiate our subjectivities, our research will be imprinted with our own biases and assumptions. This can lead to observations that are interpreted through the perspective of the observer, rather than the observed; are insensitive to race, class, culture, or gender; have difficulty hearing marginalized voices; tend to dichotomize what is seen; and do not respect the power of language.

Remember: it is quite easy to see the things you expect to see and hear the things you want to hear. It's like when you get a new car and you suddenly see that model everywhere you go. The cars were always there – you just never noticed them before. And I know that much of the feedback I give students is positive, but every bit of (constructive!) criticism seems to loom 10 times larger in their brains. Before you go out in the field, it is well worth consciously brainstorming your own expectations.

You can then brainstorm a range of alternatives, so that you are less likely to observe and reflect on your observations in ways that confirm what you already suspect.

Recording

There are actually two quite different strategies for recording observations. The first involves the capture of raw data by things like photography, audio and/or video recording. This allows observations to be 'preserved' in a raw form so that they can be reviewed and used at a later date. These methods, however, demand the use of 'equipment' and can be considered intrusive. The second strategy is note taking or journaling. These methods can capture anything from descriptive and formal accounts of space, actors, acts, and events to much more interpretive narrative accounts that include goals, feelings, and underlying 'stories'. The form also varies and can range from coded schedules and quantitative tallying to qualitative pictures, concept maps, and jotted ideas.

The recording method (or methods) you will need to adopt will vary depending on the level of participation, openness, and structure in your observational processes. For candid studies, the use of an observation schedule that you fill in as observations occur might be appropriate, as would the use of photography and audio video recording. For studies that involve high levels of immersion and are perhaps covert, you might want to note, journal, doodle, or map your observations when you are removed from your observational setting and have a level of privacy. Your circumstances may also see you looking to employ a combination of the above. Regardless of the methods you choose to adopt, it is important to record your data in as systematic a fashion as possible. After all, this is data you will need to analyse in the future.

Authenticating

It can be hard to assess whether you have been able to control for your biases and generate credible data by reflection alone. There are, however, a number of strategies that can be used to ensure thoroughness in data collection, and confirm the authenticity of reflections. Thoroughness can be achieved through broad representation, prolonged engagement, persistence, crystallization, saturation, peer/supervisor review of your process, and full explication of method. Strategies for confirmation include informant/member checking and triangulation (see Chapter 8, Box 8.2).

WORKING WITH EXISTING 'TEXTS'

Evidence of where we have been and what we have done is absolutely everywhere. We document it in a million ways, we research it, report on it, log it, video it, journal it, blog it, leave our fingerprints on it, draw it, photograph it, write poetry about it, capture it in song, send postcards, write letters, send e-mails and texts, talk about it on

Facebook, etc. Traces of social activity literally surround us – and it is these traces (which go well beyond the written word) that social scientists refer to as 'text'.

Now if you look at these traces or 'texts' as data, you begin to realize just how data rich our world is. So it is worth thinking twice about producing even more of it without at least considering what is already out there. The challenge is knowing what you are looking for; knowing options for finding it; knowing whether or not you can trust it; and having some sense of what you can do with it.

Now it might sound a bit strange, but when it comes to textual analysis, clearly and succinctly articulating what you are after in terms of 'data' is something that you can actually overlook. When you conduct a survey, the process of designing and developing your questionnaire demands you work through your data needs. The same is true of interviewing. Question development is actually an exercise in clarifying what you think your respondents can offer. But when analysing text you are working with documents, records, data sets, and artefacts not produced expressly for your purposes, so it is easy to skip this articulation step and take a somewhat haphazard approach to data collection.

Textual analysis, however, demands the same consideration as any other data collection method. You need to assess your research question and/or hypothesis and ask yourself, 'What data am I after, and how will it contribute to my understanding?' You need to know what you are looking for – and think it through with the same rigour you would put into developing a questionnaire, interview schedule, or observation checklist.

Options and possibilities

Once you know what you are looking for, you will need to know where you can find it and how you can get your hands on it. As shown in Table 12.2, 'texts' can refer to almost any human/social artefact and cover a huge array of data types that might be derived from an organization, an individual, or perhaps a family. Your text might also be located on the television, at the movies, at a school, or at a museum or park. It may be in the public domain, or it might be private. It may be held by other researchers, local government, national government, or international agencies. And getting your hands on it may involve writing away for it, going to the library, making a personal appeal, or going into the field.

Given this diversity, the key to success is being prepared. You will need to know well in advance where your data sources are located; who the gatekeepers might be; how to best approach them; whether or not you will need to use a sampling strategy; and whether the collection of sensitive or private data will require ethics approval.

Issues and complexities

There are some real advantages in exploring pre-produced texts. Existing texts allow you to:

- explore what people have actually produced in the real world
- capitalize on the vast amount of data already out there

TABLE 12.2   BROAD-RANGING 'TEXTS'

What type of texts will you be exploring?

Official data and records – while you may have to work at getting access, it may be worth exploring:

- *International data* held by organizations such as the United Nations, World Bank, or World Health Organization
- *National data* held by many federal or national governments and government departments, e.g. National Census data
- *Local government data* such as state of environment reports, community surveys, water quality data, land registry information, etc.
- *Non-governmental organization data* collected through commissioned or self-conducted research studies
- *University data*, which is abundant and covers just about every research problem ever studied
- *Archival data* such as records of births, deaths, marriages, etc.

Organizational communication, documents, and records – generally official communication that includes, but is not limited to:

- websites
- press releases
- catalogues, pamphlets, and brochures
- meeting agendas and minutes
- inter- and intra-office memos
- safety records
- sales figures
- human resource records
- client records (these might be students, patients, constituents, etc., depending on organization type)

Personal communication, documents, and records – personal and often private communication that includes, but is not limited to:

- letters and e-mails
- journals, diaries, and memoirs
- Facebook/MySpace sites
- blogs
- mobile phone texts
- sketches and drawings
- poetry and stories
- photographs and videos
- medical records
- educational records
- household records, e.g. cheque book stubs, bills, insurance documents, etc.

The media/contemporary entertainment – data here is often examined in relation to questions of content or portrayal, e.g. the content of personal ads, how often male characters are shown crying, or how often sexual assault has made the national news over the past two years. Data can come from:

- websites
- newspaper or magazine columns/articles/advertisements
- YouTube content
- news programmes and current affairs shows
- TV dramas, sitcoms, and reality shows
- commercials
- music videos
- biographies and autobiographies

(Continued)

TABLE 12.2   *(Continued)*

What type of texts will you be exploring?

The arts – the arts have captured and recorded the human spirit and condition over the ages in every corner of the globe, making them perfect for comparing across both culture and time. Societal attitudes are well captured in:

- paintings, drawings, and sketches
- photography
- music
- plays and films

Social artefacts – these include any product of social beings. Examples of social products or social traces are extremely broad ranging and can include things like:

- garbage
- graffiti
- children's games
- rites and rituals
- jokes
- T-shirt slogans
- tools
- crafts
- videos (YouTube has created a huge and accessible database here)

- collect for rich, in-depth qualitative data and standardized, quantifiable data – as well as both verbal and non-verbal data
- eliminate the need for physical access to research subjects, which can reduce costs as well as minimize stress for both researchers and research subjects
- eliminate worries related to: building trust; getting people to act naturally; role playing; and figuring out how attributes such as race, gender, ethnicity, class, and age of researcher and researched might confound data collection
- be neutral and not a force for change
- overcome the expectation that 'real' research demands interviews and surveys.

That is a pretty long list, which will hopefully pique your interest in exploring data traditionally underutilized. But there are some challenges associated in working with pre-produced texts. Pre-produced texts require you to:

- work through data not expressly generated to answer your particular research question(s)
- make sure your own biases do not colour your interpretations and understandings
- avoid taking records out of context
- protect the needs of an uninformed researched, i.e. protection of privacy, anonymity, and/or confidentiality
- question a text's origin/agenda – remember that some sources are by their nature subjective, i.e. media coverage, personal communication, or 'party line' material with an express political agenda, and even authoritative texts with an explicit goal of unbiased knowledge can be tainted by subjectivities.

In fact, because you are working with existing data, assessing credibility is essential. Ask yourself if the pre-existing data you are working with is unbiased, complete, and accurate. Does it give a full account? You also need to be able to recognize whether your data was produced with a particular agenda in mind (e.g. political campaign paraphernalia, promotional materials, or even surveys that have been produced by those with a vested interest). It may be tempting to treat the printed word as truth and to treat artefacts as conclusive evidence, but all data needs to be viewed with a critical eye.

Credibility will also rest on how well you are able to manage your own subjectivities. How you 'read' and make sense of your data will be coloured by your own researcher reality. You need to ensure that your biases do not colour your interpretations and understandings, and that your data is interpreted within its original context. Strategies for ensuring credibility are similar to those used to authenticate observations and include: well-designed and reviewed methods; broad representation that explores multiple sources of data; crystallization and saturation that sees a full 'story' come together; triangulation of unobtrusive data with other data sources; and, if possible, checking and comparing notes with an insider or other researcher (see Chapter 8, Box 8.2).

The process of textual analysis

Because textual analysis does not involve document production, the steps involved differ somewhat from other methods of data collection. In order to carry out textual analysis you need to: plan for all contingencies; gather your 'texts'; review their credibility; interrogate their witting and unwitting evidence; reflect and refine your process; and, finally, analyse your data. Box 12.3 provides the steps/checklist for the process of textual analysis.

BOX 12.3   STEPS FOR EXPLORING PRE-PRODUCED 'TEXTS'

A: PLANNING – CONSIDERATION OF 'WHO', 'WHERE', 'WHEN', 'HOW', AND 'WHAT'

The success of your analysis will hinge on the forethought you put into the planning process.

1 **Population and sample/respondent/participants** – in textual analysis this involves creating a list of 'texts' you wish to explore and understanding who they will speak for. If the breadth of texts you wish to explore is overly wide, you will need to develop an appropriate sampling strategy (see Chapter 10).
2 **Access** – how you will locate and access texts. You will also need to consider any language or cultural barriers that might keep you from fully drawing from your texts.
3 **Your biases** – recognizing and controlling for subjectivities in ways that can best ensure you explore 'texts' with an open mind.

(Continued)

(Continued)

4 **Your skills** – how you might develop the skills/resources needed to carry out your analysis.

5 **Credibility** – consider strategies for ensuring credibility (see Chapter 8, Box 8.2).

6 **Data** – knowing exactly what it is you are looking for or trying to find in your texts.

7 **Ethics/ethics approval** – consideration of any ethical dilemmas inherent in your project, and getting appropriate ethics approval, i.e. seeking approval to explore texts that might be classified, in confidence, sensitive, or private.

8 **Contingencies** – the unexpected, the unplanned, and the unfortunate. This means having a back-up plan ready to go if your original plan does not pan out.

B: GATHERING – PULLING 'TEXTS' TOGETHER

9 **Gather relevant 'texts'** – most of the texts outlined in Table 12.2 can be collected, but a few will require you to go out in the field; for example, you may want to look at graffiti, museum exhibits, or waste, *in situ*.

10 **Organize** – for collected text, you will want to develop and employ an organization and management scheme.

11 **Copy** – make copies of original text for the purpose of annotation.

C: REVIEWING – PRELIMINARY TEXTUAL INVESTIGATION

12 **Confirm authenticity** – assess the authenticity and credibility of the 'text'.

13 **Explore the text's agenda** – review the text and consider any inherent biases.

D: INTERROGATING – DELVING INTO YOUR TEXT

14 **Background information** – extract background information on author/creator, audience, purpose, style as appropriate to the text being explored.

15 **Ask questions 'about' the text** – Who produced it? What did they produce it for? What were the circumstances of production? When, where, and why was it produced? What type of data is it? Basically, you want to explore any background information that is available (sometimes called the latent content or unwitting evidence).

16 **Explore content** – this will vary by the type of text and as discussed in the next section can involve qualitative and quantitative processes. The key to success here is outlining what you plan to extract from the text well in advance (see step 6 above).

E: REFLECTING AND REFINING

17 **Learn and improve as you go** – view document analysis as an iterative and ongoing process.

18   **Review the process** – reflect on any difficulties associated with gathering the texts, reviewing the sources, and exploring the content.

19   **Review your notes** – reflect on any difficulties you might encounter in making sense of your record.

20   **Make modifications** – based on your own review of the process and the quality of the data generated.

21   **Keep reviewing and refining** – keep refining until you are comfortable with the process and data collected.

22   **Major issues?** – if there are major issues you will need to openly discuss them with your supervisor and consider modifications.

F: ANALYSING DATA – MAKING SENSE

23   **Analysis** – data collected in textual analysis can be quantitative (through various modes of tallying and more in-depth statistical analysis – see Chapter 13) or can be much more qualitative (through deeper reflective processes – see Chapter 14). Remember: analysis should work towards addressing your research questions in insightful ways.

Delving into documents, history, artefacts, and secondary data

Because 'texts' can cover such a wide array of material, there are several defined methods for their analysis. While each follows the basic steps outlined in Box 12.3, document analysis, historical analysis, analysis of artefacts, and secondary data analysis all involve their own tricks of the trade.

Document analysis

DOCUMENT ANALYSIS
Collection, review, interrogation, and analysis of various forms of written text as a primary source of research data.

By far the most common text a researcher is likely to analyse is documents (both Web-based and hardcopy), so the above advice on textual analysis is all highly relevant. There are, however, two issues worth delving into a bit deeper. The first is the issue of bias. In document analysis, pre-existing documents are treated as a primary a source of data. But because they are pre-existing texts, you will need to thoughtfully consider the issue of subjectivity. The credibility of the data you generate will, in part, be dependent on recognition of the bias/purpose of the author. It may be tempting to treat the printed word as truth, but if you do, you will need to ask whose truth? A second source of bias lies with you as the researcher. As with any method (and as discussed in Chapter 3), how you read and draw from the documents will be coloured by your own researcher reality.

The second issue relates to mining your documents for data. Once you locate, acquire, and assess the credibility of your documents, you will be ready to extract the data. Now the first step is to ask yourself questions about the document. This refers to questions related to the author, audience, circumstances of production, document type, whether it is a typical or exceptional example, the style, tone, agenda, political purpose, whether it contains facts, opinions, or both; basically any background information related to the document. This is sometimes called the latent content or 'unwitting' evidence. Answers to these questions may lie within the document itself, i.e. document type, tone, and style, or may require further investigation, i.e. information about the author or the document's genre.

The next step involves exploration of the 'witting' evidence or the content within the document. There are a couple of ways you can do this. The first is by using an 'interview technique', while the second involves noting occurrences, a method akin to formal structured observation:

- *The interview* – In 'interviewing' your documents, you are, in a sense, treating each document as a respondent who can provide you with information relevant to your enquiry. The questions you ask will be dependent on the nature of your enquiry and on document type. As with an interview, you will need to determine what it is you want to know, and whether your document can provide you with the answers. You then need to 'ask' each question and highlight the passages in the document that provide the answer. Organizing your responses can be done by using a colour-coded highlighting system or you can turn to qualitative data management programs such as NVIVO or NUD*IST to help you with document indexing.
- *Noting occurrences* – Noting occurrences is a process that quantifies the use of particular words, phrases, and concepts within a given document. As in formal structured observations, the researcher determines what is being 'looked for' and notes the amount, the frequency, and often the context of the occurrence. This can also be referred to as 'content analysis', and is taken up in more depth in Chapter 14.

Historical analysis

HISTORICAL ANALYSIS
Collection, review, interrogation, and analysis of various forms of data in order to establish facts and draw conclusion about past events.

Historical analysis is a specific form of textual analysis that can include any and all forms of 'text' covered in Table 12.2, and generally involves all the steps covered in Box 12.3. The main point of distinction, however, is that historical analysis has a quite defined purpose of establishing facts and drawing conclusions about the past. While this goal may seem straightforward, this is actually a multi-pronged goal that involves:

- *Ascertaining what actually happened* – Sometimes the myth or the legend is not based on facts, or at least a full array of facts.
- *Ascertaining why it happened* – Historical analysis goes beyond 'what' and asks about multiple realities, circumstances, context, and conditions. There is an attempt to understand situated complexity.
- *Understanding implications* – Historians believe the past is the key to unlocking the future; historical analysis therefore attempts to link analysis of the past to present conditions and future possibilities.

To accomplish these goals researchers turn to a wide variety of sources that can be *primary*, e.g. the *testimony* of those who were witness to events, or *social bookkeeping*, which refers to records that survived from the past. They might also turn to sources considered *secondary,* i.e. that is accounts of the past that were not generated within the historical period being explored, namely someone else's account/analysis of the past.

The challenges here are: (1) ensuring the authenticity and credibility of the resources used; (2) gathering enough data for an account to be considered complete; and (3) finding trends and patterns among what might be disparate and contradictory evidence.

Analysis of cultural artefacts

CULTURAL ARTEFACT ANALYSIS
Collection, review, interrogation, and analysis of various human-made objects in order to ascertain information about the culture of the objects' creator(s) and users.

When we interact with the world we leave our mark. Evidence of where we have been and what we have been up to is everywhere. And as any crime scene investigator will tell you, through this evidence we reveal something about ourselves.

Beyond the written word, evidence of our interactions includes the things we leave behind as well as the wear and tear we cause. In the world of social science research, we refer to these as measures of erosion or accretion:

- *Erosion* – Explores wear and tear. In a crime scene this might mean looking at footprints or skid marks. In the world of social science we might look at how worn seats are to determine where people most prefer to sit on the train, or determining patient reading preferences by examining the condition of waiting room magazines.
- *Accretion* – Explores what people leave behind. For example, if we go back to the crime scene we might look for DNA or a dropped matchbook. In the social science world we attempt to determine if staff are conforming with waste disposal policy by looking through hospital garbage bins or we might study toilet door graffiti to examine attitudes to promiscuity.

This type of exploration often goes unconsidered by project students, but it can offer huge insight in certain types of research. Historical research, for example, might be illuminated by exploration of artefacts such as dwellings, tools, art, etc.; in fact just about anything that sheds light on the social condition of the period being explored. Cross-cultural studies can also be enhanced through this type of exploration. Comparing children's games or the marriage ceremonies of different cultures, for example, can be extremely enlightening.

In fact you could argue that understanding any culture can be enhanced by exploring its physical evidence or its 'tracks'. One contemporary example here is 'carbon footprinting', or the estimate of the carbon produced by an individual, household, or business (and thereby its contribution to global warming). This measure of accretion has actually become newsworthy and a part of everyday discourse.

Secondary data analysis

> **SECONDARY DATA ANALYSIS**
> Collection, review, interrogation, and analysis of existing data sets in order to answer questions not previously or adequately addressed.

Data collection is such an entrenched part of research processes that we sometimes forget that the data we seek may have already been collected. There is a tremendous amount of hard data out there and censuses, large-scale surveys, and organizational records can all potentially hold the answers to research questions. Capitalizing on these data sets makes sense. Using secondary data allows you to 'skip' data collection processes and all the stress, cost, and time they take. It can also allow you to work with samples that might otherwise have been inaccessible, or samples much larger than you would have been able to generate on your own. But remember: secondary data is only as good as its collection processes – and you have no control over these.

Now perhaps the most crucial step in secondary analysis is knowing exactly what you are looking for – that is, having a clearly articulated research question and knowing what types of data might answer that question. When it comes to secondary analysis, this can actually be more difficult than you might realize. When you are working with an existing data set, you skip the process of design, including working through decisions about population, samples, questions, response categories, etc. You also do not get to explore data as it comes in. And both of these processes offer tremendous opportunity for conceptual work. In secondary analysis, you need to consciously think through such issues, even if design and preliminary data were done by others. Only then will you be in a position to assess the relevance of an existing data set to your research question.

The basic steps of secondary analysis are:

1   *Locating data* − Knowing what is out there and whether you can gain access to it. A quick Internet search, possibly with the help of a librarian, will reveal a wealth of options.
2   *Evaluating relevance of the data* − Considering things like the data's original purpose, when it was collected, population, sampling strategy/sample, data collection protocols, operationalization of concepts, questions asked, and form/shape of the data.
3   *Assessing credibility of the data* − Establishing the credentials of the original researchers, searching for full explication of methods including any problems encountered, determining how consistent the data is with data from other sources, discovering whether the data has been used in any credible published research.
4   *Analysis* − This will generally involve a range of statistical processes as discussed in Chapter 13.

FURTHER READING

Observation studies and textual analysis represent an incredible range of possibilities, options, and diversity in working with indirect data. While this chapter has attempted to guide you through the basics, if you intend to go down this track you will probably need to do a bit more reading.

Observation

DeWalt, K. M. and DeWalt, B. R. (2001) *Participant Observation: A Guide for Fieldwork*. Lanham, MD: AltaMira Press.

Gillham, B. (2008) *Observation Techniques: Structured to Unstructured*. London: Continuum International.

Hume, L. and Mulcock, J. (eds) (2004) *Anthropologists in the Field: Cases in Participant Observation*. Irvington, NY: Columbia University Press.

Lofland, J. and Lofland, L. H. (2003) *Analyzing Social Settings: A Guide to Qualitative Observation and Analysis*. Belmont, CA: Wadsworth.

Rosenbaum, P. R. (2002) *Observational Studies*. New York: Springer.

Document analysis

Prior, L. (2003) *Using Documents in Social Research*. London: Sage.

(Continued)

(Continued)

Rapley, T. (2008) *Doing Conversation, Discourse and Document Analysis.* London: Sage.

Historical analysis

Danto, E. A. (2008) *Historical Research.* Oxford: Oxford University Press.
Mahoney, J. and Rueschemeyer, D. (eds) (2003) *Comparative Historical Analysis in the Social Sciences.* Cambridge: Cambridge University Press.

Cultural artefact analysis

Lee, R. M. (2000) *Unobtrusive Methods in Social Research.* Buckingham: Open University Press.
Schiffer, M. (1999) *The Material Life of Human Beings: Artifacts, Behavior and Communication.* London: Routledge.
Webb, E. J., Campbell, D. T., Schwartz, R. D., and Sechrest, L. (1998) *Unobtrusive Measures: Nonreactive Research in the Social Sciences.* Dallas: Houghton Mifflin.

Secondary analysis

Best, S. J. and Krueger, B. S. (2004) *Internet Data Collection.* Thousand Oaks, CA: Sage.
Kiecolt, K. J. and Nathan, L. E. (1985) *Secondary Analysis of Survey Data.* London: Sage.
Myatt, G. J. (2006) *Making Sense of Data: A Practical Guide to Exploratory Data Analysis and Data Mining.* New York: Wiley-Interscience.
Stewart, D. W. and Kamins, M. A. (1992) *Secondary Research: Information Sources and Methods.* London: Sage.

CHAPTER SUMMARY

- Indirect data is data that exists regardless of a researcher's questioning, prompting and probing. It is found in social situations, documents, databases, and artefacts and is not created by the researcher for research processes.
- Observation relies on a researcher's ability to gather data through his or her senses and can range from non-participant to participant, candid to covert, and structured to unstructured.

- Observation allows researchers to document actual behaviour rather than responses related to behaviour. The observed, however, can act differently when surveilled. Researchers' observations can also be biased by their own worldviews.
- Observation is sometimes treated casually, but is a method that needs to be treated as rigorously as any other and should include planning, observing, recording, reflecting, and authenticating.
- Taking the world in through our senses needs to be tackled systematically in order to ensure we take in a full range of sensory inputs, keep biases in check, and aim for saturated understanding. This takes practice, so reflecting on ongoing practice is essential.
- Recording observations can involve preservation of raw data through audio recordings, photographs, and videos or capturing impressions through note taking and journaling. Observations can be quite subjective so it is important to confirm through strategies that ensure thoroughness and confirmation.
- Existing 'texts' refer to traces of social activity that includes official data and records, electronic/Internet material, corporate data, personal records, the media, the arts, and social artefacts.
- Working with existing texts allows researchers to be neutral, capitalize on existing data, explore what people produce, and eliminate the need for physical access to research subjects. But researchers need to work through data not expressly generated for their particular research question(s).
- Textual analysis involves: planning for all contingencies; gathering 'texts'; reviewing credibility; interrogating witting and unwitting evidence; reflecting and refining your process; and finally analysing data.
- Document analysis refers to the exploration of various forms of written text as a primary source of research data. In doing this, researchers need to consider both the original author's bias and their own. Mining documents for data involves asking questions about the background of a document as well as its contents.
- Historical analysis refers to the exploration of various forms of data in order to better understand the past, including what happened, why it happened, and its implications. Data includes testimony, social bookkeeping, secondary accounts, and social artefacts. Gathering a full range of credible evidence can be a challenge.
- Cultural artefact analysis refers to the exploration of various human-made objects in order to ascertain information about the culture of the objects' creator(s) and users. Measures include those of erosion, i.e. wear and tear, and accretion, i.e. things people produce or leave behind.
- Secondary data analysis refers to the exploration of existing data sets. While this can save time and resources, you do not develop and 'own' the data. Before any statistical analysis is attempted you need to assess both the relevance and credibility of your data sources.

13
ANALYSING QUANTITATIVE DATA

CHAPTER PREVIEW

* Moving from raw data to significant findings
* Managing data and defining variables
* Descriptive statistics
* Inferential statistics
* Presenting quantitative data

MOVING FROM RAW DATA TO SIGNIFICANT FINDINGS

> **All meanings, we know, depend
> on the key of interpretation.**
> *George Eliot*

It's easy to fall into the trap of thinking the major hurdle in your research project is data collection. And yes, as covered in the previous chapters, gathering credible data is certainly a challenge – but so too is making sense of it. That intimidating mound of data you have managed to collect cannot really tell you anything until you have gone through a systematic process of interrogation and interpretation. In fact, just as English novelist George Eliot states, the key to meaning is 'interpretation'.

Keeping a sense of the overall project

I think one of the most important challenges in interpreting quantitative data is staying on top of it the whole way through your analysis. Alvin Toffler is once reputed to have said, 'You can use all the data you can get, but you still have to distrust it and use your own intelligence and judgement.' In fact, there can be a real temptation to

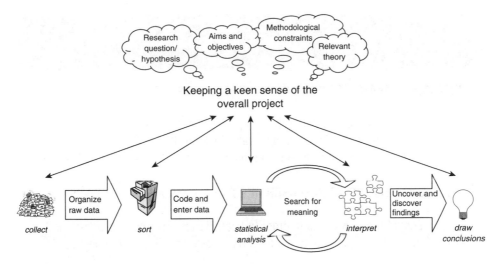

FIGURE 13.1   THE PROCESS OF REFLECTIVE ANALYSIS

relinquish control of the data to your computer – and without a doubt, there are evermore powerful and user-friendly statistics programs that can help you manage and analyse your data. But it is important to remember that there is *no* substitute for the insight, acumen, and common sense you need to manage the process. Computer programs might be able to facilitate analysis and do the 'tasks', but it is the researcher who needs to work strategically, creatively, and intuitively to get a 'feel' for the data, to cycle between that data and existing theory, and to follow the hunches that can lead to significant findings – both expected and unexpected. Researchers cannot afford to get lost in a swarm of numbers and lose a sense of what they are trying to accomplish. Keeping a keen sense of their overall project is imperative.

Figure 13.1 depicts analysis as a process that is much more comprehensive and complex than simply plugging numbers into a computer. Reflexive analysis involves staying as close to the data as possible – from initial collection right through to the drawing of final conclusions. It is a process that requires you to: manage and organize your raw data; systematically code and enter your data; engage in reflective statistical analysis; interpret meaning; uncover and discover findings; and, finally, draw relevant conclusions, all the while keeping an overall sense of the project that has you consistently moving between your data and your research questions, aims and objectives, theoretical underpinnings, and methodological constraints.

It is important to remember that even the most sophisticated analysis is worthless if you are struggling to grasp the implications of your findings to your overall project. To do this you need to conduct your analysis in a critical, reflexive, and iterative fashion that cycles between your data and your overarching frameworks. Rather than hand your thinking over to a computer program, the process of analysis should see you persistently interrogating the data, and the findings that emerge from that data. Stay engaged. It's not that hard to produce an amazing array of 'findings', but not know what it all means. Box 13.1 runs through a series of questions you should ask before and during data interrogation. The questions are designed to help you keep your eye on the bigger picture.

BOX 13.1   QUESTIONS FOR KEEPING THE BIGGER PICTURE IN MIND

QUESTIONS RELATED TO YOUR OWN EXPECTATIONS

- What do I expect to find, i.e. will my hypothesis bear out?
- What don't I expect to find, and how can I look for it?
- Can my findings be interpreted in alternative ways? What are the implications?

QUESTIONS RELATED TO RESEARCH QUESTION, AIMS AND OBJECTIVES

- How should I treat my data in order to best address my research questions?
- How do my findings relate to my research questions, aims, and objectives?

QUESTIONS RELATED TO THEORY

- Are my findings confirming my theories? How? Why? Why not?
- Does my theory inform/help to explain my findings? In what ways?
- Can my unexpected findings link with alternative theories?

QUESTIONS RELATED TO METHODS

- Have my methods of data collection and/or analysis coloured my results? If so, in what ways?
- How might my methodological shortcomings be affecting my findings?

Doing statistical analysis

It was not long ago that 'doing' statistics meant working with formulae, but I cannot believe in the need for everyone attempting a research project to master formulae. Doing statistics in the twenty-first century is more about your ability to use statistical software than your ability to calculate means, modes, medians, and standard deviations – and look up *p*-values in the back of a book.

OK, I admit these programs do demand a basic understanding of the language and logic of statistics. But focusing on formulae is like trying to learn to ride a bike by being taught how to build one. Sure, being able to perform the mechanics can help you understand the logic of application (and there are many excellent resources that can help you build that knowledge), but if your primary goal, like most students tackling a project, is to be able to undertake relatively straightforward statistical analysis your needs will include understanding: (1) how to manage your data; (2) the nature of variables; (3) the role and function of both descriptive and inferential statistics; (4) appropriate use of statistical tests; and (5) effective data presentation.

Now while this chapter will do its best to help you through the above, you are well advised to supplement your reading with some hands-on practice (even if this is simply playing with the mock data sets provided in stats programs). Very few students can get their heads around statistics without getting into some data – so success depends on getting your hands dirty by working with relevant statistical programs. For this type of knowledge 'to stick', it needs to be applied.

The other piece of advice is to ask for help. When you get deeper into the mysteries of statistics, particularly inferential statistics and multivariate analysis, it becomes hard for even experienced researchers to know the best way forward. If your analysis is likely to reach this level of sophistication, it is worth seeking the help of a statistics specialist. In fact in many universities, doctoral candidates doing high-level stats are not only allowed to, but also sometimes encouraged to, have their data analysed by an expert. But even if you are outsourcing (which generally requires funding), there is no getting around a need to know the basics. You will still need to run your own preliminary analysis, direct the higher level outsourced analysis, understand and interpret results, and be knowledgeable enough to ask critical questions.

MANAGING DATA AND DEFINING VARIABLES

There are two important steps that sit between the raw quantitative data you have managed to collect and your ability to take on statistical analysis. These are effectively and efficiently managing your data so that you can build a full database and defining your data as variables in relation to both cause and effect and measurements scales.

Data management

Data can build pretty quickly, and you might be surprised by the amount you have managed to collect. The challenge is employing a rigorous and systematic approach to data management that will allow you to build or create a data set that can be managed and utilized throughout the process of analysis. Box 13.2 runs through five steps I believe are essential for effectively managing your data.

BOX 13.2   DATA MANAGEMENT

STEP 1: FAMILIARIZE YOURSELF WITH APPROPRIATE SOFTWARE

This involves accessing programs and arranging necessary training. Most universities have licences that allow students certain software access, and many universities provide relevant short courses. Programs themselves generally contain comprehensive

(Continued)

(Continued)

tutorials complete with mock data sets. Programs you are likely to come across include:

- **SPSS** – sophisticated and user-friendly (www.spss.com)
- **SAS** – often an institutional standard, but some feel it is not as user-friendly as SPSS (www.sas.com)
- **Minitab** – more introductory, good for learners/small data sets (www.mini tab.com)
- **Excel** – while not a dedicated stats program, it can handle the basics and is readily available on most PCs (Microsoft Office product).

STEP 2: LOG IN YOUR DATA

Data can come from a number of sources at various stages throughout the research process, so it is well worth keeping a record of your data as it is collected. Keep in mind that original data should be kept for a reasonable period of time; researchers need to be able to trace results back to original sources.

STEP 3: SCREEN YOUR DATA FOR ANY POTENTIAL PROBLEMS

This includes a preliminary check to see if your data is legible and complete. If done early, you can uncover potential problems not picked up in your pilot, and make improvements to your data collection protocols.

STEP 4: ENTER THE DATA

There are actually two steps involved in data entry. The first is to define your variables. Figure 13.2 depicts an SPSS Variable View window, which requires you to input variable information such as name, measurement type, labels, values, etc.

The second step is to systematically enter your data into a database. While your data can be entered as it comes in or after it has been collected in its entirety, other than for the purpose of a trial run, full analysis does not take place until after data entry is complete. Figure 13.3 depicts an SPSS data entry screen.

STEP 5: CLEAN THE DATA

This involves combing through the data to make sure any entry errors are found, and that the data set looks in order. When entering quantified data it is easy to make mistakes – particularly if you're moving fast, i.e. typos. It is essential that you go through your data to make sure it is as accurate as possible.

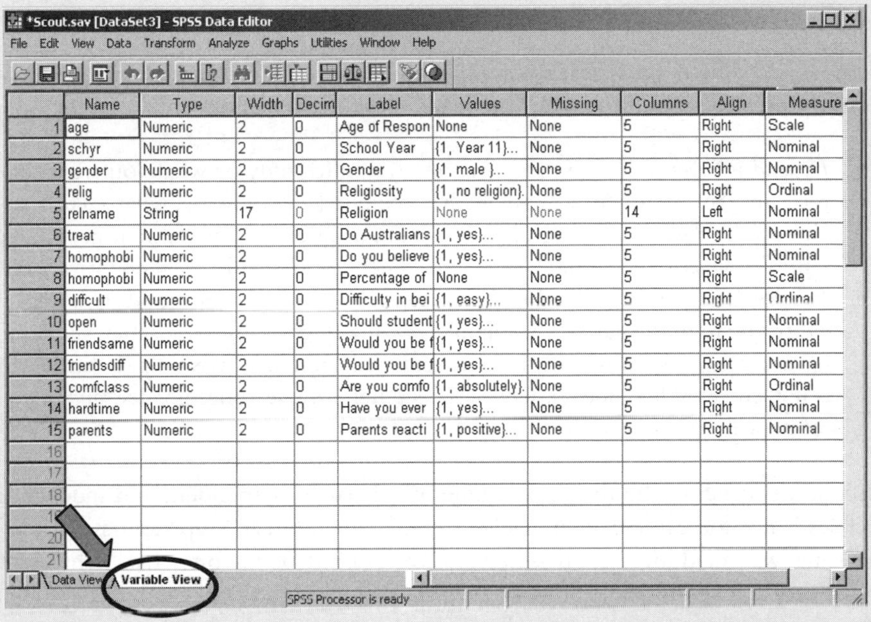

	Name	Type	Width	Decim	Label	Values	Missing	Columns	Align	Measure
1	age	Numeric	2	0	Age of Respon	None	None	5	Right	Scale
2	schyr	Numeric	2	0	School Year	{1, Year 11}...	None	5	Right	Nominal
3	gender	Numeric	2	0	Gender	{1, male }...	None	5	Right	Nominal
4	relig	Numeric	2	0	Religiosity	{1, no religion}.	None	5	Right	Ordinal
5	relname	String	17	0	Religion	None	None	14	Left	Nominal
6	treat	Numeric	2	0	Do Australians	{1, yes}...	None	5	Right	Nominal
7	homophobi	Numeric	2	0	Do you believe	{1, yes}...	None	5	Right	Nominal
8	homophobi	Numeric	2	0	Percentage of	None	None	5	Right	Scale
9	diffcult	Numeric	2	0	Difficulty in bei	{1, easy}...	None	5	Right	Ordinal
10	open	Numeric	2	0	Should student	{1, yes}...	None	5	Right	Nominal
11	friendsame	Numeric	2	0	Would you be f	{1, yes}...	None	5	Right	Nominal
12	friendsdiff	Numeric	2	0	Would you be f	{1, yes}...	None	5	Right	Nominal
13	comfclass	Numeric	2	0	Are you comfo	{1, absolutely}.	None	5	Right	Ordinal
14	hardtime	Numeric	2	0	Have you ever	{1, yes}...	None	5	Right	Nominal
15	parents	Numeric	2	0	Parents reacti	{1, positive}...	None	5	Right	Nominal

FIGURE 13.2 SPSS VARIABLE VIEW

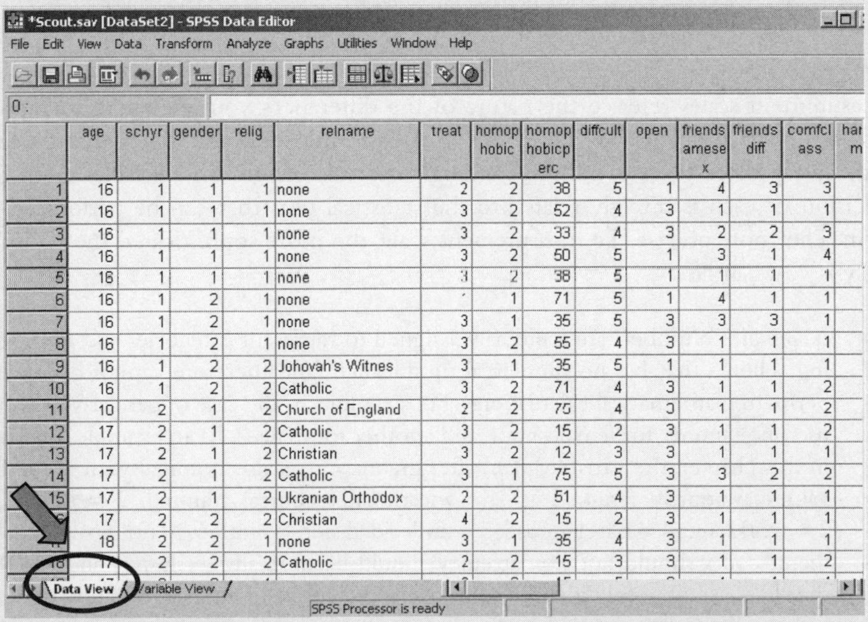

	age	schyr	gender	relig	relname	treat	homophobic	homophobicperc	diffcult	open	friendsamesex	friendsdiff	comfclass	har m
1	16	1	1	1	none	2	2	38	5	1	4	3	3	
2	16	1	1	1	none	3	2	52	4	3	1	1	1	
3	16	1	1	1	none	3	2	33	4	3	2	2	3	
4	16	1	1	1	none	3	2	50	5	1	3	1	4	
5	16	1	1	1	none	3	2	38	5	1	1	1	1	
6	16	1	2	1	none	[illegible]	1	71	5	1	4	1	1	
7	16	1	2	1	none	3	1	35	5	3	3	3	1	
8	16	1	2	1	none	3	2	55	4	3	1	1	1	
9	16	1	2	2	Johovah's Witnes	3	1	35	5	1	1	1	1	
10	16	1	2	2	Catholic	3	2	71	4	3	1	1	2	
11	10	2	1	2	Church of England	2	2	75	4	3	1	1	2	
12	17	2	1	2	Catholic	3	2	15	2	3	1	1	2	
13	17	2	1	2	Christian	3	2	12	3	3	1	1	1	
14	17	2	1	2	Catholic	3	1	75	5	3	3	2	2	
15	17	2	1	2	Ukranian Orthodox	2	2	51	4	3	1	1	1	
16	17	2	2	2	Christian	4	2	15	2	3	1	1	1	
17	18	2	2	1	none	3	1	35	4	3	1	1	1	
18	17	2	2	2	Catholic	2	2	15	3	3	1	1	2	

FIGURE 13.3 SPSS DATA VIEW

Understanding variables – cause and effect

A key way to differentiate variables is through cause and effect. This means being able to clearly identify and distinguish your dependent and independent variables:

- *Dependent variables* – The things you are trying to study or what you are trying to measure. For example, you might be interested in knowing what factors cause chronic headaches, a strong income stream, or levels of achievement in secondary school – headaches, income, and achievement would all be dependent variables.
- *Independent variables* – The things that might be causing an effect on the things you are trying to understand. For example, reading might cause headaches; gender may have a role in determining income; parental influence may impact on levels of achievement. The independent variables here are reading, gender, and parental influence.

While understanding the theoretical difference between dependent and independent variables is not too difficult, being able to readily identify each type comes with practice. One way of doing this is simply to ask what depends on what. Achievement *depends* on parental influence or income *depends* on gender. As I like to tell my students, it does not make sense to say gender depends on income unless you happen to be saving for a sex-change operation!

Understanding variables – measurement scales

Measurement scales refer to the nature of the differences you are trying to capture within a particular variable. There are four basic measurement scales that become respectively more precise: nominal, ordinal, interval, and ratio (see Table 13.1). The precision of each is directly related to the statistical tests that can be performed on them. The more precise the measurement scale, the more sophisticated the statistical analysis you can do.

- *Nominal* – Numbers are arbitrarily assigned to represent categories and are a coding scheme that has no numerical significance (and therefore cannot be used to perform mathematical calculations). For example, in the case of gender you would use one number for female, say 1, and another for male, 2. In an example used later in this chapter, the variable 'plans after graduation' is also nominal with numerical values arbitrarily assigned as 1 = vocational/technical training, 2 = university, 3 = workforce, 4 = travel abroad, 5 = undecided, and 6 = other. In nominal measurement, codes should not overlap (they should be mutually exclusive) and together should cover all possibilities (be collectively exhaustive). The main function of nominal data is to allow researchers to tally responses in order to understand population distributions.
- *Ordinal* – This scale rank orders categories in some meaningful way; there is an order to the coding. Magnitudes of difference, however, are not indicated. Take, for example, socio-economic status (lower, middle, or upper class). Lower class may

TABLE 13.1   MEASUREMENT SCALES

	Nominal	Ordinal	Interval	Ratio
Classifies	✓	✓	✓	✓
Orders		✓	✓	✓
Equidistant units			✓	✓
Absolute zero				✓

denote less status than the other two classes but the amount of the difference is not defined. Other examples include air travel (economy, business, first class), or items where respondents are asked to rank-order selected choices (biggest environmental challenges facing developed countries). Likert-type scales, in which respondents are asked to select a response on a point scale (e.g. 'I enjoy going to work': 1 = strongly disagree, 2 = disagree, 3 = neutral, 4 = agree, 5 = strongly agree), are ordinal since a precise difference in magnitude cannot be determined. Many researchers, however, treat Likert scales as interval because it allows them to perform more precise statistical tests. In most small-scale studies this is not generally viewed as problematic.

- *Interval* – In addition to ordering the data, this scale uses equidistant units to measure difference. This scale does not, however, have an absolute zero. An example here is date: the year 2009 occurs 44 years after the year 1965, but time did not begin in AD 1. IQ is also considered an interval scale even though there is some debate over the equidistant nature between points.

- *Ratio* – Not only is each point on a ratio scale equidistant, but there is also an absolute zero. Examples of ratio data include age, height, distance, and income. Because ratio data is 'real' numbers, all basic mathematical operations can be performed.

DESCRIPTIVE STATISTICS

As the name implies, descriptive statistics are used to describe the basic features of a data set and are key to summarizing variables. The goal is to present quantitative descriptions in a manageable and intelligible form. More specifically, descriptive statistics provide measures of central tendency, dispersion, and distribution shape. Such measures vary by data type (nominal, ordinal, interval, ratio) and are standard calculations in statistics programs.

Measuring central tendency

One of the most basic questions you can ask of your data centres on central tendency. For example, what was the average score on a test? Do most people lean left or right on the issue of abortion? Or what do most people think is the main problem with our health care system? In statistics, there are three ways to measure central tendency: mean, median, and mode – and the example questions above respectively relate to

TABLE 13.2   CENTRAL TENDENCY FOR 'AGE OF PARTICIPANTS'*

Data related to age of participants in a local youth group	
Raw data	12, 12, 10, 9, 12, 15, 11, 12, 11, 11, 15, 16, 17, 12, 13, 13, 14, 11, 10, 9, 9, 8, 13, 14, 12, 14, 15, 13, 13, 10, 9, 13, 14, 13, 9
N (no. of cases)	35
Mean (average)	12.11
Median (midpoint)	12
Mode (most common value)	13

* Figures generated with SPSS.

these three measures (see e.g. Table 13.2). While measures of central tendency can be calculated manually, all stats programs can automatically calculate these figures.

- *Mean* – The mathematical average. To calculate the mean, you add the values for each case and then divide by the number of cases. Because the mean is a mathematical calculation, it is used to measure central tendency for interval and ratio data, and cannot be used for nominal or ordinal data where numbers are used as 'codes'. For example, it makes no sense to average the 1s, 2s, and 3s that might be assigned to Christians, Buddhists, and Muslims.
- *Median* – The midpoint of a range. To find the median you simply arrange values in ascending (or descending) order and find the middle value. This measure is generally used in ordinal data, and has the advantage of negating the impact of extreme values (e.g. one extreme salary of $3 million will push average income levels up – but it will not affect the midpoint). Of course, this can also be a limitation given that extreme values can be significant to a study.
- *Mode* – The most common value or values noted for a variable. Since nominal data is categorical and cannot be manipulated mathematically, it relies on mode as its measure of central tendency.

Measuring dispersion

While measures of central tendency are a standard and highly useful form of data description and simplification, they need to be complemented with information on response variability. For example, say you had a group of students with IQs of 100, 100, 95, and 105, and another group of students with IQs of 60, 140, 65, and 135. Then the central tendency, in this case the mean, of both groups would be 100. Dispersion around the mean, however, will require you to design the curriculum and engage learning with each group quite differently. There are several ways to understand dispersion, which are appropriate for different variable types. As with central tendency, statistics programs can automatically generate these figures (Table 13.3).

- *Range* – This is the simplest way to calculate dispersion, and is the highest minus the lowest value. For example, if your respondents ranged in age from 8 to 17, the range would be 9 years. While this measure is easy to calculate, it is dependent on extreme values alone, and ignores intermediate values.

TABLE 13.3   DISPERSION FOR 'AGE OF PARTICIPANTS'*

Data related to age of participants in a local youth group	
Raw data	12, 12, 10, 9, 12, 15, 11, 12, 11, 11, 15, 16, 17, 12, 13, 13, 14, 11, 10, 9, 9, 8, 13, 14, 12, 14, 15, 13, 13, 10, 9, 13, 14, 13, 9
N (no. of cases)	35
Range (spread of the data)	8 to 17 = 9
Inner quartile range (spread between 25th and 75th %)	10 to 14 = 4
Variance (spread around the mean)	4.93
Standard deviation (square root of variance)	2.22

* Figures generated with SPSS.

- *Quartiles* – This involves subdividing your range into four equal parts or 'quartiles' and is a commonly used measure of dispersion for ordinal data, or data whose central tendency is measured by a median. It allows researchers to compare the various quarters or present the inner 50% as a dispersion measure. This is known as the inner quartile range.
- *Variance* – This measure uses all values to calculate the spread around the mean, and is actually the 'average squared deviation from the mean'. It needs to be calculated from interval and ratio data and gives a good indication of dispersion. It is much more common, however, for researchers to use and present the square root of the variance, which is known as the standard deviation.
- *Standard deviation* – This is the square root of the variance, and is the basis of many commonly used statistical tests for interval and ratio data. As explained below, its power comes to the fore with data that sits under a normal curve.

Measuring the shape of the data

To understand a data set fully, central tendency and dispersion need to be considered in light of the shape of the data, or how the data is distributed. As shown in Figure 13.4, a normal curve is 'bell shaped'; the distribution of the data is symmetrical, with the mean, median, and mode all converging at the highest point of the curve. If the distribution of the data is not symmetrical, it is considered skewed. In skewed data the mean, median, and mode fall at different points.

Kurtosis characterizes how peaked or flat a distribution is compared with 'normal'. Positive kurtosis indicates a relatively peaked distribution, while negative kurtosis indicates a flatter distribution.

The significance in understanding the shape of a distribution is in the statistical inferences that can be drawn. As shown in Figure 13.5, a normal distribution is subject to a particular set of rules regarding the significance of a standard deviation, namely that:

- 68.2% of cases will fall within one standard deviation of the mean
- 95.4% of cases will fall within two standard deviations of the mean
- 99.6% of cases will fall within three standard deviations of the mean.

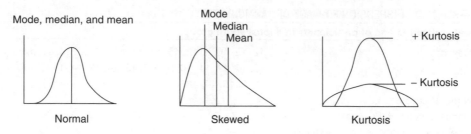

FIGURE 13.4 SHAPE OF THE DATA

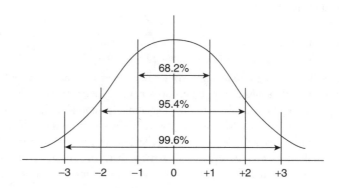

FIGURE 13.5 AREAS UNDER THE NORMAL CURVE

So if we had a normal curve for the sample data relating to 'age of participants' (mean = 12.11, s.d. = 2.22) (see Tables 13.2 and 13.3), 68.2% of participants would fall between the ages of 9.89 and 14.33 (12.11−2.22 and 12.11+2.22). Table 13.4 shows the actual curve, skewness, and kurtosis of our sample data set.

These rules of the normal curve allow for the use of quite powerful statistical tests and are generally used with interval and ratio data (sometimes called parametric tests). For data that does not follow the assumptions of a normal curve (nominal and ordinal data), the researcher needs to call on non-parametric statistical tests in making inferences.

INFERENTIAL STATISTICS

While the goal of descriptive statistics is to describe and summarize the characteristics of your sample, the goal of inferential statistics is to draw conclusions that extend beyond your immediate data/sample. For example, inferential statistics can be used to test various hypotheses about the relationship between different variables or, perhaps more importantly, to allow you to estimate characteristics of a population from sample data. In other words, inferential statistics allow you to generalize.

TABLE 13.4   SHAPE OF THE DATA FOR 'AGE OF PARTICIPANTS'*

Data related to age of participants in a local youth group

Raw data	12, 12, 10, 9, 12, 15, 11, 12, 11, 11, 15, 16, 17, 12, 13, 13, 14, 11, 10, 9, 9, 8, 13, 14, 12, 14, 15, 13, 13, 10, 9, 13, 14, 13, 9
N (no. of cases)	35
Histogram (distribution)	

Std Dev. = 2.22
Mean = 12.1
N = 35.00

Skewness (symmetricality)	0.070
Kurtosis (flatness)	−0.562

* Figures and histogram generated with SPSS.

Questions suitable to inferential statistics

So exactly what can inferential statistics tell us? Well, inferential statistics, as shown in Box 13.3, can help us interrogate our data at a number of levels.

BOX 13.3   QUESTIONS FOR INTERROGATING QUANTITATIVE DATA USING INFERENTIAL STATISTICS

HOW DO PARTICIPANTS IN MY STUDY COMPARE TO A LARGER POPULATION?

These types of question compare a sample with a population. For example, say you are conducting a study of students doing a particular university course. You might ask if the percentages of males or females in your sample, or their average age, or their interests are statistically similar to university students across the country. To answer such questions you will need access to population data for this larger range of students.

(Continued)

(Continued)

ARE THERE DIFFERENCES BETWEEN TWO OR MORE GROUPS OF RESPONDENTS?

Questions that compare two or more groups are very common and are often referred to as 'between subject'. I'll stick with a student theme here: for example, you might ask if male and female students are likely to have similar interests; or whether students of different ethnic backgrounds are likely to do different courses; or whether students studying at different campuses have different grade point averages.

HAVE MY RESPONDENTS CHANGED OVER TIME?

These types of questions involve before and after data with either the same group of respondents or respondents who are matched by similar characteristics. They are often referred to as 'within subject'. An example of this type of question might be, 'Have final-year students' study habits changed since their first year at university?'

IS THERE A RELATIONSHIP BETWEEN TWO OR MORE VARIABLES?

These types of questions can look for relationships and correlations, or cause and effect. Examples of relationship questions might be, 'Is there an association between time spent studying and satisfaction with university?' Or, 'Is there a correlation between students' gender and the extracurricular activities they are involved in?' Questions looking for cause and effect differentiate dependent and independent variables. For example, 'Does satisfaction depend on study time?' Or, 'Does stress depend on the course taken?' Cause and effect relationships can also look to more than one independent variable to explain variation in the dependent variable (multivariate analysis). For example, 'Does satisfaction with university course depend on a combination of length of study habits, age, and career aspirations?'

Statistical significance

As discussed, the goal of inferential statistics is to be able to generalize beyond a sample. But because the data is still limited to a sample, it is impossible to say with 100% conviction that any generalization is without the potential for error. What inferential statistics do allow you to do, however, is assess the probability that an observed difference is more than a fluke or chance finding, and is in fact statistically significant.

Statistical significance generally refers to a '*p*-value', which assesses the actual probability that your findings are more than coincidence. Conventional *p*-values are .05, .01, and .001, which tell you that the probability your findings have occurred by chance is 5/100, 1/100, or 1/1,000 respectively. Basically, the lower the *p*-value, the more confident researchers can be that findings are genuine. Keep in mind that researchers do not usually accept findings that have a *p*-value greater than .05 because the probability that findings are coincidental or caused by sampling error is too great.

Understanding and selecting the right statistical test

There is a baffling array of statistical tests out there that can help you answer the types of questions highlighted in Box 13.3. And while it is important to understand the underlying logic that drives the most common statistical tests (see Table 13.5 below), programs such as SPSS and SAS are capable of running such tests without your needing to know the technicalities of their mathematical operations. The problem of knowing which test is right for your particular application, however, still remains. Luckily, you can turn to a number of test selectors now available on the Internet (see Bill Trochim's test selector at www.socialresearchmethods.net/kb/index.htm) and through programs such as MODSTAT and SPSS.

But even with the aid of such selectors (including the tabular one I offer below), you still need to know the nature of your variables (independent/dependent), scales of measurement (nominal, ordinal, interval, ratio), distribution shape (normal or skewed), the types of questions you want to ask, and the types of conclusions you are trying to draw.

Box 13.4 explains the distinction between univariate (one variable), bivariate (two variable), and multivariate (three or more variable) analysis, while Table 13.5 covers common tests for undertaking such analyses. Table 13.5 can be read down the first column for univariate data (the column provides an example of the data type, its measure of central tendency, dispersion, and appropriate tests for comparing this type of variable with a population). It can also be read as a grid for exploring the relationship between two or more variables. Once you know what tests to conduct, your statistical software will be able to run the analysis and assess statistical significance.

BOX 13.4   UNIVARIATE, BIVARIATE, AND MULTIVARIATE ANALYSIS

UNIVARIATE

The goal of univariate analysis is to provide a clear picture of the data through examination of one variable at a time. It is a cornerstone of a descriptive study and consists of measures of central tendency, dispersion, and distribution as discussed under descriptive statistics. While univariate analysis does not look at correlation, cause and effect, or modelling, it is an essential preliminary stage in all types and levels of statistical analysis.

(Continued)

(Continued)

BIVARIATE

The goal of bivariate analysis is to assess the relationship between two variables; for example, whether there is a relationship between education level and television viewing habits, or gender and income. As covered in Table 13.5, the range of tests that are used to explore such relationships is quite extensive and varies by variable type. The most common tests are cross-tabulations (Chi squared) (used for two nominal variables), ANOVA (used for one nominal and one ratio variable), and correlations (used for two ratio variables).

MULTIVARIATE

The goal of multivariate analysis is to explore relationships between three or more variables. This allows for a level of sophistication that offers researchers the opportunity to explore cause and effect, as well as test theories and build/ test models. With multivariate analysis not only can researchers explore if a dependent variable is dependent on two or more independent variables (i.e. income is dependent on both gender and educational attainment), but also it allows them to acknowledge the relationship between the dependent variables (i.e. the relationship between gender and educational attainment). Some of the methods used in multivariate analysis are factor analysis, elaboration, structural equation modelling, MANOVA, multiple regression, canonical correlation, and path analysis. It is worth noting that statistics specialists are often called on at this level of analysis.

PRESENTING QUANTITATIVE DATA

When it comes to presenting quantitative data, there can be a real temptation to offer graphs, charts, and tables for every single variable in your study. But it is important to resist this temptation and actively determine what is most important in your work. Your findings need to tell a story related to your aims, objectives, and research questions.

Now when it comes to how your data should be presented, I think there is one golden rule: your presentation should not be hard work for the reader. Most people's eyes glaze over when it comes to statistics, so your data should not be hard to decipher. You should not need to be a statistician to understand it. Your challenge is to present your data graphically and verbally so that meanings are clear. Any graphs and tables you present should ease the task for the reader. So while you need to include adequate information, you do not want to go into information overload. Box 13.5 covers the basics of graphical presentation, while Box 13.6 looks at the presentation of quantitative data in tabular form.

TABLE 13.5   SELECTING STATISTICAL TESTS

Univariate	Bi/multivariate		
	Nominal	**Ordinal**	**Interval/Ratio** (Assumption of normality – if not normal use ordinal tests)
Nominal 2-point scale, e.g. gender: 1 = female, 2 = male	Compare two or more groups: **chi squared**	Compare two groups: **Mann–Whitney** three or more groups: **Kruskal–Wallis**	Compare two or more groups: **ANOVA** followed by *t*-test
3-point scale, e.g. religion: 1 = Catholic, 2 = Protestant, and 3 = Jewish Central tendency: **mode** Dispersion: **frequency**	Compare within same group over time: 2 pts: **McNemar test** 3 + pts: **Cochran's Q**	Compare within same group over two times: 2 pts: **Wilcoxon signed-rank test** 3+ pts: **Cochran's Q** three or more times (2+ pts): **Friedman's test**	Compare within same group over times (2+ pts): **ANOVA followed by** *t*-test
Compare sample with population: **chi squared**	Relationship with other variables: yes/no: **chi squared** Relationship strength: 2 pts: **phi** 3+ pts: **lambda**	Relationship with other variables: Yes/no: **chi squared** Relationship strength: 2+ pts: **lambda**	Relationship with other variables: yes/no: **Pearson's product moment correlation** Relationship strength: **F-test** With two or more independent and 1 dependent variables: **MANOVA** 2+ dependent variables and 3+ groups: **multiple regression** or **path analysis**
Ordinal TV viewing, order of preference: 1 = sitcoms, 2 = dramas, 3 = movies, 4 = news, 5 = reality TV *or* Likert scale, 1 = strongly disagree, 2 = disagree 3 = neutral, etc.		Relationship with other variables:	Relationship with other variables:
Central tendency: **median**		small sample, <10: **Kendall's tau**	**Jaspen's coefficient of multiserial correlation**
Dispersion: **interquartile range**		Larger sample: **Spearman's rho**	With the interval/ratio variable as dependent: **ANOVA**

(Continued)

TABLE 13.5 *(Continued)*

Univariate		Bi/multivariate	
	Nominal	Ordinal	Interval/Ratio (Assumption of normality – if not normal use ordinal tests)
Compare sample with population: **Kolmogorov–Smirnov**		With one variable as dependent: **Somer's *d***	
Interval/ratio			
Interval, e.g. IQ score Ratio, e.g. real numbers, age, height, weight			Relationship with other variables – no dependent/ independent distinction: **Pearson's product moment correlation**
Central tendency: **mean**			
Dispersion: **standard deviation**			With one independent and one dependent variable: **Pearson's linear correlation**
Compare sample with population: ***t*-test**			With two or more independent and 1 dependent variables: **multiple regression**
			With two or more independent and two or more dependent variables: **canonical correlation**

BOX 13.5   GRAPHS APLENTY

THE POWER OF GRAPHS

As they say, a picture is worth a thousand words, so a good graph can go a long way in communicating your findings.

SAMPLE DATA

In order to run you through the most commonly used graphs in quantitative analysis, I mocked up a four-variable data set in SPSS using a hypothetical example of survey data from 60 students (30 males and 30 females) about to graduate from high school:

Gender 1 = female 2 = male	Grade Point Average (out of possible 4)	Plans after graduation 1 = vocational/ technical training 2 = university 3 = workforce 4 = travel 5 = undecided 6 = other	Importance of university 1 = not at all unimportant to 7 = essential
1	3.10	2	7
2	2.60	3	2
1	1.30	3	2
2	3.60	5	6
2	1.50	1	1
Etc. (60 cases in all)			

EXPLORING 'PLANS AFTER GRADUATION'

'Plans After Graduation' is a nominal variable so bar and pie graphs tend to work well. The line graph, however, does not work because it is better suited to showing change over time – which is not what we are trying to do.

Bar Graph

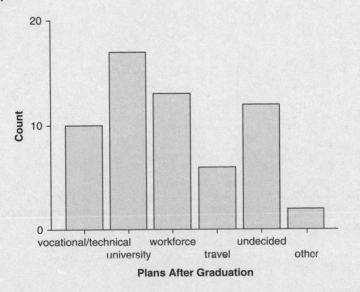

(Continued)

(Continued)

Pie Graph

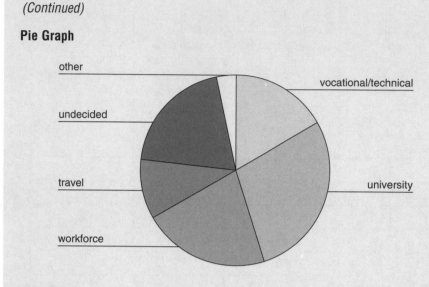

Line Graph

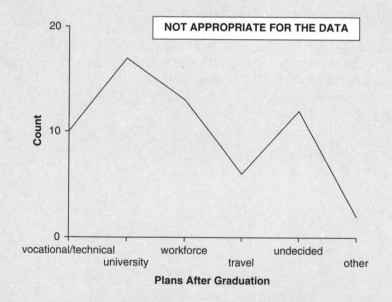

This type of graph would be better suited for data that showed something like changes in a student's GPA (Grade Point Average) over their high school career (GPA would sit on one axis and year of study on the other).

Clustered Bar Graph

A clustered bar graph allows you to compare the distribution of a nominal variable for two or more groups. In this example, 'Plans After Graduation' is compared by gender.

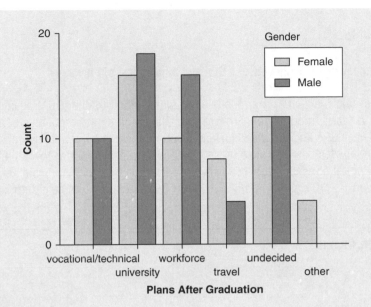

EXPLORING GPA

A histogram is appropriate for showing the distribution of interval and ratio data. Here we can see the distribution of GPA (a ratio variable), complete with mean, standard deviation, and the plotting of a normal curve.

Histogram with normal curve

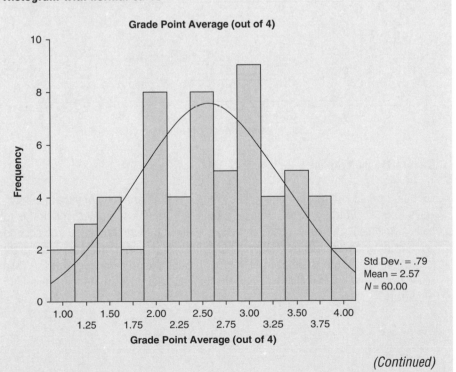

(Continued)

(Continued)

Exploring the relationship between GPA and 'Importance of University'

In this example, a scatter graph is used to plot a *ratio* variable (GPA) against an *ordinal* variable (Importance of University). The graph shows a positive correlation between GPA and perceived university importance: that is, while the relationship is not perfect, as GPA goes up so too does perceived importance. To find out the exact level of association you can run a Pearson's correlation, which shows a .773 correlation, significant at the .01 level (you are 99% sure the pattern is not a fluke).

SCATTER GRAPH

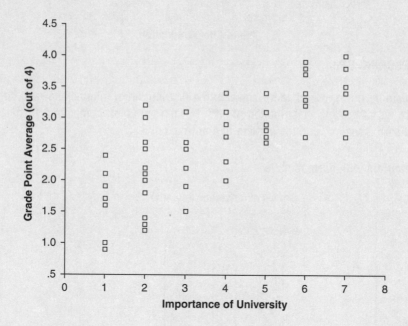

Generating the graphs

OK – so how do you go about generating these types of graphs? Well there are two ways to go about this and both involve sitting in front of a computer. The first is to have someone in the know show you what to do, and then practise it. The second is to sit down by yourself and have a play with a stats program. Most have great interactive online tutorials that can take you through the process from A to Z. While reading can give you familiarity, I truly believe that the best way to learn this kind of stuff is by doing.

PRESENTING COMPLEXITY WITH SIMPLICITY

Tables are generally more complex than graphs because they attempt to summarize the relationship between a number of variables (multivariate analysis). And because this summary can involve multiple statistical operations, statistics programs rarely spit tables out in a ready-to-use form. Now you can use an automatic table generator (you can find these on the Internet – one example is TableMaker at www.bagism.com/tablemaker), and this can certainly help, but the chances are you will still need to do some manual manipulation. The challenge here is walking the line between enough and too much information.

RULES OF THUMB

Your tables should not: (1) give your readers a headache; (2) make their eyes glaze over; or (3) make them even more confused. While your tables should not stand alone (you will need to walk your readers through them) they should be something that the non-specialist can engage with and learn from. Your tables will be most effective if: you can provide clear and adequate information; you do not assume too much knowledge; and you keep them as simple as possible.

SOME EXAMPLES

Below are three examples taken from a study I did sometime ago on the process of giving up religion. Table 1 simply outlines the criteria I used to classify three distinct processes of religious disaffiliation and the percentage of my sample ($n = 80$) that fell into these categories. While this information is pretty self-explanatory and could have been presented in a non-tabular form, I thought the table allowed readers to get a quick sense of the distinctions I was trying to make.

TABLE 1   CLASSIFICATION OF DISAFFILIATION JOURNEY AND DISTRIBUTION

Type of disaffiliation journey	Classification criteria
Angry rebellion 30%	A tone of: weariness; anger; irritated disgust, perhaps not with life, but at least with God or religion A journey of reaction or rebellion
Discontented doubt 29%	Empty, melancholic, depressive intellectualism Confused detachment wherein religion becomes deconstructed to the point of irreconcilable doubt and emptiness
Open exploration 41%	Without a reactionary basis, or a confused intellectualism A willingness to expand the realms of spiritual possibility beyond immediate experience and frames of reference

(Continued)

(Continued)

Table 2 is a bit more complex because it looks at the frequency distribution (cross-tabulation) of these three types of disaffiliation journey by both gender and religion. It also shows, through Chi squared statistics, that religion is significant, i.e. the distribution is not even. You cannot assume that your readers will know what this means, so it is up to you to walk them through your table. An example of this type of walk-through (the italic text) is given below.

TABLE 2   FREQUENCY DISTRIBUTIONS FOR DEMOGRAPHIC VARIABLES BY TYPE OF JOURNEY

	Rebellion	Doubt	Exploration	Significance
Gender				
Female	50.0	45.8	46.9	
Male	50.0	54.2	53.1	
	100.0	**100.0**	**100.0**	
Religion				
Protestant	29.2	50.0	46.9	*
Catholic	70.8	50.0	53.1	
	100.0	**100.0**	**100.0**	

*Chi squared test of significance $p < .05$.
All numbers expressed as percentages.

As shown in this table, those having gone through each of the three disaffiliation journeys are as likely to be male as female. The results for religion, however, are somewhat more interesting. Catholics and Protestants tend to go through journeys of discontented doubt and open exploration in similar proportions. Those whose journeys are more rebellious in nature, however, are somewhat more likely to have a Catholic heritage.

The complexity of Table 3 is even greater because I attempt to compare certain characteristics of the three disaffiliation journeys. In other words, I want to show if there is a statistically significant distinction between the types of journey in relation to: how old individuals were when they first doubted their faith; how long the process took; whether it was still ongoing at the time of interview; and how intense the process was. The complexity of the table meant I definitely had to walk readers through it.

TABLE 3   MEAN SCORES AND SIGNIFICANCE FOR PROFILE VARIABLES BY TYPE OF JOURNEY*

	Rebellion	Doubt	Exploration	Reb–Dbt	Reb–Expl	Dbt–Expl
Age first doubt	20.88	19.58	16.94		*	
Process length	4.42	10.83	5.62	*		*
Process ongoing	0.08	0.35	0.15	*		*
Intensity	0.70	0.42	0.32	*	*	

*One-way ANOVA $p < .05$.

The figures in this table point to varying and distinct patterns of disaffiliation for each type of journey. Those on a rebellious path generally complete an intense and relatively short journey away from faith. For those whose journey is marked by discontented doubts, however, the process is quite lengthy, lasting an average of almost 11 years, with one-third still in the process of moving away from religion at the time of interview. The journey for this discontented group, however, is not as intense as that of the rebellious contingent. Those whose journey out of faith is characterized by open exploration, on the other hand, go through a relatively short and often finalized process of disaffiliation that begins earlier in life. The process of disaffiliation is not generally seen as intense.

A FINAL WORD

Good tables do take time to construct, and if you struggle at the high end of word processing, creating tables can be extraordinarily frustrating. But if you can manage to create tables that are well constructed and well explained, they can be an exceedingly important and effective communication tool.

FURTHER READING

Works on quantitative analysis are virtually unending, so for this list I have pulled together those that are fairly recent (unless seminal), very practical, and highly applied.

General social science statistics

Donnelly Jr, R. A. (2007) *The Complete Idiot's Guide to Statistics.* New York: Alpha Books.

Hardy, M. A. and Bryman, A. (eds) (2004) *Handbook of Data Analysis.* London: Sage.

Salkind, N. J. (2007) *Statistics for People Who (Think They) Hate Statistics.* London: Sage.

Sirkin, R. M. (2005) *Statistics for the Social Sciences.* Thousand Oaks, CA: Sage.

Program specific

Bissett, D. (2007) *Automated Data Analysis Using Excel.* Boca Raton, FL: Chapman & Hall/CRC Press.

(Continued)

(Continued)

Bryman, A. and Cramer, D. (2008) *Quantitative Data Analysis with SPSS 14, 15 & 16: A Guide for Social Scientists.* London: Routledge.

Carver, R. H. (2003) *Doing Data Analysis with MINITAB 14.* Pacific Grove, CA: Duxbury Press.

Der, G. and Everitt, B. S. (2008) *Handbook of Statistical Analyses Using SAS.* Boca Raton, FL: CRC Press.

Greasley, P. (2008) *Quantitative Data Analysis with SPSS.* Buckingham: Open University Press.

CHAPTER SUMMARY

- Data interpretation is a major hurdle in any research study. Effective data analysis involves: keeping your eye on the main game; managing your data; engaging in the actual process of analysis; and effectively presenting your data.
- Being able to do statistics no longer means being able to work with formulae. It is much more important for researchers to be familiar with the language and logic of statistics, and be competent in the use of statistical software.
- Data management involves: familiarizing yourself with appropriate software; systematically logging in and screening your data: entering the data into a program; and, finally, 'cleaning' your data.
- Different data types demand discrete treatment, so it is important to be able to distinguish variables by both cause and effect (dependent or independent) and their measurement scales (nominal, ordinal, interval, and ratio).
- Descriptive statistics are used to summarize the basic features of a data set through measures of central tendency (mean, mode, and median), dispersion (range, quartiles, variance, and standard deviation), and distribution (skewness and kurtosis).
- Inferential statistics allow researchers to assess their ability to draw conclusions that extend beyond the immediate data. For example, if a sample represents the population; if there are differences between two or more groups; if there are changes over time; or if there is a relationship between two or more variables.
- Statistical significance is generally captured through a 'p-value', which assesses the probability that your findings are more than coincidence. The lower the p-value, the more confident researchers can be that findings are genuine.
- Statistical analysis can be univariate, i.e. exploring one variable at a time; bivariate, i.e. exploring the relationship between two variables; or

multivariate, i.e. exploring the relationship between three or more variables. Multivariate analysis allows for the most sophisticated data interrogation.

- Selecting the right statistical test relies on knowing the nature of your variables, their scale of measurement, their distribution shape, and the types of questions you want to ask.
- Presenting quantitative data often involves the production of graphs and tables. These need to be (1) selectively generated so that they make relevant arguments, and (2) informative yet simple so that they aid the reader's understanding.

14
ANALYSING QUALITATIVE DATA

CHAPTER PREVIEW

- The promise of qualitative data
- The logic of QDA
- The methods of QDA
- Specific QDA strategies
- Presenting qualitative data

THE PROMISE OF QUALITATIVE ANALYSIS

> **"** **Not everything that can be counted counts,**
> **and not everything that counts can be counted. "**
> *Albert Einstein*

You may think of Einstein as an archetypal 'scientist', but, as I have come to find, he's archetypal only if this means scientists are extraordinarily witty, insightful, political, creative, and open-minded. Which, contrary to the stereotype, is exactly what I think is needed for groundbreaking advances in science. So when Einstein himself recognizes the limitations of quantification, it is indeed a powerful endorsement for working with qualitative data.

Yes, quantitative data and the use of statistics is a clearly defined and effective way of reducing and summarizing data. But statistics rely on the reduction of meaning to numbers. And when meanings are intricate and complex (which is often the case), reduction can be incredibly difficult. There can be a loss of 'richness' associated with the process.

This concern has led to the development of a plethora of qualitative data analysis (QDA) approaches that aim to create new understandings by exploring and interpreting complex data from sources such as interviews, group discussions, observation, journals, archival documents, etc., without the aid of quantification. But the literature related to these approaches is quite thick, and wading through it in order to find appropriate and

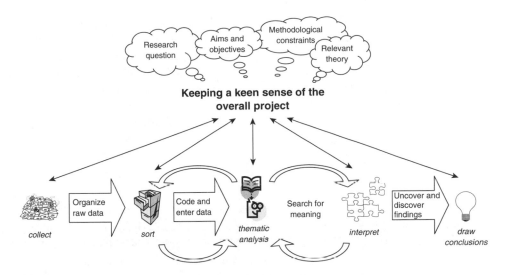

FIGURE 14.1   THE PROCESS OF REFLECTIVE ANALYSIS

effective strategies can be a real challenge. Many students end up: (1) spending a huge amount of time attempting to work through the vast array of approaches and associated literature; (2) haphazardly selecting one method that may or may not be appropriate to their project; (3) conducting their analysis without any well-defined methodological protocols; or (4) doing a combination of these points.

So while we know there is inherent power in words and images, the challenge is working through options for managing and analysing qualitative data that best preserve richness, yet crystallize meaning. I think the best way to go about this is to become familiar with both the logic and methods that underpin most QDA strategies. Once this foundation is set, working through more specific, specialist strategies becomes much easier.

Keeping the bigger picture in focus

In methods literature, we tend to dichotomize quantitative and qualitative analysis. But when it comes right down to it, the underlying logic is very similar. As shown in Figure 14.1, the process of reflective qualitative analysis requires researchers to: (1) organize their raw data; (2) enter and code that data; (3) search for meaning through thematic analysis; (4) interpret meaning; and (5) draw conclusions – all the while keeping the bigger picture, i.e. research questions, aims and objectives, methodological constraints, and theory, clearly in mind. While this is very much in line with quantitative analysis, the main points of difference are the use of thematic, rather than statistical, analysis, and a closer more entwined relationship between entering and coding data, data analysis, and interpretation. Rather than being three distinct, ordered steps, qualitative analysis demands a more organic process that sees these three steps all influencing each other and working in overlapping cycles.

As with quantitative analysis, it is easy to get lost in the detail and lose focus. It is therefore extremely important to keep asking yourself questions that can help you maintain an overarching perspective. As fully articulated in Box 13.1 in the previous chapter, this means asking yourself questions related to: (1) your own expectations – both what you expect and do not expect to find; (2) research questions, aims, and objectives – how you can work with your data so that it helps you achieve your project's stated goals; (3) theory – how your data confirms your theories, how theory can help explain your data, and whether your data is pointing to alternative theories; and (4) methods – how the methods employed might affect results.

From raw data to significant findings

In the world of qualitative analysis, raw data can be extremely messy. You might be facing a host of digital recordings, a mound of interview transcripts, a research journal (which can range from highly organized to highly disorganized), scribbled notes, highlighted documents, photographs, videotapes, mind maps – in fact the array is almost endless. And there is no doubt that a mound of messy data is extremely intimidating, especially if you are new to qualitative analysis.

As highlighted in Box 14.1, the best advice is to be systematic. No matter how reflexive and iterative you intend your analysis to be, you still need to approach the management of your data with methodical rigour.

BOX 14.1   QUALITATIVE DATA MANAGEMENT

While managing qualitative data is essential, it is worth noting that it is almost impossible to 'manage' qualitative data without engaging in some level of analysis. The process of organizing your data, e.g. deciding how you will group it, will see you engaging with your data and making decisions that will have an effect on analysis, and should therefore be recognized as a part of analysis.

STEP 1: FAMILIARIZE YOURSELF WITH APPROPRIATE SOFTWARE

As discussed in the next section, there is some debate as to the necessity for all project students to use specialist software for QDA, but it is certainly worth becoming familiar with available tools. Programs worth exploring include:

- **NU*DIST, NVIVO, MAXqda, The Ethnograph** – used for indexing, searching and theorizing text.
- **ATLAS.ti** – can be used for images as well as words.
- **CONCORDANCE, HAMLET, DICTION** – popular for content analysis.
  (Information on all of the above is available at www.textanalysis.info)
- **CLAN-CA** – popular for conversation analysis *(http://childes.psy.cmu.edu)*.

As with quantitative software, most universities have licences that allow students access to certain qualitative programs. Universities may also provide relevant short courses.

STEP 2: LOG IN YOUR DATA

It is rare that qualitative comes in at the same time, or in the same form, and can end up being a lot messier than a pile of questionnaires, so it is wise to keep track of your qualitative data as it is collected. It is well worth noting the respondents/ source, data collection procedures, collection dates, and any commonly used shorthand.

STEP 3: ORGANIZE YOUR DATA SOURCES

This involves grouping like sources, making any necessary copies, and conducting an initial cull of any notes, observations, etc., not relevant to the analysis. As well as organizing, this process allows you to screen your data. If done early, you can uncover potential problems not picked up in your pilot, and make improvements to any ongoing data collection protocols.

STEP 4: READ THROUGH AND TAKE OVERARCHING NOTES

It is extremely important to get a feel for qualitative data. This means reading through your data as it comes in and taking a variety of notes that will help you decide on the best way to sort and categorize the data you have collected. This is where data management and data analysis become highly blurred since any notes related to emerging themes *are* analysis.

STEP 5: PREPARE DATA FOR ANALYSIS/TRANSCRIPTION

If using a specialist QDA program, you will need to transcribe/scan your data so that it is ready to be entered into the relevant program. If you plan on manually analysing your qualitative data, you still need to go through this step so that you can print out your interviews, photographs, etc. You need to be able to actually put your hands on your data.

STEP 6: ENTER DATA/GET ANALYSIS TOOLS PREPARED

If you are using QDA software, you will need to enter your electronic data into the program. If you are manually handling your data, you won't need to 'enter' your data, but you will need to arm yourself with qualitative analysis tools such as index cards, whiteboards, sticky notes, and highlighters. In both cases analysis tends to be ongoing and often begins before all the data has been collected/entered.

QDA software

It was not long ago that QDA was done 'by hand' with elaborate filing, cutting, sticky notes, markers, etc. But quality software (as highlighted in Box 14.1) now abounds and 'manual handling' is no longer necessary. QDA programs can store, code, index, map, classify, notate, find, tally, enumerate, explore, graph, etc. Basically, they can: (1) do all the things you can do manually, but much more efficiently; and (2) do things that manual handling of a large data set simply will not allow. While becoming proficient in the use of such software can mean an investment in time (and possibly money), if you are working with a large data set you are likely to get that time back.

But if QDA programs are so efficient and effective, why are they so inconsistently called on by researchers working with qualitative data? Well, there are three answers here. First, a lack of familiarity – researchers may not be aware of the programs, let alone what they can do. Second, the learning investment is seen as too large and/or difficult. Third, researchers may realize, or decide, that they really don't want to do that much with their qualitative data; they may just want to use it sparingly to back up a more quantitative study.

My advice? Well, you really need to think through the pros and cons here. If you are working with a small data set and you cannot see any more QDA in your future, you may not think it will pay to go down this path – manual handling might do the trick. But if you (1) are after a deeper level of rigorous qualitative analysis, (2) have to manage a large data set, or (3) see yourself needing to work with qualitative data in the future, it is probably worth battling the learning curve. Not only is your research process likely to be more rigorous, but you will probably save a fair bit of time in the long run.

To get started with QDA software, I would recommend talking to your supervisor/ lecturer to find out what programs might be most appropriate for your goals and data. I would also have a look at relevant software websites (see Box 14.1); there is a lot of information here and some sites even offer trial programs. Finally, I would recommend that you take appropriate training courses. NU*DIST and NVIVO are both very popular and short courses are pretty easy to find.

THE LOGIC OF QDA

Whether you are working with qualitative or quantitative data, the main game of any form of analysis is to move from raw data to meaningful understanding. In quantitative methods, this is done through statistical tests of coded data that assess the significance of findings; coding the data is preliminary to any analyses and interpretation. In qualitative analysis, understandings are built by a more tangled and creative process of uncovering and discovering themes that run through the raw data, and by interpreting the implication of those themes in relation to your research questions.

Balancing creativity and focus

There is no doubt that good qualitative analysis demands a degree of openness, a high level of curiosity, and a willingness to accept fluidity. Qualitative analysis demands that you think your way through analysis and work your data so that it yields significant meaning. And such meaning may not be handed to you on a silver platter. As Isaac Asimov once said, 'The most exciting phrase to hear in science, the one that heralds new discoveries, is not "Eureka!" (I found it!) but "That's funny …".'

At the same time, however, we are not talking about airy–fairy metaphysical exploration. We are talking about science, with all the protocols and rigour thereof. As shown in Box 14.2, there is a real need for researchers to actively work between creativity and rigour. Creativity needs to be managed. You never want the cost of creativity to be credibility.

BOX 14.2   BALANCING CREATIVITY AND RIGOUR

Think outside the square … yet stay squarely on target.
Be original, innovative, and imaginative … yet know where you want to go.
Use your intuition … but be able to share the logic of that intuition.
Be fluid and flexible … yet deliberate and methodical.
Be inspired, imaginative and ingenious … yet realistic and practical.

Moving between inductive and deductive reasoning

Moving from raw data, such as transcripts, pictures, notes, journals, videos, documents, etc., to meaningful understanding is a process reliant on the generation/exploration of relevant themes; and these themes can either be discovered (through inductive reasoning) or uncovered (through deductive reasoning). So what do I mean by this?

Well, you may decide to explore your data inductively from the ground up. In other words, you may want to explore your data without a predetermined theme or theory in mind. Your aim might be to discover themes and eventuating theory by allowing them to emerge from the data. This is often referred to as the production of grounded theory or 'theory that was derived from data systematically gathered and analysed through the research process' (Corbin and Strauss 2007: 12).

In order to generate grounded theory, researchers engage in a rigorous and iterative process of data collection and 'constant comparative' analysis that finds raw data brought to increasingly higher levels of abstraction until theory is generated. This method of theory generation (which shares the same name as its product – grounded theory) has embedded within it very well-defined and clearly articulated techniques for data analysis (see readings at the end of the chapter). And it is precisely this clear articulation of grounded theory techniques that have seen them become central to many QDA strategies.

Students who only engage in grounded theory literature, however, can fall prey to the false assumption that QDA is always inductive. But this need not be the case. Discovering themes is not the only QDA option. You may, for example, have predetermined (a priori) themes or theory in mind – they might have come from engagement

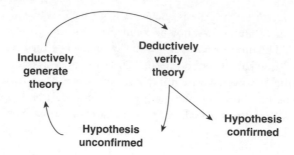

FIGURE 14.2   CYCLES OF INDUCTIVE AND DEDUCTIVE REASONING

with the literature; your prior experiences; the nature of your research question; or from insights you had while collecting your data. In this case, you are trying to uncover data deductively. You are mining your data for predetermined categories of exploration in order to support 'theory'. Rather than theory emerging from raw data, theory generation depends on progressive verification.

As shown in Figure 14.2, another likely possibility is that you will end up engaging in cycles of inductive and deductive reasoning. For example, you may design your study so that theory can emerge through inductive, ground-up processes, but as those theories begin to emerge from the data, it is likely that you will move towards a process of deductive confirmation. In this case, theory generation depends on ongoing verification. On the other hand, the credibility of those testing hypotheses through deductive verification can depend on their willingness to acknowledge the unexpected that just might arise from their data. Researchers need to be able to generate alternative explanations inductively.

THE METHODS OF QDA

When it comes to QDA, the most important thing to recognize is the pressing need for ongoing rich engagement with the documents, transcripts, images, and texts that make up your raw data. This will involve lots of reading and rereading that needs to start right from the point of data collection and continue through processes of data management, data analysis, and even the drawing of conclusions. As articulated more fully bellow and drawn out even further in Box 14.3, analysis then involves: (1) identifying biases and noting overall impressions; (2) reducing (an evil word I know, but an essential step in moving from messy raw data to rich understanding), organizing, and coding your data; (3) searching for patterns and interconnections; (4) mapping and building themes; (5) building and verifying theories; and (6) drawing conclusions.

There are two important things to note here. The first is that while the goal is to move from raw data to rich theoretical understanding, this process is far from linear. Qualitative data demands cycles of iterative analysis. The discovery of anything interesting will take you back to an earlier step including rereading, reviewing, and re-engaging. The second thing to note is related to the notion of reduction. Students

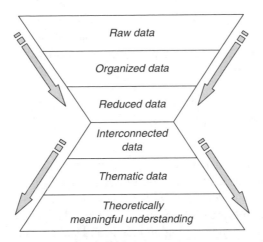

FIGURE 14.3   WORKING WITH QUALITATIVE DATA: DRILLING IN AND ABSTRACTING OUT

can get a bit worried when I tell them that part of the process is 'reducing'. They think this is antithetical to QDA's goal of preserving richness.

Well, richness is important, but qualitative analysis involves more than just preserving richness. Good qualitative analysis actually requires you to build it. Put it this way: raw data may be rich, but it is also messy and not publishable. If publishing in a journal, for example, you need to move from up to 1,000 or more pages of raw data to a 10-page article and this necessarily involves processes of reduction that make the data manageable and understandable. But you will also want to make the data meaningful. So after processes of reduction, you will want to find interconnections, develop themes, and build theories. As shown in Figure 14.3, getting to the point of meaningful understanding means abstracting your data back outwards so that it tells a full and powerful story that is in rich dialogue with theory.

Identifying biases/noting impressions

Because it is difficult to completely separate the process of data collection from analysis (you simply do not have the ability to constrain all thinking processes while engaged in listening to people's stories), you tend to analyse as you go. But this can be hazardous, since interpretations are always entwined with a researcher's biases, prejudices, worldviews, and paradigms – both recognized and unrecognized, conscious and subconscious.

Because of these biases, a good way to start your analysis is to list as many of your assumptions and preconceived notions as possible. In addition to bringing forward conscious recognition of biases that might need to be managed through the analysis process, it will also help you elicit potential categories for exploration.

The second step is to engage in careful reading of all collected data, with 'general impression' notes recorded throughout the reading process. The objective here is to get an overall feel for the data and begin a process of holistically looking at disparate sources of data as an overarching story. As well as various topics, this might involve identifying feelings and emotions. If you were exploring experiences of divorce, for example, anger, frustration, and hurt would be as important as division of property or custody arrangements.

Reducing and coding into themes

The next stage of analysis is to undertake a line-by-line examination of all data sources. This involves systematic drilling of the raw data in order to build up categories of understanding. The idea is to reduce your data and sort it into various themes. If you are doing your analysis manually, a good approach is to make multiple copies of transcripts that you can highlight, cut, and stack into relevant piles and play around with as your analysis progresses. If you are using QDA software, your program will allow you to undertake a comparable process, electronically.

As discussed above, this can be highly disconcerting. Suddenly your rich data is sorted and stacked into what may seem like superficial heaps. But remind yourself that this is just one stage in your analysis – and that this is a stage that you can revisit as your insights grow.

Now what you are looking for in this line-by-line exploration are categories and themes, but this might be alluded to in several ways: that is, through the words that are used; the concepts that are discussed; the linguistic devices that are called upon; and the non-verbal cues noted by the researcher:

- *Exploring words* – Words can be explored through their repetition, or through exploration of their context and usage (sometimes called key words in context). Specific cultural connotations of particular words can also be important. Patton (2001) refers to this as 'indigenous categories', while Corbin and Strauss (2007) refer to it as 'in vivo' coding. When working with words, researchers often systematically search a text to find all instances of a particular word (or phrase), making note of its context/meaning (see content analysis in Table 14.1 on page 270). Several software packages such as DICTION or CONCORDANCE can quickly and efficiently identify and tally the use of particular words and even present such findings in a quantitative manner.
- *Exploring concepts* – To explore concepts, researchers generally engage in line-by-line or paragraph-by-paragraph reading of transcripts, engaging in what grounded theory proponents refer to as 'constant comparison'. In other words, concepts and meaning are explored in each text and then compared with previously analysed texts to draw out both similarities and disparities. The concepts you explore can arise from the literature, your research question, intuition, or prior experiences. Concepts may also be derived from 'standard' social science categories of exploration, i.e. power, race, class, gender, etc. To find these you read through your text and deductively uncover the themes. The other option is to look for concepts to emerge inductively from your data without any preconceived notions (the practice of grounded theory). With predetermined categories, researchers need to be wary of 'fitting' their data to their expectations, and not

being able to see alternative explanations. However, purely inductive methods are also subject to bias since unacknowledged subjectivities can impact on the themes that emerge from the data. As discussed above, working towards meaningful understanding often involves both inductive and deductive processes.

- *Exploring linguistic devices* – Metaphors, analogies, and even proverbs are often explored because of their ability to bring richness, imagery, and empathetic understanding to words. These devices often organize thoughts and facilitate understanding by building connections between speakers and an audience. Once you start searching for such linguistic devices, you will find they abound in both the spoken and written word. Qualitative data analysts often use these rich metaphorical descriptions to categorize divergent meanings of particular concepts.

- *Exploring non-verbal cues* – One of the difficulties in moving from raw data to rich meaning is what is lost in the process. And certainly the tendency in qualitative data collection and analysis is to concentrate on words rather than the tone and emotive feeling behind the words, the body language that accompanies the words, or even words not spoken. Yet this world of the non-verbal can be central to thematic exploration. If your raw data, notes, or transcripts contain non-verbal cues, it can lend significant meaning to content and themes: exploration of tone, volume, pitch, and pace of speech; the tendency for hearty or nervous laughter; the range of facial expressions and body language; and shifts in any or all of these can be central in a bid for meaningful understanding.

Looking for patterns and interconnections

Once your texts have been explored for relevant themes, the quest for meaningful understanding moves to an exploration of the relationship between and among various themes. For example, you may look to see if the use of certain words and/or concepts is correlated with the use of other words and/or concepts. Or you may explore whether certain words/concepts are associated with a particular range of non-verbal cues or emotive states. You may also look to see if there is a connection between the use of particular metaphors and non-verbal cues. And, of course, you may want to explore how individuals with particular characteristics vary on any of these dimensions.

Interconnectivities are assumed to be both diverse and complex, and can point to the relationship between conditions and consequences, or how the experiences of the individual relate to more global themes.

Mapping and building themes

As your range of patterns and interconnections grows, it is worth 'mapping' your data. Technically, when deductively uncovering data related to 'a priori' themes, the map would be predetermined. However, when inductively discovering themes using a grounded theory approach, the map would be built as you work through your data. In practice, however, the distinction is unlikely to be that clear, and you will probably rely on both strategies to build the richest map possible.

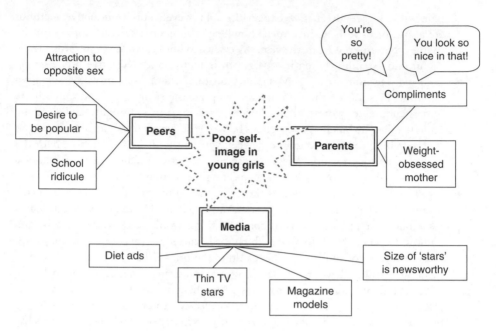

FIGURE 14.4   MAPPING YOUR THEMES

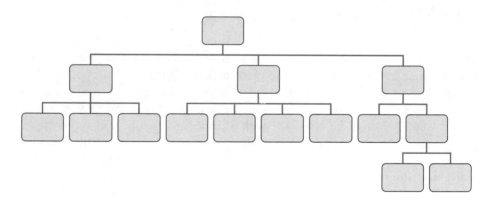

FIGURE 14.5   QDA 'TREE STRUCTURE'

Figure 14.4 offers a map exploring poor self-image in young girls built through both inductive and deductive processes. That is, some initial ideas were noted, but other concepts were added and linked as data immersion occurred. It is worth noting that this type of mind map can be easily converted to a 'tree structure' that forms the basis of analysis in many QDA software programs (see Figure 14.5).

At this stage, it is also a good idea to turn back to the literature, both past research studies and broader theoretical writings, and see how they might inform your data given the categories of understanding that have begun to emerge. This simultaneous engagement with the text and existing literature allows you to build much greater depth of understanding. Not only are you able to explore the content of your data, but also how and why that content is related to theory.

This then moves your data from piles sorted under simple categories of reduction to understandings that sit under much more meaningful themes. Mapping becomes an exercise that involves engaging themes in a dialogue and juxtaposing the themes (as well as the tensions among the themes) with relevant research and theoretically oriented literature. Reductive processes have thus expanded back out at a much more sophisticated level.

Developing theory

While your analysis may culminate with thematic mapping, the conceptualization and abstraction involved can become quite advanced and can go from model building to theory building. In other words, rich mapping is likely to spurn new ideas – that 'hey, you know what might be going on here' moment. It is quite exciting when you suddenly realize you are not just taking from the literature, but that you are ready to contribute back.

Drawing conclusions

Drawing conclusions is your opportunity to pull together all the significant/important findings of your study and consider why and how they are significant/important. It is about clearly summarizing what your data reveals and linking this back to your project's main questions, aims, and objectives. Your findings will need to be considered in relation to both current literature and your study's methodological constraints, and should clearly point to your overarching arguments. Remember: clarity is important, but do not force fit your findings to portray a world without ambiguity and complexity.

In addition to summary, you can also consider sharing your findings, insights, and ideas in the form of an original framework or model. Such devices not only add clarity to your reporting, but also help you establish your credibility as a researcher able to make original contributions back to the literature.

BOX 14.3   STEPPING YOUR WAY THROUGH EFFECTIVE QDA

I thought it would be a good idea to take you through a brief example of how the steps outlined above might unfold in practice. One of my daughters suggested that a common point of reference might be music videos. So for the purpose of this exercise imagine you want to undertake a study that explores music videos of the past three years and that you managed to record the top 30 videos of that period. Analysis might unfold as follows:

(Continued)

(Continued)

STEP 1: IDENTIFYING BIASES/NOTING OVERALL IMPRESSIONS

We all have them. You might, for example, think that music videos objectify women, that they have shallow lyrics, and that country music videos are the most inane. Doing this fully is extremely important. If you do not acknowledge preconceived notions and actively work to neutralize them, you are likely to find exactly what you expect to find!

The next step is to watch all 30 videos and take notes of overall impressions, perhaps related to content, lyrics, dancers, movement, emotions, style (these categories may derive from your own interests, insights or the literature).

STEP 2: REDUCING AND CODING INTO THEMES

This involves watching each video in turn and noting everything you possibly can related to the categories you noted/generated in step 1 as well as any other categories you inductively uncover along the way. When it comes to lyrics for Video 1, for example, you might find themes of cheating, heartbreak, and trust. In this way, you build both categories and subcategories that are likely to expand as you work your way through each video.

STEP 3: SEARCHING FOR PATTERNS AND INTERCONNECTIONS

You are likely to have overlapping themes across your 30 videos – so this step asks you to search for commonalities and divergences. For example, you may find that the video with the most explicit content comes from videos featuring bands rather than female artists, or that the dancers feature most heavily in country videos.

STEP 4: MAPPING AND BUILDING THEMES

One small section of a preliminary map might be as follows:

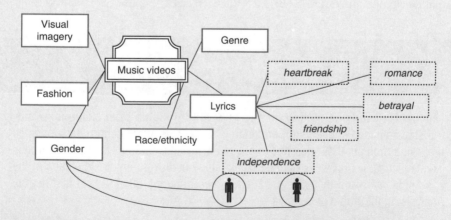

From here you would: (1) continue mapping all the main themes (genre, gender, etc.); (2) create even more subcategories as appropriate (e.g. under independence you might put males/females) and (3) map various interconnections. Don't forget to call on the literature in doing these tasks.

Now if you did not have clear boundaries on your study at the onset, you will probably come to realize that doing qualitative analysis of all aspects of music videos is a *huge* task that may not be manageable – so you may decide to narrow in on one or two particular interesting areas, say, for example, gender. Remember: it is much better to do a really rigorous job on a smaller scale than a crappy job on a bigger scale.

STEP 5: BUILDING AND VERIFYING THEORIES

This is your 'hey, you know what might be going on here' moment that will hopefully dawn on you as you watch your videos for the 103rd time and play around with your maps for the 72nd time. Who knows? You may just come up with a mind-blowing theory that sets the music industry on fire.

STEP 6: DRAWING CONCLUSIONS

You are likely to find out much more through the processes than you could possibly share, so you will need to decide what is most significant/important and link this back to your project's main questions, aims, and objectives in the most compelling and credible way.

SPECIFIC QDA STRATEGIES

To this point, I have been treating QDA as a homogeneous approach with underlying logic and methods, and I have not really discussed the distinct disciplinary and paradigmatic approaches that do exist. But as mentioned at the start of this section, a number of distinct approaches have developed over the past decades. Each has its own particular goals, theory, and methods – and each will have varying levels of applicability to your own research. Now while I would certainly recommend delving into the approaches that resonate with you, it is worth keeping in mind that you don't have to adopt just one approach. It is possible to draw insights from various strategies in a bid to evolve an approach that best cycles between your data and your own research agenda.

Table 14.1 is not designed to be comprehensive enough to make you an expert on any particular branch of QDA, but it does provide a comparative summary of some of the more commonly used strategies. You can explore these strategies further by delving into the readings offered at the end of the chapter.

PRESENTING QUALITATIVE DATA

Not many books adequately cover the presentation of qualitative data, but they should. Students often struggle with the task and end up falling back on what they

TABLE 14.1   COMPARING SPECIALIST QDA STRATEGIES

Content analysis

'To interpret meaning in speech
and text'

- Can involve linguistic 'quantification' where words and text' are units of analysis that are tallied
- Can also refer to thematic analysis through coding
- Taken up in studies where occurrence is assumed to indicate important trends. For example, analysing the newsworthiness of a particular topic, or looking at an individual's subconscious references to a particular concept

Discourse analysis

'To interpret language as it is situated in a socio-historic context'

- Rather than focus on simply what is said, discourse analysis explores language as it constitutes and embodies a socio-historic context tied to power and knowledge
- Analysis necessarily involves data exploration that is 'critical'; in other words, it challenges the dominant ideology
- Taken up in studies where 'text' is assumed to have real political power and has influence on social consciousness

Narrative analysis

'To interpret the "stories" of individuals'

- Data collection and interpretation is often iterative with focus on story building
- Metaphors seen as important
- Taken up in studies where there is a belief that it is helpful to draw out an individual's story. Usually involving a small sample and is often called on in phenomenological research

Conversation analysis

'To understand the structure and construction of conversation'

- Painstakingly transcribed conversations are explored for structural organization of speech
- Turn-taking between speakers and sequential ordering of utterances are of particular importance in understanding conversation
- Often taken up in ethnomethodological studies that look at how individuals create meaning through dialogue

Semiotics

'To interpret the meanings behind signs and symbols'

- Involves identification of 'cognitive domains' – or the learning skills and mental processes used to make meaning
- Attempts to deconstruct specific meanings in order to reconstruct understanding
- Taken up in linguistics and humanities – social researchers using semiotics often attempt to understand how signs are created and used to affect social consciousness

Hermeneutics

'To interpret text in a dialogic fashion'

- Involves moving in and out of text using a 'hermeneutic spiral', or a process that cycles in on richer understandings by altering viewpoints
- Focus on alternative perspectives – global vs detailed, conventional vs critical, etc.
- Often used in the study of literature including historical document, novels, lyrics, artworks, and theatre. Taken up when there is an assumption that meaning is a product of the relationship between author and audience

Grounded theory

'To generate theory directly from data'

- Highly inductive (analytic induction)
- Use of 'constant comparative method' to explore each data source in relation to those previously analysed

TABLE 14.1   *(Continued)*

	• Taken up by researchers who believe it is important to cast aside all preconceived notions and simply let the data tell the story
Visual analysis 'To interpret still and moving images'	• Can involve the logic of all of the strategies above, the point of difference being the analysis of images rather than words
	• Can also involve gathering people's opinions on, and reactions to, particular images, clips, artwork, etc. When photographs are used this is called photo elicitation
	• Taken up by researchers who argue the importance of images to full social understanding – something increasingly recognized in our MySpace, YouTube, TV, DVD, world

are most familiar with, or what they can find in their methods books (which are often quantitatively biased). So while students working on a qualitative project may only have three cases, five documents, or eight interviews, they can end up with some pseudo-quantitative analysis and presentation that includes pie charts, bar graphs, and percentages. For example, they may say 50% feel … and 25% think, when they are talking about a total of only four people.

This simply isn't where the power of qualitative data lies. The power of qualitative data is in the actual words and images themselves – so my advice is to use them. If the goal is the rich use of words, then avoid inappropriate quantification and preserve/capitalize on language. Now I think the best way to preserve and capitalize on words and images is through storytelling. What you need here is a clear message, argument or storyline, and to selectively use your words and/or images in a way that gives weight to that story. The qualitative data you present should be pointed and powerful enough to draw your readers in.

An example is probably the best way to get this across. To do this, I'll go back to my own study on religious disaffiliation. Now for this study, I actually conducted in-depth interviews with 80 'apostates' (those who had given up religious faith), so I was able to effectively quantify and present the data in tabular form (which I shared with you in the previous chapter – Box 13.6). But while this quantification definitely makes for a nice summary, it is the words and stories of the apostates themselves that are most compelling.

BOX 14.4   AN EXAMPLE OF QUALITATIVE DATA PRESENTATION

This example centres on the individuals whose processes of religious disaffiliation are best represented not by angry rebellion or open exploration, but by 'discontented doubts'. In my research such individuals were labelled 'egoistic apostates', one of three types of apostate (apostates being individuals who have given up religious faith) identified through the research.

(Continued)

(Continued)

THE EGOISTIC APOSTATE

The common road

Egoistic apostates have a difficult time reconciling religion with the condition of the world or the condition of themselves. Processes of disaffiliation are inscribed with introspection, negative self-reflection, and an emptiness that leads to a sense of disenchantment with God, religion, and, at times, the self. Apostasy tends to be an intense intellectual exercise in confusion and detachment. The following narrative captures the essence of egoistic disaffiliation:

> I was starting to have a really hard time; I think it was in year eight. My parents were fighting a fair bit, and … God didn't seem to want to help. My life at times has not been easy … I have been depressed, I have had some mighty lows and as a youth it was during these lows that I really doubted God. It's hard to believe in anything when you do not believe in yourself and I wanted to turn to God, but he didn't reach out. I often felt that God was not there for me … It made me wonder whether he existed at all, I used to think about that all the time. Was he there? Did he just not care about me? (Interview No. 13)

Quite telling in this egoistic passage is a clearly articulated sense of disenchantment with both God and religion. The statements 'God did not seem to want to help' and 'he didn't reach out' show both disenchantment with familial religion and painful internalization of God's rejection of a personal relationship. Focus is placed on the self, and there is clear indication of the emptiness associated with religious doubts.

For egoistic apostates, the process of disaffiliation tends to be an introspective journey of doubt and questioning arising from a very personalized sense of disappointment. The hallmark of the egoistic journey is a meditative and intellectual focus accompanied by a sense of alienated loss. The following narrative further illustrates the point:

> I was sort of isolated as a child, I lived in a safe cocoon of ignorance, I didn't think that my parents really … that I really ever felt that what they did or thought was right, but I didn't really know why. When I went to uni and met a few people that made me question things for the first time. All the inconsistencies that go along with the church. I had never really looked at religion objectively; I don't even think I looked at it at all. Anyway, it's depressing. I mean you just have to look at the opulence of the church as compared to that of the poor who they say they want to help, and you, ah, realize that there may be a problem with the idea of God. I really … I had a hard time with that revelation; I mean I just think that, well that nothing makes sense. I just don't know. (Interview No. 67)

This passage clearly shows a sense of disenchantment with the notion of God and religion. The 'inconsistencies' of the church leave this egoistic apostate with an internalized sense of disenchantment. The hypocrisy perceived in the church leads to a loss of religion that is quite mournful. The statement 'I really ... I had a hard time with that' shows a sense of lost confusion that is difficult to resolve; God and religion are thoughtfully considered to the point of vulnerable uncertainty.

Divergent paths

While lost and confused introspection is a common theme in egoistic journeys away from faith, the journey can still take somewhat divergent paths. For example, the depressed introspection that marks the egoistic respondent's journey can be associated with reactionary pain and anger:

> I was sixteen when I started to doubt the traditional church and a traditional God. There is just so much suffering in the world. How could there be a God who would allow so many people to die and, so many children to suffer? ... How could we make sense of the world if there is a God who is such a strong father, yet such an absolute bastard? God made no sense. Either he is mean and vindictive or there is no God. I myself think that there is no male God. No religion that I have ever heard of really captures the essence of this world. I was completely disenchanted with religion, and with what it tries to give me ... the more I looked, the more I realized that the Christian faiths were all bastions of greed and oppression. It is such a waste, on both a personal and social level. That's why I became an atheist. (Interview No. 38)

For this respondent, egoistic disenchantment is the result of a resentful recognition of 'suffering in the world'. The perceived 'greed and oppression' of Christianity leads to both anger and alienation. For example, words such as 'mean', 'vindictive', and 'bastard' point to angry reactionism, while an egoistic sense of personalized alienation and emptiness is pointed to by the phrases '[i]t is such a waste' and 'I was completely disenchanted'. This respondent thus presents a simultaneous sense of mourning and anger.

Anger, however, is not the only construct associated with egoistic apostasy. Many egoistic journeys actually have a strong rational and logical component. In this case, disenchantment is coupled with a rational reflection on familial faith. The following narrative is indicative:

> I can't remember what exactly started me on the path, but I think that it is just all the problems in the world. Holy wars always spun me out. King Arthur and all that. I mean Holy–War isn't that an oxymoron? Anyway, I think I just gave up the notion of God, God first. There can be no God in this world, and then, I mean look at it. Old people handing money to preachers over the phone and people still going to war. I don't get it, never will, how can you not have some serious question of both religion and God, how can you not let it get to you? I mean I

(Continued)

(Continued)

really let that worry me ... once I gave up on God, well then you can start to really see religion for what it is ..., it is a mess. Yeah, it may be hard, but once you think about it logically, what else can you do but let religion go? (Interview No. 68)

For this respondent, the egoistic, emotive components of the process appear to be tempered with a sense of logic. Egoism is present, particularly at the start of the apostatic journey. This egoism, however, has been negotiated with a less emotive plea to the intellect; that is, to 'think about it logically'.

Concluding remarks

A journey in which both God and religion are examined and deconstructed on a personal level with a relatively acute sense of disenchantment, loss, confusion, and emptiness may best characterize egoistic apostasy. From this common ground, however, the journey can take various paths, including journeys tainted with angry reactionism, and journeys that incorporate a sense of rationality and logic.

FURTHER READING

When it comes to QDA there are a huge amount of options, so it is well worth delving into some reading.

General qualitative analysis

Auerbach, C. and Silverstein, L. B. (2003) *Qualitative Data: An Introduction to Coding and Analysis*. New York: NYU Press.
Boyatzis, R. E. (1998) *Transforming Qualitative Information: Thematic Analysis and Code Development*. London: Sage.
Grbich, C. (2007) *Qualitative Data Analysis: An Introduction*. London: Sage.
Miles, M. and Huberman, A. (1994) *Qualitative Data Analysis: An Expanded Source Book*. Thousand Oaks, CA: Sage.
Silverman, D. (2006) *Interpreting Qualitative Data: Methods for Analysing Talk, Text and Interaction*. London: Sage.

Content analysis

Franzosi, R. (ed.) (2008) *Content Analysis*. London: Sage.
Kripppendorf, K. (2003) *Content Analysis: An Introduction to Its Methodology*. London: Sage.

Kripppendorf, K. and Bock, M. A. (2008) *The Content Analysis Reader.* London: Sage.
Neuendorf, K. A. (2001) *The Content Analysis Guidebook.* London: Sage.

Discourse analysis

Fairclough, N. (2008) *Analysing Discourse: Textual Analysis for Social Research.* Cambridge: Cambridge University Press.
Hoey, M. (2000) *Textual Interaction: An Introduction to Written Discourse Analysis.* London: Routledge.
Van Dijk, T. A. (2008) *Society and Discourse: How Social Contexts Influence Text and Talk.* Cambridge: Cambridge University Press.
Wodak, R. and Meyer, M. (eds) (2002) *Methods of Critical Discourse Analysis.* London: Sage.

Narrative analysis

Clandinin, D. J. (ed.) (2006) *Handbook of Narrative Inquiry: Mapping a Methodology.* London: Sage.
Clandinin, D. J. and Connelly, F. M. (2004) *Narrative Inquiry: Experience and Story in Qualitative Research.* San Francisco: Jossey-Bass.
Herman, L. and Vervaeck, B. (2005) *Handbook of Narrative Analysis.* Lincoln, NE: University of Nebraska Press.
Riessman, C. K. (2007) *Narrative Methods for the Human Sciences.* London: Sage.

Conversation analysis

Hutchby, I. and Woofit, R. (2008) *Conversation Analysis.* Cambridge: Polity Press.
Liddicoat, A. J. (2007) *An Introduction to Conversation Analysis.* London: Continuum International.
Ten Have, P. (2007) *Doing Conversation Analysis: A Practical Guide.* Thousand Oaks, CA: Corwin Press.

Semiotics

Chandler, D. (2007) *Semiotics: The Basics.* London: Routledge.
Danesi, M. (2007) *The Quest for Meaning: A Guide to Semiotic Theory and Practice.* Toronto: University of Toronto Press.
Gottdiener, M., Lagopoulos, A., and Boklund-Lagopoulos, K. (eds) (2003) *Semiotics.* London: Sage.

(Continued)

(Continued)

Hermeneutics

Cohen, M. Z., Kahn, D. L., and Steeves, R. H. (2000) *Hermeneutic Phenomenological Research. A Practical Guide for Nurse Researchers.* Thousand Oaks, CA: Sage.

Herda, E. (1999) *Research Conversations and Narrative: A Critical Hermeneutic Orientation in Participatory Inquiry.* New York: Praeger.

Seebohm, T. M. (2005) *Hermeneutics. Method and Methodology.* New York: Springer.

Grounded theory

Bryant, A. and Charmaz. K. (2007) *The SAGE Handbook of Grounded Theory.* London: Sage.

Corbin, J. and Strauss, A. (2007) *Basics of Qualitative Research: Techniques and Procedures for Developing Grounded Theory.* London: Sage.

Glaser, B. and Strauss, A. (1967) *Discovery of Grounded Theory.* Chicago: Aldine.

Visual analysis

Banks, M. (2001) *Visual Methods in Social Research.* London: Sage.

Helmers, M. (2005) *The Elements of Visual Analysis.* White Plains, NY: Longman.

Rose, G. (2007) *Visual Methodologies: An Introduction to the Interpretation of Visual Methods.* London: Sage.

Van Leeuwen, T. and Jewitt, C. (eds) (2001) *Handbook of Visual Analysis.* London: Sage.

QDA programs

Bazeley, P. (2007) *Qualitative Data Analysis with NVivo.* London: Sage.

Lewins, A. and Silver, C. (2007) *Using Software in Qualitative Research: A Step-by-Step Guide.* London: Sage.

West, M. D. (2001) *Theory, Method, and Practice in Computer Content Analysis.* Norwood, NJ: Ablex Press.

CHAPTER SUMMARY

- Qualitative data analysis (QDA) creates new understandings by exploring and interpreting complex data from sources such as interviews, group discussions, observation, journals, archival documents, etc., without the aid of quantification.
- Analysis should be approached as a critical, reflexive, and iterative process that cycles between data and an overarching research framework.
- Managing qualitative data involves: familiarizing yourself with appropriate software; developing a data management system; systematically organizing your data: making overarching notes; preparing transcriptions; and finally (if using QDA software) entering the data.
- The logic of QDA involves balancing creativity and focus while uncovering and discovering themes that run through the raw data.
- QDA generally involves: identifying biases and noting impressions; reducing, organizing, and coding; searching for patterns and interconnections; mapping and building themes; building and verifying theories; and drawing conclusions.
- As you work through your text you might find yourself exploring everything from words to concepts, linguistic devices, and non-verbal cues.
- There are a number of paradigm/discipline-based strategies for QDA including: content, discourse, narrative, and conversation analysis; semiotics; hermeneutics; and grounded theory. Visual analysis intersects with all of these and reminds researchers of the importance of images.
- Effective presentation of qualitative data can be a real challenge. You will need to have a clear storyline, and selectively use your words and/or images to give weight to your story.

15
THE CHALLENGE OF WRITING UP

CHAPTER PREVIEW

- The writing challenge
- Research as communication
- The writing process
- The need for exposure
- The final word

THE WRITING CHALLENGE

> **I always write a good first line, but I have trouble in writing the others.**
> *Molière*

I have not come across many students who consider writing up an easy or hassle-free process. In fact, writing up is almost always approached with a sense of apprehension and wariness. And in many ways this is justified. For one thing, this could just well be the biggest single piece of academic writing you have ever attempted. Second, there are major consequences attached to the quality of your write-up – research is often judged not by what you did, but by your ability to report on what you did. Finally, you probably are not too practised in the art of writing research reports. This is likely to be new terrain.

So I know there is a good chance you wish this whole research thing could happen without the need to write it up. But that is not the reality. This is something you have to tackle. Luckily there are quite a few practical strategies for negotiating the writing process in a way that improves the overall quality of the project, and makes the task less daunting. If you can: (1) make a start; (2) see writing as part and parcel of the research journey rather than just an account of that journey; (3) craft a good story that engages others in your research; and (4) accept the need to draft and redraft, you can produce and submit a research account that will impress examiners and maybe even make a real contribution back to the literature.

BOX 15.1   THE PERILS (AND JOYS) OF WRITING!

It is not easy:

Composition is, for the most part,
an effort of slow diligence and steady perseverance.
Samuel Johnson (1709–84), English author

No pen, no ink, no table, no room, no time, no quiet,
no inclination.
James Joyce (1882–1941), Irish author

Writing … a combination of ditch-digging,
mountain-climbing, treadmill and childbirth.
Edna Ferber (1887–1968), US writer

But then again:

Writing is a dreadful Labour, yet not so
dreadful as Idleness.
Thomas Carlyle (1795–1881), Scottish essayist and historian

Writing is a sweet, wonderful reward.
Franz Kafka (1883–1924), German author

RESEARCH AS COMMUNICATION

If there were only one piece of advice I could give to someone tackling a writing project it would be to view writing as an exercise in communication. Now you may think the ultimate goal in writing up your project is simply reporting on what you did and what you found, but there is much more to it than this. The ultimate goal is to explain, illuminate, and share your research with others. You need your readers to understand your research journey and appreciate its consequences.

When you view writing as a communication process you recognize that good writing demands consideration of your readers. It is worth remembering that very few people (yourself probably included) have the ability to sit through a monotonous monologue or stay engaged in dry and turgid writing – they need to be mentally, intellectually, and/or emotionally involved. For an audience to appreciate what you have to say, you need to engage their thinking, predict their questions, and respond to their enquiries. They may not be able to respond iteratively, but it is their response that gauges your success.

Knowing and engaging your audience

A major factor in effective research communication is the ability to connect with your readers and this starts with knowing who they are:

- *Who am I writing for?* – Writing should be a communication process with your readers, and this means writing with your readers in mind. Consider whether your readers will be limited to academics or if your work is likely to be read by other groups such as community leaders, community members, managers, politicians, practitioners, etc.
- *What do they know?* – In most forms of writing the challenge is starting where readers are, not over or under their heads. This means considering what your readers are likely to know about your topic, as well as what they know about research processes. You need to 'add value' to what people already know without losing them in the process. The challenge in student writing is somewhat different. In this case, your readers are likely to know as much or even more about your topic as you do – and are likely to be charged with the responsibility of judging your work. The trick here is not being the 'expert' but tackling your writing in a way that impresses your readers with your engagement, logic, and insights.
- *What are their expectations?* – The expectation of academics, assessors, or examiners is not that you will blow them away with your incredible knowledge (although that would be nice!), but that you are able to show thoughtful engagement with relevant literature and logically sound research processes. The other thing they will definitely expect is polished work. You simply cannot impress with spelling mistakes, typos, and missing references.

Finding an appropriate structure and style

One of the biggest challenges in writing up a research report is knowing how best to organize it. Now this will be determined by a number of factors including the advice of your supervisor, your own sense of comfort, and, perhaps most importantly, the paradigm you are working under. Studies that sit under the positivist umbrella, say a study with a quantitative methodology, generally use a traditional format and formal style. But with a more qualitative methodology, there is some debate on how to best capture what you have done and find a voice that best reflects that paradigm.

The traditional format

When it comes to research reports, there is certainly a traditional structure that is recognized, accepted, expected, and often advocated. This is the 'introduction, literature review, methods, findings, discussion, conclusion' format that dominates the literature. And it is quite easy to see why so many researchers adopt this approach. Not only does it tend to be expected, but it also answers reader's questions in a sequence quite natural to the flow of a normal conversation. As shown in Table 15.1, project-related questions and their respective answers can easily structure a report or thesis that readily falls into a traditional format.

While this format may not be appropriate for all approaches to research, it is a format that undeniably limits the work readers need to do to make sense of your write-up, and therefore your research – something that should never be underestimated, regardless of

TABLE 15.1 THE STANDARD CONVERSATION

The questions	The answers that structure the chapters/sections of the conventional report
So tell me what your research is about?	Title Abstract Introduction • research question(s) • hypothesis (as appropriate)
And why did you choose this particular topic/question?	Introduction • rationale
What do you hope to achieve?	Introduction • aims and objectives
I really don't know much about this, can you fill me in?	Background • literature review (recent literature and prior research) • theory (current and seminal as appropriate) • context (social, cultural, historic, and geographic)
How exactly did you go about doing your research?	Research design/approach • methodological approach (framework) • methods (techniques/procedures) • limitations
And what did you find out?	Findings/results/emergent story • text, tables, graphs, charts, themes, quotes, etc. Discussion • analysis, interpretation, and meaning of findings
How would you explain the relevance/importance of what you have done?	Conclusion • implications • significance • recommendations (particularly important in applied research)

whether your goal is examination, publication, or broad dissemination. It is also a format that does allows some flexibility. For example, the voice you adopt and the emphasis you place on each section will vary in accordance with the specifics of your projects.

Alternative formats

Depending on the nature of the paradigm you are working under, your comfort zone, your research topic, your methods, and your readers, you might decide that an alternative structure will best get your message across. Alternative structures for writing up your research report can be based on:

- *Chronology* – Describing how the events within your research project unfolded over time.
- *Theory building* – Describing how theory was inductively generated, and allowing that theory to build throughout your report.
- *Findings first* – Providing readers with your conclusions up front, and then describing how you got there.

Any one of these formats, a combination of the above, or in fact something completely original, might be better suited to your project than the traditional structure.

But it is crucial that you consider whether your readers will be familiar with and/or accepting of something considered alternative.

Two cases where the 'risks' of alternative formats are minimized, and perhaps even rewarded, are:

- When you are using a format that is accepted as appropriate for your particular paradigmatic, disciplinary, or methodological approach; for example, the use of a 'theory-building structure' for studies that have adopted a grounded theory approach, or perhaps a 'chronological structure' for a case study exploring change.
- When you know (or can confidently assume) that your readers are likely to be open to a more creative structure. If your write-up is to be assessed, consider whether your examiner(s) are likely to be open to the alternative, i.e. they have written, or have students who have written, in alternative ways. If they are firmly planted in the positivist tradition, you may want to reconsider your approach or, if possible, your examiner. If your goal is to have your research published, the key will be to find a journal for which the alternative is quite standard.

Now if you decide to buck the system, and go with a structure that is new to your readers, you need to take great care that the logic of that structure becomes self-evident as your readers progress through your account. You cannot afford for them to get 'lost' as you take them through your research project. In fact, it is absolutely crucial that your readers do not end up scratching their heads and questioning the credibility of your entire research project just because they are unfamiliar or uncomfortable with the way you have chosen to write it up.

THE WRITING PROCESS

Traditionally, research has been a three-step process: (1) write and submit a research proposal; (2) conduct the research; (3) write up the report. And while less and less academics advocate this process, it is a process whose legacy seems to linger in the practice of many supervisors and their students. For the inexperienced researcher, however, this can be perilous. For many, 'writing' can be a huge obstacle. If you leave it until the end, you risk writer's block, which can lead to inevitable delays and even put completion at risk.

More commonly advised (if not entirely practised) is to approach writing as a process central to every stage of the research journey. Writing should be considered an activity that progresses as your research progresses. For example, if you formulate even your most initial ideas in written form, you will have begun to produce notes for the first draft of your 'introduction' and 'methods'; and annotating your sources can lead to preliminary drafts of your 'literature review'. These sections can then be redrafted as you go through the process of data collection. Similarly, preliminary analysis, note taking, and writing throughout data collection will provide you with a good start on 'findings'.

Keep in mind that even if you are a procrastinator and you are not that keen on writing as you go, it is a highly attractive option compared with facing the daunting prospect of having to start your writing from scratch when you complete your data collection and analysis. Write as you go and avoid leaving it all until the very end. If you can force yourself to see writing as part and parcel of the research process rather than just an account of that process, you will never have to face what looks like an insurmountable obstacle.

Writing as analysis

As well as a head start on report production, 'writing as you go' can actually be part of analysis. Very few people can formulate finalized ideas in their heads without committing them to paper. Ideas almost always evolve as you write, and in this way each draft of your writing will drive the evolution of your ideas. Writing, for example, can be central to the construction and interpretation of meaning. It can move you from the production of specific descriptive understandings, through to broader synthesis, and on to crafting significant, relevant, logical, and coherent storylines. In fact, many find writing and rewriting the key to bringing storylines into focus.

Now while this is true for all types of research (it is virtually impossible to evolve ideas if they stay planted in the realm of the mind), it is particularly relevant to research that sits under post–positivist (subjectivist, interpretivist, or constructivist) paradigms that demand iterative engagement with narrative, discourse, and/or text. As you work through each draft, understandings evolve and your analysis goes one step deeper.

Constructing your 'story'

So why am I using the word 'story'? Well, I am using it because good stories grab reader interest, hold that interest, have a strong plot, take readers on a journey, and lead them to logical, yet sometimes surprising, conclusions. The other implication of stories is that people simply won't read them if they are boring, tedious, long-winded, and pretentious. Yes, your write-up needs to report on your research, but it should do more: it should unfold, it should engage, and it should tell an interesting story. Now as the author of that 'story', there are a number of things you need to do:

1   *Think of your research account as a 'conversation'* – Now I realize conversations are two way, but you can apply this even in writing. You may not be there to see or hear a response, but you should be trying to engage your readers as if they are listening. In fact, if you can give relevant information, predict questions, and respond to enquiries, your writing will become 'interactive'. Remember that readers who feel involved are the most engaged.

2   *Become familiar with the craft* – Very few authors are not avid readers. One of the most effective things you can do is find 'good' examples of what you intend to

write. As you read through your literature, take note of not just content, but also structure and style. Also have a look at theses or reports that have been well received. These examples may not be prototypes, but they can certainly give you some sense of the shape of your end product.

3   *Find a voice* – There is likely to be a tension between 'engaging storytelling' and 'take me seriously reporting'. How to best negotiate this tension will depend on you, your goals, and your readers' expectations. The more you know about these elements, the better placed you will be to find an effective voice. Now the general rule of thumb is to avoid use of first person so that your research does not appear to be tainted with personal bias and subjectivities. But even within the positivist paradigm, this convention is relaxing (i.e. using first person to give personal opinion will not be well received, but using 'I' to report factually on things you did is now more commonly accepted). Objectivity is no longer seen as reliant upon masking a researcher's role. Under post-positivist paradigms, recognition of researcher role is paramount so there aren't really any hard and fast rules against use of first person. In fact, many 'qualitative' researchers use a highly reflexive first-person voice to outline their personal story, agendas, biases, etc., very early in their report/thesis. This, however, can leave some struggling to negotiate formality, as they move between a relaxed conversation and a logical/comprehensive research account. The key is a confident and consistent style that will be deemed appropriate to your project.

4   *Develop your structure* – Decide on a structure and work up an appropriate outline for your write-up early on. The more you know about where you want to go, the easier it will be to set a course that can help you get there. Remember that your structure can always be modified as your thinking evolves.

5   *Craft the storyline* – Whether you opt for a traditional or alternative structure, your report will need to take your readers through a clear, coherent, and hopefully compelling storyline with a beginning, a middle, and an end. It needs to engage your readers, pique their interest, and take them through your research journey in a way that unfolds the story and logically leads to your conclusion. A good idea is to use Table 15.1 as a checklist that can help you assess if your storyline will logically answer the questions readers are likely to ask. Some good tips for beginning this process include: writing a creative working title; constructing one or more draft outlines; and writing a one-page abstract (a task many researchers find exceptionally difficult, but extremely focusing).

6   *Be ready to make convincing arguments* – It is essential that you write purposefully. The quality and credibility of your write-up is largely dependent on your ability to construct logical and convincing arguments. Whether we are talking about your study's rationale, a review of the literature, or the presentation of methods, findings, and conclusions, the process of research demands more than simple summary and reporting. It is a process reliant on the ability of the author to convince, reason, and argue a case – as well, of course, as your ability to back up your arguments with appropriate data and references.

7   *Write/construct your first draft* – You can think about it, and you can keep thinking about it, and you can think about it some more, but it will not happen unless you do it. If you have constructed writing as part of the research process rather than its product, the bones of your first draft will be there for you to put together and flesh out. If, however, you have followed the 'write-up after' approach, you will

need to gather your notes and put it all down on paper. Regardless of approach, students generally find they need more time than they initially thought to write up that first draft.

8   *Get appropriate feedback* – Reader expectations can vary widely, so do not wait until the last minute to find out that your approach is inappropriate. Be sure to pass a draft of your write-up to someone who either has some experience in research, or has some insights into reader expectations.

9   *Be prepared to redraft* – This should be an expectation. In fact, as discussed below, very few people can get away with submitting a second draft or even third draft, let alone a first.

Developing each section/chapter

So let's get specific and talk about the writing needs within each section/chapter of your project write-up. Now I have decided to focus on the 'traditional' format, since it is the one most projects will adopt/adapt and the sections within it are likely to show up in some form even if you choose an alternative structure. As for the length of your document – well, regardless of whether the expectation is 20 or 350 pages, the expected sections are basically the same. Obviously the depth will vary dramatically, but the actual structure and guidelines for effective construction vary very little.

The front end

In Chapter 5, I went through each section expected in a research proposal. Now when it comes to the front end of your project write-up, you can draw on this work to build various sections expected in your final write-up:

- *Title* – This is something I wouldn't work on again until you have written up your entire project. At that stage you can take a look at the clear, concise, and unambiguous title you constructed for your proposal and see if it still fits or if it can be reworked to better match your project.
- *Summary/abstract* – Abstracts are so condensed that they are hard to get right. But they are extremely informative to your processes. If you wrote one for your proposal, have a look at it now. If your learning is as rich as it should have been over the course of your research, you are likely to want to do a complete rewrite. I advise my students to take this on before writing their discussion and conclusion so that they can think through how they might focus their argument. But I also suggest that they go over it again at the very end so that it completely and utterly matches the body of their work from aims and objectives through to methods, findings, discussion, and conclusions.
- *Research question/hypothesis* – Given the emphasis in this book on the importance of a well-defined research question, I am hoping this is something that has been very close to you throughout your research project. Now is your last chance to really nail the articulation of what you attempted to find out.

- *Introduction/rationale* – If you wrote this up for your proposal, you will now need to revisit, strengthen, and expand. Keep in mind that, as highlighted in Chapter 5, the main job of this section is to introduce your topic and convince readers that the problem you want to address is significant and worth exploring (which is why a few existing stats related to the extent/depth of the problem can be effective). This section should give some context to the problem (and in a more humanities-oriented write-up even some indication of your relationship to the problem), and lead your readers to a 'therefore' conclusion that sets up your aims and objectives. The trick is to write purposefully.

- *Aims/objectives* – If you are writing these for the first time have a look at the advice in Chapter 5. If you have already articulated these, this is your opportunity to make sure you have a goodness-of-fit between what you set out to do and what you eventually did. You may need to rewrite completely (particularly if your project took a turn in an unexpected direction) or simply refine and tighten.

- *Overview of the study* – A common convention in a thesis write-up is to give a brief and straightforward overview of each thesis chapter. This is usually done in one or two paragraphs per chapter and can cover not only content, but purpose and argument. Paragraphs are likely to start with: Chapter One introduces … Chapter Two discusses … The purpose of the chapter is two-fold … Chapter Three outlines … The chapter goes on to argue …

All of the above usually sit in the preliminary pages (title and abstract) and first section/chapter.

- *Literature review* – Hopefully you will come to the final write-up stage with a draft literature review in hand. If not, *start now!*, and follow the fairly detailed advice in Chapter 6. If you have a draft, review, add any new research, and try to find and tighten lines of argument. Remember that the goal here is to review past research in order to show a place for your own research processes. Depending on the nature of your project, as well as covering past research, your literature review may have a section that situates your study in a conceptual or theoretical framework.

- *Background* – This is a fairly straightforward chapter/section that offers the reader contextual information about your research setting, culture, political arena, etc. For example, if your study were on the threats of tourism on the traditional culture of Palau, you would need to offer your readers context regarding Palau's geography; tourism potential, history, and culture; as well as tourism trends. Remember to include only what a reader needs in order to work through your thesis. If it is not essential, don't include it.

The research design section

The research design section of your thesis is really the crux of your report. It is what defines your project as a true research study. It is how credibility will be judged – both the credibility of your project and the credibility of you as a social scientist.

- *Methodology* – Most research design sections of social science and certainly humanities write-ups will demand you engage with methodology, or the overarching framework you have used to situate your study within the paradigm(s) of science. Now this section can be quite theoretical and have you delving into the debates on paradigm outlined in Chapter 1. At this level, methodology situates understandings of truth, objectivity, and the construction of knowledge and the researcher might be integral to the discussion. This is also where you situate your study in terms of 'qualitative' and 'quantitative' approaches such as action research, experimental design, and phenomenology.

- *Methods* – All research design sections include methods comprising information on how you found respondents, i.e. population and sample/sampling procedures; data collection methods, i.e. surveying, interviewing, and document analysis; and methods of analysis, i.e. statistical or thematic analysis. These sections are relatively straight-forward reports of what you did (as compared with your proposal, which is what you were going to do).

- *Limitations/delimitations* – As discussed in Chapter 5, you will need to clearly artic-ulate all factors that have had an impact on your research processes/results. While it is crucial that you offer full disclosure here, try to avoid being overly apologetic. You need to offer strong justification for what you did and why your data is cred-ible in spite of any constraints.

- *Ethical considerations/approval procedures* – Finally you will need to review: all ethical considerations; the processes you adopted in order to ensure the emotional, physical, and intellectual well-being of your study participants; and the approval processes you may have gone through. Again this is a relatively straightforward reporting-type section.

The back end

- *Findings* – Findings are the presentation of the answers you have found to your key questions. They are not raw data nor the full abstraction of your data back to theory. Rather, this is a summative description of data that you find most significant. It is therefore important to resist the temptation to summarize the answer to every question you asked in your research processes. What you need to present is what is most key, interesting, educative, informative, and best makes the case regarding your research question/hypothesis. But avoid doing too much with this informa-tion. Abstraction generally waits until the discussion section. The presentation of quantitative and qualitative data is covered in Chapters 13 and 14 respectively.

- *Discussion* – This is where you get to make something of your data. The structure here is almost always thematic and tied to the storylines that have emerged from your data. It is your opportunity to take what you discovered in your findings and argue their implications/significance. So while the findings section may be fairly straightforward reporting, the discussion section/chapter is made up of purposeful arguments, arguments that emerge from your findings and show that you have met your aims and objectives. Now to do this well, you are likely to find yourself work-ing iteratively with both your data and the literature.

There are actually three ways you can handle the findings and discussion sections/chapters. The first is to offer one (or more) findings sections followed by one (or more) discussion sections. This means you present all the findings first, with all the discussion to follow. The second approach is thematic organization with findings and discussion related to one particular theme found within one section/chapter. This is repeated for as many strategic themes as you might have. The third approach is again thematic, but with less distinction between findings and discussion. These types of chapters are generally found in more humanities-oriented projects and are highly thematic in their organization.

- *Conclusion* – Drawing conclusions is all about clearly summarizing what your research processes have revealed and linking this back to your project's main questions, aims, and objectives in the most compelling and credible way. This is generally a tight section/chapter (and should be, given the work your 'discussion' has done). You do not tend to introduce new material in the conclusion other than the possibility of practical recommendations (common in applied research) or an original framework or model. This would be appropriate if you've begun to conceptualize a bigger picture in a fairly sophisticated manner.
- *References* – Perfection! Nothing less is expected or accepted. Take the time to do this right – it's a good time to be anal.

From first to final draft

> "What is written without effort is in general read without pleasure. "
> *Samuel Johnson*

Whether you decide to write in a way that is formal or casual, traditional or alternative, dry or emotive, there is a common denominator. Regardless of format, style, or voice your final work needs to be highly polished and unarguably professional – you cannot afford to come across as an amateur. Your authority can actually be enhanced or destroyed, not only by the quality of your research, but by its presentation. And I honestly do not know anyone who can accomplish this without working through a number of drafts. Bottom line? Be ready (1) to seek and take advice; and (2) to draft, redraft, and redraft again.

Seeking and utilizing feedback

There really is no way around it. If you want to move from a first to a final draft, you need to take the sometimes uncomfortable step of seeking quality feedback. Now you might think this would be a straightforward process, but that is not always the case. A PhD candidate of mine, for example, once submitted a preliminary draft of a chapter to a co-supervisor for comment. After a nervous wait of over two months, we found that the eventuating comments were all related to minor editing, i.e. spelling, grammar, and even proper margins for quotes. And while that might be really helpful for a final draft, it was completely useless at the first-draft stage where ideas, concepts, and logic were the things that needed to be reviewed.

This really brings home the need to ask the right people for advice, and to be specific in your requests. You need to know where you are in the process and ask for comments related to your current needs. A good strategy here is to ask your readers to comment on the same questions you need to ask yourself as you work through various drafts of your document (see questions in the next section). If it is a first draft, you will probably want advice on overall ideas, arguments, logic, and structure, while later stages will see you seeking suggestions for consistency, coherence, readability, and, finally, copy editing.

This means that you may not always go to the same person for advice. One professor I work with, for example, is excellent at broadening ideas, but is extremely sloppy. I do not think he could edit a children's picture book. Others will be great at the nitty-gritty detail – but will not be able to engage with the bigger picture. Now while the advice of your supervisor(s) can be invaluable, so too can the advice of colleagues, peers, and family. In fact, at some stage, it is worth asking a non-specialist to read your work to see if the logic makes sense to him or her – because it should. And don't forget to try to get a sense of timeframe. It can take some readers months to get back to you.

Now knowing who to ask and what to ask is one thing, but being willing to hand over what you have written is another. What if your secret fears of not being good enough are validated? Handing over is always exposing, but keep in mind that fears of incompetence are often a crisis of confidence – not a lack of ability. And besides, it is better to find out if you are off track early, than wait until you have invested a huge amount of time in an iffy direction.

OK, say you have managed to ask the right person the right questions and you get your draft back. If you are lucky, it is full of constructive, relevant, and thought-provoking comments. You should be happy – not only has someone put in a lot of time and effort, but they have provided you with a road map for moving forward. But, of course, you're human. So instead of being happy, you are devastated. In fact, you may feel insulted, frustrated, and even incompetent. You are not alone here. Personally, I wish feedback on my own work was limited to validation of just how clever I am. But what I really need – like it or not – is criticality. Validation simply doesn't move you forward. You need to accept advice and not take criticism personally. If you do, writing up will become an emotional minefield.

So now that you have the advice, what do you do with it? Well, unreflexive incorporation is just as bad as blanket dismissal. You need to mentally take the feedback on board, consider it in light of the source, and work through the implications that the advice has for what you are trying to say. And of course this is particularly important if you find yourself getting conflicting advice. Talk to your supervisor/lecturer, but remember that it is your work and you are the one who needs to make the final call.

Drafting and redrafting

There is no doubt that the journey from first draft to submission can be long and challenging. In fact, contrary to the desire of just about every fibre in your body, you may find that your final document does not retain much from that first draft. The irony, of course, is that you could not get to that final draft without that first draft and all the drafts in between.

Now as you work through various drafts, you will be tightening up different aspects of your writing (see Box 15.2). But you can approach this in any number of ways. Some like to work sentence by sentence in a slow and diligent fashion, while others do not want to break a stream of consciousness – they try to get new ideas down on paper all at once, to be cleaned up later on. As long as you find a process that works for you, there is nothing wrong with developing your own approach. It is the end result that counts.

Box 15.2 offers a number of checklists for helping you get to a quality end product. While it may seem somewhat tedious, almost all good writers do go through some variation of this process (see Box 15.3).

BOX 15.2   CHECKLISTS FOR THE REDRAFTING PROCESS

REWORKING THE FIRST DRAFT

It would be nice if your first draft were it. But it rarely works that way. When you step back and take stock, you are likely to find that the process of writing itself has evolved your ideas, and that your thoughts have moved beyond what you initially managed to capture on paper. As you work through your first draft ask yourself:

- ☑ Is this making sense? Does the logic flow? Do I need to alter the structure?
- ☑ Am I using a 'voice' I am comfortable with?
- ☑ Do I need to incorporate more material/ideas – or are sections really repetitive?
- ☑ Am I happy with my overall argument, and is it coming through?
- ☑ Does each chapter or section have a clear and obvious point or argument?
- ☑ Have I sought and responded to feedback?

REWORKING THE SECOND DRAFT

Once you are happy with the overall ideas, arguments, logic, and structure, it is time to fine-tune your arguments and strive for coherence and consistency. In doing this, ask yourself:

- ☑ How can I make my points and arguments clearer? Do I 'waffle on' at any point? Am I using lots of jargon and acronyms? Should I incorporate some/more examples?
- ☑ Do I want to include some/more diagrams, photos, maps, etc.?
- ☑ Is the structure coherent? Are there clear and logical links between chapters/sections?
- ☑ Is there consistency within and between chapters/sections? Do I appear to contradict myself at any point? Is my voice used consistently throughout the work?

☑ Is the length on target?
☑ Have I sought and responded to feedback?

MOVING TOWARDS THE PENULTIMATE DRAFT

Being ready to move towards a penultimate draft implies that you are reasonably happy with the construction and logic of the arguments running throughout and within your document. Attention can now be turned to fluency, clarity, and overall readability. Ask yourself:

☑ Are there ways I can further increase clarity? Are my terms used consistently? Have I got rid of unnecessary jargon?
☑ Are there ways I can make this read more fluently? Can I break up my longer sentences? Can I rework my one-sentence paragraphs?
☑ Are there ways I can make this more engaging? Can I limit the use of passive voice? Do I come across as apologetic? Are my arguments strong and convincing?
☑ Am I sure I have protected the confidentiality of my respondents/participants?
☑ Have I guarded against any potential accusations of plagiarism? Have I checked and double checked my sources, both in the text and in the references or bibliography?
☑ Have I written and edited any preliminary and end pages, namely title page, table of contents, list of figures, acknowledgements, abstract, preface, appendices, and references?
☑ Have I thoroughly checked my spelling and grammar?
☑ Have I done a word count?
☑ Have I sought and responded to feedback?

PRODUCING THE FINAL DRAFT

You would think that if you did all the above, your final document would be done. Not quite; you now need to do a final edit. If it is a large work and you can fund it, you might want to consider using a copy editor. It is amazing what editorial slip-ups someone with specialist skills can find, even after you have combed through your own work a dozen times. Some things you may want to ask prior to submission are:

☑ Have I looked for typos of all sorts?
☑ Have I triple checked spelling (especially those things that spell checkers cannot pick up, like typing 'form' instead of 'from')?
☑ Have I checked my line spacing, fonts, margins, etc.?
☑ Have I numbered all pages, including preliminary and end pages, sequentially? Have I made sure they are all in the proper order?
☑ Have I checked through the final document to make sure there were no printing glitches?

BOX 15.3   I WISH I COULD WRITE LIKE YOU …

When students read something I have written they tend to say things like, 'I wish I could write like you, but I'm just not a good writer.' 'You sound so easy and natural – my stuff is just a mess.'

Well, let me tell you a little bit about my easy, natural style.

Take this book as an example. With each and every chapter it takes me up to, I would say, four or five attempts before I find a start I am happy with (and this is usually just the quote and first couple of paragraphs). Once I am comfortable with how I will start, I rewrite it three or four times – sentence by sentence – until I feel like it is pretty good. Only then do I move on to the next section.

The next time I sit down to write, I reread that first bit and work through it a couple more times. Only at this stage do I feel like it is beginning to sound easy and natural – so I move on. This painstakingly slow process is repeated throughout the entire chapter until I get through it all.

When a full draft of the chapter is finished, I review it again, make more modifications, and, when happy, give it to a reader who is tough, but whose opinion I respect. Undoubtedly he will have comments, and I will take them into consideration and modify the text as I see fit.

Now when the entire book is complete I will look at all the chapters in context to make sure the whole thing nests together well. Again more modification is guaranteed. I will then do a copy edit and send it off to my publisher. Done? Not quite … from there Sage Publications will help me with more reviews (and possible modifications), professional copy editing, layout, and design, and final proofing – and this is what you will eventually see.

If only an easy and natural style came easily and naturally!

THE NEED FOR EXPOSURE

> ❝ It is of great importance that the general public be given the opportunity to experience, consciously and intelligently, the efforts and results of scientific research. Restricting the body of knowledge to a small group deadens the philosophical spirit of a people and leads to spiritual poverty. ❞
> *Albert Einstein*

A tremendous amount of effort goes into the conduct of rigorous and credible research. So the last thing you want to do is go through the whole research process and not capitalize on your achievements. But this can actually be the rule rather than the exception. An unbelievable amount of research ends up as nothing more than a thesis/report sitting somewhere on a shelf. OK, as a student researcher your immediate goal may be a grade or even a degree, but do not forget that the ultimate goal of research is to contribute to a body of knowledge, and your findings cannot add to a body of knowledge if they are not disseminated.

Unfortunately, conducting a research project, even if it is done well, in no way assures wide dissemination. Take, for example, the PhD thesis, probably the most prestigious piece of academic research writing there is. Sadly, it can also be the most poorly disseminated. Most theses are read by the author, a reviewer or editor, the supervisor or supervisory panel, and examiners. At the high end, that is about seven or eight people – not a lot of dissemination for a work that usually takes four or more years. Now this does not mean that research dissemination will not happen, but it does remind us that we need to take defined steps to facilitate it.

Attending conferences

There are three good reasons for attending conferences. The first is to expose yourself to an incredible array of cutting-edge research and researchers. The Web has really made the search for relevant conferences quite easy. You are likely to be amazed at the depth and breadth of topics being discussed and researched. The second reason is to network. Whether you plan to pursue a job or a higher degree, knowing who's out there and having an opportunity to meet them can be invaluable to your future. The third reason (and one of my favourites) is the opportunity for fun. Making and catching up with friends, exploring new regions of the state, country, or world, getting away – when you put it all together it is an experience not to be missed.

Giving presentations

While you might find it intimidating, presenting your work can be extremely rewarding. It is an amazing opportunity to get feedback as well as a sense of your work's potential impact. Now most students are incredibly anxious before a presentation, but generally happy they did it afterwards. Presentation can be made:

- *Within the university system* – It can be within a class, as part of a seminar series, or as part of a post graduate group.
- *At conferences* – Conference presentations can give heightened profile to both you and your work. Not only do they allow you to disseminate your work, but they also give you experience and confidence in this type of forum, help you generate new research ideas, and, of course, allow you even more inroads when it comes to networking.
- *To various stakeholder groups* – If your study is relevant to a community group, local government authority, or particular workplace, it is well worth sharing your findings. As well as getting your research out there, networking is again a bonus.

Writing and submitting articles

If you have undertaken a major project, you might want to consider publication. In fact, if you are pursuing a PhD, it is well worth trying to publish some of your work as you go. Not only can it focus your thesis, but it can also be invaluable for your career. Now the ultimate in publication is a single-authored work in an international refereed journal, and this is a worthy goal. But it is one that can be quite difficult for the inexperienced researcher to achieve. Another option is co-authorship. Quite often, your supervisor will be willing to co-author a work, which will give you expert advice and put more weight behind your submission. Just be sure to openly discuss issues of primary authorship.

THE FINAL WORD

So, you have reached the end of the journey – or at least the end of this book. Hopefully, your research journey will continue. So what last words of wisdom do I have for you? Well, I don't think I will take that on by myself. In fact, I think I will leave it to Albert Einstein:

> Einstein on continuing the journey:
> *The important thing is not to stop questioning.*
> Einstein on overcoming challenges:
> *In the middle of difficulty lies opportunity.*
> Einstein on the sometimes confusing research process:
> *If we knew what it was we were doing, it would not be called research, would it?*
> Einstein on the joys of being a professional researcher:
> *If I had only known, I would have been a locksmith.*

Good luck with your project. Hopefully you will become a research addict and be back for more!

FURTHER READING

There are three types of reading I would recommend to those at the final stages of writing up a project. The first is the internal documents produced by your university. Subject/course outlines, style guides, and manuals produced by and for your institution/programme will not only provide you with hard and fast criteria, but also likely steer you in directions that meet with more general expectations. The second is readings that act as examples. If you know what 'product' you are trying to produce, finding a few effective examples can offer a world of learning. Finally, the third type of reading (rec-

Booth, W. C., Colomb, G. C., and Williams, J. M. (2008) *The Craft of Research.* Chicago: University of Chicago Press.

Clark, I. L. (2006) *Writing the Successful Thesis and Dissertation: Entering the Conversation.* Englewood Cliffs, NJ: Prentice Hall.

Evans, D. and Gruba, P. (2003) *How to Write a Better Thesis.* Melbourne: Melbourne University Press.

Garson, G. D. (2001) *Guide to Writing Empirical Papers, Theses, and Dissertations.* Boca Raton, FL: CRC Press.

Glatthorn, A. A. and Joyner, R. L. (2005) *Writing the Winning Thesis or Dissertation: A Step-by-Step Guide.* Thousand Oaks, CA: Corwin Press.

Mulvaney, M. K. and Jolliffe, D. A. (2004) *Academic Writing: Genres, Samples, and Resources.* White Plains, NY: Longman.

Pyrczak, F. and Bruce, R. R. (2007) *Writing Empirical Research Reports: A Basic Guide for Students of the Social and Behavioral Sciences.* Glendale, CA: Pyrczak.

Strunk Jr, W. and White, E. B. (2008) *Elements of Style.* Boston, MA: Allyn & Bacon.

Wolcott, H. F. (2008) *Writing Up Qualitative Research.* London: Sage.

Woods, P. (2005) *Successful Writing for Qualitative Researchers.* London: Routledge.

CHAPTER SUMMARY

- Because your write-up will be a considerable piece of academic work with major consequences attached to its quality, the writing process can be intimidating. There are, however, practical strategies that can improve the quality of your work and make the task less daunting.
- The goal of your write-up is to share your research with others. It should be thought of as a communication process or a 'conversation' that demands consideration of your readers.
- To write effectively you need to know your audience – including who they are, what they know, and what their expectations might be.
- Your write-up can follow a standard structure that follows the introduction, literature review, methods, findings, then conclusion format, or it can follow an alternative structure that may better suit a particular project's aims and objectives. While alternative structures can allow more creative flexibility, the standard format gives readers what they tend to expect.
- Once considered an activity that commenced when research was complete, writing up is now commonly recommended as a practice that should be incorporated throughout the research process.
- Writing itself can be a form of analysis central to the construction and interpretation of meaning. It can also be instrumental in the development of significant, relevant, logical, and coherent storylines.

interpretation of meaning. It can also be instrumental in the development of significant, relevant, logical, and coherent storylines.

- Your research write-up should unfold as an interesting story. As the author of that story you need to: think of writing as a conversation; become familiar with the craft; find a voice; develop a structure: create a storyline; make convincing arguments; and get down to the business of writing and rewriting.

- Because each section of your write-up serves a different purpose, the writing required within each section varies. Overall, however, you will need to write purposively and convincingly.

- Preparing your document for submission involves getting appropriate feedback. This requires both specific and appropriate requests and a willingness to, if not welcome, then at least accept, criticality.

- Moving from first to final draft is a multi-stage process that sees you working systematically through the development of logic and argument, coherence and consistency, fluency and readability, and, finally, copy editing.

- The ultimate goal of any research project is to add to a body of knowledge. Once your project is complete, it is worth thinking about broader dissemination including attending conferences, giving presentations, and writing/submitting papers.

BIBLIOGRAPHY

Aldridge, A. (2001) *Surveying the Social World: Principles and Practice in Survey Research.* Buckingham: Open University Press.

Andrews, R. (2003) *Research Questions.* London: Continuum International.

Atkinson, P., Coffey, A., Delamont, S., Lofland, J., and Lofland, L. (eds) (2007) *Handbook of Ethnography.* London: Sage.

Auerbach, C. and Silverstein, L. B. (2003) *Qualitative Data: An Introduction to Coding and Analysis.* New York: NYU Press.

Balatti, J., Gargano, I., Goldman, M., Wood, G., and Woodlock, J. (2004) *Improving Indigenous Completion Rates in Mainstream TAFE – An Action Research Approach.* Leabrook, South Australia: NCEAR.

Banks, M. (2001) *Visual Methods in Social Research.* London: Sage.

Bazeley, P. (2007) *Qualitative Data Analysis with NVivo.* London: Sage.

Berger, P. and Luckmann, T. (1967) *The Social Construction of Reality: A Treatise in the Sociology of Knowledge.* New York: Anchor.

Best, S. J. and Krueger, B. S. (2004) *Internet Data Collection.* Thousand Oaks, CA: Sage.

Bickman, L. (ed.) (2000) *Research Design.* London: Sage.

Bissett, D. (2007) *Automated Data Analysis Using Excel.* Boca Raton, FL: Chapman & Hall CRC Press.

Boghossian, P. A. (2006) *Fear of Knowledge: Against Relativism and Constructivism.* Oxford: Oxford University Press.

BonJour, L. (2005) *The Structure of Empirical Knowledge.* Cambridge, MA: Harvard University Press.

Booth, W. C., Colomb, G. C., and Williams, J. M. (2008) *The Craft of Research.* Chicago: University of Chicago Press.

Boyatzis, R. E. (1998) *Transforming Qualitative Information: Thematic Analysis and Code Development.* London: Sage.

Bradburn, N. M., Sudman, S., and Wansink, B. (2004) *Asking Questions: The Definitive Guide to Questionnaire Design.* Hoboken, NJ: Jossey-Bass.

Bronowski, J. (1971) 'An interview with Jacob Bronowski', *Encounter Magazine.* June: 8–9.

Brown, J. R. (1996) *The I in Science: Training to Utilize Subjectivity in Research.* Oslo: Scandinavian University Press.

Brown, S. G. and Dobrin, S. I. (eds) (2004) *Ethnography Unbound: From Theory Shock to Critical Praxis.* Albany, NY: State University of New York Press.

Bryant, A. and Charmaz, K. (2007) *The SAGE Handbook of Grounded Theory.* London: Sage.

Bryman, A. (2008) *Social Research Methods.* Oxford: Oxford University Press.

Bryman, A. and Cramer, D. (2008) *Quantitative Data Analysis with SPSS 14, 15 & 16: A Guide for Social Scientists.* London: Routledge.

Burr, V. (2003) *Social Constructionism.* New York: Psychology Press.

Carey, S. S. (2003) *A Beginner's Guide to Scientific Method.* Belmont, CA: Wadsworth.

Carver, R. H. (2003) *Doing Data Analysis with MINITAB 14.* Pacific Grove, CA: Duxbury Press.

Cavana, R. L., Delahaye, B. L., and Sekaran, U. (2001) *Applied Business Research: Qualitative and Quantitative Methods.* New York: John Wiley & Sons.

Chandler, D. (2007) *Semiotics: The Basics.* London: Routledge.

Clandinin, D. J. (ed.) (2006) *Handbook of Narrative Inquiry: Mapping a Methodology.* London: Sage.

Clandinin, D. J. and Connelly, F. M. (2004) *Narrative Inquiry: Experience and Story in Qualitative Research.* San Francisco: Jossey-Bass.

Clark, I. L. (2006) *Writing the Successful Thesis and Dissertation: Entering the Conversation.* Englewood Cliffs, NJ: Prentice Hall.

Coghlan, D. and Brannick, T. (2004) *Doing Action Research in Your Own Organization.* London: Sage.

Cohen, M. Z., Kahn, D. L., and Steeves, R. H. (2000) *Hermeneutic Phenomenological Research. A Practical Guide for Nurse Researchers.* Thousand Oaks, CA: Sage.

Coley, S. M. and Scheinberg, C. A. (2000) *Proposal Writing.* London: Sage.

Conee, E. and Sider, T. (2005) *Riddles of Existence: A Guided Tour of Metaphysics.* Oxford: Oxford University Press.

Corbin, J. and Strauss, A. (2007) *Basics of Qualitative Research: Techniques and Procedures for Developing Grounded Theory.* London: Sage.

Coulon, A. (2000) *Ethnomethodology.* London: Sage.

Creswell, J. W. (2008) *Research Design: Qualitative, Quantitative and Mixed Methods Approaches.* London: Sage.

Creswell, J. W. and Plano Clark, V. L. (2006) *Designing and Conducting Mixed Methods Research.* London: Sage.

Cryer, P. (2006) *The Research Student's Guide to Success.* Buckingham: Open University Press.

Danesi, M. (2007) *The Quest for Meaning: A Guide to Semiotic Theory and Practice.* Toronto: University of Toronto Press.

Danto, E. A. (2008) *Historical Research.* Oxford: Oxford University Press.

de Certeau, M. (2002) *The Practice of Everyday Life.* Berkeley, CA: University of California Press.

de Vaus, D. (2009) *Research Design in Social Research.* London: Sage.

Denzin, N. and Lincoln, Y. (2005) *The Sage Handbook of Qualitative Research.* Thousand Oaks, CA: Sage.

Denzin, N. K. (2003) *Performance Ethnography: Critical Pedagogy and the Politics of Culture.* London: Sage.

Denzin, N. K. and Lincoln, Y. S. (eds) (2007) *Strategies of Qualitative Inquiry.* Thousand Oaks, CA: Sage.

Der, G. and Everitt, B. S. (2008) *Handbook of Statistical Analyses Using SAS.* Boca Raton, FL: CRC Press.

DeWalt, K. M. and DeWalt, B. R. (2001) *Participant Observation: A Guide for Fieldwork.* Lanham, MD: AltaMira Press.

Dillman, D. A. (2006) *Mail and Internet Surveys: The Tailored Design Method.* Hoboken, NJ: John Wiley & Sons.

Donnelly Jr, R. A. (2007) *The Complete Idiot's Guide to Statistics.* New York: Alpha Books.

Dorofeev, S. and Grant, P. (2006) *Statistics for Real-Life Sample Surveys: Non-Simple-Random Samples and Weighted Data.* Cambridge: Cambridge University Press.

Evans, D. and Gruba, P. (2003) *How to Write a Better Thesis.* Melbourne: Melbourne University Press.

Fairclough, N. (2008) *Analysing Discourse: Textual Analysis for Social Research.* Cambridge: Cambridge University Press.

Fals Borda, O. and Rahman, M. A. (1991) *Action and Knowledge: Breaking the Monopoly with Participatory Action Research.* New York: Intermediate Technology/Apex Press.

Feynman, R. (1997) *Surely You're Joking, Mr. Feynman!* New York: W. W. Norton.

Fink, A. (2004) *Conducting Research Literature Reviews: From the Internet to Paper.* Thousand Oaks, CA: Sage.

Fitzpatrick, J. L., Sanders, J. R., and Worthen, B. R. (2003) *Program Evaluation: Alternative Approaches and Practical Guidelines.* New York: Allyn & Bacon.

Fowler Jr, F. J. (2008) *Survey Research Methods.* London: Sage.

Francis, D. and Hester, S. (2004) *An Invitation to Ethnomethodology.* London: Sage.

Franzosi, R. (ed.) (2008) *Content Analysis.* London: Sage.

Freire, P. (1970) *Pedagogy of the Oppressed.* New York: Herder & Herder.

Galvan, J. L. (2005) *Writing Literature Reviews: A Guide for Students of the Social and Behavioral Sciences.* Glendale, CA: Pyrczak.

Garfinkel, H. (1967) *Studies in Ethnomethodology.* Englewood Cliffs, NJ: Prentice Hall.

Garson, G. D. (2001) *Guide to Writing Empirical Papers, Theses, and Dissertations.* Boca Raton, FL: CRC Press.

Gauch Jr, H. G. (2002) *Scientific Method in Practice.* Cambridge: Cambridge University Press.

Geertz, C. ([1973] 2000) *The Interpretation of Cultures.* New York: Basic Books.

Gerring, J. (2006) *Case Study Research: Principles and Practices.* Cambridge: Cambridge University Press.

Gillham, B. (2005) *Research Interviewing: The Range of Techniques.* Buckingham: Open University Press.

Gillham, B. (2008) *Observation Techniques: Structured to Unstructured.* London: Continuum International.

Glaser, B. and Strauss, A. (1967) *Discovery of Grounded Theory.* Chicago: Aldine.

Glatthorn, A. A. and Joyner, R. L. (2005) *Writing the Winning Thesis or Dissertation: A Step-by-Step Guide.* Thousand Oaks, CA: Corwin Press.

Glucksmann, M. (aka Ruth Cavendish) (2009) *Women on the Line.* London: Routledge.

Gorard, S. (2003) *Quantitative Methods in Social Science.* London: Continuum International.

Gottdiener, M., Lagopoulos, A., and Boklund-Lagopoulos, K. (eds) (2003) *Semiotics.* London: Sage.

Grbich, C. (2007) *Qualitative Data Analysis: An Introduction.* London: Sage.

Greasley, P. (2008) *Quantitative Data Analysis with SPSS.* Buckingham: Open University Press.

Greene, J. C. (2007) *Mixed Methods in Social Inquiry.* Hoboken, NJ: Jossey-Bass.

Greenwood, D. and Levin, M. (2006) *Introduction to Action Research: Social Research for Social Change.* Thousand Oaks, CA: Sage.

Groves, R. M., Fowler, F. J., Couper, M. J., Lepkowski, J. M., Singer, E., and Tourangeau, R. (2004) *Survey Methodology.* New York: John Wiley & Sons.

Guba, E. (ed.) (1990) *The Paradigm Dialog.* London: Sage.

Gubrium, J. F. and Holstein, J. A. (2001) *Handbook of Interview Research: Context and Method.* London: Sage.

Hakim, C. (2000) *Research Design.* London: Routledge.

Hall, G. and Longman, J. (2008) *The Postgraduate's Companion.* London: Sage.

Hammersley, M., Foster, R., and Gomm, R. (2000) *Case Study Method: Key Issues, Key Texts.* London: Sage.

Hancock, D. R. and Algozzine, R. (2006) *Doing Case Study Research: A Practical Guide for Beginning Researchers.* New York: Teachers College Press.

Hardy, M. A. and Bryman, A. (eds) (2004) *Handbook of Data Analysis*. London: Sage.

Hart, C. (2000) *Doing a Literature Review*. London: Sage.

Hart, C. (2001) *Doing a Literature Search*. London: Sage.

Hazelrigg, L. E. (1989) *Social Science and the Challenge of Relativism: A Wilderness of Mirrors: On Practices of Theory in a Gray Age*. Gainesville, FL: University Press of Florida.

Helmers, M. (2005) *The Elements of Visual Analysis*. White Plains, NY: Longman.

Herda, E. (1999) *Research Conversations and Narrative: A Critical Hermeneutic Orientation in Participatory Inquiry*. New York: Praeger.

Herman, L. and Vervaeck, B. (2005) *Handbook of Narrative Analysis*. Lincoln, NE: University of Nebraska Press.

Herr, K. G. and Anderson, G. L. (2005) *The Action Research Dissertation: A Guide for Students and Faculty*. London: Sage.

Hesse-Biber, S. N. and Yaiser, M. L. (2004) *Feminist Perspectives on Social Research*. New York: Oxford University Press.

Hoey, M. (2000) *Textual Interaction: An Introduction to Written Discourse Analysis*. London: Routledge.

Hood, S., Mayall, B., and Oliver, S. (eds) (1999) *Critical Issues in Social Research: Power and Prejudice*. Buckingham: Open University Press.

Hume, L. and Mulcock, J. (eds) (2004) *Anthropologists in the Field: Cases in Participant Observation*. Irvington, NY: Columbia University Press.

Hurston, Z. N. (1942) *Dust Tracks on a Road*. New York: Harper Collins.

Hutchby, I. and Woofit, R. (2008) *Conversation Analysis*. Cambridge: Polity Press.

IMNRC (2002) *Integrity in Scientific Research: Creating an Environment That Promotes Responsible Conduct*. Washington, DC: National Academies Press.

International Labour Organization (2005) *Facts on Safe Work*. Geneva: ILO. Web page at www.ilo.org/public/english/bureau/inf/download/wssd/pdf/health.pdf.

Israel, M. and Hay, I. (2006) *Research Ethics for Social Scientists*. London: Sage.

Jacquette, D. (2002) *Ontology*. Montreal: McGill–Queen's University Press.

Janesick, V. (2007) 'The dance of qualitative research design: metaphor, methodolatry, and meaning', in N. K. Denzin and Y. S. Lincoln (eds), *Strategies of Qualitative Inquiry*. Thousand Oaks, CA: Sage. pp. 35–55.

Kiecolt, K. J. and Nathan, L. E. (1985) *Secondary Analysis of Survey Data*. London: Sage.

Kindon, S. (2008) *Participatory Action Research Approaches and Methods: Connecting People, Participation and Place*. London: Routledge.

King, N. and Horrocks, S. (2009) *Interviews in Qualitative Research*. Thousand Oaks, CA: Sage.

Kolb, D. A. (1984) *Experiential Learning: Experience as the Source of Learning and Development*. Englewood Cliffs, NJ: Prentice Hall.

Kripppendorf, K. (2003) *Content Analysis: An Introduction to Its Methodology*. London: Sage.

Kripppendorf, K. and Bock, M. A. (2008) *The Content Analysis Reader*. London: Sage.

Kvale, S. and Brinkman, S. (2008) *InterViews: Learning the Craft of Qualitative Research Interviewing*. London: Sage.

Lee, R. M. (2000) *Unobtrusive Methods in Social Research*. Buckingham: Open University Press.

Leedy, P. D. and Ormond, J. E. (2004) *Practical Research: Planning and Design*. Englewood Cliffs, NJ: Prentice Hall.

Lehmann, E. L. and Romano, J. P. (2005) *Testing Statistical Hypotheses*. New York: Springer.

Levy, P. S. and Lemeshow, S. (2008) *Sampling of Populations: Methods and Applications*. New York: Wiley-Interscience.

Lewin, K. (1946) 'Action research and the minority problems', *Journal of Social Issues*, 2: 34–6.

Lewins, A. and Silver, C. (2007) *Using Software in Qualitative Research: A Step-by-Step Guide*. London: Sage.

Liddicoat, A. J. (2007) *An Introduction to Conversation Analysis.* London: Continuum International.

Locke, L. F., Spirduso, W. W., and Silverman, S. J. (2007) *Proposals That Work: A Guide for Planning Dissertations and Grant Proposals.* London: Sage.

Lofland, J. and Lofland, L. H. (2003) *Analyzing Social Settings: A Guide to Qualitative Observation and Analysis.* Belmont, CA: Wadsworth.

Macfarlane, B. (2008) *Researching with Integrity: The Ethics of Academic Research.* London: Routledge.

Machi, L. A. (2008) *The Literature Review: Six Steps to Success.* Thousand Oaks, CA: Corwin Press.

Macrina, F. L. (2005) *Scientific Integrity: Text and Cases in Responsible Conduct of Research.* Herndon, VA: ASM Press.

Madison, D. S. (2005) *Critical Ethnography: Method, Ethics, and Performance.* London: Sage.

Mahoney, J. and Rueschemeyer, D. (eds) (2003) *Comparative Historical Analysis in the Social Sciences.* Cambridge: Cambridge University Press.

Marshall, C. and Rossman, G. (2006) *Designing Qualitative Research.* London: Sage.

Maxim, P. S. (1999) *Quantitative Research Methods in the Social Sciences.* Oxford: Oxford University Press.

Mayo, E. (1933) *The Human Problems of an Industrial Civilization.* New York: Viking Press.

McIntyre, A. (2007) *Participatory Action Research.* London: Sage.

McIver, J. P. and Carmines, E. G. (1981) *Unidimensional Scaling.* London: Sage.

McNiff, J. (2002) *You and Your Action Research Project.* Oxford: Taylor & Francis.

McNiff, J. and Whitehead, J. (2002) *Action Research: Principles and Practice.* London: Routledge.

Mertens, D. M. and Ginsberg, P. E. (2008) *The Handbook of Social Research Ethics.* London: Sage.

Miles, M. and Huberman, A. (1994) *Qualitative Data Analysis: An Expanded Source Book.* Thousand Oaks, CA: Sage.

Mitchell, M. L. and Jolley, J. M. (2006) *Research Design Explained.* Belmont, CA: Wadsworth.

Moore, N. (2006) *How to do Research: A Practical Guide to Designing and Managing Research Projects.* London: Facet.

Moustakas, C. (2000) *Phenomenological Research Methods.* London: Sage.

Mulvaney, M. K. and Jolliffe, D. A. (2004) *Academic Writing: Genres, Samples, and Resources.* White Plains, NY: Longman.

Munhall, P. L. and Chenail, R. J. (2007) *Qualitative Research Proposals and Reports: A Guide.* Sudbury, MA: Jones & Bartlett.

Myatt, G. J. (2006) *Making Sense of Data: A Practical Guide to Exploratory Data Analysis and Data Mining.* New York: Wiley-Interscience.

Neuendorf, K. A. (2001) *The Content Analysis Guidebook.* London: Sage.

Neuman, W. L. (2005) *Social Research Methods: Qualitative and Quantitative Approaches.* Boston, MA: Allyn & Bacon.

Ogden, T. E. and Goldberg, I. A. (eds) (2002) *Research Proposals: A Guide to Success.* New York: Academic Press.

O'Leary, Z. (2001) 'Conversations in the kitchen', in A. Bartlett and G. Mercer (eds), *Postgraduate Research Supervision: Transforming (R)elations.* New York: Peter Lang. pp. 195–8.

O'Leary, Z. (2001) *Reaction, Introspection and Exploration: Diversity in Journeys out of Faith.* Kew, Victoria: Christian Research Association.

O'Leary, Z. (2004) *The Essential Guide to Doing Research.* London: Sage.

O'Leary, Z. (2005) *Researching Real-World Problems: A Guide to Methods of Inquiry.* London: Sage.

O'Leary, Z. (2007) *The Social Science Jargon Buster: The Key Terms You Need to Know.* London: Sage.

Oliver, P. (2003) *The Students' Guide to Research Ethics.* Buckingham: Open University Press.

Orr, L. L. (1998) *Social Experiments: Evaluating Public Programs with Experimental Methods.* London: Sage.

Oxford English Dictionary (2007) Oxford: Oxford University Press.

Pan, M. L. (2007) *Preparing Literature Reviews: Qualitative and Quantitative Approaches.* Glendale, CA: Pyrczak.

Patton, M. Q. (2001) *Qualitative Research and Evaluation Methods.* Thousand Oaks, CA: Sage.

Phelps, R., Fisher, K., and Ellis, A. H. (2007) *Organizing and Managing Your Research: A Practical Guide for Postgraduates.* London: Sage.

Prior, L. (2003) *Using Documents in Social Research.* London: Sage.

Psillos, S. (1999) *Scientific Realism: How Science Tracks Truth.* London: Routledge.

Punch, K. (2005) *Introduction to Social Research.* London: Sage.

Punch, K. (2006) *Developing Effective Research Proposals.* London: Sage.

Pyrczak, F. and Bruce, R. R. (2007) *Writing Empirical Research Reports: A Basic Guide for Students of the Social and Behavioral Sciences.* Glendale, CA: Pyrczak.

Ramazanoğlu, C. with Holland, J. (2002) *Feminist Methodology: Challenges and Choices.* Thousand Oaks, CA: Sage.

Rao, P. S., Rao, R. S., Poduri, S. R. S., and Miller, W. (2000) *Sampling Methodologies with Applications.* New York: Lewis.

Rapley, T. (2008) *Doing Conversation, Discourse and Document Analysis.* London: Sage.

Rea, L. M. and Parker, R. A. (2005) *Designing and Conducting Survey Research: A Comprehensive Guide.* Hoboken, NJ: Jossey-Bass.

Reason, P. and Bradbury, H. (2006) *Handbook of Action Research.* London: Sage.

Reinharz, S. (1992) *Feminist Methods in Social Research.* New York: Oxford University Press.

Rescher, N. (2005) *Reason and Reality: Realism and Idealism in Pragmatic Perspective.* Lanham, MD: Rowman & Littlefield.

Ridley, D. (2008) *The Literature Review: A Step by Step Guide for Students.* London: Sage.

Riessman, C. K. (2007) *Narrative Methods for the Human Sciences.* London: Sage.

Robinson, D. (2004) *Introducing Empiricism.* New York: Totem Books.

Robson, C. (2002) *Real World Research.* Oxford: Blackwell.

Roethlisberger, F. J. and Dickson, W. J. (1939) *Management and the Worker: An Account of a Research Program Conducted by the Western Electric Company, Hawthorne Works.* New York: John Wiley & Sons.

Rose, G. (2007) *Visual Methodologies: An Introduction to the Interpretation of Visual Methods.* London: Sage.

Rosenbaum, P. R. (2002) *Observational Studies.* New York: Springer.

Rossi, P. H., Freeman, H. E., and Lipsey, M. W. (2003) *Evaluation: A Systematic Approach.* Thousand Oaks, CA: Sage.

Royse, D., Thyer, B. A., Padgett, D. K., and Logan, T. K. (2005) *Program Evaluation: An Introduction.* Florence, KY: Brooks Cole.

Rubin, H. J. and Rubin, I. S. (2004) *Qualitative Interviewing: The Art of Hearing Data.* Thousand Oaks, CA: Sage.

Rudestam, K. E. and Newton, R. R. (2007) *Surviving Your Dissertation: A Comprehensive Guide to Content and Process.* London: Sage.

Salkind, N. J. (2007) *Statistics for People Who (Think They) Hate Statistics.* London: Sage.

Saris, W. E. and Gallhofer, I. N. (2007) *Design, Evaluation, and Analysis of Questionnaires for Survey Research.* New York: Wiley-Interscience.

Schaeffer III, R. L. and Mendenhall, W. (2005) *Elementary Survey Sampling.* Belmont, CA: Duxbury.

Schick, T. (ed.) (1999) *Readings in the Philosophy of Science: From Positivism to Postmodern.* Columbus, OH: McGraw-Hill.

Schiffer, M. (1999) *The Material Life of Human Beings: Artifacts, Behavior and Communication.* London: Routledge.

Seebohm, T. M. (2005) *Hermeneutics. Method and Methodology.* New York: Springer.

Seidman, U. (2006) *Interviewing as Qualitative Research: A Guide for Researchers in Education and the Social Sciences.* New York: Teachers College Press.

Shulman, J. and Asimov, I. (eds) (1988) *Isaac Asimov's Book of Science and Nature Quotation.* New York: Weidenfeld & Nicolson.

Silverman, D. (2006) *Interpreting Qualitative Data: Methods for Analysing Talk, Text and Interaction.* London: Sage.

Sinfield, M. (1995) 'Women with AIDS: a phenomenological study', *Australasian Annual Conference, Society for HIV Medicine,* 16–19 November, 7: 61.

Sirkin, R. M. (2005) *Statistics for the Social Sciences.* Thousand Oaks, CA: Sage.

Steinmetz, G. (ed.) (2005) *The Politics of Method in the Human Sciences: Positivism and Its Epistemological Others.* Durham, NC: Duke University Press.

Steup, M. and Sosa, E. (eds) (2005) *Contemporary Debates In Epistemology.* Oxford: Blackwell.

Stewart, D. W. and Kamins, M. A. (1992) *Secondary Research: Information Sources and Methods.* London: Sage.

Stringer, E. (2007) *Action Research.* Thousand Oaks, CA: Corwin Press.

Strunk Jr, W. and White, E. B. (2008) *Elements of Style.* Boston, MA: Allyn & Bacon.

Tarling, R. (2005) *Managing Social Research: A Practical Guide.* London: Routledge.

Tashakkori, A. and Teddlie, C. (eds) (2002) *Handbook of Mixed Methods Social and Behavioral Research.* London: Sage.

Tavers, M. (2001) *Qualitative Research Through Case Studies.* London: Sage.

Ten Have, P. (2004) *Understanding Qualitative Research and Ethnomethodology.* London: Sage.

Ten Have, P. (2007) *Doing Conversation Analysis: A Practical Guide.* Thousand Oaks, CA: Corwin Press.

Thomas, J. (1993) *Doing Critical Ethnography.* Newbury Park, CA: Sage.

Thompson, S. K. (2002) *Sampling.* New York: John Wiley & Sons.

Tortu, S., Goldsamt, L. A., and Hamid, R. (eds) (2001) *A Practical Guide to Research and Services with Hidden Populations.* Boston, MA: Allyn & Bacon.

Trochim, W. M. (2009) *The Research Methods Knowledge Base.* Web page at www.socialresearchmethods.net/kb/index.htm.

Troman, G., Jeffrey, B., and Walford, G. (eds) (2005) *Methodological Issues and Practices in Ethnography.* Greenwich, CT: JAI Press.

Van Dijk, T. A. (2008) *Society and Discourse: How Social Contexts Influence Text and Talk.* Cambridge: Cambridge University Press.

Van Leeuwen, T. and Jewitt, C. (eds) (2001) *Handbook of Visual Analysis.* London: Sage.

Van Manen, M. (1997) *Researching Lived Experience: Human Science for an Action Sensitive Pedagogy.* Albany, NY: State University of New York Press.

Wainer, H. (2000) *Drawing Inferences from Self-selected Samples.* Mahwah, NJ: Lawrence Erlbaum.

Wallerstein, I. (2001) *Unthinking Social Science: The Limits of Nineteenth-Century Paradigms.* Philadelphia: Temple University Press.

Webb, E. J., Campbell, D. T., Schwartz, R. D., and Sechrest, L. (1998) *Unobtrusive Measures: Nonreactive Research in the Social Sciences.* Dallas: Houghton Mifflin.

Weber, M. ([1904] 1949) 'Objectivity in social science and social policy', in M. Weber, *The Methodology of the Social Sciences.* New York: Free Press.

Webster, M. and Sell, J. (eds) (2007) *Laboratory Experiments in the Social Sciences.* Boston, MA: Academic Press.

Wengraf, T. (2001) *Qualitative Research Interviewing: Semi-Structured, Biographical and Narrative Methods.* London: Sage.

West, M. D. (2001) *Theory, Method, and Practice in Computer Content Analysis.* Norwood, NJ: Ablex Press.

White, P. (2009) *Developing Research Questions: A Guide for Social Scientists.* Basingstoke: Palgrave Macmillan.

Wholey, J. S., Hatry, H. P., and Newcomer, K. E. (eds) (2004) *Handbook of Practical Program Evaluation.* Hoboken, NJ: Jossey-Bass.

Willer, D. and Walker, H. (2007) *Building Experiments: Testing Social Theory.* Stanford, CA: Stanford University Press.

Williams, M. (2001) *Problems of Knowledge: A Critical Introduction to Epistemology.* Oxford: Oxford University Press.

Wodak, R. and Meyer, M. (eds) (2002) *Methods of Critical Discourse Analysis.* London: Sage.

Wolcott, H. F. (2008) *Writing Up Qualitative Research.* London: Sage.

Wolcott, H. F. (2008) *Ethnography: A Way of Seeing.* Lanham, MD: AltaMira Press.

Woods, P. (2005) *Successful Writing for Qualitative Researchers.* London: Routledge.

Yin, R. K. (2008) *Case Study Research: Design and Methods.* Thousand Oaks, CA: Sage.

Zahavi, D. (2007) *Subjectivity and Selfhood: Investigating the First-Person Perspective.* Cambridge MA: The MIT Press.

INDEX

access, 196
act, 64
action learning, 15
action research, 102, 145–52
  challenges of, 151–2
  cycles of, 149–50
  key elements, 148–50
  participatory action research, 154
  scope of , 147–8
aims, 64
analysis, 230–53
  data management, 233–5
  qualitative, 256–71
  quantitative/statistical, 232–5
annotated bibliography, 79–81
anonymity, 41
auditability, 39, 43
authenticity, 43
autonomy, 41

basic research, 137
bivariate analysis, 244–6
Boolean operators, 77
breaching experiments, 124
broad representation, 115
budgets, 65–6

case study, 174
cases, 173–7
  opportunities, 174–5
  selection of, 175–7
census, 181
central tendency, 237–8
  mean, 238
  median, 238
  mode, 238
class, 31
coercion, 41
concept mapping, 48–52
conclusions, 267
confidence interval, 164
confidence level, 164

confidentiality, 41
content analysis, 270
conversation analysis, 270
coverage error, 166
credibility, 29, 114–5
critical ethnography, 155–6
criticality, 153
cross sectional surveys, 181
crystallization, 114
cultural artefact analysis, 225–6

data, 232–5, 256–71
  management of, 233–5
  presentation of, 244, 246–53,
    269, 271–4
  qualitative, 256–71
  quantitative/statistical, 232–5
data analysis programs, 234–5, 258–60
  qualitative programs, 258–60
  quantitative programs, 234–5
data collection, 180–205, 208–27
  direct, 180–205
  existing data, 111–12
  experimentation, 107–10
  indirect, 208–27
  interviewing, 194–205
  observation, 209–17
  surveying, 180–94
  textual analysis, 73–4, 217–27
deception, 41
deductive logic, 261–2
delimitations, 65
dependability, 37, 43
dependent variables, 108, 236
descriptive statistics, 237–40
discourse analysis, 270
dispersion, 238–9
  quartiles, 239
  range, 238–9
  standard deviation, 239–40
  variance, 239
dissemination, 292–4

'doability', 97
document analysis, 223–4
drafting, 67–8, 288–92
   final drafts, 291
   first drafts, 290
   penultimate drafts, 291
   second drafts, 290–1

emancipatory research, 152–6
   critical ethnography, 155–6
   issues in, 156
   participatory action research, 154
emergent design, 68–9, 101–2
empiricism, 4–6
epistemology, 4–6
   equity, 42
erroneous assumptions, 168–9
ethical responsibilities, 40–2, 65, 109
   anonymity, 41
   autonomy, 41
   coercion, 41
   competence, 41
   confidentiality, 41
   conscientiousness, 41–2
   deception, 41
   equity, 42
   honesty, 42
   inducement, 41
   informed consent, 41
   legal obligations, 40
   moral obligations, 40–1
   no harm, 41
   right to discontinue, 41
   voluntary involvement, 41
ethics approval, 42
ethnicity, 35
ethnography, 115–20
   conduct of, 117–18
   strengths and challenges, 119–20
ethnomethodology, 123–6
   conduct of, 124–5
   strengths and challenges, 125–6
evaluation research, 137–45
   challenges, 142–5
   formative evaluation, 140–1
   outcome evaluation, 138–40
   politics of, 141–2
   process evaluation, 140–1
   summative evaluation, 138–40
existing data, 111–12
experimental design, 107–10
   conduct of, 107–10
   strength and challenges, 110
   quasi experimental design, 109
   random control trial, 109
   single group design, 109
explication of method, 115

feedback, 288–9
feminist 'methodology', 126
feminist approaches to research, 126–7
focus groups, 196

Gantt chart, 21, 65
gender, 31, 35
generalizability, 39, 43
graphs, 244–50
grounded theory, 101, 270–1
Guttman Scaling, 188–9

hermeneutics, 270
histogram, 241, 249
historical analysis, 224–5
hypothesis, 55–6, 64
hypothetico-deductive method, 106

independent variables, 108, 236
indicators of 'good' research, 29–43
   auditability, 39, 43
   authenticity, 43
   dependability, 37, 43
   ethicality, 43
   generalizability, 39, 43
   neutrality, 43
   objectivity, 43
   reliability, 37, 43
   representativeness, 39, 43
   reproducibility, 43
   subjectivity with transparency, 43
   transferability, 39, 43
   validity, 43
inductive logic, 261–2
inferential statistics, 240–4
inducement, 41
informed consent, 41
integrity, 29–44
   in the production of knowledge, 29–39, 43–4
   and the researched, 40–4
interviewing, 194–205
   capturing responses, 203–4
   issues and complexities, 196–8
   process, 199–205
   prompts and probes, 204
   translation, 199, 201–2
   types of, 195–6

key informants, 171–3
   opportunities, 171
   selection of, 172
   types of, 172
key words, 77
kurtosis, 239–41

legal obligations, 40
Likert scaling, 187–8

limitations, 37–8, 65
literature, 71–87
    annotating, 79–81
    importance of, 71–2
    managing, 77–81
    role of, 72–4
    sourcing, 75–7
    types of, 75–6
literature reviews, 64, 73–4, 81–7
    coverage, 82–3
    purpose, 81–2
    writing process, 83–6

managing subjectivities, 30–3
mean, 238
measurement scales, 236–7
    interval, 237
    nominal, 236
    ordinal, 236–7
    ratio, 237
median, 238
member checking, 115
methodological design, 88–9
    checklist, 100–1
    emergent design, 68–9, 101–2
methodology, 88–9, 92–4, 104–35, 135–59
    action oriented, 145–52
    emancipatory, 152–6
    evaluative, 137–45
    mixed, 127–31
    qualitative, 104–6, 113–27
    quantitative, 104–6, 106–13
    quantitative/qualitative divide, 104–6
methods, 63, 65, 73–4, 88–9, 94–5, 98–9
mixed methodology, 127–31
    arguments for, 127–8
    challenges and obstacles, 130–1
    perspectives and strategies, 128–30
mode, 238
moral obligations, 40–1
multivariate analysis, 244–6

narrative analysis, 270
neutrality, 43
non-parametric tests, 240
non-random samples, 168–71
    convenience sampling, 170–1
    handpicked sampling, 170
    snowball sampling, 170
    volunteer sampling, 170
non response bias, 167
normal curve, 239–40

objectives, 64
objectivity, 43
observation, 209–17
    issues and complexities, 211–13

observation cont.
    process, 213–17
    types of, 209–11
ontology, 4–6
operationalizing concepts, 186–8

panel study, 182
paradigm, 4–8
parametric tests, 240
participant observation, 210
participatory action research, 154
peer review, 115
persistent observation, 115
phenomenology, 119–23
    conduct of, 120–2
    phenomenological
        descriptions, 121
    strengths and challenges, 122–3
politics, 27–8
population, 161, 163
population studies, 110–13
    gathering primary data, 112–13
    strengths and challenges, 113
    working with existing data, 111–12
positivism, 4–6
post-positivism, 4–6
power, 27–8
problem based learning, 15
prolonged engagement, 115
prompts and probes, 204
proposal, 61–70
    elements of, 64–6
    role of, 61–4
    writing, 66–8

qualitative data, 256–74
    analysis of, 256–71
    presentation of, 269, 271–4
qualitative data analysis, 256–71
    content analysis, 270
    conversation analysis, 270
    data management, 258–9
    discourse analysis, 270
    grounded theory, 270–1
    hermeneutics, 270
    logic and methods, 260–9
    narrative analysis, 270
    presentation of 269, 271–4
    semiotics, 270
    software, 259–60
    thematic analysis, 262–9
    visual analysis, 270
quantitative data, 230–53
    analysis of, 230–46
    presentation of, 244, 246–53
quartiles, 239
quasi experimental design, 109

race, 31
radical views, 153
random control trial, 109
random samples, 166–8
    cluster sampling, 168
    multistage cluster sampling, 168
    simple random sampling, 167
    stratified sampling, 167
    systematic sampling, 167
range, 238–9
rationale, 64, 73–4
realism, 6
recommendations, 288
referencing, 66
reflexivity, 7–8
relativism, 6
reliability, 37, 43
representativeness, 39, 43
reproducibility, 43
research questions, 46–60, 62, 64
    characteristics of, 56–9
    checklist, 59
    developing, 48–55, 73–4
    importance of, 46–7
    from question to answers, 89–97
researcher roles, 96
respondents, 160–79

samples, 161–9
    non-random samples, 168–70
    random samples, 166–8
    sample frame, 163
    sampling strategies, 165–9
    selection of, 162–6
    size of, 163–5
saturation, 114
scientific method, 106
secondary data analysis,
        226–7
semiotics, 270
skewness, 239–41
social constructivism, 6
stakeholders, 139–42, 143
standard deviation, 239–40
statistical analysis, 230–53
    bivariate analysis, 244–6
    descriptive statistics, 237–40
    inferential statistics, 240–4
    multivariate analysis, 244–6
    presentation of, 244, 246–53
    selecting statistical tests, 243–6
    univariate analysis, 243–6
statistical significance, 242–3
subjectivism, 6
subjectivity, 30–3, 43
survey instruments, 186–94
    background information, 193
    concept operationalization, 186–8

survey instruments *cont.*
    instruction, 193
    layout and design, 194
    organization and length, 193
    question formulation, 188–90
    response categories, 191–3
survey questions, 188–93, 171–3
    closed questions, 191–2
    formulation, 188–90
    open questions, 191
surveying, 180–94
    instrument, 186–94
    issues and complexities, 182–3
    process, 183–6
    types of, 181–2

tables, 251–3
textual analysis, 73–4, 217–27
    cultural artefact analysis, 225–6
    document analysis, 223–4
    historical analysis, 224–5
    issues and complexities, 218–21
    process of, 221–3
    types of, 218, 219–20
    secondary data analysis, 226–7
theory, 65, 73–4
Thurstone scaling, 188–9
time management, 20–2
title, 64
tools, 88–9
transferability, 39, 43
translation, 201–2
trend survey, 181–2
triangulation, 115
trust, 35–6
truth, 34

univariate analysis, 243–6
unwitting bias, 168–9

validity, 43
variables, 108–9, 236–7
    dependent, 108, 236
    independent, 108, 236
variance, 239
visual analysis, 270

writing, 279–94
    as analysis, 283
    audience, 279–80
    as communication, 279–82
    dissemination, 292–4
    drafting, 288–92
    feedback, 288–9
    process of, 282–92
    sections of, 285–8
    storylines, 283–5
    structure, 280–2